Family Life in the Age of Shakespeare

Recent Titles in
The Age of Shakespeare

Religion in the Age of Shakespeare
Christopher Baker

FAMILY LIFE IN THE AGE OF SHAKESPEARE

Bruce W. Young

THE AGE OF SHAKESPEARE

GREENWOOD PRESS
WESTPORT, CONNECTICUT • LONDON

Library of Congress Cataloging-in-Publication Data

Young, Bruce Wilson.
Family life in the age of Shakespeare / Bruce W. Young.
p. cm. — (The age of Shakespeare, ISSN 1936–6388)
Includes bibliographical references and index.
ISBN 978–0–313–34239–4 (alk. paper)
1. Shakespeare, William, 1564–1616—Criticism and interpretation.
2. Family in literature. 3. Domestic drama, English—History and criticism.
4. Family—England—History—16th century. 5. Family—England—History—17th century. 6. Home in literature. I. Title.
PR3069.F35Y68 2009
822.3'3—dc22 2008036700

British Library Cataloguing in Publication Data is available.

Library of Congress Catalog Card Number: 2008036700
ISBN: 978–0–313–34239–4
ISSN: 1936–6388

First published in 2009

Greenwood Press, 88 Post Road West, Westport, CT 06881
An imprint of Greenwood Publishing Group, Inc.
www.greenwood.com

Printed in the United States of America

The paper used in this book complies with the Permanent Paper Standard issued by the National Information Standards Organization (Z39.48–1984).

10 9 8 7 6 5 4 3 2 1

To my parents, Daren and Ruth Young

CONTENTS

PREFACE

For centuries Shakespeare's readers and viewers have been intrigued by his treatment of family life. Modern readers in particular wonder how changes in family life since Shakespeare's time should affect our interpretation of the plays. Were brides commonly as young as Juliet? Did parents normally force their children into unwanted marriages as the Capulets try to do with their daughter? Would an early modern father have been content, as Egeus seems to be in *A Midsummer Night's Dream*, to see his daughter die or become a nun because she failed to accept the husband he chose? Were families generally as miserable and self-destructive as Hamlet's and King Lear's are made out to be?

The purpose of this book is to answer such questions and in general to provide historical and other kinds of information about family life that will enhance readers' appreciation and understanding of Shakespeare. The book is intended especially for students and general readers, who often come to the plays and poems eager to learn but inadequately prepared to appreciate and understand all Shakespeare has to offer. For many, obstacles to full appreciation and understanding include misconceptions about marriage and family life in Shakespeare's time—misconceptions that, unfortunately, Internet sites, popular books on Shakespeare, and even some professional critics and scholars have aided in promoting. Some misconceptions, such as the mistaken view that Shakespeare's contemporaries married very young and that marriage arrangements were commonly forced on couples against their will, are still widespread among students and general readers, despite abundant evidence to the contrary. And other erroneous beliefs, such as in the supposedly common brutality of fathers and husbands, are maintained by many writers who should know better.

The information provided here is divided into chapters in such a way that the book can serve as a reference. The first two chapters present historical information about family life, the first with background on its development up to the Renaissance, the second looking in detail at family life in Shakespeare's time. Besides correcting misconceptions, the information in these chapters should help readers understand both specific practices and general attitudes related to family, as well as the importance of family in social and political life of the past and its central role in the predominant conception of reality.

Chapter 3 examines Shakespeare's uses of family in his poems and plays, with abundant examples that show the dramatic and thematic functions that family serves as well as variations between different kinds of plays. Chapter 4 explores family life as interpreted in Shakespearean productions from Shakespeare's time to the present, illustrating how particular directors and actors have dealt with details related to family life and how, in various cultures and media (including film), the understanding and treatment of family issues have changed over time. Chapter 5 surveys Shakespearean scholarship and criticism dealing with family and related issues, with some attention to earlier criticism but focusing on the controversies that have marked Shakespearean criticism during the twentieth century and into the twenty-first.

The main chapters just described are followed by a selection of primary documents, each introduced and set in context. These documents are drawn mainly from sixteenth- and seventeenth-century England and include various kinds of items—excerpts from sermons, discourses, handbooks on family life, legal documents, ballads, pamphlets on gender controversies of the period, and so on—which together provide a fascinating and illuminating window on life in the period as experienced and understood by men and women from various social classes and religious persuasions. This selection of primary documents is followed by a glossary defining major terms used in the book and by a bibliography citing print and electronic sources. For ease in use, the bibliography is divided into topical categories.

This book does not assume any specialized historical or critical background on the part of readers or anything beyond a general knowledge of Shakespeare. Historical and critical materials are presented as clearly and accessibly as possible. At the same time, the book is packed with information, providing accurate and up-to-date details about virtually all aspects of family life in Shakespeare's time, including courtship, marriage, child-rearing, domestic loss, inheritance, and sibling and extended family relations. Other books on Shakespeare—almost all of them addressed to scholars—have dealt with limited aspects of family life or with family in a narrow group of plays, such as the history plays or late romances. By contrast, this book examines family life as a whole in connection with the broad range of Shakespeare's works, as well as in connection with Shakespearean performance and criticism from the 1600s to the present.

Besides appearing in a separate section near the end of the book, documents from Shakespeare's time provide specific evidence for the description of family life I offer in earlier chapters. In addition, a few illustrations drawn from paintings, engravings, photographs, and other sources appear throughout the book to provide a visual sense of family life in Shakespeare's time as well as a record of some important moments in Shakespearean productions over the centuries.

In all these ways—through information on many aspects of family life and on its treatment on stage and in film, supported by illustrations and by evidence from primary sources and from recent historical study—this book attempts to make readers aware of both the familiarity and the unfamiliarity, even strangeness, of Shakespeare's treatment of family. I hope to assist readers in discovering the connections between their own experiences and the plays' depictions of family life. But I also intend to help readers see the disparities—the ways family life in the plays, and with it family life in Shakespeare's time, differs radically from family as we know it now.

Obviously, being aware of both the similarities and the differences is crucial if we hope, as readers and viewers, to understand Shakespeare aright. But this awareness also has a bearing on how effectively the plays are performed—how well, that is, particular performances can help audiences identify with the characters and actions on stage but at the same time remain aware of the distance between events on the stage and their own familiar lives. And so, along with its other purposes, this book can serve as a source of information for directors and actors. One example of how this book can be helpful to such readers is in the information it gives about customs depicted in the plays that are no longer commonly practiced or understood—for instance, the custom (marked by particular gestures on the part of both parents and children) of giving and receiving parental blessings, a custom that is mentioned or appears, often with powerful effect, in over half of Shakespeare's plays. Not only do I explain this custom and its role in daily life in Shakespeare's time, but I also show how Shakespeare himself uses the custom and how it has been used—or sometimes has been ignored or misunderstood—in later productions of the plays.

Besides its intrinsic interest for most readers and viewers, family holds a place of high dramatic and thematic importance in almost all of Shakespeare's plays, from the happy endings of the comedies and romances to the horrors portrayed in the tragedies. Despite the various ways family functions in the plays, there has been a long tradition of oversimplifying Shakespeare's picture of family life. Many readers and viewers—and even some professional critics—have insisted on viewing Shakespeare's treatment of family in either an unrealistically positive or an overly negative light. Recent critics have mainly erred in the negative direction. As a result, much Shakespearean criticism over the past 30 or 40 years has been unbalanced and inaccurate in its view of family in Shakespeare's plays and in Shakespeare's time. This has been due in part to the influence of early work by historians of the family that has since been corrected by better and more sympathetic historical research. Some critics still depend on Philippe Ariès, for instance, despite the fact that historians now reject some of his central assertions about the treatment of children in the past. Another writer, Lawrence Stone, has been especially influential on Shakespearean criticism even though most historians consider his work on English family life deeply flawed. Some articles and books by Shakespearean critics still refer to his assertions that marriages in the past were loveless, that parents did not grieve greatly over their children's deaths, and that the brutal disciplining of children was widely accepted. Most historians of family life would now say that these assertions are at best suspect and at worst simply wrong. As evidenced by the bibliography found later in this book, I refer to some of the best recent studies, including books by Ralph A.

Houlbrooke, Linda A. Pollock, Alan Macfarlane, and David Cressy. These and other studies give a richer and more accurate picture of family life in the past than was available only a generation ago. Unfortunately, many Shakespearean critics have not caught up with the historians' progress, and as a result, students who dip into Shakespearean criticism for general understanding or help in writing papers often come away with a distorted rather than enriched view of family life in Shakespeare's works and in his world.

Thus, one of my chief aims in this book is to provide a balanced approach to family life in the age of Shakespeare. As I summarize how family was experienced in the past and then explore Shakespeare's various uses of family, I seek to balance the negatives that were undoubtedly present in the period—conflict, anxiety, domination, and so on—with the equally well-documented positives. These include the ideals of sacrifice, generosity, and mutual respect and the aspiration for loving, happy family life shared by many in Shakespeare's time. The result, I hope, is that readers will come away from this book better equipped to experience and interpret the richness and variety of Shakespeare's works.

Quotations from Shakespeare are from *The Riverside Shakespeare*, 2nd edition, edited by G. Blakemore Evans (Boston: Houghton Mifflin, 1997). Unless otherwise indicated, biblical quotations are from the Authorized or King James Version. Through most of the text, when I have quoted from older sources, including sixteenth- and seventeenth-century documents, I have retained the original spelling, but I have expanded contracted forms of "the," "that," and certain other words; have modernized the use of u/v and i/j; and have not generally followed the use of italics and other typefaces in the originals. In the Primary Documents section, however, the selections have been more thoroughly modernized for ease in reading.

I am grateful to all who have contributed to this project: David Paxman, who gave the manuscript a careful reading; colleagues from around the world with whom I have discussed the issues raised in this book; librarians and other personnel at the Shakespeare Centre Library, the British Film Institute, the British Library, the Bodleian, the Folger Shakespeare Library, the Houghton Library, the Huntington Library, and other institutions where I have done research; research assistants who have aided my work on family life for many years and especially Emily Dyer, Rachel Ebeling, Veronica Goosey, and Jessica Green, who have worked with me on this project; and George Butler, my editor at Greenwood Press, who has answered dozens of questions and given vital guidance. I am also grateful to Brigham Young University, which has provided time and other resources to encourage my work. Above all, I am grateful for my family—my parents, parents-in-law, children, and other relatives who have taken an interest in the project and my wife, Margaret Blair Young, a brilliant but generous critic and a faithful friend. Without the encouragement, patience, and kindness she and others have provided, I could never have written this book.

1

BACKGROUND

Much in family life of the past is unfamiliar to us. Marriages that might shock us now—for instance, between an uncle and a niece—were common in some cultures. Many other features of family life, including gender roles, inheritance customs, and the family's political role, have changed over time. Yet much is familiar as well. Family has always been associated with the great rites of passage: birth, coming of age, death. Family relationships have always aroused strong emotions. And family has always had both a social function and a powerful role in forming personal identity.

Though in contrast to older cultures, family life in Shakespeare's time may seem relatively familiar, it has its share of unexpected features—features that we will better understand if we trace them to their origins in earlier periods. At least three sources of cultural influence helped shape family life in Shakespeare's time: Greek and Roman civilization, biblical tradition going back to Hebrew and Christian antiquity, and the Germanic cultures from which the English originated. Each of these cultures differs from the others on such matters as gender roles, availability of divorce, the age gap between husbands and wives, and relative freedom in choice of marriage partners. At the same time, these cultures have much in common, often revealing aspects of family life that have held true for centuries, sometimes persisting into our own time. Among these aspects are the centrality of the nuclear family and the importance of familial love and loyalty. Along with changes and continuity in family life itself, there have been changes in the role family has played in political life and in each culture's understanding of the world. A look at these cultures will thus help us see both what is distinctive in early modern family life and what connects it with life in other periods.

ANCIENT GREECE AND ROME

Family life in ancient Greece and Rome illustrates a principle that applies in part to Shakespeare's time, certainly more than it does to the modern world: namely, that—in contrast to the modern view of family as a private set of associations among autonomous individuals—families in traditional cultures functioned both as parts of the larger community and as units from which individuals derived their identities.

Ancient Greece

Though family life in ancient Greece had important personal functions—for instance, it was a place where emotional bonds were formed and where individuals received practical and religious instruction—the family's most important role was to serve as the foundation of the social structure. Family life varied from one ancient Greek city-state to another, but in every city-state, people viewed themselves as belonging to a *polis*, or community—a social unit in which all citizens participated and whose laws and customs were binding on all. The *polis* in turn was made up of smaller units based on kinship, the smallest being the individual family or household. Groups of related families formed what were known as *gene* (singular: *genos*). Several *gene* formed a phratry (a "brotherhood" or clan), and the phratries were grouped into *phylae*, or tribes.

Each household included parents, children, and often additional members, such as slaves or unmarried female relatives. The father was the head of the household and was responsible for representing the family in public affairs, providing dowries for his daughters and sometimes for other relatives, caring for his aged parents, carrying on the family's religious traditions, and keeping ancestral lands intact. A father's public functions included helping to defend the city and ensuring the continuation of his family, an essential role given that each family was an integral part of the *polis* as well as the means by which traditions were handed on.

Men were the main or only participants in some of the most important activities of ancient Greece, including warfare, athletic competition, and the feasting and poetry recitation that took place at gatherings known as symposia. Women's activities, with the notable exception of religious worship, were confined mainly to the home. In cities, a portion of the house was often reserved exclusively for women and children, and women did not generally go out in public unsupervised, except during festivals. In addition to bearing and raising children, wives also managed household affairs and supervised the family's slaves. Besides work inside the home, women also played a prominent role in religious worship, some serving as priestesses.

At least in Athens, there seems to have been a wide difference in age between husbands and wives, with marriage taking place between a man of about 30 and a woman of about 14 or 15, a much wider age gap than was common in Shakespeare's time. Upon marriage, the bride became part of her husband's family. Marriage was preceded, sometimes several years earlier, by a betrothal arranged by a young woman's father or guardian. The marriage itself was accompanied by various ceremonies, including sacrifice, ritual baths taken by the bride and groom, feasting, and a procession leading the bride to her husband's house, with attendants carrying torches and singing wedding songs, including the *epithalamion* (literally, "at the bridal chamber") that was imitated by poets in Shakespeare's time.

Greek marriages were monogamous. Marriages between close relatives, such as cousins or uncles and nieces, were not prohibited and in fact were sometimes required in order to perpetuate a family line. Marriage relationships between parents and children or between children of the same mother, however, would have been considered incestuous. Divorce was relatively common (for instance, it could result if a couple were unable to have children), and those who were widowed or divorced often remarried.

It is hard to know how much companionship existed in an average Greek marriage, though there is evidence that it was sometimes present despite age differences and other obstacles. Greek literature includes depictions of romantic love in marriage, sometimes along with the problems such love could cause in producing divided loyalties. Epitaphs include tender expressions of love between husband and wife (for instance, one pictures a wife bidding farewell to her husband, "dearest of men," and the husband acknowledging that, as she loved him, so he "loved [her] in return" and now longs for her [Pomeroy 10–11]). Nevertheless, as Simon Hornblower has pointed out, it appears that "the prevailing homosexual ethos of the gymnasia and of the symposium helped to reduce the cultural value attached to women and to the marriage bond" (248). Attitudes may have been different, however, among the poor and in the countryside, where there was probably freer association of men and women. Furthermore, the strong distinction between male and female roles did not hold in all Greek city-states. In Sparta, for instance, women participated in athletics and other public activities.

Childbirth took place in the home. As in ancient cultures generally, infant mortality was high, perhaps 30 or 40 percent in the first year. As a result, an average Athenian family probably included about two sons and one daughter. In Sparta, weak or deformed infant boys were regularly abandoned. In Athens, where abandonment of girls was more common, some abandoned infants were rescued and either raised by foster parents or sold into slavery.

Children who remained in the family underwent a purification ceremony a few days after birth. As in many other cultures, including Shakespeare's, Athenian infants were swaddled, that is, wrapped in strips of cloth. Mothers generally nursed their children, but some infants were nursed by other women. Much in the life of children and parents would be familiar to us even today. There is a good deal of evidence for childhood play, including games, toys, and dolls. Despite the practice of abandoning infants, the ancient Greeks—especially mothers—apparently loved their children, and parents grieved deeply when children who were part of the family died. Parents evidently took delight in their small children, despite being aware of their physical, moral, and intellectual immaturity.

As they grew up, both boys and girls participated in religious rituals. Much education took place within the home, with boys and girls preparing for their different roles. Schooling was not compulsory, but many boys attended school beginning about age 6 or 7. At infancy and at adolescence a boy could be enrolled in his father's phratry. Young men became citizens at about age 18 and acquired further adult privileges and responsibilities at about age 30. This pattern of education and change in status, based mainly on life in Athens in the classical period (c. 500–300 B.C.), did not hold for all city-states, in particular for Sparta, where boys left home at age 7 and received lengthy military training.

Besides variations among the Greek city-states, changes in family life also took place over time. In later times, particularly in the Hellenistic period beginning in the late 300s B.C., men married at a younger age, family life became a more private matter, and women were more likely to play a prominent role in the public sphere. In all periods of Greek culture, however, family was considered a vitally important institution and was associated with such ideals as loyalty and love. Though tension certainly existed in some families, harmony between parents and children was valued—Mark Golden quotes an ancient Greek proverb, "How sweet is concord between parents and children" (104)—as was harmony between brothers. Though men and women had very different roles in ancient Greece, the close bond that developed between brothers and sisters in childhood often continued later in life. When ancient Greeks lived long enough to have grandchildren, there also seems to have been affection between grandchildren and grandparents. And though husbands and wives in many ways lived separate lives, many marriages appear to have been loving ones.

Several Greek writers discussed family life at length, and some even questioned traditional ideas about the family. Among these writers, three especially—Xenophon, Plato, and Aristotle—influenced thinking on the subject in Shakespeare's day. Xenophon, the most traditional of the three, wrote a treatise titled *Oeconomicus* describing the different roles of husband and wife in managing the household and carrying out other family duties. This treatise was often quoted in early modern England to support arguments for natural differences between men and women. Plato and Aristotle, whose ideas on family life were more complex and challenging than Xenophon's, were also frequently quoted and discussed.

In *The Republic*, Plato has Socrates propose the abolition of private family life. In an ideal state the rulers should be forbidden "to live together in separate households, and all the women should be common to all the men; similarly, children should be held in common, and no parent should know its child, or child its parent" (168). Children would thus belong to the entire community. Plato may have based this proposal on life in Sparta, where family connections were similarly broken down. The reason Plato gives for abolishing private families is that they pose the danger of disunity. Presumably, with families living in separate households, individuals would care more about themselves and their immediate kin than about the community as a whole. In the ideal society, by contrast, rather than indulging in "his own private joys and sorrows" and having his interests divided between the state and the family, a citizen should view anyone he meets "as related to him" (179, 178). All private interests would thus be replaced by a desire for the good of the whole community.

Plato's student Aristotle disagreed with his teacher's proposal. He argued that the community, or *polis*, is necessarily made up of private households, which perform certain functions essential to the life of the larger community. It is in households that individuals—who are joined together by natural bonds—first learn to associate ethically with others and are thus prepared for life in the *polis*. At the same time, for a family to perform its functions, family life needs the support of the larger community, with its laws and shared way of life. According to Aristotle, family life in itself is not a cause of social disunity. Rather, caring for oneself and one's family becomes the basis for caring about the community as a whole. Furthermore, Aristotle argues, if children belonged to the whole community, individual members of the community would feel *less* responsible for caring for and educating the children because they would not feel strongly tied to any of them. Families and the community are thus both necessary to each other, and together they enable individuals to enjoy a life of virtue and happiness.

Plato's radical proposal was likely intended as a critique of Athenian life, in which families were becoming a source of social disunity rather than cohesion. But his proposal, as well as Aristotle's response, shows that even in ancient Greek culture, where membership in the larger community was of central importance, the family played a different but also vitally important role. Though families performed public functions and were connected with the larger community, they also had a private dimension: relationships within the family were among the closest and strongest; husbands and wives were bonded by affection and responsibility; and parents not only loved and cared for their children but also saw them as in some special way "their own," even as extensions of the parents' as well as the family's identity. Family life among the ancient Greeks thus not only had functions peculiar to their time and culture but also had much in common with family life as it has been experienced throughout human history.

Ancient Rome

Family life was, if anything, even more central to ancient Roman life than it was for the ancient Greeks. Family was the focus of much in Roman law and culture, including mythic and legendary stories, and terms from family life were used in the political and religious spheres. Greg Woolf notes, for instance, that Roman deities were often referred to as "Mother" or "Father" and that a leader might be honored by being called the *pater patriae* or "Father of the Fatherland" (80). The Romans saw themselves as constituting a kind of large-scale family. Like the Greeks, the ancient Romans saw the family (in the sense of the household) as playing an important public role. Especially during certain periods, such as the reign of Augustus, the state encouraged childbearing and sought to discourage celibacy and adultery. Families were expected to inculcate traditional values and prepare children for participation in the community. Family connections served important functions in many political and economic activities and helped establish one's social rank.

Yet despite many similarities, there were significant differences between Greek and Roman family life. For instance, whereas ancient Greeks normally married close relatives (a practice known as endogamy), the Romans practiced exogamy—that is, they married nonrelatives. Also, Roman brides were older than Greek ones. To some extent these differences reflect a general difference between what some scholars have called "Eastern" (or "non-European") and "Western European" types of marriage. Ancient Greeks were closer to the Eastern type, with endogamous marriages, very young marriage for women, greater separation between men and women, and exclusion of women from public life. Though ancient Romans were strongly influenced by Greek culture, the greater mingling of the sexes, slightly older age of brides, and practice of exogamy associate the Romans with the Western European family type.

One of the most important features of family life in ancient Rome was the power of the father, or *paterfamilias*, who had authority over all his living descendants as well as his slaves and former slaves. This authority theoretically included power over life and death (though this power was rarely exercised), as well as control of property and the power to dissolve his children's marriages and even convene court sessions to try family members for misdeeds. Romans referred to the authoritarian *paterfamilias* as an ideal, and the notion, though to some extent a myth, served important social functions. Yet the image of the all-powerful *paterfamilias* is certainly exaggerated; in reality his authority was limited in various ways (for instance, he often counseled with other family members in making decisions), and the relatively short life span of ancient Romans meant that a *paterfamilias* could wield his authority for only a limited period. Still, whatever the limits on his power, the *paterfamilias* was the main authority figure for an extended familial group and might exercise authority over a wider group than would have been the case in ancient Greece. Besides referring to a household or to a group connected by common lineage, the word *familia* could also mean all the persons and property over which a *paterfamilias* had authority. Family members in this sense included slaves and former slaves, who might live in various locations and who were often employed by aristocrats and other men of influence and wealth in governing, managing property, and carrying out economic enterprises.

Despite these extended uses of *familia*, however, life within a household had much in common with family life in other times and cultures. The strongest bonds were within the nuclear family—that is, the family made up of a husband and wife and their children—and in most cases each nuclear family lived in a separate household. Most households, however, would also have included slaves, and some included foster children. Though the *paterfamilias* theoretically controlled the property of his descendants, in practice adult children often lived independently, using an allowance provided by the *paterfamilias*. Upon his death, property was divided among all his children, both sons and daughters, and each son became a *paterfamilias* in his own right.

As in ancient Greece, marriage in ancient Rome was monogamous, though some men had mistresses. The age difference between husband and wife was probably somewhat smaller in ancient Rome than in ancient Greece. Marriage generally took place between a man in his later twenties and a woman in her later teens or early twenties, though in aristocratic families the bride and groom would commonly have been younger. Certain conditions had to be met for a valid marriage. For instance, the groom had to be at least 14 and the bride at least 12 (the same ages prescribed in Shakespeare's time), both had to be citizens, and they could not be too closely related. Also, though the parents of the bride and groom generally arranged the marriage, the couple's consent to the arrangement was required. Still, despite being able to object under certain circumstances (for instance, a daughter might object to marrying a man of "unworthy character"), the couple was normally expected to submit to their parents' (especially their fathers') wishes.

Though men were dominant in the public sphere, the women of ancient Rome played a greater public role than ancient Greek women had. In particular, wealthy women and female members of the imperial household might wield great influence. Many upper-class women were well educated. Depending on their social class, women had a choice of various occupations, and many women controlled a certain amount of property. Nevertheless, women could not hold public offices, and they were generally praised for their roles as wives and mothers and for such virtues as chastity, modesty, and obedience.

There is evidence of a great range of attitudes toward marriage among the ancient Romans, from complaints to expressions of tenderness and devotion, some of these in epitaphs composed by one spouse after the other's death. It is clear that for many, marriage was a close relationship. There also seems to have been a strong bond between parents and children and between siblings. Such family devotion—called *pietas*—was highly valued by ancient Romans.

Eight or nine days after birth (eight for girls and nine for boys), a child received a name and underwent the *lustratio*, a ceremony of protection and purification. As with the Greeks, newborns in ancient Rome were wrapped in swaddling bands. Though mothers were viewed as having a strong emotional bond with their children, by the late first century A.D., most children in wealthy families were nursed by wet nurses rather than by their own mothers. Like the Greeks, ancient Romans sometimes abandoned their infant children, who were often found and raised as slaves. Yet there is much evidence of affection between parents and children. One source, for instance, notes that "small children were often referred to as *deliciae*," meaning "sweethearts," and epitaphs and other evidence show that parents enjoyed seeing their children play and grieved at their death (Le Glay et al. 142; French 20–21; Nielsen 204). Most families had no more than two or three children who lived past infancy. Because in some families, no children survived to adulthood, it was fairly common for a man to adopt a son (usually someone who was already an adult) to carry on the family line.

Young children enjoyed playing with a variety of toys, games, and pets. As they grew older, children were introduced to more serious activities. Schools were available for children, including girls, at least to some extent, but were not compulsory. Wealthier families might employ tutors in the home to teach their children. There was no uniform age at which Roman boys officially became adults, but the transition took place sometime during the teenage years, usually between ages 14 and 16. The father marked this transition to adulthood by taking his son, along with a group of the father's friends, to be enrolled as a citizen. In addition, the son began wearing the *toga virilis*, or toga of manhood.

For many ancient Romans, one important function of family was to give them a sense of continuity over time. Inscriptions on monuments and tombstones indicate that Romans of various social classes felt it important to preserve the family name and remember those who had died. In particular, during the yearly festivals of Parentalia and Feralia, the tombs of ancestors were honored. Such practices were among the ways Romans identified with relatives beyond their immediate families.

Another way Romans identified with extended family members was through a social grouping known as the *gens* (plural: *gentes*). Each *gens* was a group of families that claimed common ancestry. Sometimes translated "clan," the *gens* was in some ways comparable to the Greek *genos* (also a group of related families). But though both had some religious functions and helped establish social status, the two institutions differed in many ways. For instance, unlike the Greek *gene*, which could be grouped into *phylae* or tribes, the Roman *gentes* were not part of larger family groups. And there was no ceremony for admission to a *gens* as there was for admission to a *genos*. Furthermore, the Roman practice of not marrying close relatives (the opposite being common for the ancient Greeks) meant that a husband and wife would not belong to the same *gens*.

Despite the collapse of the Roman Empire in the late 400s A.D., Roman law and custom continued to have some influence throughout the Middle Ages and into the early modern period. In addition, several writers from the ancient Roman world helped shape later attitudes about family, especially beginning in the Renaissance or early modern period, when Latin literature was intensely admired and imitated. For instance, Virgil's *Aeneid*, written in the first century B.C., puts great emphasis on family relationships and provides memorable images of family devotion, especially that of Aeneas, the epic's hero, carrying his father on his back out of the burning city of Troy.

Cicero, another Roman writer from the first century B.C. who was greatly admired during the Renaissance, wrote about family and other subjects in his book *De Officiis* (meaning *On Duties* or *On Obligations*). Although he presents friendship as the ideal relationship, he emphasizes the moral obligations that come with family bonds. Our first duty, he argues, is to our country and our parents, "for their services have laid us under the heaviest obligation; next come children and the whole family, who look to us alone for support and can have no other protection; finally, our kinsmen, with whom we live on good terms and with whom, for the most part, our lot is one" (61; 1.58). According to Cicero, family bonds derive from our natural instincts. The first and closest of these bonds, that of husband and wife, leads to the creation of a home and then to the bond between parents and children and between brothers and sisters, with further connections arising between families as the children leave home and marry. Family relationships are thus the source of social relationships in general. As Cicero puts it, the household "is the foundation of civil government, the nursery, as it were, of the state" (57; 1.54).

Besides Virgil, Cicero, and others who wrote in Latin, many from this period wrote in Greek, the language of educated people throughout the Mediterranean world. One of these was Plutarch, a writer of the first century A.D. best known for his *Lives of the Noble Greeks and Romans*, a source Shakespeare used for several plays set in ancient Rome. Plutarch also wrote a work titled *Moralia*, which includes (along with pieces on dozens of other topics) advice on educating children, discourses praising fraternal and paternal love, a dialogue arguing for the superiority of heterosexual over homosexual love and for the bonding power of sex in marriage, and advice for newlyweds. This advice encourages loyalty and unity of mind as well as of bodies and property, explains how to avoid anger and discord and how to nurture mutual affection, counsels the husband to respect and honor his wife and to govern through love, and urges both to do all things through mutual consent.

Another group of works from the ancient Roman world—long prose narratives now usually called "Greek romances" or "Greek novels"—were to have a strong influence on Shakespeare and other early modern writers and, through them, on the modern conception of love and marriage. These works, written between the first and third centuries A.D., tell of long-lost children, strange adventures, and lovers who are separated and, after many trials, finally reunited. The relevance of these works for later attitudes toward marriage and family lies in their romanticized view of young love, their emphasis on fidelity and love in marriage, and, in some, their depiction of joyful family reunions. Shakespeare was among the writers who helped transmit these attitudes to later generations, basing several of his plays—for instance, *The Comedy of Errors*, *Pericles*, and *The Winter's Tale*—directly or indirectly on the "Greek romances."

Both literary works of this sort and other evidence about family life in ancient times reveal that, despite many differences between life then and now, there is much we can relate to, including the emphasis on the nuclear family and the notion that family life should be harmonious and happy, with relationships marked by mutual respect, loyalty, and affection. There is plenty of evidence that these ideals were not always attained, along with equally impressive evidence that the ideals were aspired to and sometimes experienced. Family was clearly an institution of central importance in ancient Greece and Rome, depended on for educating children and preparing them for life in the community. Family also served important economic functions related to the activities of daily life and to the transmission of property from one generation to another. But family had more than just pragmatic functions. Children were desired and valued for their own sake. Marriage was seen as a relationship of friendship and affection as well as one of procreative and economic necessity. Much religious worship was carried on within families, and family relationships were treated by many as sacred. Families helped link individuals to the past and future. And family helped give individuals a sense of significance and belonging.

HEBREW AND CHRISTIAN ANTIQUITY

The ancient Greeks and Romans helped shape family life in Shakespeare's time through the ideas of their philosophers and other writers, through political institutions and laws, and through some specific customs that survived through the centuries. Yet in some ways the ancient Hebrews and early Christians had an even greater impact. Christianity became a dominant cultural force during late antiquity and throughout the Middle Ages. And though ancient Hebrew family life had little if any direct influence on family life in Shakespeare's time, it had enormous indirect influence through the Bible, which became one of the most authoritative sources for the standard understanding and practice of family life.

Ancient Hebrews

The Bible includes a wide variety of material relevant to family: frequent genealogical lists that show the close link between personal identity and family descent; commandments, doctrines, and stories with doctrinal implications; and other reflections of family life among the Hebrews and early Christians who transmitted the biblical text. The Bible begins with the story of Adam and Eve, whose marriage, as the first human one and as one authorized by God himself, became the defining, archetypal pattern for all subsequent marriages. They are commanded to "multiply, and replenish the earth" (Genesis 1:28). The fact that God creates Eve from one of Adam's ribs means that she is "bone of [his] bones, and flesh of [his] flesh," with the following lesson being drawn: "Therefore shall a man leave his father and his mother, and shall cleave unto his wife: and they shall be one flesh" (Genesis 2:23–24). The ideal unity of a married couple was founded on this biblical story, as was the idea that neither male nor female is complete alone.

The family of Adam and Eve also became archetypal, setting a pattern for all future families. This pattern has both its positive side—for instance, Adam and Eve's nurturing and teaching of their children—and its negative side. The first murder, Cain's killing of his brother Abel, took place within this family and, as an image of family conflict, was the subject of a good deal of later commentary and literary representation. In *Hamlet*, for instance, Shakespeare refers to Cain and Abel and has King Claudius reflect on the resemblance between the biblical story and his own murder of his brother: "It hath the primal eldest curse upon't, / A brother's murther" (3.3.37–38).

Much of Genesis, the first book of the Bible, focuses on family life and especially on its problems, including conflict between husband and wife (for instance, Isaac and Rebekah's conflict over who should be the birthright son) and between brothers (for instance, Joseph's persecution by his brothers followed by his eventually forgiving them and saving them from famine). Stories with a family dimension—such as the stories of Noah, Abraham, Isaac, Jacob, and Joseph and his brothers—received plentiful commentary throughout the Middle Ages, and many were portrayed on stage in the English mystery plays of the 1300s to 1500s.

Later books of the Bible include similar stories—for instance, the accounts of Ruth and Esther, of King David's adultery, of David's relationship with his son Absalom, and of Job and his family. The story of Jephthah from the book of Judges, in which he finds himself forced by a vow to sacrifice his daughter, is one of many biblical stories to which Shakespeare refers. In addition to such stories, the Bible presents direct and symbolic teaching relevant to family life. The book of Proverbs has much advice on family life, including counsel to obey and respect parents and a description of an ideal wife. The Ten Commandments include injunctions against adultery and against coveting "thy neighbour's wife," as well as the command to honor father and mother (Exodus 20:12, 14, 17). The books of Leviticus and Deuteronomy give specific instructions on incest, divorce, and other matters that were to influence rules and practices throughout the Middle Ages and even, with modification, into our own time. The Hebrew scriptures sometimes refer to God as a father and thus as the model of compassionate but demanding love that earthly fathers ought to imitate. Furthermore, God is repeatedly called the husband of Israel, and prophets denounce the Israelites for being like an unfaithful wife.

As the Bible and other evidence make clear, the ancient Hebrews had a strong sense of family solidarity and greatly valued relationships within both the nuclear and the extended family. Biblical stories of family conflict and reconciliation reveal the problems of family life but also the great value put on restoring harmony when it was lost. The ancient Hebrews undoubtedly found personal satisfactions in family life. Yet because all of Israel was viewed as being under covenant with God, personal interests were supposed to be subservient to fulfilling the terms of that covenant. Therefore, whatever its personal value, family was also seen as an instrument for achieving larger purposes.

Ancient Hebrews identified strongly with their ancestral families, traced through the male line, and saw themselves as part of a great extended family, the nation of Israel. Within that greater family, individuals were members of one of the 12 tribes of Israel. Individuals within a given tribe were members of smaller groups of kin descended from a common ancestor. The Hebrew term for such a group, *mišpāḥâ,* is sometimes translated "clan," but some prefer "residential kinship group" because the group's members generally lived in the same area (Meyers 13).

Archeological evidence has shown that the early inhabitants of ancient Israel lived in villages, each made up of about 50 to 150 people belonging to several extended families, all part of the same clan or *mišpāḥâ*. Each extended family or "father's house"—*bêt-'āb* in Hebrew—would have had up to about 15 members, including a husband and wife and their children and grandchildren, sometimes along with servants and other unrelated members, all living in a family compound with two or three houses surrounding a courtyard. Though they saw themselves as members of the "father's house," it is likely that each married son and his immediate family lived in a separate structure within the family compound.

The marriage practices of the ancient Hebrews show a preference for endogamy (marriage with relatives), though with certain limitations. The biblical rules against incest prohibited sexual relations within the immediate family and also within certain relationships formed through marriage, including between a man and his sister-in-law or daughter-in-law. But marriage between other close relatives was possible, including between an uncle and a niece. There appears to have been a preference for marrying within the same tribe and especially for marrying fellow Israelites. However, the strong condemnation by several biblical writers of marriages with foreign wives shows that marriages to foreigners sometimes took place. Such marriages were condemned primarily because a foreign spouse with different religious beliefs and practices might lead one away from fidelity to Israel's God.

Most marriages were monogamous, but some men, mainly among the elite, practiced polygamy (meaning "many marriages") or, more precisely, polygyny (having "many wives"). Some men also had concubines, that is, women who were not wives in the full sense but who were viewed as belonging to a particular man and who might bear him children. Some polygamous relationships were likely the result of a practice known as levirate marriage (from the Hebrew word *lēvir,* meaning "brother-in-law"), in which a near kinsman, sometimes a brother, married the widow of a man who died without having children. The purpose of levirate marriages was apparently to provide an heir to carry on the family line of a childless man and also to keep his land within the extended family.

The father was recognized as having the ultimate authority to arrange marriages for his children. But in practice a son might be involved in the process of selecting a wife (for instance, he might approach the father of a prospective bride). And it appears that mothers were sometimes involved as well and that daughters' wishes were at times taken into consideration. Determining the average age of marriage is difficult, and ages certainly varied with location and over time. But common ages for marriage seem to have been in the late twenties (or sometimes later) for men and in the mid- to late teens for women.

Marriage was usually preceded by betrothal, which was taken so seriously that the couple were considered essentially married even before the wedding took place. The wedding was accompanied by various ceremonies, including a procession and feasting. Once married, the couple had different but equally important roles. Men might, among other things, be farmers, shepherds, warriors, or (if of the appropriate lineage) priests. Besides bearing and raising children, women engaged in many domestic and agricultural tasks requiring great skill. As a family's mother, a woman—though subordinate to her husband—was honored, and she often exerted a strong influence in the family.

Despite biblical indications that companionship and mutual aid were important purposes of marriage along with procreation, marriages among the ancient Hebrews may have often been something other than the intimate partnership valued in the modern world. For the ancient Hebrews, the ideal wife would have beauty, virtue, and domestic skills and would be obedient and faithful to her husband. The ideal husband would honor and care for his wife and would do so from a position of superior authority. Though ideally marriages would be loving and harmonious, there is some evidence that blood relationships were emphasized more strongly than the marriage bond. With very few restrictions, a husband could divorce his wife. However, despite scriptural permission for divorce, one of the later prophets condemned the practice (Malachi 2:16). Remarriage after divorce was common.

Children were highly valued in ancient Hebrew families. For one thing, they guaranteed the continuation of the family line. Women considered childlessness a reproach and a cause of grief; being able to have children was a source of honor and joy. At birth, infants were washed and wrapped in swaddling bands. Nursing, whether by a wet nurse (for the wealthy) or by the mother herself, might last as long as three years. Children were expected to have great respect for parental authority, but that authority was supposed to be used in the child's interest. Parents were an important source of both religious and practical instruction. Parents were also believed to have the power to bless or curse their children, a belief that persisted into Shakespeare's time and that Shakespeare alludes to in many of his plays. The ancient book of Sirach (also known as Ecclesiasticus) warns that "a father's blessing strengthens his children's houses, but a mother's curse uproots their foundations" (3:9, New English Bible). The Hebrew custom of giving a blessing, sometimes taking place as a parent was dying and in later periods as a regular part of Sabbath observance, was a formal act patterned after the blessings given by ancient biblical figures such as Isaac, Jacob, and Joseph. These men, while placing hands on the recipient's head, pronounced words of blessing that were viewed as influencing their sons and their sons' descendants. In a similar way, blessings given by Jewish parents, especially by fathers, were viewed as having divine sanction.

In the Bible, a father's blessing is sometimes associated with the birthright, the right to carry on the family line. Though this right usually belongs to the oldest son, it was sometimes deliberately or inadvertently transferred to a younger son. In contrast to the common practice of Shakespeare's time, inheritance among the ancient Hebrews was not governed strictly by primogeniture—that is, the oldest son did not inherit the entire estate. However, though the inheritance was divided among the sons, the oldest son was given a double portion. If a couple had no sons, the inheritance was divided among the daughters, but they were expected to marry within the tribe so that the property would not go to outsiders.

Early Christians

The earliest Christians were Jews and, soon after, non-Jews whose marriage and family patterns would have been those of their cultures of origin. Their new religion, however, certainly influenced their attitudes and practices related to family life. Over time, Christian teachings as recorded in the Bible became the basis for laws and customs throughout Europe.

The Christian scriptures of the New Testament repeat many of the teachings of the Hebrew scriptures—for instance, the injunctions against adultery and other sexual misconduct and the counsel to honor parents. The New Testament, especially in the epistles of Paul, gives additional emphasis to love, forbearance, and forgiveness within the family: parents are to love their children, and husbands and wives are to love each other. At the same time, the New Testament states even more strongly than the Hebrew scriptures that loyalty to family should not compete with loyalty to God. Jesus is quoted as saying that he has come to "set a man at variance against his father, and the daughter against her mother, and the daughter in law against her mother in law." He further teaches, "He that loveth father or mother more than me is not worthy of me: and he that loveth son or daughter more than me is not worthy of me" (Matthew 10:35, 37). Family is thus one of the settings in which one can live a Christian life, but family loyalties should not take priority over loyalty to God.

On the subject of marriage, the New Testament presents contrasting ideas. On the one hand, it emphasizes unity and a kind of equality between husband and wife. On the other, it teaches that the husband is "the head" of the wife. Paul teaches, "Neither is the man without the woman, neither the woman without the man, in the Lord" (1 Corinthians 11:11) and indicates that husband and wife are spiritual equals. Marriage is called "honourable" and the marriage bed "undefiled" (Hebrews 13:4), and Paul (though sometimes read as having a negative view of marriage) counsels husband and wife to freely respond to each other's desire for sexual relations (1 Corinthians 7:2–5). More than once, the New Testament quotes the verse in Genesis about a man leaving his father and mother and becoming "one flesh" with his wife (Matthew 19:5; Mark 10:7–8; Ephesians 5:31). When Jesus quotes this verse, he adds, "What therefore God hath joined together, let not man put asunder" (Matthew 19:6). Moses allowed divorce "because of the hardness of your hearts," but Jesus expects a higher standard of his followers: divorce is wrong except as a consequence of fornication (Matthew 19:8–9). These words from the New Testament led to divorce being prohibited within the Catholic Church and later within the Church of England.

Several New Testament passages call the husband "the head" of the wife or otherwise refer to his authority in the family. Paul writes, "For the husband is the head of the wife, even as Christ is the head of the church" (Ephesians 5:23; see also 1 Corinthians 11:3). Peter counsels wives to "be in subjection" to their husbands (1 Peter 3:1). Though some recent scholarship has shown that "head" can mean "source" and imply nurturing and life-giving power as well as authority, these passages have usually been interpreted as implying authority on the husband's part and obedience on the wife's. (For a defense of the translation "source," see Fee 502–5; Kroeger 267–83; Mickelsen and Mickelsen 97–110.) Some of these passages, however, temper this hierarchical view with suggestions of equality and mutual submission. Paul speaks of "submitting yourselves one to another" and writes that, just as the wife should submit herself to her husband, so the husband should love his wife and give himself for her, as Christ did for the Church (Ephesians 5:21, 25).

New Testament teachings both accommodated and sought to reform the practices of those who became Christians. Both responses were necessary because, to an extent, early Christians shared the customs and attitudes of the cultures in which they lived. In several ways, however, the Christian view and practice of family life were distinctive. Christians were expected to follow a strict code of sexual morality and to be examples of self-restraint and purity in a decadent world. Notably, this expectation was the same for both men and women. Most early Christians were probably monogamous. They were expected to be faithful to their marriage partners and were counseled to avoid divorce. Because they were supposed to show charity—that is, patience, kindness, humility, compassion, and goodwill—toward all, including their enemies, Christians were certainly expected to be charitable in their family life as well.

But perhaps what made early Christians most distinctive was their sense of being called to something higher than an ordinary worldly life and their willingness to endure persecution for their faith. In theory at least, family was not their highest value or central focus; in fact, they must be willing to sacrifice family loyalties, if required, in order to be loyal to God. Though most continued to live in traditional family units, early Christians saw themselves as belonging to a larger family, one encompassing all followers of Christ. Early Christians therefore called each other "brother" and "sister." This view that all Christians belong to a single family is founded on statements made by Jesus, such as this one: "For whosoever shall do the will of my Father which is in heaven, the same is my brother, and sister, and mother" (Matthew 12:50). Among other things, this view led early Christians to care for widows, orphans, and others who lacked families of their own.

After the period of intense persecution ended and Christians became accepted and even dominant within the Roman Empire, Christian ideas about marriage and family became increasingly influential. Yet this influence became complex and in some ways contradictory as Christian thought developed during late antiquity and the Middle Ages. To a degree, Christian influence strengthened marriage and family life and moved them somewhat closer to modern expectations, leading to a greater sense of the unique value of each child, greater equality between the sexes, a growing emphasis on marital affection and free choice of a partner as the basis for marriage, the opportunity (previously unavailable under Roman law) for slaves to enter into valid marriages, and emphasis on the permanence of marriage accompanied by opposition to divorce. As part of this process, marriage became a sacrament sanctified by the Church.

At the same time, by emphasizing asceticism and especially sexual purity, St. Augustine and other early Christian thinkers seemed to devalue marriage and exalt virginity as the ideal Christian condition. This ideal came to be connected with monasticism, a practice that began among some devout Christians in late antiquity and grew into a thriving institution during the Middle Ages. New Testament passages calling for spiritual-mindedness and self-restraint came to be interpreted as condemning sexual indulgence of all kinds, including in marriage. Though Christian authorities expressed various views during the Middle Ages, some asserted that all sexual relations were sinful to a degree, especially if engaged in for any purpose other than procreation. Some writers were especially vigorous in their opposition to widows' remarrying. And some denigrated not only marriage but women in general, as a source of temptation and as inferior to men in various respects. Alongside this misogynistic tradition, however, were contrasting views expressed by writers who idealized women, considered them different from but complementary to men, or emphasized the spiritual equality of men and women.

During late antiquity and the Middle Ages, the Church as an institution gradually came to set the rules that governed marriage and family life. Because these matters had previously been handled mainly by the families themselves, the growing power of the Church lessened the power of families. Yet some families, endowed with wealth or political power, were influential even while the Church grew in importance, and such families continued to emphasize family loyalty. In contrast, Christian thinkers focused on the ideal of the entirety of mankind—or at least of all Christians—forming a single family. St. Augustine used this ideal as one reason for the laws against incest. If marriage were allowed between people closely related, then kinship ties would remain within relatively small groups, each group lacking such ties with other groups. But if (as the laws against incest required) marriage between close relatives were prohibited, then spouses would need to be sought outside of one's own kindred. As a result, "the social tie would not be confined to a small group but would extend more widely to connect a large number with the multiplying links of kinship." More people, that is—including people previously not closely related—would be "bound by intimate ties," the ties of marriage and other family relationships. The social harmony thus promoted through "the affection of kinship" would reflect and anticipate the unity of the heavenly city toward which Christians were aiming (*City of God* 623–24).

Using biblical precepts combined with Roman law and custom as well as influences from other sources, the Church sought to regulate divorce and prohibit a variety of other practices, including abortion, infanticide, and the abandonment and sale of children. Customs and attitudes changed slowly, and despite the highly spiritual emphasis of Christian thinkers in late antiquity and the Middle Ages, marriage and family life for most people remained ordinary, practical realities largely unaffected by theoretical speculation. Still, Christianity had a pervasive influence that gradually transformed many people's conception of marriage and family.

As the Roman Empire grew weaker, Germanic customs and attitudes came to have an influence as well, especially in northern and western Europe. With the gradual Christianization of Europe, Roman and biblical influences combined with the native Germanic traditions to form what we now call the culture of medieval Europe.

EARLY GERMANIC CULTURE: FROM PRE-CHRISTIAN TO CHRISTIAN EUROPE

Before their conversion to Christianity, the Germanic peoples of Europe were made up of several tribes, each functioning as an economic and military unit and sometimes united by a common religious cult. Kinship, especially close kinship, was very important to life within a tribe but generally was not the source of a tribe's identity. In fact, several elements of ancient Germanic life tended to weaken the role of kinship: the importance of the retinues surrounding military chieftains, the ability of strong leaders to draw together people not closely related, and feuds and other conflicts within a tribe that might lead to permanent divisions.

The retinue—often called "comitatus" by scholars, following the practice of ancient Roman writers—consisted of the followers of a chieftain, who depended on the retinue for military and other services and who in return provided for the retinue's needs and divided with them the spoils of battle. This relationship between a chieftain and his followers became the basis for the more complicated feudal system that developed in medieval Europe. A chieftain's retinue might include close relatives, but it was not limited to them.

Feuds were the standard means for resolving conflicts and regulating behavior. Those closely related to a person who had been injured or killed were supposed to exact revenge on or monetary payment from the offender. This duty helped reaffirm the bonds between extended family members. Yet such feuds weakened the tribe as a whole, sometimes leading to the creation of a new tribe as one group separated from the rest.

Recent scholarship suggests that, despite the obligation to take part in feuds and other customs involving kinship ties, extended families did not form independent units among the early Germanic peoples. Though most members of a tribe would have been more or less distantly related, common descent was not the main source of a tribe's identity, and extended families were not the main social units within a tribe. Traditional theories have emphasized the supposedly central role in Germanic culture of clans or large groups with common ancestry. But there is little evidence that such clans existed, and they were certainly not an important element of social organization. As A. C. Murray concludes, "kinship was a crucial factor in all aspects of barbarian activity, but its uses and groupings were fluid, and probably on the whole not long lasting" (64).

The most important family relationships among the early Germanic peoples were within the individual household. Fathers were the main figures of authority, but wives also played an important and respected role. The ancient Roman historian Tacitus describes how, during battles, Germanic warriors were encouraged and cared for by their wives and mothers. He also notes that during times of peace, women did most of the work of managing the household. Along with the children, they apparently did most of the household chores as well. Children were valued, and according to Tacitus, limiting or destroying one's offspring was considered shameful. Mothers apparently breast-fed their own children rather than using nurses. Besides parents and children, a household might include slaves, but slavery was not common, and according to Tacitus, slaves normally had households of their own. Polygamy and concubinage were rare but existed, at least among the upper classes.

Marriage customs varied over time. Tacitus notes that at the time of marriage, husband and wife gave gifts to each other, in part to symbolize the partnership onto which they were about to embark. Apparently, marriages involved affection but were also a way of forming alliances between families. Tacitus emphasizes the importance of women's virtue and the rarity of adultery among the early Germans, but he certainly does this in part as a critique of Roman decadence.

In the earliest times, Germanic customs included marriage by capture (that is, men would marry women they captured in battle) and marriage by sale (a man would pay a family in exchange for a wife). Gradually, "the sale of the bride was converted to sale of the family's rights over her" and then finally "to a token payment balanced by a growing custom of giving money to the bride herself" (McNamara and Wemple 128). In addition to this bride gift, women also received a "morning gift" from their husbands following the consummation of the marriage. By means of these gifts, women during the early medieval period could come into possession of a significant amount of money and property. Germanic customs did not require the giving of a dowry by the bride's father, but some parents gave dowries, probably influenced by Roman customs.

Though family life mainly took place within individual households, extended families played important roles as well, not as independent social units but as groups with whom a person identified and with whom he or she was bound by shared obligations, including the obligation already discussed to take part in feuds. According to Murray, "the basic kin group of society" among early Germans was "the bilateral kindred"—that is, a relatively small group of relatives to whom a person was related through both father and mother (223). Malcolm Todd estimates that this group consisted of between 20 and 50 households (31).

Among the customs involving the extended family were those related to inheritance. Various tribes had different inheritance customs. For instance, primogeniture (inheritance by the firstborn, usually the firstborn son) was an occasional but not a usual practice. In most tribes, a family's possessions went to all the children upon the parents' death. If a couple had no children, the inheritance went first to the deceased's brothers and then (if there were no brothers) to paternal and maternal uncles, either in that order or possibly with the inheritance divided between both groups of uncles.

Despite the authority of fathers, then, inheritance and other practices indicate that both parents played an important role in defining a person's familial identity. In fact, a special bond seems to have existed between a man and his maternal uncles—or, viewed from the uncles' point of view, between a man and his sister's sons. The Roman historian Tacitus refers to this bond among the early Germans, and there is much evidence for its persistence among Germanic peoples throughout the Middle Ages. Though theories assuming a matriarchal structure in early German culture have been shown to be without foundation, it is clear that kinship ties through both the maternal and paternal lines were important.

Traditional life among the early Germans changed as they came into contact with other peoples. Such contact began at least as early as 100 B.C., when Germanic tribes began to engage in military conflict and other encounters with the Romans. As the Roman Empire weakened, many Germanic tribes—who up until then had lived mainly in northern and eastern Europe—migrated toward the south and west. This led to further contact with Romans, who enlisted some of the Germans to help defend the empire. By A.D. 476, the lands that had formed the western portion of the empire, including Italy, had come under the control of Germanic rulers. As the Roman Empire collapsed and as Germanic tribes established themselves in various areas and merged with earlier inhabitants, the groups that were eventually to become the nations of modern Europe began to take shape.

The conversion of the Germanic tribes to Christianity took place mainly between the 300s and 700s. This conversion, as well as their assimilation with other peoples of Europe, had profound effects on the Germanic peoples' way of life and understanding of the world, including changes in practices and attitudes related to family life. Among these changes were attempts to prohibit polygamy and concubinage, monastic life as an alternative to marriage and family life, and various changes in marriage and inheritance customs. Many of these changes came with the spread of Christianity and the growing power of the Church, which sought to set and enforce rules related to marriage and family life. Nevertheless, Church leaders often complained of practices without being able to end them. Other changes came as Germanic customs were influenced by contact with the customs of other peoples.

Marriage and inheritance customs, already existing in various forms throughout Europe, changed over the centuries that followed. Though sons were given preference in inheritance, the trend from the sixth century through the eighth was to loosen restrictions on inheritance by women. As some families gained wealth and property, the women in those families came to exercise considerable power in the public sphere. They shared in ruling kingdoms and other political units, helped defend their lands, and played other important roles in public life.

The dividing of estates that resulted from looser rules of inheritance led, however, to the weakening of great families. In response, Europe of the tenth and eleventh centuries saw a movement toward primogeniture: rather than being divided among the children, a family's entire estate would go to the oldest son. During this same period, a daughter's dowry—money or property given by her family when she married—came to replace her rights to inheritance. This series of changes helped protect the power of great families but reduced the economic independence of women.

Though many aspects of family life remained the same from the time of the early Germanic tribes to the formation of the medieval kingdoms, much also changed. Life in a medieval household was less rudimentary and less focused on warfare than it had been for Germanic families in earlier periods. Over time, Roman laws, attitudes, and customs influenced those of Germanic peoples. Christianity in particular came to have a profound influence, with the Church setting rules and seeking to influence behavior connected with marriage and family life. The important role of kindred, at first weakened by the power of Germanic kings and their retinues, would later grow as some families came to amass wealth and property and would change further with changing inheritance customs.

Yet even with these changes, the nuclear family—a household made up of parents and children—remained the focus of family life among the Germanic peoples and their descendants through the entire ancient and medieval periods. And contrary to common stereotypes, family life was commonly marked by affection between husband and wife and between parents and children. Though some children—offered to the Church, abandoned, or raised by a foster family—grew up outside of their family of birth, the evidence for parental attachment to children is abundant. Much literary and other evidence points to love and affection between husbands and wives as well.

Indeed, modern readers may be surprised at how familiar many medieval attitudes concerning marriage will seem. As Shannon McSheffrey points out, most historians dealing with the later Middle Ages acknowledge that "affection, attraction, and personal choice were major considerations in making a marriage," though practical matters were important as well (154–55). Even in the earlier Middle Ages, though forced marriages apparently took place, authorities noted the importance of the consent of the couple as well as the parents in contracting a marriage. By the 1100s, the free consent of the bride and groom was established as essential to a valid marriage, one of the reasons offered being that "those whose body is one ought to be of one spirit" (Urban II, qtd. by Noonan 421). Religious authorities emphasized procreation and avoiding fornication as primary purposes for sexual relations in marriage and noted circumstances under which sexual passion might be sinful, yet many also taught that moderate sexual pleasure in marriage was good, in part because it helped build unity and friendship between husband and wife.

FAMILY LIFE IN MEDIEVAL ENGLAND: FROM THE ANGLO-SAXONS TO EARLY MODERN TIMES

Much that has just been said about family life among Germanic peoples is also true of England during the Middle Ages, given that England's population during this time was largely Germanic. Before its invasion by Germanic tribes—the Angles, Saxons, and Jutes—in the A.D. 400s, the area we now call England was inhabited by Celtic peoples who had undergone a period of Roman rule. Because the invaders were Germanic tribesmen from an area of northern Europe outside of the realm of Roman influence, the culture they established in England was thoroughly Germanic, and because of its relatively isolated location, England would remain more Germanic in culture than the rest of Europe through the greater part of the Middle Ages. John Blair argues that a good deal of what Tacitus wrote of the early Germans in the first century A.D. applies accurately to the Anglo-Saxons and that even their conversion to Christianity left much in their customs and outlook intact (4–5).

Early Anglo-Saxon settlements were small—much smaller than the ones the invaders had left on the European continent—and often included a few related families, each living in a separate house. The membership of an average household would probably have been fairly small and would have consisted mainly of a nuclear family living in a single dwelling. Though the number of members of a household would have changed with births, deaths, and other events, an average household might have included the parents and perhaps two to four children. According to Sally Crawford, "the actual surviving number of offspring of any one mother rarely exceed[ed] four or five" (113). Occasionally, others (including servants or relatives) may have been part of a household, but it is hard to determine how often. In any case, it is not likely that extended families normally joined together to form single households, and only upper-class households would have included many members beyond the nuclear family.

We don't know the average age of marriage, but given the very low life expectancy of Anglo-Saxons, marriages may have taken place somewhat earlier than in Shakespeare's time. Average life expectancy was about 25 years or less, but that can be accounted for mainly by infant and childhood mortality. A person surviving adolescence could expect to live several decades longer. Crawford has assembled evidence suggesting that although some women (especially from well-to-do families) married in their teens, most women gave birth during their twenties, indicating that marriage often did not take place until the late teens or early twenties (109–12). Men may have been on average a little older than their wives. As with other Germanic peoples, Anglo-Saxon wives received a bride gift upon marriage and a morning gift after the marriage's consummation.

Most Anglo-Saxons were farmers, and husbands and wives both would have worked to sustain the household and farm. Most of women's work, however, took place inside the home, including textile production. They also managed and protected household goods. As a result, they were associated with keys, which were often attached to their belts. Men's work included planting, harvesting, dairy work, and related crafts, but sometimes women engaged in such farm labor as well. Men also took part in military activity.

As with earlier Germanic peoples, a person's kin included relatives on both the mother's and the father's sides of the family. People generally recognized only close relatives (especially parents, grandparents, siblings, uncles, aunts, nephews, and nieces) as kin, while "more distant relatives fade into obscurity" (Crawford 109). The bond between a man and his maternal uncles was especially strong. This bond, which again goes back to earlier Germanic times, brought mutual affection and obligation, including the uncle's duty to protect the interests of his sisters' sons. Among the sources of evidence for this bond are legal documents and such literary works as *Beowulf* and *The Battle of Maldon*.

Another survival from earlier periods was the obligation of kinsmen to exact revenge or compensation for offenses. When a person was killed or injured, Anglo-Saxon law allowed the offender or his family to pay *wergild* (literally, "man gold") to the victim's family, the amount depending on the victim's social rank. If the *wergild* was not paid, a blood feud could result. Though Shakespeare drew largely from Greek and Roman sources for his depictions of revenge, these ancient Germanic traditions exercised some influence as well.

The conversion of the Anglo-Saxons to Christianity during the late 500s and 600s brought about changes in family life, but there was also much continuity. Baptism now became an important ritual, usually performed soon after a child's birth. Burial now often took place in churchyards rather than in ancestral burial grounds. The Church sought to regulate sexual behavior and various family matters and in particular opposed marriage within the prohibited degrees of kinship (which constituted incest), polygamy and concubinage, and divorce. Among the early Anglo-Saxons, marriage had been loosely defined and included marriages between close kin and polygamy among some of the elite, including kings. But by the time of King Alfred in the late 800s, marriage had become "a sacred and indissoluble union," at least in theory, and it was much clearer which offspring counted as legitimate (Crawford 66). Yet complaints about polygamy continued late into Anglo-Saxon times.

In several ways the Church contributed to a weakening of kinship obligations. The Church became a source of authority apart from kinship ties. Some parents dedicated children to monastic life. The Church also introduced the concept of spiritual kinship, which involved the practice of having godparents outside of the family who were responsible for the spiritual welfare of a child. But though such practices resulted in some de-emphasis on kinship ties, they helped strengthen social bonds in general, connecting non-related families with each other and introducing children to helpful associations outside the nuclear family.

Another practice with a similar effect was fosterage. Already a traditional practice among Anglo-Saxons before their conversion to Christianity, fosterage consisted of sending children to live in other homes. This was sometimes done out of necessity, such as when one or more of the children's biological parents died. But even when both parents were living, fosterage often provided children with training and established connections between families. Bonds of affection and loyalty often developed between children and their foster parents.

English culture changed dramatically with the Norman Conquest, though immediate changes in family life were probably minimal. The Normans were descendants of Vikings who had settled during the early 900s in an area in northwest France that came to be known as Normandy. In 1066, William, Duke of Normandy, invaded England to assert his right to the throne and defeated the Anglo-Saxon king. William became king of England, and his Norman followers replaced the Anglo-Saxon aristocracy. Over the next three hundred years, with intermarriage and changes in language and culture, the Normans and Anglo-Saxons ceased to be ethnically separate groups, so that we can speak of an English way of life by the end of the Middle Ages that combined elements from Norman and Anglo-Saxon culture.

Among the changes that came with the Norman Conquest were a more strongly centralized form of government and an increased emphasis on feudalism. Another change was that succession to the monarchy now normally took place by descent rather than by election. Though Anglo-Saxon kings were expected to have royal blood, they were actually chosen by the Witenagemot (an assembly of leading men) from among the available candidates. After the Norman Conquest, a new monarch would usually be the previous monarch's oldest son or another close family member. One result is that all English monarchs since the Norman Conquest have been descendants of William the Conqueror.

The conquest strengthened England's connections with continental Europe and thus increased the continent's influence on English culture. But family life retained many of the features it had had during previous generations, and changes were gradual. Among the changes was the introduction of surnames, which had not been used by the Anglo-Saxons. The use of surnames that fathers passed on to their children was widespread among the nobility by the late 1200s, and before long, the practice was common at lower social levels. Inheritance patterns also underwent changes. In Anglo-Saxon times, property was commonly divided equally among sons and daughters. During the later Middle Ages, by contrast, primogeniture became the dominant practice, though customs varied in different parts of England.

Primogeniture, along with other developments, brought a narrowing of women's legal rights. In contrast to Anglo-Saxon women's relative legal independence, following the Norman Conquest, married women and their property were theoretically under their husbands' control, and wives could regain their property and dowry, along with a portion of the husband's property, only after their husbands' death. Yet in practice, many women had more independence than legal theory would suggest, managing estates in the absence of their husbands, joining craft guilds, doing work on a farm, helping to run businesses, or even running businesses on their own. Women were involved in textile production, tavern keeping, baking, brewing, and a variety of other trades.

By the end of the Middle Ages, family life in England was significantly different than it had been in early Germanic times. Now most men were not warriors. Though some lived in castles and many were farm laborers, many lived in cities. In early Germanic times, family connections, along with loyalty to one's immediate lord, were the most important social relationships and the means by which conflicts were resolved or sometimes perpetuated. By the end of the Middle Ages, many institutions besides the family competed for a person's loyalty, and social order was maintained by various levels of national and local government, as well as through the associated influence of the Church.

Marriage was now both a sacrament and a legal contract, and though a union could be valid even without a religious ceremony, the Church called for the observance of certain forms, including the calling of banns (announcement that the marriage was to take place) and a wedding ceremony performed by a priest. Though the influence of parents on marriage arrangements may have been stronger in earlier times, it is likely that personal affection was a factor in the making of marriages from the early Middle Ages onward. Cnut, who ruled England in the 1000s, ordered that "no woman . . . be forced to marry a man whom she dislikes" (qtd. in McNamara and Wemple 129). By the mid-1100s, marriages in England had come to be governed exclusively by canon law (that is, the law of the Church), and by that time, it was established throughout Christian Europe that the free consent of the couple was required for a valid marriage. Authoritative writers on the subject argued that marital affection as well as free consent was essential to marriage and noted the bad results of forced marriages. Along with being forced into a marriage, certain other conditions—either party being under the age of consent (12 for girls, 14 for boys), being too closely related, or having made a vow of celibacy—made a marriage invalid, and it could be annulled for any of these reasons.

Despite the requirement of consent, parents and other authority figures could use various forms of persuasion and pressure to influence marriage arrangements, especially for children in upper-class families. Wards, whose marriages were under the control of a feudal lord, had to pay a fine if, while still a ward, they wished to refuse a marriage proposed by the lord. Yet many appear to have been willing to pay the fine. Some leading families betrothed their underage children, but the children could refuse the marriage once they reached the age of consent. Though the age of consent set a lower limit for a valid marriage, marriage in the early teens was rare. During the later Middle Ages, members of the English aristocracy sometimes married in their teens, but for most, marriage took place in the twenties.

Many customs surrounding childbirth persisted through the Middle Ages and even into Shakespeare's time. At birth, which usually took place with only women present, the child was wrapped in swaddling bands. At baptism, which followed soon after, children received the sponsorship of godparents and were named. As they grew older, small children of both sexes would be given the same kind of clothing, and eventually boys would receive breeches distinguishing them as male. Most children were breast-fed by their mothers until age two or later, but noble houses often used wet nurses.

From Anglo-Saxon times onward, children engaged in unsupervised play, probably up to age eight or later. The French historian Philippe Ariès has argued that children were treated as little adults during the Middle Ages and that childhood was not recognized as a separate stage of life. More recent historians have disputed that assertion, noting that, in fact, the English of the Middle Ages divided life into several stages, including infancy, childhood, and youth or adolescence. Though it varied over time, the age of legal responsibility was generally set at about 12 for girls and 14 for boys, that is, at the onset of puberty. It was also at this age that children were considered ready for adult religious obligations and for serious work, though tasks suitable to their ages might be given to younger children.

The degree of affection, loyalty, and happiness within a home certainly varied from one family to another, but these ideals were hoped for and often experienced, from Anglo-Saxon times onward. Though schools and other institutions had an influence by the later Middle Ages, parents continued, as they had for centuries, to be responsible for the nurture and education of their children. Fathers were legally responsible for their families, but few seem to have exercised tyrannical control. Despite high childhood mortality (even in the later Middle Ages, over 40% may have died by age 10), there is strong evidence of parental love and care, and the image many have of the commonly brutal treatment of children in past times is without foundation. King Alfred, writing in the 800s, was apparently drawing on common feelings when he wrote of the unbearable pain fathers feel at the death of a child (see Crawford 169). Infanticide was certainly not widespread during the Middle Ages, and both parents seem to have been anxious for the welfare of their children, including those suffering from deformities or illness. Literary and pictorial evidence going back to the Anglo-Saxon period clearly demonstrates affection between parents and children. There is also evidence of strong bonds between siblings and between grandparents and grandchildren. Though corporal punishment was used throughout the Middle Ages, parents were often criticized for being too indulgent with their children. The ritual blessing of children by their parents, an act that expressed concern and affection, can be traced at least to the 1200s in England and may go much further back.

Although children in the poorest families generally stayed at home to help with the work of the household or farm, others (especially those who lived in cities) were often sent elsewhere at about the time of puberty to work as servants or apprentices. Boys in wealthier families might continue their schooling during their teenage years to train for careers, and in the highest classes children might be sent to live in great households to serve and receive training. Whether or not the children remained at home, the parent–child bond seems to have endured, and parents who sent their children away for service or apprenticeship clearly did so for their children's benefit, hoping to ensure their readiness for adulthood.

The period of over a thousand years from the Anglo-Saxon invasions until Shakespeare's time obviously saw great changes in attitudes and customs related to family life, some of these the result of religious and political changes and others coming with the growth of cities and the increasing complexity of economic and social life. What is remarkable, though, is how much remained the same. Family continued to mean parents and children, connected with a small group of other kin, and despite the conflict that marred family life at times, most desired and many experienced familial bonds of affection, loyalty, and mutual support.

REFERENCES

Ariès, Philippe. *Centuries of Childhood: A Social History of Family Life*. Trans. Robert Baldick. New York: Vintage Books, 1962.

Augustine of Hippo. *City of God*. Trans. Henry Bettenson. Penguin Classics. London: Penguin Books, 1984.

Blair, John. *The Anglo-Saxon Age: A Very Short Introduction*. Oxford: Oxford University Press, 2000.

Cicero, Marcus Tullius. *De officiis*. With an English translation by Walter Miller. London: W. Heinemann; New York: Macmillan, 1913.

Crawford, Sally. *Childhood in Anglo-Saxon England*. Stroud, UK: Sutton Publishing, 1999.

Fee, Gordon D. *The First Epistle to the Corinthians*. The New International Commentary on the New Testament. Grand Rapids, MI: Eerdmans, 1987.

French, Valerie. "Children in Antiquity." *Children in Historical and Comparative Perspective: An International Handbook and Research Guide*. Ed. Joseph M. Hawes and N. Ray Hiner. Westport, CT: Greenwood Press, 1991. 13–29.

Golden, Mark. *Children and Childhood in Classical Athens*. Baltimore: Johns Hopkins University Press, 1990.

H[ornblower], S[imon]. "Greek and Roman Civilizations, Ancient: Ancient Greek Civilization." *The New Encyclopædia Britannica: Macropædia*. 15th ed. Chicago, IL: Encyclopædia Britannica, 2005.

Kroeger, C. C. "The Classical Concept of *Head* as 'Source.'" Appendix III in *Equal to Serve: Women and Men in the Church and Home*. By Gretchen Gaebelein Hull. Old Tappan, NJ: Fleming H. Revell, 1987.

Le Glay, Marcel, et al. *A History of Rome*. Trans. Antonia Nevill. 2nd ed. Malden, MA: Blackwell, 2001.

McNamara, Jo Ann, and Suzanne Wemple. "The Power of Women through the Family in Medieval Europe: 500–1100." *Feminist Studies* 1 (1973): 126–41.

McSheffrey, Shannon. "'I will never have none ayenst my faders will': Consent and the Making of Marriage in the Late Medieval Diocese of London." *Women, Marriage, and Family in Medieval Christendom: Essays in Memory of Michael M. Sheehan, C.S.B*. Ed. Constance M. Rousseau and Joel T. Rosenthal. Studies in Medieval Culture 37. Kalamazoo: Western Michigan University-Medieval Institute Publications, 1998. 153–74.

Meyers, Carol. "The Family in Early Israel." *Families in Ancient Israel*. Ed. Leo G. Perdue, Joseph Blenkinsopp, John J. Collins, and Carol Meyers. The Family, Religion, and Culture. Louisville, KY: Westminster John Knox, 1997. 1–47.

Mickelsen, Berkeley, and Alvera Mickelsen. "What Does *Kephale* Mean in the New Testament?" *Women, Authority and the Bible*. Ed. Alvera Mickelsen. Downers Grove, IL: InterVarsity Press, 1986. 97–110.

Murray, Alexander Callander. *Germanic Kinship Structure: Studies in Law and Society in Antiquity and the Early Middle Ages*. Toronto: Pontifical Institute of Mediaeval Studies, 1983.

Nielsen, Hanne Sigismund. "Interpreting Epithets in Roman Epitaphs." *The Roman Family in Italy: Status, Sentiment, Space*. Ed. Beryl Rawson and Paul Weaver. Canberra: Humanities Research Centre; Oxford: Clarendon Press: 1997. 169–204.

Noonan, John T., Jr. "Power to Choose." *Viator* 4 (1973): 419–34.

Plato. *The Republic*. Trans. Desmond Lee. 2nd ed. London: Penguin, 1974, 2003.

Plutarch. *Moral Essays*. Trans. Rex Warner. Harmondsworth, UK: Penguin, 1971. (Translation of Plutarch's *Moralia*.)

Pomeroy, Sarah B. *Families in Classical and Hellenistic Greece: Representations and Realities*. Oxford: Clarendon Press, 1997.

[Sirach.] Ecclesiasticus or The Wisdom of Jesus Son of Sirach. *The New English Bible with the Apocrypha*. New York: Oxford University Press, 1971.

Tacitus. *Germania*. Trans. J. B. Rives. Oxford: Clarendon Press; New York: Oxford University Press, 1999.

Todd, Malcolm. *The Early Germans*. 2nd ed. Malden, MA: Blackwell, 2004.

Virgil. *The Aeneid of Virgil: A Verse Translation*. Trans. Allen Mandelbaum. Berkeley: University of California Press, 1971.

Woolf, Greg, ed. *Cambridge Illustrated History of the Roman World*. Cambridge: Cambridge University Press, 2003.

Xenophon. *Oeconomicus: A Social and Historical Commentary*. Trans. Sarah B. Pomeroy. Oxford: Clarendon Press; New York: Oxford University Press, 1994.

2

FAMILY LIFE IN SHAKESPEARE'S WORLD

Shakespeare lived and wrote during the late 1500s and early 1600s, roughly in the middle of what is known as the early modern period (c. 1500–1700). England during this time was a place of brilliant literary accomplishment, intellectual ferment, intense nationalism, and political and religious turmoil. All these events and conditions influenced family life, and family life in turn became a topic of discussion and literary representation.

Family in early modern England is sometimes loosely referred to as "patriarchal." For two reasons, however, this term is best avoided. The first is that many specialists use the term for a family structure definitely *not* found in early modern England (namely, one in which several generations live in a single household under the authority of the eldest living male ancestor). The second reason is that in popular usage, *patriarchal* connotes male domination and even brutality, associations that seriously distort and oversimplify the picture of family life in the period. Many studies that use the terms *patriarchal* and *patriarchy* end up being circular because they assume rather than demonstrate the very features of family life they associate with these words.

Most changes in marriage and family life from the Middle Ages to the early modern period were gradual. But certain watershed events—such as the introduction of printing, the revival of interest in ancient Greek and Latin civilization, and the Protestant Reformation—led to more obvious changes. For one thing, the invention of the printing press led to the publication of scores of treatises, handbooks, sermon collections, and pamphlets, and as a result, discussion of issues related to gender, marriage, and family now took place in print and involved many more participants, women as well as men, than would have been the case a century or two earlier. The early modern period also saw a movement toward stronger central government in England, and this along with religious changes helped transform some of the rules governing family life and how these rules were enforced.

Yet for the most part, family life in early modern England was much the same as it had been in the late Middle Ages. The English family continued to be a prime example of the Western European type in which men and women mingled with relative freedom and in which there was not a wide age gap between husbands and wives. Kinship continued to be essentially bilateral, as it had been since early Germanic times; that is, people considered relatives on both the mother's and the father's sides of the family to be kindred. The use of surnames, which had begun in the later Middle Ages, was now well established. The Church—first the Roman Catholic and then the Anglican—continued to play an important role in setting rules and providing ceremonies related to marriage and family life. As a result of such rules, marriage was monogamous, divorce was virtually nonexistent, and marriages were exogamous—that is, marriage with close relatives was prohibited. The age of marriage changed little through the late Middle Ages and early modern period, and a valid marriage continued to require the consent of the couple. As had been true throughout the Middle Ages, each nuclear family (made up of a father, a mother, and unmarried children) normally lived in a separate household, and despite the importance of extended family relationships, the closest bonds were within the nuclear family. There was little change in customs related to inheritance, betrothal and marriage, or child-rearing. Gender roles remained much the same, as did the experience of childhood and the transitional events leading to adult status.

Besides its close connection with the later Middle Ages, family life in Shakespeare's time had much in common with even older cultures. Indeed, with the Renaissance and Reformation and their reemphasis on the writers of classical antiquity and on the Bible, the influence of older cultures became even stronger. Family was centrally important for the ancient Greeks, Romans, and Hebrews, and it continued to be so in early modern England. Furthermore, to a great extent, all of these cultures shared a common outlook, what might be called the traditional picture of the world. An important feature of this traditional picture was the assumption that individuals were not essentially separate, self-governing beings. Rather, individual identity was defined by membership in one's family and community and one's place in the cosmos.

Though we have not entirely abandoned this view, our conception of reality has changed fundamentally since the Middle Ages. As a result, we misinterpret much about family life in the past unless we learn not only about the practices of everyday life but also about how people viewed the family's role in the cosmos and the community.

The age of Shakespeare was a time of transition during which the traditional outlook continued, even dominated, and yet was also challenged. The challenges came in various forms, including the beginnings of modern science and philosophy and movement toward greater religious and political freedom and pluralism. Such changes eventually led to the decline of the traditional outlook and to a split between the public sphere (where a more secular outlook prevailed) and the private sphere (the sphere of religious belief and personal relationships).

Shakespeare and other writers used the tension between newer and older views to help provide interest and dramatic conflict to their works. But for most of these writers, the traditional view continued to be authoritative and strongly affected how they dealt with virtually every issue, including those related to family life.

FAMILY, COMMONWEALTH, COSMOS

Family was central to the experience of Shakespeare's contemporaries in ways that many of us may find hard to understand. Besides its moral and religious dimensions, family was believed to have a political and even a cosmic role far more significant than most moderns acknowledge. In the traditional view, the world was thought of as being made up of several related entities: the individual human being, the family, the state or commonwealth, and finally the entire cosmos. Each smaller entity was viewed as both "a part and a pattern" of each larger one: that is, each smaller entity not only formed part of the larger ones but also resembled them in structure and function. Thus, individuals were necessarily members of families, families made up the state or commonwealth, and commonwealths were part of the cosmos. Between each of these levels, an elaborate system of correspondences or resemblances could be observed. This view is summed up by Sir John Hayward:

> The whole worlde is nothinge but a greate state; a state is no other then a greate familie; and a familie no other then a greate bodye. As one God ruleth the worlde, one maister the familie, as all the members of one bodye receive both sense and motion from one heade, . . . so . . . one state should be governed by one commaunder. (B4)

Elements of this view—for instance, the naturalness of monarchy—were subject to dispute, especially during the political conflicts of the 1600s. But for those who accepted the traditional view, the correspondences it proposed were more than mere accidents. Instead, they demonstrated the order by which the whole universe was governed. These correspondences were felt to be part of a great system of interrelations—ranging from the "little world of man" (or "microcosm") to the "great world" (or "macrocosm") of which he was part—in which all created things were interdependent and all were ultimately dependent on God.

Another way of thinking about the interconnectedness of the world was to view it as resembling a body or organism. The influential clergyman William Perkins, writing about 1600, claimed that "all societies of men are bodies. A family is a body and so is every particular church a body and the commonwealth also" (*Treatise* 449). In using the metaphor of the body, he had in mind the diverse roles and functions performed by the various members of the commonwealth, roles differing in dignity but all equally necessary (like the organs of a body) to the functioning of the whole. Indeed, the body of society would die or be seriously impaired by the loss of any of its members. Conversely, no member of the social organism could expect to find identity or life outside the organism; to cut off a foot would be to kill it.

The family, too, is like a body. Just as the organs and limbs of a body are connected and interdependent, so the members of the family are connected physically—they are of the same "flesh and blood"—and are also bound together by ties of emotional and practical interdependence. Far from diminishing the value and individuality of family members, this condition of being members of a single organism gives each (at least in theory) a particular and irreplaceable value. The family's successful existence requires that each member perform a role or function different from that of other members of the family (the father, for instance, being the "head"). These roles, some based on gender and some on age but all based on bonds that were viewed as natural, brought with them widely shared expectations, though many of the details were subject to negotiation and dispute.

Like the natural and social worlds, family life was held to be organized hierarchically. Any given family would have been expected to conform to a hierarchical structure, with the father at the head, assisted by the mother, and with children and servants accepting the father and mother as "governors" and themselves as "subjects." Yet this hierarchical view, especially as applied to the family, allowed for more nuance and flexibility than moderns tend to imagine. For one thing, one's role in the family hierarchy would have varied over time. Family life was thus a process as well as a structure. Furthermore, one's position in the structure brought responsibilities as well as privileges. In particular, those who governed were supposed to act for the good of those lower in degree.

Family was of course not the only social institution of early modern England to which people belonged, yet it played a crucial role as a source and foundation on which the larger institutions depended. Families, viewed both as creations of and as conduits for the cosmos's life-giving powers, helped bring human society into being. Furthermore, the family, besides being the first and smallest institution in which human beings participated, was also seen as the model for all larger ones, including the state and the Church. Thus, just as private families have fathers, so "princes," according to a writer from the late 1500s, are "the publike fathers of their countries" (Bilson 249). Similarly, private fathers are, in a sense, like kings.

The father, it was believed, served as head of the family by the appointment of nature and God. But he was not to misuse his authority and in fact was supposed to govern his family for the good of all and especially to provide physically and spiritually for his children. The happiness of the commonwealth was thought to depend on the proper carrying out of these functions. Thomas Pickering, echoing the ancient Roman writer Cicero, explained that because the family is "the Seminarie [literally, the seed-bed] of all other Societies, it followeth that the holie and righteous government thereof, is a direct meane for the good ordering, both of Church and Common-wealth" (3).

In addition to serving a social function, the family was also thought of as being connected to the whole order of the universe. Family relationships give structure and significance to time, connecting individuals with the past and future. "Marriages do turne mutability into the image of eternity," wrote William Secker, by "spring[ing] up new buds, when the old are withered" (21). As another writer noted, by having offspring, parents "continue their name, and

A family receives religious instruction. From *Tenor of the Whole Psalmes in Foure Partes* (London, 1563), Tenor part, t.o. verso. This item is reproduced by permission of The Huntington Library, San Marino, California.

posterity upon earth" and "represent and shadow, in some sort, immortality, by deriving life from the root into the branches, from the father to the sonne, and his sonnes sonne, from generation to generation" (Griffith 238).

Besides linking past, present, and future, family also connected earth with heaven. In loving and serving their children, parents were supposed to imitate God's perfect love. In various ways—through instruction and example and through the daily practice of giving a ritual blessing—parents could convey heavenly grace to their children. God himself was thought of as the father of nature and of humankind. A father should therefore, in the words of Matthew Griffith, "represent [the] Majesty of God, at home" (8).

This godlike role of parents—especially fathers—could certainly be abused. Yet the analogy between God's authority and a father's was not supposed to be taken as an excuse for tyranny. Fathers resemble God in power, but they should also resemble him in love. They should have the same fatherly care for their children that God has for his. Henry Smith, a popular London preacher contemporary with Shakespeare, explained that "they which are called fathers, are called by the name of God, to warne them that they are in stead of God to their children, which teacheth all his sonnes." The father should be a teacher and a model, for "what example have children but their parentes?" (79). Like every "good governour," in the words of another writer, a father "must governe for the good of those that bee under him" (Dod 81).

The roles of fathers and other family members were thought of as being "natural"; that is, they were defined by the nature of reality, which in turn had been established by God. In fact, during this period, the word *nature* had several related meanings: it could refer to the universe as a whole, to the force that sustains the universe, to human nature, and specifically to the feelings that should exist within a family, especially between parents and children. Thus, love and loyalty within a family were called "natural," and the word *nature* itself could refer to proper family feelings and behavior. Conflict and disloyalty in a family were called "unnatural" because they were departures from the ideal founded in nature.

Although proper family life was understood to derive from the very nature of things, at the same time Shakespeare and his contemporaries recognized that individual families were imperfect. The standard explanation for the gap between the "natural" ideals and the imperfections of daily life was the Fall—that is, the fall of Adam and Eve that led to a fallen and imperfect condition for all of their descendants. In fact, it was believed that the human fall had affected all of earthly reality. As Theodore Spencer puts it (summarizing the traditional view), "when Adam fell, Nature fell too" (25). The fallen or imperfect condition of human beings in this world, coupled with the free will with which God has endowed them, allows them to depart from nature in its ideal sense and become unnatural. Therefore, the "naturall love" of family members for each other, though necessary, is not enough; it must, as John Newnham argued, be "augmented and confirmed by" the divine gift of "charitie" (2).

Furthermore, many regarded nature, even at its best (including family life), as intrinsically inferior to the eternal realities of heaven and as potentially in competition with God for human loyalty. Readers of the Bible were aware that Christ had warned his disciples not to love family members more than they loved him. Religious writers of Shakespeare's time took this warning seriously and reminded their contemporaries that family loyalty must be secondary to their loyalty to God. Still, despite being aware that family loyalty could compete with loyalty to God, most religious writers of the period put a high value on family and saw it as one of the instruments God could use to strengthen the Church and encourage Christian living. Many in Shakespeare's time would have shared the view, expressed by Martin Luther and others, that marriage is a school of faith and love in which Christian attributes can be exercised and developed.

For Shakespeare and his contemporaries, family was an essential part of the structure of reality and was thought of ideally as part of a harmonious system that included the state and the cosmos. Yet at the same time, family life as actually experienced was imperfect, troubled at times by jealousy, antagonism, and other evils. In practice, the ideals associated with "natural" family feelings and behavior served as norms against which human imperfection could be judged. Yet these were clearly ideals to which many in early modern England aspired and that they sometimes managed to experience.

FAMILY AS HOUSEHOLD AND LINEAGE

The word *family* was understood in Shakespeare's time as having two primary senses: that of household and that of lineage. In neither of these senses did it coincide precisely with what we now call the nuclear family. Writing in the early 1600s, Matthew Griffith used the word "Familie" to mean "all that are in the house" and noted that "house" may have several senses, including a "Tribe," a "Nation," or a "place to sleepe in" (2–3). In this last sense, a "family" will be, as William Perkins puts it, a "society of certain persons having mutual relations one to another under the private government of one," these persons including parents, children, servants, and anyone else living in the household (*Christian Oeconomy* 416). Thus, though each household had a nuclear family at the core, and though relationships within the nuclear family were the strongest and most enduring, others also participated in the life of the household, including servants and sometimes friends and relatives. Of course the largest households would have been those of the wealthy. But even many of Shakespeare's less than wealthy contemporaries had a servant or two. The head of the household was thus the master of servants as well as the father of children.

Yet this tendency of early modern households to include some members outside of the immediate family should not mislead us into thinking that households were commonly very large or multigenerational. As it probably had been through much of the Middle Ages, the average household size in early modern England was around four or five, though a good many households were slightly larger, and any given household's size would have varied over time. Mothers on average bore six or seven children, but the death of about a quarter of these by age 10 and the departure of many for apprenticeship or service as teenagers meant that there were usually no more than two or three children at home at one time. Occasionally one of the spouses' widowed parents or another relative might join the household. But perhaps only 1 in 20 households—according to some studies, even fewer—contained relatives other than the parents and children.

Family in its other sense—that of lineage—was an important factor in establishing a person's identity, especially if the family was wealthy or prominent. For some, belonging to a great and ancient family was a source of pride. Because surnames came from the father, most identified more readily with their father's line. But maternal connections were often important as well, in some cases remarkably so. In general, English kinship was decidedly bilateral—that is, individuals recognized and valued relatives on both their father's and mother's sides and usually did not strongly distinguish between them. Those endowed with noble lineage through either the paternal or the maternal line were warned that they must maintain the family's reputation through a virtuous life. "Remember," wrote Sir Henry Sidney to his son Philip, "the noble blood you are descended of by your mother's side: and think that only by virtuous life and good action you may be an

A family at the dinner table. From *A Pleasant Countrey New Ditty* (London, 1625). Pepys Library, Magdalene College, Cambridge.

ornament to that illustrious family" (qtd. in Arber 1:42). Some worried that a fall in fortune or virtue could stain or even ruin "an ancient house."

In addition to blood relatives, relatives through marriage were also important as sources of friendship or practical support. A man's father-in-law, for instance, might help him financially and socially. To an extent, one's "spiritual kindred" were important as well. A network of spiritual kinship linked the godparents chosen to be responsible for a child's religious education with the child and the child's parents, who were in turn linked with the godparents' children. Though spiritual kinship became somewhat less important after the Protestant Reformation, it continued as an important concept and institution in most parts of England during this period. Still, personal identity was most closely tied to one's parents and other ancestors and, to some extent, to one's siblings. One might find friendship or support among any of one's relatives. But relationships would have been closest and strongest among immediate family members—those, that is, who lived together in a household—and especially between husband and wife.

HUSBANDS AND WIVES

Many modern readers and viewers of Shakespeare assume that Shakespeare's contemporaries married very young and were regularly forced into loveless marriages. Surprisingly, some modern historians have promoted exactly this view. Virginia Woolf, in a well-known chapter in *A Room of One's Own*, describes her attempt to discover the lived realities behind Shakespeare's fictions and tells of turning to G. M. Trevelyan's *History of England* for answers. According to Trevelyan,

> Wife beating was a recognised right of man, and was practised without shame by high as well as low. . . . The daughter who refused to marry the gentleman of her parents' choice was liable to be locked up, beaten and flung about the room, without any shock being inflicted on public opinion. Marriage was not an affair of personal affection, but of family avarice. . . . Betrothal often took place while one or both of the parties was in the cradle, and marriage when they were scarcely out of the nurses' charge. (qtd. in Woolf 42)

Influenced by Trevelyan, Woolf guesses that women in Shakespeare's time were married at age "fifteen or sixteen" (46).

In fact, as abundant evidence proves, Trevelyan was wrong about the age at which Shakespeare's contemporaries married as well as about most of his other pronouncements on marriage and family life.

Arranged marriages, in the sense of marriages in which the wishes of the couple are not considered, were in fact rare and might be held invalid if it could be shown that either the bride or the groom did not give consent. Such marriages were called "forced" or "enforced" marriages. Of course parents sometimes applied pressure, in extreme cases threatening to disown a disobedient child. But a wide variety of writers condemned excessive parental pressure and the unhappy marriages that could result. In a sermon on marriage, Bishop Edwin Sandys argued that both the parents' consent and that of the bride and groom were necessary:

> And, as the parents' or tutors' consent is to be had in all good and lawful marriages, so it is against the duty of good parents, either to keep their children longer unmarried than is convenient, or through an over-great desire of enriching them (which is the common disease) to marry them against their liking. . . . There can be no lawful and commendable match, where there wanteth full consent and agreement of the parties whom it most concerneth. (326–27)

Of course, such a statement implies that forced marriages sometimes took place, as indeed they did. Still, the legal standard, according to Henry Swinburne, a seventeenth-century authority on the subject, was this: "without Consent [meaning the consent of the couple] there cannot be any Matrimony" (51). The principle that a valid marriage required the consent of the couple was not new to early modern England, having been established as part of Church law throughout Europe by the 1100s. This legal standard meant that a marriage to which the bride or groom did not consent could be prevented from happening, and even if it did take place but was not consummated, it could be annulled. Though attempts to resist a forced marriage must have been difficult given that the couple's inheritance and place in their families were at stake, such attempts were sometimes successful, and the right of a couple to reject a proposed match seems to have been generally accepted.

But marriages were often "arranged" in another sense: that is, the parents normally were involved in the process that culminated in the marriage of their children. Parents were involved because it was recognized that the interests of two families, not simply of two individuals, were at stake. Furthermore, it was felt that, in undertaking something as momentous as marriage, young people needed the counsel that wise and loving parents would give. Therefore, though parents' approval was not required for a valid marriage, there was a strong expectation that a prospective bride or groom would seek and obtain such approval.

Young people who sought to avoid an unwanted match or who were simply determined to marry contrary to their parents' wishes sometimes resorted to clandestine (i.e., secret) marriage. William Gouge, in a seventeenth-century treatise, describes a situation remarkably similar to that found in several of Shakespeare's plays:

> It oft falleth out, that when parents or other friends have provided a good match for their daughter, or for some other under their governement, and all things on all parts well concluded, the wedding day appointed, and all things fitted and prepared for the solemnizing of the wedding, some desirous to forestall that mariage, by secret and cunning devices get the bride away a few daies before, if not on the very morning of the intended wedding day, and mary her out of hand to another. That which maketh men so bold is, that they know a clandestine mariage being consummate shall stand firme in law. (203)

As Gouge notes, such marriages were valid despite the lack of parental consent. Yet they were also, as R. C. Bald has pointed out, both an "offence against the canon law" and "a serious breach of the social code" (130–31). Such marriages, in other words, while valid, would have been undertaken in an illegal way. The legal consequences of a clandestine marriage involving a bride under 16 are summarized by seventeenth-century writer Michael Dalton: "The taking away of a maide under sixteene yeares of age, without the consent of her parents or governors, or contracting mariage with her, or deflowring her, is no felony, but yet shall be punished with long imprisonment, without baile, or with grievous fine" (248). One well-known instance of a secret marriage is that of John Donne and Ann More in 1601, following which Ann's furious father succeeded in having Donne briefly imprisoned. Yet the Lord Keeper reminded the bride's father (according to Izaak Walton) that "errors might be overpunished," and Donne was in fact released when the marriage was proven valid. Even so, Walton himself lamented the "mischief" and "passion" of the kind of love that would lead to a clandestine marriage; one ought, he says, to obtain "the allowance of those friends, whose approbation always was, and ever will be necessary, to make even a vertuous love become lawful" (see Bald 128–40).

Most marriages took place with parental knowledge and consent, as well as with the consent of the bride and groom, and were preceded by a period of courtship. Courtship, at least for the better-off families of the period, was a formal procedure involving a woman, a suitor, and the woman's parents. The suitor would obtain permission from the woman's father to woo her. Once her heart was won (and with the parents' approval confirmed and other necessary arrangements made), the marriage could take place.

But not all courtship was as formal as this. Diaries and other records from the period indicate various ways a courtship might proceed. Sometimes friends or relatives invited a man or woman to consider a prospective partner. Often a man engaged the help of a third party in some stages of the courtship, and sometimes letters were exchanged between a couple. A couple might meet at the house of friends or family and become better acquainted over dinner or in other group settings or might find private occasions to talk. As courtship progressed, they might take walks or go to fairs or other social gatherings together and often began to show affection by kissing or holding hands. As matters became serious, a couple commonly exchanged gifts and love tokens—such as rings, ribbons, and gloves—with the man often taking the lead in giving such gifts. But even with the couple taking an active role in the courtship, friends and especially family were also involved, seeking to protect the couple's and the families' interests and working out financial arrangements. Even at lower social levels, obtaining the parents' and especially the father's consent was generally part of the courtship process.

Though men were normally the suitors, women sometimes took a more active role. A broadside ballad titled *The Wooing Maid* portrays a woman inviting the attention of suitors ("I use all the motives my sex will permit me, / To put men in mind, that they may not forget me") and incidentally evokes some of the settings in which courtship may have taken place, including weddings, dances, and other "merry meetings" (Parker stanzas 4–5). But, as the ballad itself suggests, for a woman to have taken the lead in wooing was unusual and would probably not have met with social approval. Even without taking the leading role, however, a woman might resist or encourage a suitor's advances.

In fact, Shakespeare's contemporaries often talked of both the man and the woman choosing a spouse. For both, the proper grounds were commonly said to

A man courting a woman. From *A Delicate New Ditty* (London, c. 1630). Pepys Library, Magdalene College, Cambridge.

be affection coupled with being well-matched in rank, age, temperament, and religious conviction. Wealth was certainly often a consideration (moralists often said it was given exaggerated importance), but virtue, shared belief, and a capacity for harmony and love were supposed to be given greater weight. Falling in love appears to have been a common precursor to marriage. Though people were aware that passionate love was dangerous and needed to be tempered with reason and self-restraint (for one thing, it could lead as easily to a disastrous as to a happy marriage), still most felt that marriage should be preceded by mutual attraction and affection.

Before a marriage could take place, a dowry and jointure would have to be negotiated. The dowry, also called the "portion," was money, property, or sometimes goods provided by the family of the bride to the groom. The jointure, lands or income provided by the groom or the groom's family, was intended to support the wife after her husband's death. Both families thus contributed funds or property needed for the couple's independence and future security.

Along with negotiating the dowry and jointure, the families would also appoint the day of marriage, usually at least two or three weeks away so that preparations could be made and the banns could be read in church on three Sundays or holy days preceding the wedding. One reason for the reading of the banns was to assure that no impediments existed that would prevent the marriage—for instance a pre-contract or a relationship between the prospective bride and groom within the forbidden degrees that would make the marriage incestuous.

The concept of forbidden degrees of kinship had its roots in the early Middle Ages and even earlier: it was based partly on prohibitions found in the ancient Hebrew scriptures. The medieval Catholic Church, however, had gone much further than the biblical prohibitions and eventually created an elaborate set of rules forbidding marriages even between those related very distantly by blood or marriage (including those having a common ancestor as far back as seven generations, later reduced to four), as well as those related by "spiritual kinship."

Beginning in the early 1500s with Henry VIII's break from the Roman Catholic Church, efforts were made in England to reduce and simplify the forbidden degrees. By the 1560s, shortly before Shakespeare was born, it was established that the forbidden degrees encompassed close relationships of consanguinity (blood relationships) and affinity (relationships established through marriage), including direct ancestors and descendants, siblings, aunts, uncles, nieces, nephews, and the spouses of any of those named (for instance, a brother-in-law or sister-in-law). Spiritual kinship was no longer an impediment to marriage. Because, even with modifications, the rules were complex, charts noting whom one could not marry were published. (See example, page 39.)

Incest even beyond the nuclear family was considered contrary to the laws of God and was viewed as "infectynge and corruptinge the maners of the people" and violating the holiness of marriage (*Determinations* 19v). Little mention was made of physical defects that might result from incest, though at least one English writer of the 1600s alluded to the "hereditary diseases" marriage among close kin might produce (Burton 1:206). The most common argument against incest,

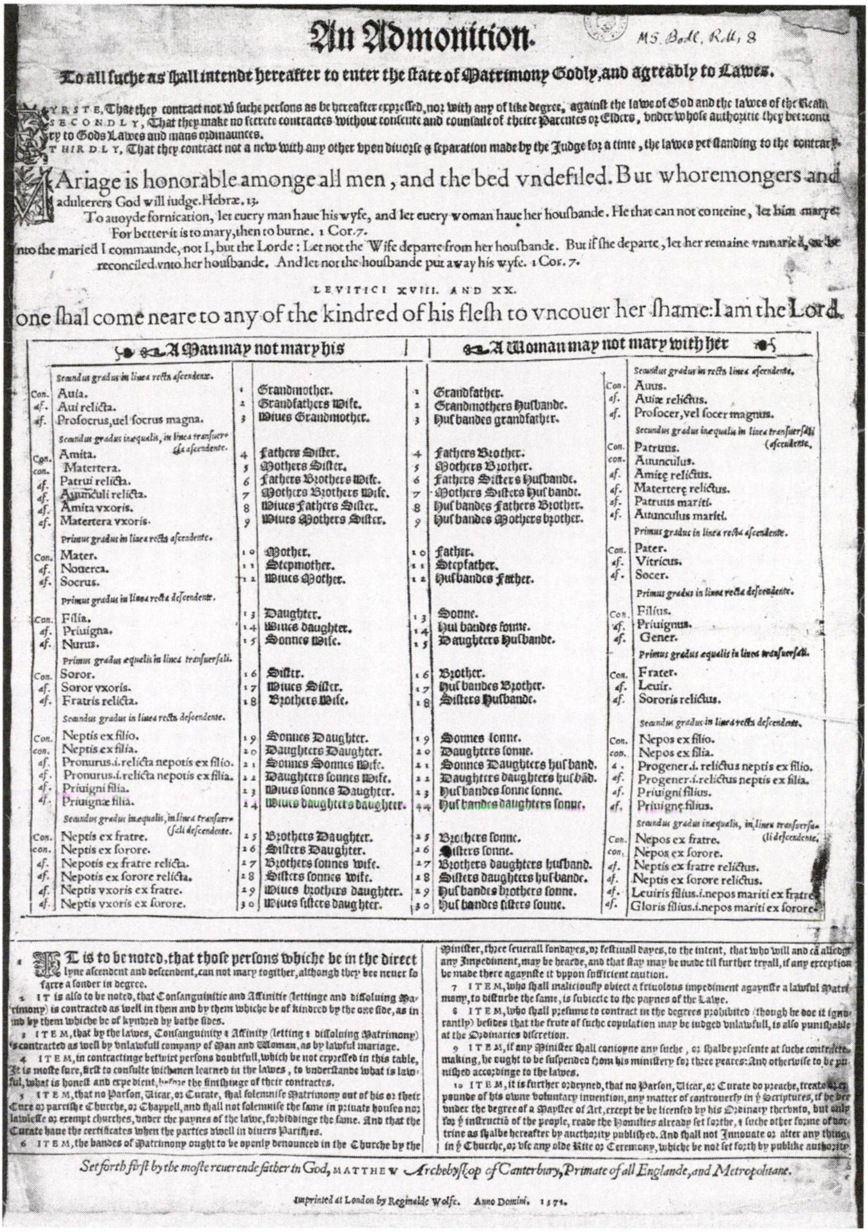

An Admonition.

MS. Bodl. Rolls 8

To all ſuche as ſhall intende hereafter to enter the ſtate of Matrimony Godly, and agreably to Lawes.

FYRSTE, That they contract not wͭ ſuche perſons as be hereafter expreſſed, nor with any of like degree, againſt the lawe of God and the lawes of the Realm.

SECONDLY, That they make no ſecrete contractes without conſente and counſaile of theire Parentes or Elders, under whoſe authoritie they be contrary to Gods Lawes and mans ordinaunces.

THIRDLY, That they contract not a new with any other upon divorſe & ſeparation made by the Judge for a time, the lawes yet ſtanding to the contrary.

MAriage is honorable amonge all men, and the bed vndefiled. But whoremongers and adulterers God will iudge. Hebræ. 13.

To auoyde fornication, let euery man haue his wyfe, and let euery woman haue her houſbande. He that can not conteine, let him marye: For better it is to mary, then to burne. 1 Cor. 7.

Unto the maried I commaunde, not I, but the Lorde: Let not the Wife departe from her houſbande. But if ſhe departe, let her remaine vnmaried, or be reconciled vnto her houſbande. And let not the houſbande put away his wyfe. 1 Cor. 7.

LEVITICI XVIII. AND XX.

None ſhal come neare to any of the kindred of his fleſh to vncouer her ſhame: I am the Lord.

	A Man may not mary his				A Woman may not mary with her		
	Secundus gradus in linea recta aſcendente.						*Secundus gradus in recta linea aſcendente.*
Con.	Auia.	1	Grandmother.	1	Grandfather.	Con.	Auus.
af.	Aui relicta.	2	Grandfathers Wife.	2	Grandmothers Huſbande.	af.	Auiæ relictus.
af.	Proſocrus, uel ſocrus magna.	3	Wiues Grandmother.	3	Huſbandes grandfather.	af.	Proſocer, vel ſocer magnus.
	Secundus gradus inæqualis, in linea tranſuerſa aſcendente.						*Secundus gradus inæqualis in linea tranſuerſali aſcendente.*
Con.	Amita.	4	Fathers Siſter.	4	Fathers Brother.	Con.	Patruus.
con.	Matertera.	5	Mothers Siſter.	5	Mothers Brother.	con.	Auunculus.
af.	Patrui relicta.	6	Fathers Brothers Wife.	6	Fathers Siſters Huſbande.	af.	Amitę relictus.
af.	Auunculi relicta.	7	Mothers Brothers Wife.	7	Mothers Siſters Huſbande.	af.	Materterę relictus.
af.	Amita vxoris.	8	Wiues Fathers Siſter.	8	Huſbandes Fathers Brother.	af.	Patruus mariti.
af.	Matertera vxoris.	9	Wiues Mothers Siſter.	9	Huſbandes Mothers brother.	af.	Auunculus mariti.
	Primus gradus in linea recta aſcendente.						*Primus gradus in linea recta aſcendente.*
Con.	Mater.	10	Mother.	10	Father.	Con.	Pater.
af.	Nouerca.	11	Stepmother.	11	Stepfather.	af.	Vitricus.
af.	Socrus.	12	Wiues Mother.	12	Huſbandes Father.	af.	Socer.
	Primus gradus in linea recta deſcendente.						*Primus gradus in linea recta deſcendente.*
Con.	Filia.	13	Daughter.	13	Sonne.	Con.	Filius.
af.	Priuigna.	14	Wiues daughter.	14	Huſbandes ſonne.	af.	Priuignus.
af.	Nurus.	15	Sonnes Wife.	15	Daughters Huſbande.	af.	Gener.
	Primus gradus æqualis in linea tranſuerſali.						*Primus gradus æqualis in linea tranſuerſali.*
Con.	Soror.	16	Siſter.	16	Brother.	Con.	Frater.
af.	Soror vxoris.	17	Wiues Siſter.	17	Huſbandes Brother.	af.	Leuir.
af.	Fratris relicta.	18	Brothers Wife.	18	Siſters Huſbande.	af.	Sororis relictus.
	Secundus gradus in linea recta deſcendente.						*Secundus gradus in linea recta deſcendente.*
Con.	Neptis ex filio.	19	Sonnes Daughter.	19	Sonnes ſonne.	Con.	Nepos ex filio.
con.	Neptis ex filia.	20	Daughters Daughter.	20	Daughters ſonne.	con.	Nepos ex filia.
af.	Pronurus. i. relicta nepotis ex filio.	21	Sonnes Sonnes Wife.	21	Sonnes Daughters huſband.	af.	Progener. i. relictus neptis ex filio.
af.	Pronurus. i. relicta nepotis ex filia.	22	Daughters ſonnes Wife.	22	Daughters daughters huſbād.	af.	Progener. i. relictus neptis ex filia.
af.	Priuigni filia.	23	Wiues ſonnes Daughter.	23	Huſbandes ſonne ſonne.	af.	Priuigni filius.
af.	Priuignæ filia.	24	Wiues daughters daughter.	24	Huſbandes daughters ſonne.	af.	Priuignę filius.
	Secundus gradus inæqualis, in linea tranſuerſali deſcendente.						*Secundus gradus inæqualis, in linea tranſuerſali deſcendente.*
Con.	Neptis ex fratre.	25	Brothers Daughter.	25	Brothers ſonne.	Con.	Nepos ex fratre.
con.	Neptis ex ſorore.	26	Siſters Daughter.	26	Siſters ſonne.	con.	Nepos ex ſorore.
af.	Nepotis ex fratre relicta.	27	Brothers ſonnes wife.	27	Brothers daughters huſband.	af.	Neptis ex fratre relictus.
af.	Nepotis ex ſorore relicta.	28	Siſters ſonnes wife.	28	Siſters daughters huſbande.	af.	Neptis ex ſorore relictus.
af.	Neptis vxoris ex fratre.	29	Wiues brothers daughter.	29	Huſbandes brothers ſonne.	af.	Leuiris filius. i. nepos mariti ex fratre.
af.	Neptis vxoris ex ſorore.	30	Wiues ſiſters daughter.	30	Huſbandes ſiſters ſonne.	af.	Gloris filius. i. nepos mariti ex ſorore.

1 IT is to be noted, that thoſe perſons whiche be in the direct lyne aſcendent and deſcendent, can not mary togither, although they bee neuer ſo farre a ſonder in degree.

2 IT is alſo to be noted, that Conſanguinitie and Affinitie (lettinge and diſſoluing Matrimony) is contracted as well in them and by them whiche be of kindred by the one ſide, as in and by them whiche be of kyndred by bothe ſides.

3 ITEM, that by the lawes, Conſanguinity & Affinity (letting & diſſoluing Matrimony) is contracted as well by vnlawfull company of Man and Woman, as by lawful mariage.

4 ITEM, in contractinge betwixt perſons doubtfull, which be not expreſſed in this table, It is moſte ſure, firſt to conſulte with men learned in the lawes, to vnderſtande what is lawful, what is honeſt and expedient, before the finiſhinge of their contractes.

5 ITEM, that no Parſon, Vicar, or Curate, ſhal ſolemniſe Matrimony out of his or their Cure or pariſhe Churche, or Chappell, and ſhall not ſolemniſe the ſame in priuate houſes nor lawleſſe or exempt churches, vnder the paynes of the lawe, forbiddinge the ſame. And that the Curate haue the certificates when the parties dwell in diuers Pariſhes.

6 ITEM, the bandes of Matrimony ought to be openly denounced in the Churche by the Miniſter, three ſeuerall ſondayes, or feſtiuall dayes, to the intent, that who will and cā alledge any Impediment, may be hearde, and that ſtay may be made til further tryall, if any exception be made there agaynſte it vppon ſufficient caution.

7 ITEM, who ſhall malicioully obiect a friuolous impediment agaynſte a lawful Matrimony, to diſturbe the ſame, is ſubiecte to the paynes of the Lawe.

8 ITEM, who ſhall preſume to contract in the degrees prohibited (though he doe it ignorantly) beſides that the frute of ſuche copulation may be iudged vnlawfull, is alſo puniſhable at the Ordinaries diſcretion.

9 ITEM, if any Miniſter ſhall conioyne any ſuche, or ſhalbe preſente at ſuche contracte making, he ought to be ſuſpended from his miniſtery for three yeares: And otherwiſe to be puniſhed accordinge to the lawes.

10 ITEM, it is further ordeyned, that no Parſon, Vicar, or Curate do preache, treate or expounde of his owne voluntary invention, any matter of controuerſy in ẏ Scriptures, if he bee vnder the degree of a Mayſter of Art, except he be licenſed by his Ordinary therevnto, but only for ẏ inſtructiō of the people, reade the Homilies already ſet forthe, & ſuche other forme of doctrine as ſhalbe hereafter by auctority publiſhed. And ſhall not Innouate or alter any thinge in ẏ Churche, or vſe any olde Rite or Ceremony, whiche be not ſet forth by publike authority.

Set forth firſt by the moſte reuerende father in God, MATTHEW *Archebyſhop of Canterbury, Primate of all Englande, and Metropolitane.*

Imprinted at London by Reginalde Wolfe. Anno Domini. 1571.

This chart illustrates degrees of kinship within which marriage was forbidden. *An Admonition, to All Suche as Shall Intende Hereafter to Enter the State of Matrimony Godly, and Agreeably to Laws* (London, 1571), issued by Matthew Parker, Archbishop of Canterbury. Bodleian Library, University of Oxford. MS Bodl. Rolls 8.

deriving from St. Augustine, was that it prevented the expansion of social bonds. As a writer from the time of Henry VIII explained, marriage among close kin hinders "the propagacion and increasynge of love and charitie betwene christen people" by decreasing the number of marriages between strangers (*Determinations* 19v). This attitude implies that one of marriage's functions is to build social unity by connecting otherwise unrelated families. Thus, marrying meant expanding one's family connections. As Robert Burton put it, with marriage "the sweet company of kinsmen increaseth, the number of parents is dobled, of brothers, sisters, nephews" (3:267), for to marry is to join one's spouse's family.

Marriage was generally preceded by betrothal, also referred to in Shakespeare's time as a contract, espousal, "troth-plight" (meaning the pledging of one's faithfulness), or "handfasting" (in reference to the couple's clasping of hands as they became betrothed). Betrothal, whether done secretly or in public, was a formal agreement to marry and was taken almost as seriously as marriage itself. By taking each other by the right hand and repeating the proper words, indicating a promise in either the present or the future tense to take the other as spouse, a man and woman became betrothed. At the same time the couple often exchanged rings. Occasionally, the betrothal was made conditionally, with the conditions specified in the couple's words. Couples were strongly advised to have witnesses present to verify the betrothal, but witnesses were not required for a binding contract. To break a marriage contract without the consent of the other party was a serious offense, and a pre-contract, as it was called (meaning a previous promise to marry someone else), could prevent or invalidate a later marriage.

The seriousness of betrothal made for ambiguity in the relationship between the prospective bride and groom. Moralists strongly advised that sexual relations should not take place until the couple were married in church. Yet some betrothed couples felt that the contract made them husband and wife, and many engaged in sexual relations prior to the wedding. A good deal of prenuptial pregnancy in early modern England may be explained by this attitude. Though many considered sexual activity by a betrothed couple permissible or at least excusable, legally such activity was fornication, and during the 1600s it came to be more frequently and severely punished.

Normally, a marriage would be publicly solemnized in a church ceremony prescribed by "The Form of Solemnization of Matrimony" in the Book of Common Prayer (see Primary Document 5). This ceremony included not only the couple's vows but also the bestowing of the bride by the father and instruction by a priest. Though (after the Reformation) the Church of England no longer considered marriage a sacrament, the ceremony still called it "holy matrimony," and as part of his instruction, the priest was to note that God had instituted marriage and intended it to symbolize the mystical union of Christ and the Church. The priest went on to enumerate the three reasons for marriage: first, "the procreation of children to be brought up in the fear and nurture of the Lord"; second, "to avoid fornication" (that is, so that sexual relations could be engaged in lawfully); and finally, "for the mutual society, help, and comfort" of the couple. Marriage was thus intended to mark the founding of a family and the beginning of an enduring and mutually beneficial relationship between the man and woman. After asking whether the couple or anyone in the congregation knew of any impediment that would prevent a valid marriage, the priest asked the couple to indicate their willingness to enter into marriage and then had the bride's father or other authorized figure present her to be married. This "giving" of the bride indicated parental permission and made clear that the marriage concerned the family as a whole and not just the couple. The bride and groom then took each other by the right hand and said the prescribed words indicating their full intent to take each other as husband and wife. Following this, the groom placed a ring "upon the fourth finger of the woman's left hand." Then the priest blessed the couple to faithfully keep their vows and "remain in perfect love and peace together" and finally pronounced them "man and wife" ("The Form of Solemnization" 61–64).

Once the marriage ceremony had taken place, a feast would be provided, usually involving drinking, eating, dancing, revelry, and song. Sometimes the celebration would last for several days. Though the wedding festivities, like the wedding itself, were familial and communal events, it was recognized that, with marriage, the couple were acquiring a degree of independence. "After marriage there is," to quote Matthew Griffith, "a separation of the child from the . . . family of the Parent, and the erecting of a new family." But this "separation" does not, he insisted, mean a canceling of old ties; rather, it means a reordering of them, with primary loyalty transferred to one's spouse and children and with parents retaining an important, but now a secondary, role (321–22).

One reason marriage brought a degree of independence is that most brides and grooms were relatively mature. In fact, rather than marrying in their teens (as many moderns have assumed), most brides and grooms in early modern England were in their twenties and ready to establish a separate household. For a valid marriage to take place, both partners were required to have reached the age of consent—14 for boys and 12 for girls. A few marriages were solemnized at something near this age, but the vast majority of brides and grooms married later. The average age of marriage varied somewhat depending on location and social class, with marriages in the aristocracy taking place on average at about age 19 to 21 for women and age 24 to 26 for men, with occasional instances of much earlier marriage. But for most classes, the usual age was higher. Numerous studies confirm that the average age of marriage in England through most of the 1500s and 1600s was about 25 or 26 for women and 27 or 28 for men.

Besides being rare, very early marriages also seem to have met with general disapproval, motivated at least in part by a fear that the physical and emotional immaturity of a woman in her early teens could lead to ill effects either for her or for the marriage. According to Sir Simonds D'Ewes, who in 1626 was to marry a girl nearly 14, it was feared by the girl's grandmother "what danger might ensue to her very life from her extreme youth," the primary danger being the possibility of death in childbirth. The grandmother was also afraid that the girl's affection for her suitor "was no solid or real love grounded on judgment, and might therefore alter and lessen again after marriage" (1:319).

The relative maturity of most newlyweds and their closeness in age led to a degree of equality or at least of cooperative partnership between husbands and wives. Some modern observers have emphasized the hierarchical dimension of marriage—that is, the theoretical authority and superiority in rank of the husband. But as many scholars have noted, conceptions of hierarchy and mutuality coexisted in this period, and in practice the relationship between husband and wife varied from one family to another. (See, among others, Wrightson 90–104; Amussen 38–46; and Houlbrooke, *The English Family* 23, 26, 96–119.) Some have even argued that the treatises and sermons about a wife's role and in particular the notion that women should be "silent and obedient" reflect wishful thinking on the part of the writers rather than an accurate description of real women.

The idea that men were superior to women was certainly one view but was not the only one current in the period. Among other models was the view that men and women are complementary, that ideal virtue is a combination of typical male and female characteristics. Another view, sometimes presented by men, was that women are actually superior to men, especially in certain moral virtues. A third view emphasized the essential equality of men and women: some argued, for instance, that women and men are essentially the same in mind and soul, that in Christ there is neither male nor female, and that there will be no gender in the eternal world. Genesis was used both for and against the equality of the sexes. Although some argued that Eve's being created after Adam and succumbing first to temptation made women inferior, others argued that, as God's second creation after man, women were actually superior. Others emphasized the equality of men and women. According to William Austin, they were "made by *one workman;* of *one substance;* in *one place;* in *one day*" and so "must be *equall*, and both *alike;* or else, could they never justly be *fit*" to be companions and joint rulers over the earth (6, 44).

Although women's involvement in public life was certainly limited, the virtually universal admiration for Queen Elizabeth and her obvious skill as a ruler affected attitudes about women's roles. Aristocratic women were involved in public life as patrons of the arts, letters, and religion. Lower on the social scale, women ran shops or were employed in occupations ranging from street vendors to dairy maids. Besides running a household, women might also work as midwives, healers, schoolteachers, or printers or in a variety of other crafts and trades. Women of various classes attended both private and public theaters. A few women were admired for their scholarly accomplishments. And though the vast majority of works published in this period had male authors, women wrote and published plays, poems, treatises, and pamphlets on many subjects.

Despite the acknowledged capacities of women, most of Shakespeare's contemporaries, following biblical authority, accepted the idea that the husband is the "head" of the wife. Some pushed the husband's prerogatives even further, regarding his relation with his wife as one of supremacy or even ownership. Women's legal standing was problematic. In common law the idea that husband and wife constituted one person, embodied in the husband, deprived married women of legal existence. In practice, the idea limited women's legal rights and responsibilities but did not eliminate them completely. Women had various property rights, which they and their families often sought to protect, sometimes with the help of the courts. Contemporary observers were aware of women's poor legal standing in England but maintained that this alone did not indicate women's actual situation in social life or in the home, where they sometimes played a dominant role. Legal theory was not the main influence on the daily experience of marriage and in fact was in many respects at odds with prevailing ideals, which among other things insisted that husband and wife held all property in common. This view is apparent in the words of the marriage ceremony itself, in which the groom vows to the bride, "with all my worldly goods I thee endow" ("The Form of Solemnization" 63).

In the predominant view, the husband's headship was qualified by various limits and conditions and entailed both authority and responsibility, including the responsibility to act for the family's benefit rather than for selfish ends. Commentators pointed to language in the New Testament (e.g., Ephesians 5:21–23) that not only identified the husband as "the head" but also enjoined him to love and serve his wife just as Christ loved the Church. Writing in 1617, Rachel Speght granted that "the *Man is the womans Head*" but added that this "title" of "Supremacie" gives the man "no authoritie . . . to domineere, or basely command and imploy his wife, as a servant." Rather, by this title of "head" he is "taught the duties which hee oweth unto her," including the duties to "protect and defend his Wife from injuries," to maintain a harmonious relationship with her, and to instruct her, especially in religious matters (106).

Along with recognizing the husband's authority, some writers emphasized mutuality—even a degree of equality—in the relationship of husband and wife. "Mutuall love" and "mutuall comfort" and "helpe" were of the essence of marriage, and though marriage in a sense involved a giving up of liberty, this offering "must be mutuall and reciprocal" (Speght 106; Smith 19; Rogers 99). Many referred to husband and wife as "partners." William Perkins, though viewing the husband as the "chief head of the family," called a wife "the associate" of her husband, "not only in office and authority, but also in advice and counsel unto him" (*Christian Oeconomy* 437, 439). According to Henry Smith, "the man and wife are . . . like two oares in a boat, therefore he must divide offices and affaires . . . with her," for she is "an under-officer in his Commonweale" and therefore must be "feared and reverenced, and obeyed of her children and servants like himselfe" (52). Gouge even makes her "joynt governour with the husband of the Family" (256).

The wife commonly took charge of the servants and may often have taken the lead in disciplining children. She also carried out many essential household tasks, which required (in the words of Gervase Markham) "skill in Physicke, Cookery, Banqueting-stuffe, Distillation, Perfumes, Wooll, Hemp, Flax, Dayries, Brewing, Baking, and all other things belonging to an Houshould" (*The English Hus-wife* title page [Q1r]). Much of the husband's work was outside of the home. Yet, although the wife generally was mainly responsible for household tasks, the husband too was expected to help, though his willingness to do so would certainly have varied from one family to another.

One of historian Lawrence Stone's most influential assertions has been that, at least until the mid-seventeenth century, marriages were not based on mutual affection but mainly on a "pragmatic calculation of family interest" (180). More recent historians of family life are virtually unanimous in agreeing that Stone's assertion is wrong. The evidence is strong that what Stone calls "companionate marriage" was not a new feature of life in the later 1600s and 1700s but had long existed. Most historians conclude that love and friendship were essential elements of English marriages throughout the entire early modern period as well as long before.

In practice, of course, the quality of marriages varied, but there is evidence that in many cases the ideal of mutual love and happiness was attained with reasonable success. Ralph Houlbrooke and others have collected evidence from letters, diaries, and other sources demonstrating that many husbands and wives experienced intimate and loving companionship. In the mid-1500s, for instance, the merchant John Johnson and his wife—just one of many examples Houlbrooke provides—exchanged letters that are "characterised by conjugal endearments of great freshness and variety, apparently complete mutual confidence and a shared sense of humour" (*The English Family* 104). A century later Sir Anthony Ashley Cooper, along with describing his wife Margaret's beauty, faithfulness, religious devotion, generosity, and practical abilities, wrote that she was "of admirable wit and wisdom beyond any I ever knew, yet the most sweet, affectionate and observant wife in the world" (qtd. in Houlbrooke, *English Family Life* 69–70). Terms of endearment were common in letters throughout the period and were often used with obvious sincerity. Elizabeth Jocelin, for instance, in her prefatory epistle to *A Mothers Legacie, to Her Unborne Childe* (1624), calls Tourell Jocelin "MY TRULY loving, and most dearly loved Husband," "MINE owne deare love," "good sweet heart," "Dearest," and "Deare" and closes with "Thine inviolable" (B1–11v; see Primary Document 24).

Of course, not all marriages were happy, and most were probably marred by occasional conflict. Some experienced physical violence. However, the modern assumption that wife beating was a common and accepted practice is highly suspect. Most of those in early modern England who discussed the subject condemned domestic violence. Puritan writer William Whately justified wife beating in rare cases (if "she give just cause, after much bearing and forebearing, and trying all other ways, in case of utmost necessity, so that he exceed not measure") but argued that normally the practice is wrong "because it seemeth too imperious in him to do it, and too servile in her to suffer it" (qtd. in Amussen 42). As Susan Amussen demonstrates, other writers opposed the practice even more strictly. She summarizes William Gouge as claiming husband and wife to be so united that "in beating his wife [a husband] would be beating himself" (43). According to another source, a husband is "never to lay violent hands upon" his wife but should be her "defender, instructor, teacher, and comfort" (Clever and Dod, qtd. in Amussen 42). (For another discussion of the subject, see Primary Document 18.) Though the great majority of domestic violence was apparently directed by men against women, there is also evidence of wives' violence against husbands. In either case, violence between spouses clearly did not have social approval and could bring legal consequences.

Less violent marital conflict was probably common. In wealthier families, husbands sometimes pressured wives over property issues. Husbands and wives at all levels of society sometimes took offense, exchanged bitter words, or otherwise experienced conflict or estrangement. Adam Eyre recounts his wife's beginning one morning in 1647, "after her old manner, to brawl and revile me . . . with curses and oaths" and describes other instances of anger and cross words (qtd. in Houlbrooke, *English Family Life* 66–68). *The Homilie of the State of Matrimonie*, a sermon frequently read in church during the early modern period, laments that few marriages are "without chidings, brawlings, tauntings, repentings, bitter cursings, and fightings" (*Second Tome* 240; see Primary Document 6).

The solution most commonly offered to marital conflict was mutual forbearance and forgiveness. One of the duties of husband and wife, wrote Thomas Gataker, is "the bannishing of all Bitternes" (*Marriage Duties* 42). According to William Crompton,

> married persons should conster [i.e., construe] the actions one of another in the best sence; to say, and thinke, (if it be true in any tolerable manner,) their owne choyce [of a spouse] excels all others. . . . It is one property of love, to cover a multitude of infirmities, and sometimes to judge that excellent, which is but weakely good; wives passing by their husbands faults, husbands pardoning their wives failings, that so a good opinion may be still kept warme in the lap of mutuall affection. (29–30)

There is evidence that some husbands and wives followed such counsel and tried to acknowledge their own faults while extending patience and forgiveness to their spouse. Adam Eyre, for instance, reports that, as 1648 began, he persuaded his "wife to forbear to tell me of what is past, and promised her to become a good husband to her for the time to come." He concludes by "pray[ing] God that both she and I may leave off all our old and foolish contentions" (qtd. in Houlbrooke, *English Family Life* 68).

Whatever the actual quality of their marriages, Shakespeare's contemporaries generally looked to marital harmony as an ideal. This is true of both men and women writers of a variety of religious persuasions. Recognizing that not all marriages are happy, Rachel Speght seemed confident that such marriages are possible and pointed to love as the necessary condition: "Marriage is a merri-age, and this worlds Paradise, where there is mutuall love" (106). Many writers of the period similarly emphasized the loving intimacy and unity that ought to characterize married life. According to the Anglican clergyman Thomas Gataker, husband and wife "are neerer than Friends, and Brethren; or than Parents and Children. . . . Man and Wife are . . . the one ingraffed into the other, and so fastned together, that they cannot againe be sundred" (*Good Wife* 5). John Wing similarly affirmed that conjugal love "must be the most deare, intimate, precious and entire, that *hart* can have toward a creature" and should be surpassed only by love of God (44).

True marriage, according to the popular preacher Henry Smith, involves an intimate emotional bonding: "unlesse there be a joyning of hearts and a knitting of affections together, it is not Marriage indeed, but in shew and name" (44).

Calling husband and wife "yoake-fellowes," Speght argued that spouses should not only share the burdens of running a household but also provide emotional support by "sustayn[ing] part of ech others cares, griefs, and calamities" (105–6). According to the influential theologian William Perkins, husband and wife "are freely to communicate their goods, their counsel, their labours each to other for the good of themselves and theirs" (*Christian Oeconomy* 427). Henry Smith admonishes, "Let all things be commonn betweene them, which were private before . . . for they two are one. He may not say as husbands are wont to say, that which is thine is mine, and that which mine is mine owne, but that which is mine is thine, & my selfe to" (51–52). As Smith's words make clear, the ideal of marital union was not always achieved and sometimes even degenerated into competitive or domineering discord, especially when property was at stake. But with a good deal of social encouragement, many couples seem to have worked toward the ideal.

One way husbands and wives sought the "joyning of hearts" and "knitting of affections" that should come with marriage was through sexual union. The view that marriage in the past did not involve a loving sexual relationship or that sexual relations functioned only for procreation and were otherwise considered morally suspect is clearly mistaken. Though the early modern period had inherited from previous thinkers a traditional suspicion of sexuality, the prevailing view—encouraged by the Reformation, with its preference of marriage over lifelong celibacy—was that marriage was instituted by God and that sexual relations within marriage were not sinful. Writers of the period tended to treat the details of sexuality with reticence, yet the existing evidence makes it clear that mutual joy and affection were recognized as legitimate purposes of sexual relations within marriage. The preacher Jeremy Taylor argues that in engaging in their "mutual endearments," husband and wife must avoid excess and indulgence in merely selfish pleasure (for "he is an ill Husband that uses his Wife as a man treats a Harlot") (92–94). But Taylor views these endearments, and the pleasure involved, as good and appropriate as long as they are joined with any of their natural purposes. One of these, of course, is "a desire of children," and another is "to avoyd fornication"—that is, to provide a legitimate outlet for sexual desire. But besides these purposes, which Taylor paraphrases from the marriage ceremony, he adds two others: "to lighten and ease the cares and sadnesses of houshold affairs" and "to endear each other"—that is, to deepen and confirm the loving bond between husband and wife (92).

Other writers are even more explicit in their approval of sexual relations in marriage. A wedding sermon by William Whately argues that sexual relations, engaged in "lovingly, willingly and familiarly," are "the best means to continue and nourish" a husband's and wife's "mutuall naturall love," though he adds that such relations should also be marked by reverence and moderation (43). William Gouge similarly argues that, along with the fear of God, an essential way for spouses to achieve harmony is to "mutually delight each in other, and maintaine a pure and fervent love betwixt themselves," and he makes it clear that the delight of which he writes includes the mutually enjoyed sexual activity "which is warranted and sanctified by Gods Word, and ordained of God for this particular end." If engaged in "with good will and delight," sexual relations will help link "the affections of the maried couple more firmely together" (224).

Nonreligious writers also celebrated the sexual dimension of marriage. The poet Edmund Spenser describes a married couple's mutual sexual "joy" (*Epithalamion*, line 325; see Primary Document 11). An early seventeenth-century broadside ballad has a wife defend marriage by reminding her husband, "At night I give you kindely / a thousand kisses sweet" (*Lamentation*, "The Second Part," stanza 14; see Primary Document 20). A collection of poems, published in 1640 to celebrate the marriage of Hugh Rogers and Anne Baynton, includes several allusions to the wedding night: the "Marriage Bed" is a place of "Blisse," and "the married Paire" must not be kept "from their due joyes" (*Gamelia* 40, 12). Though such literary expressions are emotionally and rhetorically heightened, it is clear that they are not mere fantasies but reflect widely held attitudes. Such attitudes are evident in nonliterary materials from the period, including letters in which spouses expressed fervent longing and affection and "recalled or anticipated the pleasure of being in bed together" (Houlbrooke, *The English Family* 103–4).

The prevailing view, derived in part from the Bible, was that through sexual union, husband and wife become "one flesh" (see Genesis 2:24; Matthew 19:5–6; Mark 10:8; Ephesians 5:31). Sexual fidelity was therefore expected of both husband and wife, and adultery on the part of either was a serious offense. To some extent a double standard existed: that is, men effectively had greater sexual freedom than women. But almost all writers on the subject condemned the double standard, and there is strong evidence that men's sexual misconduct could seriously damage their reputations.

As the evidence for both marital love and marital conflict indicates, marriage in early modern England was a complicated institution involving discrepancies between ideals and reality as well as the complexities contributed by differences in gender roles and individual temperament. But even with these complexities, certain attitudes were common. It was widely believed, for instance, that happiness in marriage required both men and women to overcome selfishness and other failings, to offer themselves in responsibility and service to each other, and to practice daily forbearance and forgiveness. The frequency and fervor with which Shakespeare's contemporaries discussed these matters probably reflect similar efforts to put these ideals into practice. The remarkably sincere expressions of mutual love that survive from the period are evidence that these efforts sometimes, perhaps often, had the desired outcome.

PARENTS AND CHILDREN

Like marriage in Shakespeare's time, parent–child relations have also been described by some modern writers as ordinarily oppressive and violent. Describing

English family life of the late 1500s and early 1600s, Lawrence Stone asserts that the father was "a legalized petty tyrant within the home" and claims that the picture he gives "of a severe repression of the will of the child, extending to his or her choice of a spouse," is "beyond possibility of challenge" (7, 193). Yet many historians have in fact challenged Stone's assertions and have argued for a balanced view that acknowledges the predominance of parental love alongside occasional instances of tyranny and abuse.

Parents in early modern England valued their children mainly for noneconomic reasons. Though they anticipated that in old age they would be cared for and would find comfort in their children, they also desired children for their own sake and took delight in them as they grew up, referring to them in letters and diaries with endearing terms such as "sweet child." Further, almost everyone accepted the notion that parents by nature loved their children and ought to act for their good. As Nicholas Sander wrote in 1585, "the very existence of their children and nature itself is a perpetual cry unto parents to do all they can for the good of their children" (61).

Though children were often anticipated with joy, their entry into the world was perilous for both mother and child. Childbirth was an arduous experience that, in the words of David Cressy, "exposed the woman's vulnerability and summoned intimations of mortality" (28). Contemporary accounts refer to the "bitter pangs and pearsing paines" of childbirth and the risk of death (Bentley, "Fift Lampe" 106). Though death in childbirth was not likely in any given case, it was common enough to be widely feared and was certainly more common than now, with one estimate indicating it was the cause of death for about 1 out of 15 women who bore children (see Mendelson and Crawford 152). Though husbands were sometimes present, childbirth mainly involved women, with the prospective mother attended by other women and the baby normally delivered by a midwife. Following delivery, a mother enjoyed "the child-bed privilege," a period of about a month of recovery and freedom from most of her usual responsibilities.

At the end of this month, a ceremony took place called "the churching of women" (sometimes also called the "purification" or "thanksgiving of women after childbirth"). Recognizing the new mother, who was to kneel near the altar, the priest prayed for her and gave thanks to God for her survival. The woman gave thanks by offering the "chrisom cloth" in which the child was baptized or a monetary equivalent. The ceremony of churching marked a new mother's return to full social activity as well as the resumption of sexual relations with her husband. The ceremony was usually accompanied by a social gathering and feasting at home or at a tavern involving both men and women but focusing on the new mother and her female friends.

The child was usually christened within a few days of birth, most commonly on a Sunday or holy day but earlier if the child's life was in danger. At christening, the newborn was baptized, assigned godparents, and given a name, often the name of one of the godparents or of a relative. Sometimes the ceremony was followed by a celebration. Following the Reformation, many in the Church of England believed that baptism was not essential to a child's salvation and symbolized rather than guaranteed the child's entry into heaven. Yet the ritual, which incorporated the child into the body of the Church, continued to be important and expected. Because opinions varied concerning the status of unbaptized children, most parents were understandably anxious that their children not die without baptism.

As in many earlier cultures, the standard practice of Shakespeare's time was to swaddle newborn children. This ancient practice was commonly followed into the eighteenth century. Stone and others have interpreted swaddling as a form of repressive "physical imprisonment" that "contributed to a 'psychic numbing'" of the child (101). But evidence from the period suggests that parents believed they were acting in their children's interests by helping their limbs to grow straight and keeping the children from hurting themselves. Though some authorities recommended a lengthy period of swaddling, up to a year or more, the common practice in the seventeenth century seems to have been to put children in "coats" (a kind of gown-like outfit) within three months of birth.

Another common practice of the time was to hire a woman to nurse the infant. Though some modern writers have claimed that this practice showed a lack of affection and even lack of regard for children's survival, evidence indicates that wet nurses were chosen with care and that most parents were concerned about their children's welfare. But it is true that children sometimes died while in a nurse's charge, either from disease or from the nurses' "overlaying" (lying close to or on top of them, presumably accidentally) and smothering them. Though having others nurse one's children was common, especially in the upper classes, many writers of the time deplored the practice and recommended that mothers nurse their own children. Elizabeth Clinton, the Countess of Lincoln, wrote sternly of the "uncomely, and unchristian" reasons some mothers gave for using a wet nurse and argued that breast-feeding one's own children was a duty "which all mothers are bound to performe" (13, A2v; see Primary Document 22). Similarly, the author of

A priest christens a newborn child while family and friends observe. Woodcut from *A Booke of Christian Prayers* by Richard Day (London, 1581), R1v. This item is reproduced by permission of The Huntington Library, San Marino, California.

a book titled *The Office of Christian Parents* noted the common reasons for hiring a wet nurse—"wealth, pleasure," and "ease"—but argued that these "cannot excuse the mother which nurseth not her own child" (51). Other writers were more flexible. Edward Topsell asserted that "every woman being in health of bodie and minde, is bound by the word of God to nurse her owne children," but he granted that "in causes of weakenesse in the woman, danger to the child, or sicknesse in either of both, it is not only a dutie of necessitie, but of conscience, to nourish and cherish the children of other" (301, 303; see Primary Document 23).

Among the reasons offered for mothers' nursing their own children were that it is better for both the mothers' and the children's health and that it expresses "a motherly care" and creates in the children "a greater measure of child-like love" for the mother (Brathwait 361). Because children supposedly imbibed a nurse's disposition and complexion along with her milk, some writers argued for the advantages of having those qualities come from the natural mother. Yet despite the arguments of the moralists, having someone else nurse the child seems to have been a popular practice, at least among those who could afford it.

The time of weaning varied, but nursing usually continued into the child's second year and sometimes until the child was three. For boys, another turning point was "breeching," the time when they began to wear breeches instead of the gown-like coats that both boys and girls wore in earlier childhood. Breeching, sometimes accompanied by a celebration, marked the boy's symbolic entry into the world of men. This change of attire usually took place between ages five and seven, most commonly when a boy was about six. Girls continued wearing coats a few years longer and then started wearing more adult clothing.

Far from being constantly regimented and oppressed, most children in Shakespeare's time were treated affectionately by their parents and had time for play. For instance, in a letter written in 1624, Thomas Wentworth describes a child "laughinge, gapeinge and dauncinge in his father's armes to a piper that was playinge, to the great joie and comfort of the spectators, especially his father" (qtd. in Houlbrooke, *The English Family* 136). Diaries of the period refer to various sports and toys. Girls played with "babies" (i.e., dolls), while boys engaged in sports and games and played with tops and other toys. For instance, George Wither, writing in the 1620s, refers to "Ratles, Pot-guns [i.e., pop-guns], [and] the Schoole-boyes Tops" (4). Children in general played with hobby-horses (sticks with horse-like heads), balls, and other playthings. Adam Martindale wrote that until he turned six he "was all for childish play, and never thought of learning" (qtd. in Pollock 147).

Parents were cautioned not to neglect or overindulge their children, for they had a responsibility to provide instruction and discipline. A variety of sentiments were held about children's moral state. Some spoke of their innocence, others of their natural depravity. But all agreed that children needed training and instruction. Many considered the most important training to be religious. Both boys and girls would have received practical training as well, with the details dependent on social class and gender. Girls' schools existed, but boys were more likely to be sent to school. Girls were generally trained in household tasks, but some were

Portrait (1596) of Anne, Lady Pope, and her children, by Marcus Gheeraerts the Younger (National Portrait Gallery, London). The children (from left to right—Thomas, Henry, and Jane) are from her first marriage, to Henry Wentworth. Her sons are wearing "coats," gown-like outfits commonly worn by young boys. By permission of private collection, courtesy of Nevill Keating Pictures.

instructed at home in languages and other academic subjects. When they reached their teenage years or sometimes before, many children left home for service or apprenticeship in another household. According to Hugh Cunningham, census materials show that "around one-third of children were still living in the parental home at the age of fifteen or over," with "about 60 per cent of the population aged between fifteen and twenty-four" in service (98). Some modern commentators have speculated that this absence from home reduced the tension between parents and their adolescent children. The practice has also been interpreted as a sign that parents were not attached to their children. But evidence from the period indicates that parents often found it difficult to send their children from home yet felt it important to do so to help their children prepare for adult responsibilities. Many parents expressed anxiety about their absent children and were eager to see them when possible. Children of the nobility or gentry were often sent to serve in another household as young as age seven as part of their education. In other classes, entry into service or apprenticeship more often took place around the early or mid-teens.

Parents with children still at home had the task of disciplining them—that is, helping to prepare them for adult life by encouraging virtue and responsibility and correcting their misbehavior. One of parents' greatest challenges was to subdue children's natural selfishness and self-will. Along with instruction and encouragement, physical discipline was sometimes used, but it was not normally as harsh as some moderns imagine. Stone is certainly wrong when he maintains that parents' "fierce determination to break the will of the child" commonly led them to use "the harshest physical beating" and "overwhelming psychological pressures" (162, 101). Some early modern authorities advocated physical punishment for misbehavior, but even most of these counseled moderation. *The Office of Christian Parents* (see Primary Document 25) is only one of many handbooks that advised taking a middle course between "foolish indulgencie" and "hard handling" (90). Either extreme can have evil consequences: "the mamish cockling of the parents, to give the child the sway of his owne desires" can make "the parents and all the house slaves"; but if treated with excessive severity, a child may be "over-awed, learne to lie, dissemble, and to doe any wickednes in secret," or else "the heart of the child is utterly broken" (55, 90). The evidence indicates that in practice parents' correction of children was sometimes harsh, including "whipping" (a term referring to any sort of physical punishment) and the rod. But many parents, reluctant to use severe punishment, did so only rarely and sought to rely instead on instruction and persuasion.

Children were of course expected to obey their parents, but this obedience was not absolute. Many writers condemned disobedience and wrote of the evil consequences that were sure to follow it. Yet virtually all who wrote on the subject agreed that the obligation to obey had limits. John Bradford, for instance, wrote that children should honor their parents "so long as they pass not their bounds" (1:162). Thomas Pritchard cautioned parents to command only "such thinges as be honest, vertuous, and lawfull and consonant to the word of God" (31). Many warned that God should be honored and obeyed more than parents. As a writer of the 1590s put it, "we ought indeede to obay our earthly parents, yet we must not dishonour ou[r] eternall father. . . . Wee ought to love our worldly parents, yet we must not offend our heavenly father" (Gibbon 13).

According to some writers, the father, and to a lesser degree the mother, had authority within the household comparable to that of the king in a nation. But like a king, they were expected to exercise that authority justly. Other writers pointed instead to the differences between political and familial life. In a modern discussion of the period, Debora Shuger has demonstrated that, along with comparing fathers and kings, Renaissance discourse contrasted them and regularly emphasized the kind and nurturing, even the indulgent, aspects of fatherhood (218–49). Violent and tyrannical fathers would not have been viewed with approval or admiration. On the other hand, there are many admiring accounts of deep affection between parents and their children. Sources from the period overwhelmingly associate fatherhood with love and indicate that the word *fatherly* was virtually synonymous with *kindly* or *benevolent*. Clearly, the expectation was, in the words of John Newnham, that "the naturall and the kindelie love of Parentes towardes their children, is, or ought to bee, as constant and readie" as God's unfailing love (3).

Deference toward parents was an element of family life in Shakespeare's time. Yet along with deference, other attitudes were equally or even more highly prized. One clue to the nature of the parent–child bond is the early modern practice of giving parental blessings, a practice that some have interpreted as a sign of parental domination and of the distance between parents and children but that clearly had much different associations for most of those who practiced it.

The parental blessing was one of the most important and pervasive rituals of early modern England. Indeed, according to contemporary observers from France and Italy, it was a peculiarly English custom. It goes back at least to the 1200s, and probably much earlier; it appears to have been practiced after the Reformation by Catholics and Protestants, Puritans and non-Puritans alike, with little variation in form or meaning into the early seventeenth century. In "well-ordered" households the ritual took place daily, morning and evening, with children kneeling before their parents, both father and mother, and saying (to quote William Perkins), "Father I pray you bless me, Mother I pray you bless me" (*Treatise* 469), or words to that effect. Each parent would respond to the request by calling on God to bless the child, usually while placing both hands on the child's head to signify the conferring of the blessing. Along with the blessing, parents would sometimes give a child counsel intended for his or her benefit. Some continued to ask their parents for blessings into adulthood. Accounts of this practice range from the early 1500s—for instance, Sir Thomas More reportedly would kneel publicly before his aged father and ask for a blessing—into the 1600s, when a Venetian ambassador reported seeing Londoners kneel in public places, "no matter what their age," to ask a parent's blessing (*Calendar* 451).

Besides being practiced morning and evening, the blessing ritual was practiced on special occasions, for instance, at times of parting and reunion. Parents who were soon to die might also bless their children, about whose futures they would have felt particularly anxious at this time of final parting. Alice Thornton's description of her mother's death in 1659 reveals how emotionally intense a deathbed blessing might be:

> She imbraced us all severally in her armes, and kissed us, powring out many prayers and blessings for us all; like good old Jacob, when he gave his last blessing to his childeren. (112–13)

By kneeling, children expressed their respect and subordinate status and their acknowledgment of their parents as sources of their own being and identity. But kneeling also allowed the parent conveniently to place hands on the child's head and act as a kind of intermediary between heaven and earth in bestowing a blessing. Though any parent could give a blessing, the ritual had strong religious connotations and was, in the minds of many, comparable to a blessing given by a priest or, even more, to the blessings given by ancient biblical figures such as Isaac and Jacob. Thus, though it was a familiar daily practice, the ritual was connected in the minds of those who practiced it with customs of great antiquity, highly charged with religious associations. Though some writers distinguished between the truly prophetic blessings of the ancient patriarchs and the ordinary blessings of contemporary parents, others emphasized the prophetic power of either a blessing or a curse coming from a parent. As King James himself put it, "the blessing or curse of the Parents, hath almost ever a Propheticke power joyned with it" (76). References to parental cursing are much harder to find than references to blessing, and there seems to have been no particular ritual associated with a parental curse. More often, it appears, an angry or disappointed parent might simply withhold the expected blessing from a disobedient child.

Despite its association with parental power, the blessing ritual seems to have been viewed primarily as a loving act rather than as an instrument of control or domination. Giving a blessing was an expression of goodwill and was believed to be a way parents could convey divine influence that would benefit their children. The words parents spoke conveyed their generous desires for the child's welfare, while at the same time the physical contact involved in the ritual expressed mutual affection, with children sometimes kissing their parents' hands and parents not only placing hands on their children's heads but also often following the blessing with an embrace. If the ritual were not viewed as a positive act, it would be hard to explain why so many children of the period requested their parents' blessings, as they often did with obvious sincerity, even into adulthood.

Another indication of the quality of parent–child bonds in the period is the response of parents to the death of a child. Such a response would have been called for frequently because, according to one estimate, about one out of seven children died in the first year and about one out of four by age 10, usually from illness or other causes "beyond parental understanding or control" (Houlbrooke, *The English Family* 138–40). A few have argued that, because of the frequency of children's deaths and the supposed emotional distance between parents and children, parents did not grieve deeply for the loss of their children. This view is clearly mistaken. The evidence of parental grief is abundant, especially in diaries and letters. To cite one example, the diary entries written in 1648 by Ralph Josselin reveal the tenderness and anxiety he felt as his newborn son (also named Ralph) took ill and his grief at the boy's death: "This day my dear babe Ralph quietly fell asleep, and is at rest with the Lord." The next day he reports the burial: "These two days were such as I never knew before; the former for the death, and this for the burial of my dear son. . . . This little boy of ten days old when he died was buried with the tears and sorrow not only of the parents . . . but . . . of many of my neighbours" (qtd. in Houlbrooke, *English Family Life* 115–16).

For most parents, older children were even harder to part with. In 1625 Nehemiah Wallington's three-year-old daughter suddenly died: "my daughter Elizabeth, then being merry, went unto her mother and said unto her, 'What do you here, my wife?' And at night when we were abed says she to me, 'Father, I go abroad tomorrow and buy you a plum pie.' These were the last words that I did hear my sweet child speak." He describes her being "seized upon" the next morning by "the very pangs of death" and undergoing "great agonies (which was very grievous unto us the beholders)" for the next two days, "and then my sweet child died at four a clock in the morning . . . and was buried that day at night." Wallington's grief at the loss was violent: "The grief for this child was so great that I forgot myself so much that I did offend God in it; for I broke all my purposes, promises and covenants with my God, for I was much distracted in my mind, and could not be comforted, although my friends spake so comfortably unto me." His wife felt compelled to counsel him to accept God's will and consider "what abundance of joy" their daughter had now "gone into" (qtd. in Houlbrooke, *English Family Life* 142).

Those who lost loved ones were cautioned to keep their grief within proper bounds, something many found it hard to do. The common advice was to subdue excessive grief through reason, self-discipline, and contemplation of universal mutability and to endeavor to be submissive to God's will. As Thomas Gataker put it, parents should not "fasten their affections upon them [their children], that they should be unwilling to part from them, when God shall please to call for them" (*Jeroboams* 16).

Still, many writers on the subject acknowledged the appropriateness of grief and sought to offer comfort. The author of *A Handkercher for Parents Wet Eyes* (see Primary Document 29), before seeking to console a friend who has lost a "*beloved Sonne*," is careful not to blame him if he should "melt," "ake," and "be sore of such a wound and mayme as this" (I. C. 1, 6). But he encourages his friend to moderate his grief by considering that everyone suffers such losses, that God may intend to teach or test him, and that his son is certainly happy in heaven now that "God hath by death freed him . . . from the dangers and corruptions of the Age" (33, 49). Though his son really belongs to God, the grieving father can still remember him and even anticipate seeing him again in heaven: "There you shall one day see him againe face to face, in that very *House of clay*, which hee laid downe. . . . And (if that may make to the increase of your Blisse) I am perswaded, know, and enjoy him, see Heaven the richer in your Seed, his joy augmented and made fuller by yours, and yours by his" (63, 65).

According to David Cressy, many in this period anticipated being reunited with loved ones in heaven. James Cole, for instance, writing in 1629, assured his readers that "although our loving parents, husbands, wives, and children or friends are departed out of this world, yet for all that they be not therefore dead, but alive, yea they may still be called ours" (qtd. in Cressy 388). But not everyone believed that family relationships would continue after death. In fact, the scriptural statement that in the resurrection "they neither marry, nor are given in marriage" (Matthew 22:30) was taken by some to mean that in heaven all family ties would be dissolved. According to John Prime, "the respects of man & wife shalbe swalowed up as it were a candle put out at the rising of the Sunne," and "the affections toward father and mother, children and kinred, . . . shal also cease then. For they will either hinder somewhat, or doe much hurte in the quietnes of our passage" (209). If responses to a loved one's death are any indication, however, most probably hoped for some kind of continuing relationship in heaven.

For many, the loss of a spouse was a particularly hard blow. One diarist called his wife's death "the heaviest personal stroke that ever I experienced" and wrote, "Methinks I am but half myself without her" (Houlbrooke, *English Family Life* 70–71). Children also grieved at the deaths of their parents, and though such

The Saltonstall Family (c. 1636–37) by David des Granges. The painting shows Sir Richard Saltonstall, his deceased first wife (on the bed), their two surviving children (on the left), and his second wife, holding their baby. Tate, London / Art Resource, NY.

deaths were probably easier to accept than the death of one's child or spouse, there is evidence that many children grieved deeply.

But although many children honored and loved their parents both before and after their death, there is also evidence of friction between parents and children, especially as the children became adults and as the parents grew older. Conflict sometimes arose over inheritance, either because of children's impatience to receive money or property or because of their dissatisfaction with how the inheritance was divided among the siblings. Most parents sought to help their children advance in life and were reasonably generous in providing for them. Yet many (following the advice of contemporary writers) retained enough property to have some economic independence in their older years and to have continued influence over their children. Occasionally, parents used the threat of disinheritance to influence their children or carried out the threat as a punishment.

The neediness of some aged parents was a further cause of tension. The Elizabethan Poor Law, along with strong social expectation, obligated children to care for their parents when they became incapable of caring for themselves, a responsibility that some children felt to be a burden. Though it was widely held that old age should be treated with reverence as a time of wisdom and experience, some viewed the aged as useless and disagreeable. One writer pictured "a poore aged man" living with his son and daughter-in-law, who find him "troublesome" because he is irritable and unpleasant and has to be "so much waited on" (Robartes 114). Concerning at least some of the aged, it could be said, as Daniel Rogers lamented, that "when all strength and ability is gone, then are they no longer set by, but . . . despised, counted as burdens" (92).

Given such ambivalence about the aged, some parents understandably felt anxiety about how reliably and sincerely their children loved them. It was commonly said that love "descends rather than ascends"—that is, that parents are naturally more inclined to love their children than the reverse. Yet despite such anxieties, most in the period, including Shakespeare himself, affirmed the value of the parent–child bond and suggested that children's attitude toward parents ought to be one of gratitude, respect, and love. Despite much variation in the quality of parent–child relations, many children clearly possessed and acted on such positive feelings. The inappropriateness of a contrary attitude is evidenced by a popular story of the period that tells how a man's poor treatment of his father sets the stage for his son to treat him the same way. In the story, the man, whose father has given him all, degrades him gradually from a position of honor in the household to one of contempt and misery. Finally, the aged father is left with nothing but an "olde sackcloth." When he dies, his grandson—the eldest son of the man who has mistreated his father—says, "I pray you, father, give me this olde sackcloth." When asked why, the boy answers, "Forsooth, . . . it shall serve to cover you, as it did my old graund-father" (*Pasquils Jests* [1604], qtd. in Mack 29).

BROTHERS, SISTERS, COUSINS—AND INHERITANCE

As with other family relationships, great variety marked the bond between siblings in early modern England. Many experienced great affection and continuing loyalty. But there is also evidence of resentment and conflict, often over inheritance. Such conflict struck many not only as unfortunate but also as deeply troubling because siblings were supposed to have a strong natural connection as partakers of the same flesh and blood. According to one source from the period, the "enmitie which a man beareth towards his brother . . . is most prodigious and against nature" and is comparable "to cut[ting] off voluntarily a member of his owne flesh belonging to him" (La Primaudaye 223; see Primary Document 32). Sibling conflict, especially when it was severe, was thus considered "unnatural."

Brothers and sisters were taught that they should love and assist each other, and older children in particular were expected to take an interest in the welfare of their siblings. In their younger years, siblings were often close, playing and working together and sometimes, of course, quarreling. But for various reasons—including the spacing of children and the departure of older children for service—most children had few siblings at home as they grew up. At any given time, most households had three or fewer children living at home. For many, the sibling bond gradually weakened as each married and formed a new family. Yet the sense of being kindred continued, and on occasion adult siblings turned to each other in times of need.

Inheritance sometimes became a point of conflict between brothers, especially when the practice of primogeniture led to great disparity between the oldest son and his younger brothers. Primogeniture—the predominant though not the only mode of inheritance in early modern England—meant leaving the estate and, among aristocrats, the father's title to the eldest son. If a male heir was lacking, property was divided equally among the daughters. Primogeniture was practiced especially in the landed classes and apparently was more common among these classes in England than elsewhere in Europe. Though it was sometimes defended on philosophical and scriptural grounds, the main justification for primogeniture was that it prevented decay of the family's estate, for having the eldest son inherit ensured that the estate would remain intact. The practice was also viewed as strengthening social stability by encouraging the survival of great families.

Despite the dominance of primogeniture, other inheritance customs prevailed in certain areas. In Kent and a few other places, estates were divided equally among sons. (This custom, known as gavelkind, may have survived from Anglo-Saxon times.) Other customs included the dividing of estates equally among both sons and daughters and, in a few places, giving all to the youngest son or daughter.

Even where primogeniture was practiced, parents generally tried to provide as generously as they could for the younger children. This was done in part by arranging for their education or entry into an apprenticeship or by assisting them to find a position in the military or at court. In addition, parents often sought to provide for their younger children through marriage portions or "by annuities, pensions, moneys, leases, and purchased lands" (Fuller 46). As this list indicates, those who were able to might bequeath land to their younger sons, but preferably not from the original ancestral estate. Unfortunately, after a father's death, the oldest son sometimes failed to provide for his younger brothers as the father had intended. And even when the father's wishes were followed, younger sons sometimes resented their dependence on an older brother's benevolence.

The discontent of younger sons was proverbial. One reason for younger sons' discontent was their difficulty in finding a satisfactory economic and social place in the world, especially in comparison with the oldest brother. This problem seems to have been especially great in the early 1600s—during the latter half of Shakespeare's writing career—when, according to Ralph Houlbrooke, "high fertility and a dramatic expansion of the ranks of the gentry had sharpened competition for places of profit and honour" (*The English Family* 237). Though the economic hardships of many younger sons may have seemed harsh only when compared with the relative ease of their elder brothers, to the younger sons themselves the hardship felt real enough. Thomas Wilson called the state of younger brothers "of all stations for gentlemen most miserable" (24). John Earle pictured a younger brother as experiencing a double bind, tasked by his father "to bee a Gentleman" yet left with "nothing to maintaine" that station. The resentment of the younger brother could sometimes break out into open hostility: "He is commonly discontented, and desperate," according to Earle, "and the forme of his exclamation is, that Churle my Brother" (C4, C5; see Primary Document 33).

Though relatively uncommon, bastardy was another source of social tension, sometimes including conflict between siblings over inheritance and competition for parental attention. Attitudes toward bastards were mixed and ranged from sympathy to scorn. But even those who were sympathetic noted the potential for social disorder that came with bastardy, including the burden the community might have to bear in supporting illegitimate children. Despite the rarity of bastards (they constituted less than 3% of births throughout this period), some felt that to legitimize them might encourage sexual irresponsibility, which in turn might promote social disorder by weakening marital fidelity and producing offspring who would be inadequately cared for and educated. Some legal authorities argued that illegitimate children should not inherit, but fathers who chose to acknowledge their illegitimate offspring could make provision for them by will. Still, the general practice of the period was to stigmatize bastardy as a shameful, irregular, and inferior condition and to use the words *bastard* and *whoreson* as terms of derision, thereby subjecting illegitimate children to disparagement as well as to social and legal discrimination.

Obviously, illegitimate children often resented their marginal condition, which could extend even to their religious status. According to Alan Macfarlane, there was in Renaissance England "a widespread view that bastards should not be christened," with the result that their status as members of a local congregation was at least "dubious" (78–79). Even Henry Smith wrote with, for him, uncharacteristic harshness of those who bear "the shameful name of bastardes":

> God . . . did curse & not blesse such increase. Therefore we read not in all the Scripture of one Bastard that came to any good, but only *Iphtah*, and to shew that no inheritance did belong to them in heaven, they had no inheritance in earth, neither were counted of the congregation, as other were. (4, 14–15)

In a treatise on bastardy and incest, William Clerke took a more generous view, reminding readers that bastards were not at fault for the way they were born and insisting that the child of an unlawful union could be as virtuous as a legitimate child. Still, Clerke did not want to be read as encouraging adultery or incest and suggested that the offspring of unlawful unions were by nature "a base kind of people, ignoble" and more likely to go bad than legitimate children ("Preface" A1v, 4v). At the root of such concerns, both for illegitimate children themselves and for others, was the difficulty in making sense of their place in a community where so much depended on belonging to a family. Illegitimate children lacked a clear, secure place in the natural network of flesh and blood—families connected with families—that made up the commonwealth.

In addition to the bonds between spouses, siblings, and parents and children, extended family relationships were important in early modern England, though not as important as some have claimed. As Ralph Houlbrooke has shown, extended kinship was not, in fact, "the mainspring of English politics or the individual's most important source of security" in this period. It is true that some political alliances involved kinship, but these were often "fragile and volatile" (*The English Family* 45). In many instances, good feelings among extended families were damaged by disputes over inheritance and other matters. When good feelings prevailed, extended family members, especially in the middle and upper classes, maintained contact through visits and social gatherings, for instance, on the occasion of a wedding or funeral. Yet primary loyalties remained with the nuclear family, as they apparently had for centuries. Even among more closely related members of an extended family, emotional bonds varied a great deal depending on differences in temperament and opportunities for contact. Bonds with grandparents were often especially strong, with grandparents sometimes greatly involved in the lives of their grandchildren.

The word *cousin*, often abbreviated to *coz*, was commonly used to refer to kin of almost any sort (apart from direct ancestors and descendants) outside of the immediate family. At times cousins, in this general sense, could be of practical use. Though there was no guarantee that requested help would be given willingly, one might turn to cousins when in legal or financial difficulties. Kin could also be useful as sources of patronage or as helps in winning a post, but people sometimes hesitated to recommend a relative they didn't know well and were more forthcoming with advice than with other kinds of assistance. The bond between a man and his sister's sons was one of the stronger bonds among extended kin, and unmarried men in particular might take an interest in their nephews, often making them their heirs. Yet this bond does not seem to have been as deeply felt in early modern England as it was in earlier Germanic cultures.

Beyond the practical element in these relationships among extended kin, they figured as part of a person's identity. Almost without exception, Shakespeare's contemporaries viewed themselves as members of families, and they viewed these families as including kin outside of the local household and as extending backward and forward in time. Besides references to extended family in letters and diaries, plays of the period sometimes identified a character as belonging to "a virtuous house" or "an honoured stock," meaning a lineage that the character is imagined to share with others (*Yorkshire Tragedy* 2.165, 7.4). But as kinship became more distant, it also became less significant and involved a vague sense of connection rather than active relationships. Most had closer bonds with their neighbors than with their distant kin.

CHANGES OVER TIME

This chapter describes features of family life that applied to most families of early modern England, especially during Shakespeare's lifetime in the later 1500s and early 1600s. But if we take a broader view—looking at England for a century before and after Shakespeare—certain changes become apparent. These changes were largely the result of religious and political events but also included more gradual changes in attitude and custom.

One of the most significant events of the 1500s took place in 1534 when Henry VIII broke from the Roman Catholic Church after the pope failed to dissolve the king's marriage with a wife who had not produced a son. Though England returned to Roman Catholicism during the reign of Henry's daughter Mary, the Church of England became independent again when Mary's half-sister Elizabeth came to the throne in 1558 and was soon established as moderately Protestant in doctrine and practice. During Elizabeth's reign, there were disputes within the Church between Puritans, who wanted the Church further reformed, and their opponents, who favored traditional ceremonies and forms of church government. This conflict continued during the reigns of James I and Charles I and culminated in the English Civil War of the 1640s, which ended with the execution of King Charles in 1649. After two decades of rule by Parliament (part of that time under the leadership of Oliver Cromwell), the monarchy was restored in 1660. The Church continued to be moderately Protestant, but there was growing tolerance of religious differences along with a more secular attitude in much of the period's public discourse.

Among the changes that took place during the 1500s, starting during the reign of Henry VIII, was a drastic simplifying of the forbidden degrees of marriage. The break from Rome also led to the end of monasteries and brought changes in attitudes toward marriage. Soon priests were permitted to marry, and marriage rose in status in comparison with celibacy, though the standard view continued to be that either condition could be appropriate for a Christian. After the Reformation, marriage was no longer one of the seven sacraments (these were reduced to two—baptism and Holy Communion or Eucharist), but it was still considered "holy," and strong preference was given to solemnizing it in church. Some in the newly independent English Church attempted to make divorce possible under certain conditions, but their efforts were unsuccessful. Unless dissolved on the grounds of being invalid (which happened rarely), marriages ended only with the death of a spouse. Formal separation sometimes took place, but with no possibility of remarriage.

Some have speculated that Protestants' abandonment of the doctrine of purgatory affected their attitude toward ancestors and other relatives who had died. Because it was now held that people went directly to heaven or hell at death, family members could do nothing for them, and prayer for the dead was futile, if not blasphemous. Some likely found the change in doctrine difficult because it seemed to provide no way of dealing with anxiety about the dead. Others responded more hopefully, trusting in God's judgment and power to save.

Printing, introduced into England in the late 1400s, led to the publication of many sermons and treatises on marriage and family life. During the late 1500s and 1600s, many of these were written by Puritans who stressed biblical precepts, including the evils of fornication and adultery and the importance of parental responsibility, love between spouses, and children's and wives' obedience. Non-Puritans often wrote in a similar vein, also stressing religious precepts, though usually with less intensity. Though many writers, including Puritans, stressed that young people should obtain parental consent before marrying, the legal standard continued to allow marriage without parental consent or knowledge. Many were concerned about the problems presented by clandestine marriage, but the legal standard did not change until 1753, when Parliament passed Hardwicke's Marriage Act, which required that marriages be performed in church and that anyone marrying under age 21 obtain parental permission.

Printing also helped spread the influence of Renaissance thought, which had incorporated ideas from ancient Greek and Roman writers. These ideas were cited in support of various positions in the frequent discussions of gender and family that took place during the period. The direct effect of Renaissance thought on family life, however, was probably minimal, though some hold that it led to a more positive view of women and children.

Many customs related to inheritance remained the same throughout this period, including primogeniture among most of the gentry and the standard granting of a third of a deceased man's goods to his widow. Yet inheritance laws underwent some changes and refinements during the 1500s and 1600s, the most significant of these being the devising in the 1640s of the "strict settlement," which aimed to protect an estate and the rights of possible heirs by specifying what would happen to the estate under certain conditions, with trustees appointed to ensure the carrying out of the provisions. By making inheritance in the landed classes more orderly and predictable, the "strict settlement" probably reduced friction among relatives.

A custom that continued through much of this period, to many people's displeasure, was feudal wardship—that is, control over an heir's land and marriage if the father died before the heir reached age 21. That control was exercised by the feudal lord with sovereignty over the land in question; often, and increasingly during the 1500s, that meant the monarch. Though in theory unwanted marriages could not be enforced, the guardians' control over land allowed them to dispossess wards who did not follow their wishes. From the 1530s on, monarchs exploited their authority as guardians, often selling wardships to others, which usually meant that control of the land and the ward's marriage went to someone outside of the family. Complaints about this practice led to reforms, including changes under James I that made it easier for relatives to gain control of wardships. When the Court of Wards was abolished in 1646, the practice was abandoned altogether. Some have speculated that the end of feudal wardship (which of course had applied only to the landed classes) may have more strongly emphasized the legal freedom young people had to marry as they wished. But of course that freedom had existed, despite practices that complicated it, even before the Court of Wards was abolished.

The movement in England during the 1500s and early 1600s toward stronger central government, focused in the king or queen, had several effects on family life. The monarch was viewed as a kind of "parent" to the country—King James I in particular liked to compare himself to a "nursing father"—and the nation was viewed as a large-scale extended family. Because Elizabeth I never married and was idealized as "the Virgin Queen," celibacy at least temporarily regained a special status in the public mind. Elizabeth's great capacity as a ruler certainly affected attitudes about gender, though these were already varied, and by the end of her reign, attitudes remained much as they had been before.

With the increased power and administrative control exercised by the central government came a weakening of extended family ties in parts of England (such as the north) where these had been unusually strong. Other innovations, however, such as improved communication and transportation, led to greater ease of contact among relatives. On the whole, the importance of the extended family changed little during this period.

Some of the most significant changes in family life came as a result of disputes in the early 1600s between Puritans and ceremonially minded high churchmen. Especially beginning in the 1620s, Puritans and various religious dissenters questioned the importance and even the appropriateness of certain traditional ceremonies. Among these was the "churching of women," which some Puritans wanted to discontinue or simplify. High churchmen, by contrast, not only wanted the practice to continue but even tried to enforce uniformity in certain elements of the ceremony. The giving of parental blessings also came into question. Some were concerned with the Catholic and Jewish associations of the practice, and others, while acknowledging the importance of honoring parents, were troubled to see children kneel as part of the ritual and wondered whether human beings should kneel to anyone but God. A decline in the practice was already noticeable by 1657 when Bishop Robert Sanderson, lamenting the neglect of the parental blessing and other practices, offered as one cause the connection commonly made between such ceremonies and "popish" practices: "These last *two seven* years"—that is, since 1643—"the having of *God-fathers* at Baptism, *Churching* of Women, *Prayers* at the burial of the dead, Children asking their Parents *blessing*, &c., which whilome were held *innocent;* are now by very many thrown aside, as rags of *Popery*" (73–74). Many families continued the practice of giving and receiving parental blessings even beyond the mid-1600s, but the ritual probably became more informal with time, and fewer practiced it. It seems to have survived, however, into the eighteenth century and even, here and there, into the nineteenth. But the custom was no longer widely viewed as a sacred event associated with distant antiquity and linking heavenly power with life on the earth.

In some ways the decline of parental blessings and other ceremonial practices signaled a subtle but general change in outlook. Increasing emphasis on individual conscience and liberty made ceremonies associated with submission—especially submission to another human being—less attractive. Furthermore, many became less confident that such ceremonies genuinely linked heaven and earth. The religious conflicts of the mid-1600s made many in the later 1600s and 1700s suspicious of strong religious claims and especially of attempts to enforce them. The rise of modern science and scientific attitudes in the 1600s offered alternative ways of explaining the universe without reference to highly specific religious doctrines. Many intellectual historians trace characteristic modern attitudes to the mid-1600s, including the emphasis on personal freedom and the dominance of secular discourse in the public sphere.

All of these changes in attitude had an impact on the family, though probably more on how family was understood than on how it was experienced. With changes by the late 1600s toward a more secular and less unified view of the world, family was no longer commonly understood as an integral element in the structure of the cosmos and as linked to both the cosmos and the commonwealth by resemblances in structure and function. Family life was thought of as a private matter more than it had been previously. People continued to write and talk about family but no longer with the confidence that almost everyone would view its role in the structure of the universe in pretty much the same way.

Despite such changes in outlook, everyday family life did not change radically between the early 1500s and the late 1600s. Children were still expected to obey their parents, and parents were still expected to love their children. With only rare exceptions, historians of the family agree that the 1500s and 1600s did not see a significant change in emphasis from extended kinship to bonds in the nuclear family, from loveless marriages to companionate ones, or from brutal parenting to parenting based on concern for a child's welfare. The evidence is abundant that loving marriages, nurturing parents, and the bonds of the nuclear family were as valued and probably as common early in this period as late. And though family life became somewhat more informal by the end of this period, family bonds continued to be among the relationships most valued by virtually everyone. Family continued to be viewed as an essential feature of human life and as an institution contributing vitally to the nation's strength and to people's moral and religious education. During the centuries that followed, Shakespeare's plays would remind people of attitudes they shared with the past as well as of customs and beliefs that had now become unfamiliar. Our understanding and appreciation of Shakespeare's plays are enhanced as we see how they operate in both of these ways, reflecting both familiar and unfamiliar aspects of family life in the past.

REFERENCES

Amussen, Susan. *An Ordered Society: Gender and Class in Early Modern England.* New York: Columbia University Press, 1988.

Arber, Edward, ed. *An English Garner.* Vol. 1. London: Archibald Constable, 1895.

Austin, William. *Haec Homo: Wherein the Excellency of the Creation of Woman, Is Described.* London, 1638.

Bald, R. C. *John Donne: A Life.* Oxford: Oxford University Press, 1970.

Bentley, Thomas, comp. *The Monument of Matrones.* London, 1582.

Bilson, Thomas. *The True Difference Betweene Christian Subjection and Unchristian Rebellion.* Oxford, 1585.

Bradford, John. *The Writings of John Bradford,* M.A. Ed. Aubrey Townsend. 2 vols. Cambridge: Cambridge University Press, 1848–53.

Brathwait, Richard. *The English Gentleman; and the English Gentlewoman.* 3rd ed. London, 1641.

Burton, Robert. *The Anatomy of Melancholy.* Ed. Thomas C. Faulkner, Nicolas K. Kiessling, and Rhonda L. Blair. 3 vols. Oxford: Clarendon Press; New York: Oxford University Press, 1989–94.

C., I. A *Handkercher for Parents Wet Eyes, upon the Death of Children.* London, 1630.

Calendar of State Papers. Venetian. 1621–1623. Vol. 17. Ed. Allen B. Hinds. London: His Majesty's Stationery Office, 1911.
Clerke, William. *The Triall of Bastardie*. London, 1594.
Clinton, Elizabeth, Countess of Lincoln. *The Countesse of Lincolnes Nurserie*. Oxford, 1622.
Cressy, David. *Birth, Marriage, and Death: Ritual, Religion, and the Life-Cycle in Tudor and Stuart England*. Oxford: Oxford University Press, 1997.
Crompton, William. *A Wedding-Ring, Fitted to the Finger*. London, 1632.
Cunningham, Hugh. *Children and Childhood in Western Society since 1500*. London: Longman, 1995.
Dalton, Michael. *The Countrey Justice*. London, 1618.
The Determinations of the Moste Famous and Mooste Excellent Universities of Italy and Fraunce, That It Is So Unlefull for a Man to Marie His Brothers Wyfe, That the Pope Hath No Power to Dispence Therwith. London, 1531.
D'Ewes, Sir Simonds. *The Autobiography and Correspondence of Sir Simonds D'Ewes, Bart., During the Reigns of James I and Charles I*. Ed. James Orchard Halliwell. 2 vols. London: Richard Bentley, 1845.
Dod, John. *A Treatise or Exposition upon the Ten Commandements*. London, 1603.
Earle, John. *Micro-Cosmographie, or, A Peece of the World Discovered in Essayes and Characters*. London, 1628.
"The Form of Solemnization of Matrimony" (from The Book of Common Prayer, 1559). *Religion and Society in Early Modern England: A Sourcebook*. Ed. David Cressy and Lori Anne Ferrell. 2nd ed. New York: Routledge, 2005. 61–64.
Fuller, Thomas. *The Holy State*. Cambridge, 1642.
Γαμηλια [Gamelia]: On the Happy Marriage of the Most Accomplished Paire, H. R. Esq. [Hugh Rogers] and the Vertuous A. B. [Anne Baynton]. Oxford, 1640.
Gataker, Thomas. *A Good Wife Gods Gift*. London, 1623.
———. *Jeroboams Sonnes Decease: A Funerall Sermon*. London, 1627.
———. *Marriage Duties Briefely Couched Togither*. London, 1620.
Gibbon, Charles. *A Work Worth the Reading*. London, 1591.
Gouge, William. *Of Domesticall Duties. Eight Treatises*. 3rd ed. London, 1634.
Griffith, Matthew. *Bethel: or, A Forme for Families*. London, 1633.
Hayward, Sir John. *An Answer to the First Part of a Certaine Conference, Concerning Succession*. London, 1603.
Houlbrooke, Ralph A. *The English Family 1450–1700*. London: Longman, 1984.
———, ed. *English Family Life, 1576–1716: An Anthology from Diaries*. Oxford: Basil Blackwell, 1988.
James I. *Βασιλικον Δωρον [Basilikon Doron]*. London, 1603.
Jocelin, Elizabeth. *A Mothers Legacie, to Her Unborne Childe*. London, 1624.
The Lamentation of a New Married Man. London, [1628–29].
La Primaudaye, Peter de. *The French Academie*. Trans. T. Bowes. London, 1618.
Macfarlane, Alan. "Illegitimacy and Illegitimates in English History." *Bastardy and Its Comparative History*. Ed. Peter Laslett, Karla Oosterveen, and Richard M. Smith. Cambridge, MA: Harvard University Press, 1980. 71–85.
Mack, Maynard. "Rescuing Shakespeare." International Shakespeare Association Occasional Paper No. 1. Oxford: Oxford University Press, 1979.

M[arkham], G[ervase]. *The English Hus-wife*. Second part of *Countrey Contentments, in Two Books*. London, 1615.

Mendelson, Sara, and Patricia Crawford. *Women in Early Modern England, 1550–1720*. Oxford: Clarendon Press, 1998.

Newnham, John. *Newnams Nightcrowe. A Bird that Breedeth Braules in Many Families and Housholdes*. London, 1590.

The Office of Christian Parents: Shewing How Children Are to Be Governed throughout All Ages and Times of Their Life. Cambridge, 1616.

P[arker], M[artin]. *The Wooing Maid*. London, [1635?].

Perkins, William. *Christian Oeconomy*. 1609. *The Works of William Perkins*. Ed. Ian Breward. Appleford, UK: Sutton Courtenay Press, 1970. 411–39.

———. *A Treatise of the Vocations or Callings of Men*. 1603. *The Works of William Perkins*. Ed. Ian Breward. Appleford, UK: Sutton Courtenay Press, 1970. 441–76.

Pickering, Thomas. Epistle Dedicatorie. *Christian Oeconomie*. By William Perkins. London, 1609.

Pollock, Linda. *A Lasting Relationship: Parents and Children over Three Centuries*. London: Fourth Estate, 1987.

Prime, John. *A Fruitefull and Briefe Discourse in Two Bookes: The One of Nature, the Other of Grace*. London, 1583.

Pritchard, Thomas. *The Schoole of Honest and Vertuous Lyfe: Profitable and Necessary for All Estates and Degrees, to Be Trayned In*. London, 1579.

Robartes, Foulke. *The Revenue of the Gospel Is Tythes*. Cambridge, 1613.

Rogers, Daniel. *Matrimoniall Honour*. London, 1642.

Sander, Nicholas. *Rise and Growth of the Anglican Schism*. 1585. Trans. and ed. David Lewis. London: Burns and Oates, 1877.

Sanderson, Robert. *36 Sermons*. 1657. Ed. Izaak Walton. 8th ed. London, 1689.

Sandys, Edwin. *The Sermons of Edwin Sandys, D.D.* Ed. John Ayre. Parker Society 41. Cambridge: Cambridge University Press, 1842.

Secker, William. *A Wedding Ring Fit for the Finger*. London, 1658.

The Second Tome of Homilies. London, 1623.

Shuger, Debora Kuller. *Habits of Thought in the English Renaissance: Religion, Politics, and the Dominant Culture*. Berkeley: University of California Press, 1990.

Smith, Henry. *A Preparative to Mariage*. London, 1591.

Speght, Rachel. From *A Mouzell for Melastomus*. 1617. *The Paradise of Women: Writings by Englishwomen of the Renaissance*. Ed. Betty Travitsky. New York: Columbia University Press, 1989. 104–7.

Spencer, Theodore. *Shakespeare and the Nature of Man*. 2nd ed. New York: Macmillan, 1949.

Spenser, Edmund. *Epithalamion*. *The Yale Edition of the Shorter Poems of Edmund Spenser*. Ed. William A. Oram et al. New Haven, CT: Yale University Press, 1989. 659–79.

Stone, Lawrence. *The Family, Sex and Marriage in England 1500–1800*. New York: Harper & Row, 1977.

Swinburne, Henry. A *Treatise of Spousals, or Matrimonial Contracts*. London, 1686. (Written before 1624.)

Taylor, Jeremy. *The Rule and Exercises of Holy Living*. London, 1650.

Thornton, Alice. *The Autobiography of Mrs. Alice Thornton*. Ed. Charles Jackson. Surtees Society 62. Durham, UK: Andrews and Co., 1875.

Topsell, Edward. *The Reward of Religion. Delivered in Sundrie Lectures upon the Booke of Ruth*. London, 1613.

Whately, William. *A Bride-Bush*. London, 1617.

Wilson, Thomas. *The State of England Anno Dom. 1600*. Ed. F. J. Fisher. Camden Miscellany 16. London: Camden Society, 1936.

Wing, John. *The Crowne Conjugall or, the Spouse Royall*. Middleburgh, 1620.

Wither, George. *Britain's Remembrancer*. London, 1628.

Woolf, Virginia. *A Room of One's Own*. 1929. San Diego: Harcourt Brace Jovanovich, 1981.

Wrightson, Keith. *English Society, 1580–1680*. London: Hutchinson, 1982.

A Yorkshire Tragedy. 1608. *Three Elizabethan Domestic Tragedies*. Ed. Keith Sturgess. Baltimore: Penguin, 1969. 151–82.

3

FAMILY LIFE IN SHAKESPEARE'S WORKS

Family is an important concern in almost all of Shakespeare's plays and is central to many of them. The plays present husbands and wives, parents and children, and siblings and cousins interacting in a variety of ways, and the plots often focus on courtship and familial conflict. The difference between comedy and tragedy is largely a matter of how such plots work out. In the comedies, the courtship leads to marriage, and the conflicts are resolved. In the tragedies, either courtship fails to end in marriage, or the marriages are short-lived. The familial conflicts are not resolved, or if they are, the resolution comes so late that it cannot undo the tragic outcome. Particular plays, as we shall see, present interesting variations on these general patterns.

Besides comedies and tragedies, Shakespeare wrote histories and romances. Though the history plays focus on political events—in particular, events related to the royal families of England—the nature of English political life meant that family and politics were intertwined. The conflicts in the histories are usually between relatives, and the plays often end with events that strengthen or change the family line from which England's rulers come. The plays now referred to as "romances" arguably put more emphasis on family than any other group of Shakespeare's plays. They present families separated or in conflict but end with impressive scenes of restoration and reconciliation.

Whatever the genre, Shakespeare's presentation of family has continuing and widespread appeal. Yet at the same time, the plays depict customs and attitudes modern audiences may find difficult to relate to. The parental blessing ritual, unfamiliar to most now, appears or is mentioned in over half of Shakespeare's plays. Likewise, customs related to courtship, betrothal, and inheritance are often unfamiliar. Such customs sometimes reflect attitudes and beliefs that modern readers and viewers may not share. For instance, the plays present familial bonds not only as natural but as sacred. In contrast to modern ideas concerning personal autonomy, the plays depict characters whose identities are essentially and unavoidably derived from their family relationships. Furthermore, the plays often point to self-sacrifice and humility, rather than self-assertion, as the means for achieving personal fulfillment and happiness within families. Without understanding such customs and attitudes and, along with them, the centrality of family in the Renaissance conception of society and the universe, readers and viewers will miss much of the ethical and philosophical meaning of the plays. The first question we address, then, is how close Shakespeare's presentation of family life comes to the realities of his time.

SHAKESPEARE'S WORKS AND EARLY MODERN FAMILY LIFE

A brief answer to the question would be that Shakespeare's works reflect remarkably well the realities of family life in his time. Of course, he sometimes distorts and often heightens the realities. Yet the particulars of his time, including specific practices and general ideas and attitudes, remain the groundwork for his treatment of family.

Shakespeare often uses the standard Renaissance image of the family being like an organism or body. Lear uses the customary language identifying his daughters as his "flesh" and "blood" but in his anger extends it even further: "Or rather a disease that's in my flesh, / Which I must needs call mine" (*King Lear* 2.4.221–23). The daughters' ingratitude is like violence of one part of the body against another: "Is it not as this mouth should tear this hand / For lifting food to't?" (3.4.15–16). In the same play, Albany compares Lear and his daughter Goneril to parts of a single tree and argues that because she is damaging the very organism of which she is part, her mistreatment of her father will end up destroying her (4.2.31–36).

As such imagery indicates, the plays present familial connections as natural; consequently, violations of love and loyalty within the family are called "unnatural." Speaking to Hamlet, his father's ghost uses the phrase "if thou hast nature in thee," *nature* here meaning "natural affection and loyalty" (*Hamlet* 1.5.81); and because he was killed by his brother, he calls his murder "most foul, strange, and unnatural" (1.5.28). In *King Lear,* Gloucester, not realizing that his son Edmund is about to betray him, calls him his "loyal and natural boy" (2.1.84). In *The Tempest,* after calling Antonio "flesh and blood, / . . . brother mine," Prospero forgives him for his violation of the fraternal bond, "unnatural though thou art" (5.1.74–75, 78–79). The plays use the words *nature*, *natural,* and *unnatural* in connection with various family bonds—between spouses, siblings, and parents and children and even between an uncle and nephew. Coriolanus goes so far as to call "unnatural" his mother's act of kneeling before him (*Coriolanus* 5.3.182–85).

As part of his depiction of the family's place within the natural order, Shakespeare uses the microcosm-macrocosm concept in which smaller entities parallel larger ones. In *King Lear,* for instance, Gloucester views the conflict between parents and children as being related to evil omens in the heavens. The play as a whole emphasizes turmoil at various levels: along with conflict in the family, we see madness at the individual level, chaos in the kingdom, and—in the storm that Lear and others endure—violence in nature as a whole.

In Shakespeare's time, nature—and along with it, family—was viewed as having a hierarchical structure. Shakespeare rarely has characters discuss the hierarchical view of society explicitly, but it is an unspoken aspect of the background of many plays. Occasionally, the standard view is stated directly, and when it is, characters normally accept and value it. For instance, in *The Comedy of Errors*, Luciana tells her sister that "headstrong liberty"—ungoverned autonomy—"is lash'd with woe" and that in the human as in the natural world, females should accept their mates as "their lords" (2.1.15–25).

In certain plays, challenges to the hierarchical view lead to destruction. An example is the disrespect and abuse to which King Lear is subjected by two of his daughters. Yet sometimes the challenges to the standard view prove beneficial. By refusing to yield to her father's wishes, Lear's youngest daughter Cordelia eventually helps him to learn humility and genuine love. In *The Winter's Tale* and other plays, husbands submit to being taught and led by their wives or other women, and parents are nurtured and redeemed by their children. Such a role reversal occurs in *Pericles* when Marina rescues her father from madness and despair. He compares what has happened to a procreative act in which she has given him birth: "Thou . . . beget'st him that did thee beget" (5.1.195).

Like his contemporaries, Shakespeare understood the word *family* to mean both household and lineage. The households Shakespeare portrays have much in common with those in early modern England. Fathers, for instance, are figures of authority, but mothers share in the task of governing the household. In *Romeo and Juliet*, for instance, though Capulet dominates, he and his wife both exercise authority. Capulet, as might be expected, hands over to his wife the task of persuading Juliet to consider marriage. Likewise, much of the direction of the household servants is in Lady Capulet's hands. Lord Capulet himself determines the general plans (for Juliet's wedding, for instance), but both he and his wife give specific commands to the servants to see these plans carried out. There is even an indication that Capulet is out of place in the kitchen, that despite his superior authority, this is his wife's domain (4.4.6–7). Furthermore, when Capulet harshly tries to force a match on his daughter, his wife tells him, "You are too hot," and the Nurse says, "You are to blame" (3.5.175, 169), both indicating that he has exceeded his proper authority.

Shakespeare's plays often focus on royal courts or great households, which would have differed from the norm in size and composition. Yet the households in most of the plays are not much different from those of Shakespeare's time. Though many of those pictured by Shakespeare include servants and sometimes guests, there are remarkably few cases, setting royalty aside, of an unambiguously multigenerational household—one that includes grandparents or even aunts or uncles. Lear is warned not to live with his married daughters, and when he tries, the results are disastrous. The Fool's counsel that he not put himself in his daughters' power echoes contemporary advice to parents that they remain independent as long as possible. Daniel Rogers, for instance, writing in the seventeenth century, advised, "Be wise, you parents, yield not yourselves captives and prisoners to your children; no prison can be more irksome to a parent than a son or daughter's house" (*Matrimoniall Honour* 92, qtd. in Thomas 239).

In *Twelfth Night*, Olivia's household includes an uncle (the often drunken Sir Toby Belch), but his presence is something of an embarrassment, and he leaves by the end of the play. The Capulets and Montagues in *Romeo and Juliet* are something of an anomaly given that each household includes a nephew (Tybalt and Benvolio). Yet as younger relatives, their presence is less intrusive than an older relative's presence might be. Another exception, perhaps, is Leonato's household in *Much Ado about Nothing*, which includes his niece and brother. But because Leonato is the ruler of Messina, this might be considered a quasi-royal household.

As with households in early modern England, most of those portrayed in the plays consist mainly of nuclear families. The size of the households Shakespeare presents is not far from the norm either (the norm being four or five household members including servants). Because the plays often have upper-class settings, many of the households are larger than average. But some are unusually small, consisting of one parent and one child. The households in the comedies consist of an average of about two or three members related by blood or marriage, along with two or more servants. The households in the tragedies are a bit larger, averaging about three or four related members, with the number of servants varying with social class. The Fords and the Pages in *The Merry Wives*—Shakespeare's only sustained picture of contemporary middle-class life—correspond almost exactly to the norm. If each family has two servants (see 3.3.1), the Fords would have a household of four members, the Pages a household of six.

Family in the sense of lineage is an important element in many of Shakespeare's plays. Like Othello, many characters see themselves as deriving "life and being" from their lineage (*Othello* 1.2.21–22). An honorable ancestry, meaning one of high social rank, bestows honor on the descendants. In *All's Well That Ends Well*, for instance, Bertram calls his "honor" something "bequeathed down from many ancestors" (4.2.42–43). Family in the sense of lineage serves as a link to the past and the future. In several plays, a character's final "home" is specified as burial with ancestors. Juliet is placed in the family vault, with her ancestors and other relatives. Titus Andronicus brings his dead sons "unto their latest home, / With burial amongst their ancestors" (*Titus* 1.1.83–84). A very different character, the old Shepherd in *The Winter's Tale*, hopes "to die upon the bed my father died, / To lie close by his honest bones" (4.4.455–56). Lineage is thus essential to many characters' sense of identity. Except in some of the history plays, however, ancestors are usually not identified by name. Whatever the role of these more distant relatives, it is worth noting that the most important family relationships in Shakespeare, as in early modern England, were within the immediate family.

Courtship and Marriage

Shakespeare's plays reflect many specific customs involved in courtship, betrothal, and marriage. Courting couples in Shakespeare's time exchanged gifts and tokens, including rings, ribbons, and gloves, and took part in dancing and feasting. The plays give specific examples of similar details—for instance, the letters and other gifts Hamlet has given Ophelia (which she eventually returns); the ring Bertram gives his wife (thinking he is giving it to another woman) in *All's Well*; the ribbons and gloves mentioned in *The Winter's Tale* (4.4.231–34); and the feasting and other festivities in *The Winter's Tale*, *Much Ado about Nothing*, and other plays.

The qualities the characters look for in a spouse are similar to those Shakespeare's contemporaries valued, though perhaps the plays put more emphasis on physical appearance and less on religious compatibility. In *The Merchant of Venice*, Bassanio lists Portia's qualities in ascending order, indicating that virtue is the most important: she is "a lady richly left [i.e., an heiress], / And she is fair [beautiful] and, fairer than that word, / Of wondrous virtues" (1.1.161–63). In *The Winter's Tale*, Perdita echoes the words of moralists, and perhaps the feelings of many women, when she hopes her lover Florizel does not overvalue her beauty "and only therefore / Desire to breed by me" (4.4.101–3).

As in Shakespeare's time, men in the plays usually take the lead in courtship. Leontes describes having wooed Hermione for "three crabbed months . . . / Ere I could make thee open thy white hand, / And clap thyself my love" (*Winter's Tale* 1.2.102–4). On the other hand, women were not merely passive, either in the plays or in real life. In *Romeo and Juliet*, Juliet has as much to do with the progress of the courtship as Romeo does, if not more. Though Desdemona's father does not approve of her marriage, he will relieve Othello of blame "if she confess that she was half the wooer" (*Othello* 1.3.176). In the same scene, another character indicates that a proper courtship should be mutual. Though the man may take the lead, he should win affection "by request, and such fair question / As soul to soul affordeth" (1.3.113–14). Likewise, Capulet tells Paris that if he wants to marry Juliet, he must "woo her" and "get her heart" (*Romeo and Juliet* 1.2.16).

Sometimes a third party was involved in courtship. *Much Ado about Nothing* illustrates this practice by having Don Pedro woo Hero on Claudio's behalf. At the same time, the play shows the dangers such indirect courtship could run, in this case Claudio's mistaken belief that Don Pedro has won her for himself. In early modern England, some couples hid their courtship from their families; in other cases, the families were involved. Shakespeare presents examples of both kinds. One of Shakespeare's most realistic portraits of courtship is in *The Merry Wives of Windsor*, where each of Anne Page's parents assists a different suitor and where the daughter secretly pursues yet another. Besides portraying disagreement within a family, the play is realistic in picturing the involvement of both the couple and the parents and in emphasizing the standard expectation that a prospective marriage needed both parental consent and the couple's mutual love. As abundant evidence makes clear, Shakespeare's emphasis on love as part of courtship was not merely a literary fantasy but reflected the real experience of his contemporaries.

A successful courtship led, of course, to betrothal. Shakespeare alludes to the usual details of betrothal in *Twelfth Night* 5.1.156–61 (though this passage probably describes a full marriage ceremony) and in *As You Like It* 4.1.125–39, where a mock contract between Rosalind and Orlando includes the standard handclasp and wording ("I take thee . . . for wife" or "for my husband"). The plays frequently refer to the seriousness of the promise to marry. One reason Polixenes, in *The*

Winter's Tale, is eager to stop his son and Perdita before they say the necessary words is that if he does not, he may not be able to prevent their marriage. The seriousness of betrothal also made the status of the couple ambiguous. Though a betrothal could constitute a valid marriage as far as the law was concerned, the betrothed couple were under a "strong moral obligation," according to Davis Harding, "not to consummate their marriage until it had been properly solemnized" (151). Yet some felt that even without a church ceremony, betrothal made them husband and wife and rendered sexual relations permissible.

This ambiguity helps account for the situation at the beginning of *Measure for Measure*, where Claudio is to be executed for fornication with Juliet, who, he claims, "is fast my wife, / Save that we do the denunciation lack / Of outward order." Like many young men of Shakespeare's time, he has "upon a true contract / . . . got possession of [his intended's] bed" (1.2.147–49, 145–46). The reason he gives for not waiting likely resembles that of some of Shakespeare's contemporaries: the public marriage has been delayed "for propagation of a dow'r / Remaining in the coffer of her friends" (150–51)—that is, until Juliet's "friends" (the term often included relatives) could be brought to favor the match and provide a dowry. Though fornication was not a capital offense in Renaissance England as it is in this play, it was against the law and was punished, sometimes severely. Besides punishment, other possible consequences might be the birth of a child out of wedlock (as happens to Claudio and Juliet) or even the abandonment of the woman after intercourse has taken place, a misfortune that Ophelia refers to in one of her mad songs (*Hamlet* 4.5.48–66) and that was much complained of among Shakespeare's contemporaries.

The dangers of the passage from betrothal to marriage help explain why it was felt that parents should be involved. Like many parents in Shakespeare's time, Lord and Lady Capulet are eager to help their daughter find a good match. Even Juliet is concerned that the private contract she and Romeo have entered into may be "too rash, too unadvis'd, too sudden" (*Romeo and Juliet* 2.2.118). "Unadvis'd" here may allude to her failure to consult her parents on the matter. Another reason for the parents' involvement in making a match is their concern with the happiness and honor of the entire family. The importance of lineage and extended family relationships meant that, by entering into marriage, a couple affected many besides themselves. In a discussion with his son Florizel in *The Winter's Tale*, Polixenes (who is in disguise) makes this very point. After asking Florizel why he has not told his father of his plans to marry, Polixenes calls this behavior "unfilial" and says, "Reason my son / Should choose himself a wife, but as good reason / The father (all whose joy is nothing else / But fair posterity) should hold some counsel / In such a business" (4.4.406–10).

Before a marriage could take place, such matters as the dowry and jointure had to be arranged. Among the many references to dowries and jointures in Shakespeare, the most memorable include Mariana's lost dowry in *Measure for Measure*, Lear's withdrawal of Cordelia's dowry, and the handshake and golden statue provided posthumously as a jointure for Romeo and Juliet (*Romeo and Juliet* 5.3.296–99). Another is Petruchio's successful quest for a stunningly large dowry in *The*

Taming of the Shrew. As Maynard Mack points out, the dowry Baptista provides Petruchio—"the one half of [Baptista's] lands, / And in possession twenty thousand crowns," with another twenty thousand added later (*Taming of the Shrew* 2.1.121–22, 5.2.113)—would have been "an extraordinary figure in the 1590s," the twenty thousand crowns alone being "about two and half times the going portion even among the highest peerage" (19, citing Stone, *Crisis of the Aristocracy* 638). In return Petruchio promises, "I'll assure her of / Her widowhood, be it that she survive me, / In all my lands and leases whatsoever" (2.1.123–25).

Usually an interval of at least a few weeks took place between betrothal and marriage. The eagerness of several Shakespearean characters to marry suggests that even this short a time seemed long to some. Rosalind, for instance, describes the eagerness of "a young maid between the contract of her marriage and the day it is solemniz'd" (*As You Like It* 3.2.313–15). The plays do not mention the asking of the banns that was to take place during the interval, a practice intended to identify impediments that would render a marriage invalid. But the impediments themselves—including a previous contract and too close a kinship between the couple—are mentioned. The first of these impediments is referred to in *Richard III*, where Buckingham maintains that King Edward's supposed contract with Lady Lucy prior to his marriage with the queen makes the princes illegitimate (3.7.5–6, 178–79). The second impediment is at the heart of *Hamlet:* Gertrude's marriage with Claudius is incestuous because Claudius is her brother-in-law—and virtually her brother, given that "man and wife is one flesh" (4.3.52). Though the powerful (Henry VIII, for instance) sometimes obtained permission for such marriages, the relationship between Claudius and Gertrude is in fact within the "forbidden degrees" that normally prevented a marriage.

Several of Shakespeare's plays allude to the formula provided in the Book of Common Prayer for the solemnizing of marriage (see Primary Document 5). For instance, Rosalind's words to her father and to Orlando—"To you I give myself, for I am yours" (*As You Like It* 5.4.116–17)—echo "Who giveth this woman to be married unto this man?" ("The Form of Solemnization of Matrimony" 63). Interestingly, though, it is Rosalind who gives herself rather than being given to the groom by her father. Earlier in the play, while "pretending" to be herself, Rosalind noted the absence of a priest or of anyone to give away the bride as a basis for questioning Orlando's "commission" to take her as wife. The same flaw prevents Touchstone's first attempt at marrying Audrey, for though Jaques at first agrees to "give" the bride, he ends by advising a more regular ceremony, in a church where "a good priest . . . can tell you what marriage is" (4.1.138–41; 3.3.67–94). Touchstone indicates that an irregular ceremony was exactly what he wanted: the minister, named Sir Oliver Martext, "is not like to marry me well; and not being well married, it will be a good excuse for me hereafter to leave my wife" (3.3.90–94).

Once a marriage was solemnized, a wedding feast often took place. Several of Shakespeare's plays allude to or even present a wedding feast, with references to guests, food, and varying degrees of festivity. Hamlet comments bitterly that "the funeral bak'd meats" prepared for his father's funeral "did coldly furnish forth the marriage tables" when his mother remarried (*Hamlet* 1.2.180–81). *Romeo and Juliet* includes a good deal of preparation for a wedding feast that never happens. Kate and Petruchio's marriage in *The Taming of the Shrew* is followed by a feast. A *Midsummer Night's Dream* ends with wedding festivities; in fact, one of the play's early performances may have been at a wedding.

Not every marriage was an occasion for communal and familial celebration. Such celebration would not, of course, have accompanied the clandestine or secret marriages that sometimes took place in real life and that Shakespeare portrays in *Romeo and Juliet* and several of his comedies. Secret marriages were relatively rare, yet they were a cause for concern because, though valid even without a public ceremony or the involvement of a priest, they threatened to disrupt the social fabric. Yet there was also strong sentiment against forced marriages, leading to some sympathy for young people for whom a secret marriage was their only alternative. Shakespeare has Fenton, a young man in *The Merry Wives of Windsor* who has secretly married Anne Page, defend their act on the grounds that a loveless marriage will bring only misery:

> You would have married her most shamefully,
> Where there was no proportion held in love.
> The truth is, she and I (long since contracted)
> Are now so sure that nothing can dissolve us.
> Th' offense is holy that she hath committed,
> And this deceit loses the name of craft,
> Of disobedience, or unduteous title,
> Since therein she doth evitate [avoid] and shun
> A thousand irreligious cursed hours
> Which forced marriage would have brought upon her. (5.5.221–30)

As Fenton notes, even a private contract, especially if followed by a ceremony, resulted in a valid marriage. With his reference to "disobedience," Fenton acknowledges the ideal of parental involvement and consent. But he argues that a forced marriage, besides being unhappy, would not produce the union of hearts that Shakespeare and his contemporaries associated with the marriage bond.

In this play, the parents accept Fenton's argument, and harmony prevails. Such a happy result would probably not have followed a clandestine marriage so easily in real life. Shakespeare portrays and even exaggerates the negative consequences of a secret marriage in *Romeo and Juliet*, where the pressures to accept an unwanted marriage are intense—Capulet angrily threatens to disown his daughter and cast her out—and where the secret marriage leads to confusion and suicide. Another marriage without parental permission takes place in *Othello*. In this play, though the marriage wins the approval of the Duke and eventually the grudging acceptance of Desdemona's father, it produces a rift between father and daughter and is later used by Iago to provoke Othello's jealousy. With Iago's help, Othello ends up tormented by the suspicion raised early in the play by Desdemona's father: "She has deceiv'd her father, and may thee" (1.3.293).

Though many plays (especially the comedies) emphasize courtship and end before the couples are wed, Shakespeare provides some memorable pictures of married life and, even in the plays that end prior to a wedding, often refers to contemporary ideas about marriage. Shakespeare alludes, for instance, to the standard view that the husband is "head" of the wife and that the wife should submit to his authority, but he also incorporates the standard qualifications his contemporaries would have given to this view. The famous passage in *The Taming of the Shrew* in which Kate outlines the roles of husband and wife—one of the few times Shakespeare has a character state the hierarchical view in detail—asserts that the husband is "thy lord, thy life, thy keeper, / Thy head, thy sovereign" and exhorts women to "serve, love, and obey" (5.2.146–47, 164). But she also stresses the husband's obligation to serve and sacrifice: a husband is "one that cares for thee" and, for the good of his wife, "commits his body / To painful labor" (147–49). Kate also hints at the limits of husbandly authority: a wife is required to obey only a husband's "honest will" (5.2.158). Modern readers have often found Kate's speech hard to stomach, and indeed, it is possible to read the passage with at least a hint of irony. But Shakespeare's original audiences probably found Kate's advice not only acceptable but even admirable in the way she clearly details the duties of marriage and balances the husband's and wife's roles.

A more extreme view is also present in the play. Echoing those who pushed a husband's authority to the point of ownership, Shakespeare has Petruchio refer to Kate as his property—his "goods" and "chattels" (*Taming of the Shrew* 3.2.230.) Even within the play this is an extreme statement, intended as a piece of comic exaggeration. Yet legal discourse sometimes used similar language, speaking of women in terms of "property and possessions" (Mendelson and Crawford 48). Women's problematic legal situation, however, did not necessarily determine the quality of their marriages. In fact, outside of legal discourse, most who wrote about marriage described it as a relationship of mutual love and cooperation rather than of domination or ownership.

Shakespeare frequently echoes this emphasis on mutual love. Though there are some bad or problematic marriages, especially in the tragedies—in *Othello* and *Hamlet*, for instance—Shakespeare also presents many happy ones. The long-separated spouses in *The Comedy of Errors* and *Pericles* are examples. Ford has a bout of jealousy in *The Merry Wives of Windsor,* but both the Fords and the Pages have reasonably good marriages. Though we never see Shylock's deceased wife, he refers to her fondly (*Merchant of Venice* 3.1.121–23). As we shall see, Portia and Brutus (in *Julius Caesar*) apparently have an ideal marriage. And Coriolanus, though not easy to get along with in general, has a tender relationship with his wife. Shakespeare's young lovers, of course, anticipate a happy marriage and often start off with fervent expressions of mutual desire to serve and give. In *The Tempest*, for instance, Ferdinand and Miranda both offer to be each other's servants.

Some historians have suggested that Shakespeare, as the great English poet and playwright of love and marriage, presents a romanticized view of married love. Yet there is much evidence that love was an essential element of real-life marriages. Part of what makes Shakespeare's depiction of marriage effective, in fact, is that he alludes to both the ideals and the realities that characterized marriage in his time. At the end of *Henry V*, the Queen of France expresses the hope that, now that her daughter has married King Henry, France and England will be as lovingly united as a husband and wife. Yet she also acknowledges the contention to which marriages were subject:

> God, the best maker of all marriages,
> Combine your hearts in one, your realms in one!
> As man and wife, being two, are one in love,
> So be there 'twixt your kingdoms such a spousal,
> That never may ill office, or fell jealousy,
> Which troubles oft the bed of blessed marriage,
> Thrust in between the paction of these kingdoms,
> To make divorce of their incorporate league. (5.5.359–66)

Her use of religious language draws on the idea that marriage is holy and that it is God who effectively enables husband and wife to become one.

Many plays echo the prevailing notion, expressed in scripture and in many sermons and treatises of the period, that husband and wife become "one flesh." In *Romeo and Juliet*, Friar Lawrence refers to the marriage ceremony in which "Holy Church [will] incorporate two in one" (2.6.37). Hamlet repeats the standard phrase: "man and wife is one flesh" (4.3.52). And in *The Comedy of Errors*, Adriana tells her presumed husband that because they are "undividable incorporate," she is "better than [his] dear self's better part" (2.2.122–23).

In *Julius Caesar*, Brutus's wife Portia offers an especially memorable expression of the idea. She describes marriage as an intimate union, brought about by "vows of love" that "incorporate" a man and woman, making them one and requiring a full emotional, intellectual, and practical, as well as physical, partnership (2.1.272–73). Aware that Brutus is troubled, she argues that they form, as it were, a single being (she calls herself, "yourself, your half") and that they should know each other's secrets. A true wife, she suggests, is more than a practical or even sexual companion:

> Am I yourself
> But, as it were, in sort or limitation.
> To keep with you at meals, comfort your bed,
> And talk to you sometimes? Dwell I but in the suburbs
> Of your good pleasure? If it be no more,
> Portia is Brutus' harlot, not his wife.

Brutus cannot share his secret in this case, yet his response—"You are my true and honorable wife"—indicates that, in general, he accepts her argument (2.1.274, 282–88).

Though, as Portia notes, marriage involves more than sexual companionship, the plays allude to this dimension of marriage as well. In *The Tempest*, Prospero warns Ferdinand and Miranda against excessive intimacy before marriage but with no indication that sexual relations within marriage are suspect. In fact, as part of the masque that Prospero has spirits perform to celebrate the betrothal, the spirits bless the couple with "increasing," probably meaning offspring (4.1.107).

Characters in some other plays take a more indulgent view of premarital sex: Pompey, a bawd in *Measure for Measure*, worries that the strict laws of Vienna will require the authorities to "geld and splay all the youth of the city" (2.1.230–31). By the end of that play, the Duke takes a moderate stance, sparing the lives of offenders but enforcing sexual responsibility by requiring several men who have had illicit sexual relations to marry the women involved.

Shakespeare's treatment of sexual relations within marriage is generally quite positive. In *Cymbeline*, Posthumus refers to the "lawful pleasure" of the marriage bed (2.5.9). A phrase in *Coriolanus*—"the embracements of his bed where [a husband] would show most love" (1.3.4–5)—also makes clear the association of marital love and sexual relations. Similarly, Egeon, a husband in *The Comedy of Errors* who has been separated from his wife for years, recalls her "kind embracements" and makes the sexual reference explicit by describing the pregnancy that followed (1.1.43). One of the most memorable references to the "amorous rites" of marriage (as she calls them) is the speech in which Juliet eagerly anticipates her wedding night, when she and her husband will "lose a winning match, / Play'd for a pair of stainless maidenhoods" (*Romeo and Juliet* 3.2.8, 12–13).

Parents, Children, and Responses to Death

Shakespeare's plays also reflect contemporary experience and attitudes connected with childbirth and the relations of parents and children. The plays include both literal and figurative references to pregnancy, sometimes in connection with the danger of death in childbirth. The mother of Posthumus, who appears briefly to him in vision near the end of *Cymbeline*, died while giving him birth. In *Pericles*, Thaisa apparently dies while giving birth to Marina. Though she is in fact alive (and will eventually be reunited with husband and daughter), it is hard to forget the image of childbirth and its "pangs" taking place during a storm at sea. Speaking to what he thinks is the dead body of his wife, Pericles says, "A terrible child-bed hast thou had, my dear" (3.1.13–14, 56). *The Comedy of Errors* ends with symbolic childbirth. Aemilia feels she has been "in travail"—going through labor—for the 33 years of separation from her sons. Reunited with them, she feels like a woman now delivered of her "heavy burthen" (5.1.401–3). Yet despite the pains and perils of giving birth, Aemilia also describes the experience as joyful: "After so long grief, such nativity!" (407).

Childbirth left a woman in need of recovery. Hermione is pregnant through the first act and a half of *The Winter's Tale* and gives birth in prison. At her trial, she notes that the difficulties of giving birth do not end when the child is born. She has "with immodest hatred" been denied "the child-bed privilege . . . , which 'longs / To women of all fashion"—the privilege, that is, of being allowed to recover from the rigors of giving birth. Instead she has been "hurried / Here to this place, i' th' open air, before" she has "got strength of limit" (3.2.102–6). As David Cressy has shown, the phrase "child-bed privilege" refers to the customary period of about a month allowed in Shakespeare's time to women who had given birth before they were expected to resume their usual responsibilities (133).

Shakespeare refers at least once to swaddling, the ancient custom (still practiced in early modern England) of wrapping a newborn child in bands of cloth. Hamlet describes Polonius as a "great baby" who "is not yet out of his swaddling-clouts" (*Hamlet* 2.2.382–83). The phrase "a babe of clouts" in *King John* 3.4.58 probably means the same thing.

In their references to nursing, Shakespeare's plays reflect the mixed practice of the time. Lady Macbeth and Volumnia speak of nursing their children (*Macbeth* 1.7.54–55; *Coriolanus* 3.2.129), but Juliet was breast-fed by her nurse rather than her mother. Hermione did not nurse Mamillius but out of necessity does nurse Perdita (*Winter's Tale* 2.1.56, 3.2.99–100). Maynard Mack cites other examples of children not nursed by their mothers, some apparently by choice (*Richard III* 2.2.30; *2 Henry VI* 4.2.136–46), others because the mother was not available (*Pericles* 3.3.39–40; *Cymbeline* 3.3.103–4) (see Mack 9). The idea that children acquire a nurse's or mother's disposition through the milk she provides is mentioned several times (e.g., *Romeo and Juliet* 1.3.67–68; *As You Like It* 4.1.175–76; *Coriolanus* 3.2.129; *Winter's Tale* 2.1.56–58). *Romeo and Juliet* gives a clue as to how long a child was nursed and how the child would have been weaned: the Nurse remembers Juliet having been weaned at about age three, growing "teachy and fall[ing] out wi' th' dug" when she tasted the bitter wormwood that had been rubbed on her nurse's nipple (1.3.24–32). Juliet's age at weaning would not have been unusual in Shakespeare's time, but she was older than the "18 to 24 months" that some authorities recommended (Mack 10).

Shakespeare alludes to the coats worn in early childhood and to the breeching of boys at about age six or seven. In *The Winter's Tale*, Mamillius—who is probably five years old—is still "unbreech'd" (that is, he does not yet wear pants or breeches) and is still in the care of women (1.2.155–56). Perhaps he wears something like the "green velvet coat" his father remembers wearing at his age. Besides reflecting contemporary customs, this detail, with its reference to gender identity and to Mamillius's tender age, contributes to the play's complex depiction of family dynamics. For one thing, it heightens the poignancy of Mamillius's predicament as a child torn between his father and mother.

The plays reflect the mixed attitudes of Shakespeare's time about disciplining children. Shakespeare refers to whipping, though almost never in connection with parents whipping their children, and to the rod, wielded by a parent, a nurse, or a schoolmaster. Yet the interaction between parents and small children on stage is usually benign. Conflict, when it happens, is usually between parents and older children, but even here persuasion is the standard mode of discipline. Of course there are exceptions, such as *Romeo and Juliet*, where Capulet threatens violence; *Lear*, with its parental cursing and commands; and *The Taming of the Shrew*, where Kate, who virtually has the run of the household, is the violent one.

One remarkable way Shakespeare reflects family life of his time is in his use of the blessing ritual, a custom practiced daily in early modern England. At least 18 of Shakespeare's plays present or refer to parents formally blessing their children. In many cases, the customary gestures are mentioned or clearly intended. Cordelia kneels to ask for Lear's blessing. In *The Winter's Tale*, Perdita kneels first to ask a blessing from what she thinks is a statue of her mother. Later, when it is clear her mother is alive, Perdita is told, "Fair madam, kneel, / And pray your mother's blessing" (5.3.119–20). Marina kneels before Pericles, who says, "Now blessing on thee! rise, th' art my child," and before her mother, who says, "Blest, and mine own!" (*Pericles* 5.1.213; 5.3.48). Imogen kneels before her father Cymbeline and says, "Your blessing, sir" (*Cymbeline* 5.5.266). In *All's Well That Ends Well*, Bertram kneels to ask his mother's blessing before leaving home (1.1.59–75).

The plays also refer to the parents' placing their hands on the child's head. In *Titus Andronicus*, Lavinia asks to be blessed by her father's "victorious hand" (1.1.163). Cordelia asks her father to hold his "hand[s] in benediction o'er her" (*Lear* 4.7.57). (The word reads "hand" or "hands" depending on the version, but there is good evidence Shakespeare wrote "hands.") The gesture is also implied in many references to blessings falling on a child's head.

The plays use the blessing ritual in various ways, sometimes for comic effect (as in Launcelot Gobbo's request for a blessing from his "sand-blind" father [*Merchant of Venice* 2.2.36, 74]) and sometimes to underscore a character's villainy (as when Richard III receives a blessing but then mocks it by saying, "—and make me die a good old man! / That is the butt-end of a mother's blessing" [*Richard III* 2.2.109–10]). Besides being funny, Launcelot Gobbo's request for a blessing takes part in a pattern of biblical allusions in the play. Shakespeare invites us to think of Jacob, who impersonated his brother in order to obtain a blessing from his blind father Isaac (Genesis 27). In *Richard III*, Richard's mockery of his mother's blessing comes back to haunt him. His mother later curses him, whereas Richmond, the man who eventually defeats him, receives his own mother's blessing "by attorney" from his stepfather (5.3.83). This play's outcome underlines the fact that many in Shakespeare's time believed a parent's blessing and curse were both potent, even prophetic.

Shakespeare sometimes uses parental blessings to underscore a parent's role as an authority figure. This is especially true of those blessings joined with advice and coinciding with a child's "taking leave" of a parent. In *Hamlet* (1.3), for instance, Laertes receives a blessing and advice from Polonius before leaving for France, and in *All's Well That Ends Well* (1.1), Bertram receives similar blessing and advice from his mother. Sometimes a parent in Shakespeare's work uses a blessing to influence a child's behavior. For instance, in *As You Like It*, Orlando reports that his father charged his brother "on his blessing" to treat Orlando well (1.1.3–4). Yet even in these cases when a parent's authority is emphasized, the blessing ritual functions primarily as an expression of love and a way of bestowing beneficial influence on the child.

In a few instances, Shakespeare parodies the ritual to suggest familial and even cosmic disorder. For instance, when Coriolanus's mother kneels to him after he has knelt for her blessing, her reversal of their proper roles leads him to imagine universal chaos. Apart from a few unusual cases of this kind, Shakespeare's treatment of the blessing ritual is almost always positive. Cordelia's request of a blessing is an important moment in her reconciliation with Lear. In Shakespeare's late romances, all of which include one or more blessings, the ritual marks a joyful reunion, sometimes of a child and parent who have been separated for years. The parents' words of blessing express joy along with a fervent desire for the child's welfare. In *The Tempest*, for instance, on being reunited with a son he thought was dead, Alonso cries, "Now all the blessings / Of a glad father compass thee about!" (5.1.179–80). *The Winter's Tale* emphasizes the divine power that Shakespeare's contemporaries associated with the ritual. With her hands on Perdita's head, Hermione acts as an intermediary between heaven and earth, blessing Perdita with the words, "You gods, look down / And from your sacred vials pour your graces / Upon my daughter's head!" (5.3.119–23).

Another indication of the strength of familial bonds is Shakespeare's depiction (often highly dramatic) of characters' grief at the death of family members. Lear's grief as he brings his dead daughter on stage is the tragic climax of the play. In *Romeo and Juliet*, Juliet's apparent death is greeted with emotionally charged exclamations, and when she has actually died, the family's grief is deep though less dramatic. In *The Winter's Tale*, the death of Leontes's son and the apparent death of his wife break his heart and prompt him to repent. The one point at which Macduff shows uncontrolled anguish is when he learns that Macbeth has had his family killed. When told he should "dispute it like a man," he defends his emotions by saying, "I must also feel it as a man" (*Macbeth* 4.3.220–21).

Though we may suspect some dramatic exaggeration in these scenes, the records left by Shakespeare's contemporaries indicate they were often equally grief-stricken by the death of family members. Yet many also gave advice intended to alleviate such grief. (For example, see Primary Document 29.) Writers reminded their readers of the universality of death, the miseries of life, the need to submit to God's will, and the benefits of controlling emotions and preserving a contented mind. Several of Shakespeare's characters give similar advice, most memorably Claudius in his counsel to Hamlet. Claudius argues that excessive grief is "unmanly" and "shows a will most incorrect to heaven"; besides opposing God, such grief opposes both nature and reason, "whose common theme / Is death of fathers" (*Hamlet* 1.2.94–95, 103–4). The same issues sometimes arise in the comedies. In *Twelfth Night*, Feste mocks Olivia's vow to mourn seven years for the loss of her brother, telling her she is a fool to mourn for him if he is enjoying the bliss of heaven. Yet at the same time, the play invites us to sympathize with Viola and Sebastian, twins who have lost their father and each of whom thinks the other has died in the shipwreck that separated them.

Several plays present children grieving at a parent's death: the Princess of France in *Love's Labor's Lost*, Olivia (along with Viola and Sebastian) in *Twelfth Night*, Helen in *All's Well*, several characters in the history plays, and of course Hamlet and Ophelia. Though such grief is usually less intense than that of parents who have lost children, these examples indicate that many children felt strongly attached to their parents. In *Hamlet*, the loss of parents is central to the play. Hamlet's grief at his father's death motivates much of the play's action. Ophelia is so affected by her father's death that she loses her reason and eventually her life.

While representing the strength of the parent–child bond, the plays also allude to the ambivalence many of Shakespeare's contemporaries felt. For many, the parent–child relationship grew particularly complicated as parents aged.

Edmund's complaints in *King Lear* about "aged tyranny" (1.2.50) probably reflect attitudes some felt about their parents' authority and about having to wait for an inheritance. In the same play, Goneril and Regan strip their father of his independence and dignity while reminding him that he is old and foolish. On the other hand, other characters view Lear's and Gloucester's age as a reason to show reverence and compassion. Edgar and Cordelia come to the aid of their fathers and, in doing so, act in harmony with the counsel of many preachers and moralists of Shakespeare's time. Such figures reminded children that they should relieve their parents' needs not only out of compassion and respect for their authority but also in return for the benefits parents had given them, including life itself. (An example of such advice is found in Primary Document 26.) Many lines in *King Lear* echo such concepts: for instance, Lear says, "I gave you all" (2.4.250); Cordelia acknowledges, "You have begot me, bred me, lov'd me," and says, "I / Return those duties back as are right fit, / Obey you, love you, and most honor you" (1.1.96–98). Though the play later offers something higher than this almost mechanical vision of reciprocity, much of *King Lear*'s action and meaning is grounded in standard concepts about the duties of parents and children.

Siblings, Cousins, and Inheritance

Another set of conflicts in *King Lear,* involving Gloucester and his sons Edgar and Edmund, springs from issues related to bastardy and inheritance. The result of his father's adultery, Edmund resents his marginal status and may also take offense at the casual disrespect shown by his father's use of the word "whoreson" to describe him (*King Lear* 1.1.24). Discontented with being an "unpossessing bastard" (2.1.67), Edmund rejects the conventions that deprive him of inheritance and social status. Another play presents a bastard son with similar resentments: Don John in *Much Ado.* A more sympathetic version of this character type appears in *King John* in the form of Philip the Bastard.

Edmund's complaints derive not only from his illegitimacy but also from his status as a younger son. The widespread practice of primogeniture apparently produced a good deal of anxiety and resentment among younger sons in England during this period because oldest sons received the bulk of the inheritance. Besides *King Lear,* another play using the status of younger sons as a source of conflict is *As You Like It.* In this play, Duke Frederick has overthrown his brother Duke Senior, whose name means "older," and Oliver abuses his authority as the eldest son to oppress his younger brother Orlando. In presenting such conflicts, this and other plays echo the contemporary idea that fraternal conflict is unnatural. The servant Adam is so appalled by the conflict between Oliver and Orlando that he can hardly acknowledge them to be sons of the same father. Fraternal conflict is also at the core of *The Tempest,* in which Antonio has usurped his brother's dukedom, and *Hamlet,* in which Claudius has killed his brother and taken his kingdom and queen. Claudius recognizes the monstrous nature of his deed and compares it to the first murder, Cain's killing of Abel: "It hath the primal eldest curse upon't, / A brother's murder" (3.3.37–38).

The plays also portray loving bonds between siblings: among others, between the brothers in *As You Like It* after they are reconciled, between Laertes and Ophelia in *Hamlet*, between Isabella and Claudio in *Measure for Measure* (though they experience a serious falling-out along the way), between the siblings in *Cymbeline*, between Viola and Sebastian in *Twelfth Night*, and between the two sets of twins in *The Comedy of Errors*. This last plays ends with an expression of fraternal harmony: "We came into the world like brother and brother; / And now let's go hand in hand, not one before another" (5.1.425–26). Though this last example (with its emphasis on brothers) is an exception, many of the positive sibling bonds are between brother and sister, perhaps because they were spared the conflicts that questions of inheritance could bring. At least one play also shows sisters in conflict: Bianca and Katherina in *The Taming of the Shrew*. In this case, one source of conflict is rivalry over having suitors.

The plays also depict extended family relationships, again with a wide variety of positive and negative examples that reflect the varied experiences and expectations of Shakespeare's contemporaries. The history plays are filled with uncles, aunts, cousins, and other relatives, sometimes vying for political favor or the right to the throne. Hamlet's relationship with his uncle, affected by this same issue of political power, is further complicated by Claudius's marriage to Hamlet's mother and, of course, the murder of Hamlet's father. The help a relative could and sometimes did provide in early modern England is suggested by Lysander's description of his aunt in *A Midsummer Night's Dream*: "I have a widow aunt, a dowager, / Of great revenue, and she hath no child." Because "she respects [him] as her only son," Lysander believes she will help facilitate his marriage to Hermia (1.1.157–60).

Cousins, especially female cousins, are sometimes represented as being even closer than siblings. Rosalind and Celia, the daughters of the two enemy dukes in *As You Like It*, are said to share a love "dearer than the natural bond of sisters" (1.2.276). Beatrice and Hero, cousins in *Much Ado*, are devoted friends and even bedfellows—except for the fatal night when Hero is suspected of misconduct. These characters and several in other plays are cousins in the modern sense. It is worth remembering, however, that the term *cousin* was used in early modern England to refer to a broad range of kin. Shakespeare regularly has characters use *cousin* or *coz* in this broad sense, referring to a nephew, niece, uncle, or more distant kin, as well as to a cousin in the modern sense.

THEMATIC AND DRAMATIC FUNCTIONS

Though the plays reveal much about family life in early modern England, they are of course literary rather than historical works and use family for a variety of thematic and dramatic purposes. Because family relationships serve such purposes, they sometimes function more as symbols than as depictions of ordinary life. Even when the plays come close to representing life, they may simplify or exaggerate certain details related to family either to heighten the dramatic conflict or to give greater weight to particular themes. Many plays depict families in earlier periods or in locations other than England, and in these cases, the settings may influence Shakespeare's distortions of the customs or attitudes of his time. In short, despite their frequent tendency to realism, the plays sometimes give a misleading picture of certain features of family life in early modern England.

One example is the age at which some Shakespearean characters—especially the women—marry. Miranda in *The Tempest* is about 15; Perdita in *The Winter's Tale* is 16. The most famous example of an early marriage is in *Romeo and Juliet*, which places Juliet's age at 13, though she would have turned 14 if she had lived two weeks longer. This play has misled many readers and even some reputable scholars into thinking that women commonly married in their teens in Shakespeare's England. Alfred Harbage, for instance, claims that Juliet, though a bit young for marriage at just shy of 14, is not remarkably young: this was "an era," he mistakenly claims, "when seventeen or eighteen was a quite ripe marital age" (144). A careful reading of *Romeo and Juliet* reveals that in fact the play emphasizes Juliet's youth and lack of readiness for marriage. Paris's claim that there have been "happy mothers" even younger than Juliet reflects his eagerness to marry but runs contrary to cautions pronounced in the play itself—for instance, Capulet's caution, "And too soon marr'd are those so early made" (*Romeo and Juliet* 1.2.12–13). Paris's claim also contradicts the facts of life in Shakespeare's time.

Of course, the play is set in Italy, and early audiences may have imagined different expectations there than they were familiar with. But it is clear that Shakespeare deliberately lowered Juliet's age and did so to heighten the drama and emphasize the themes of haste and "rude will" (2.3.28; see Young). In earlier versions of the story, Juliet is older—16, for instance, in Arthur Brooke's poem *The Tragical History of Romeus and Juliet* and 18 in William Painter's prose version. Shakespeare certainly used Brooke's poem as a source, and even there, with the lovers older than in Shakespeare's version, they are still, Brooke reminds us, "of tender age," with Juliet "too yong to be a bryde" (lines 188, 1860). By lowering her age to 13, Shakespeare emphasizes her vulnerability even more. She is vulnerable not only to the physical and emotional dangers of early marriage and childbearing but also to the threats her father makes when she resists his attempt to arrange a marriage.

Early in the play, Capulet himself gives advice most early audiences would have found sensible: Paris cannot marry Juliet unless he wins her heart, for Capulet's "will to her consent is but a part" (1.2.17); and she is too young for marriage—"yet a stranger in the world"—and should wait at least two years before taking the step. Even that age—15 or 16—would have been much younger than the average age at first marriage in Shakespeare's time, which was 25 or 26 for women and 27 or 28 for men.

Read carefully, *Romeo and Juliet* accords well with attitudes in early modern England, where marriage in the early teenage years was rare and where young marriage was viewed as unwise and even dangerous. Yet ironically, as Peter Laslett has pointed out, Shakespeare's play is itself apparently responsible for "the widespread conviction that most girls in England married in their teens in earlier times" (3).

This and other plays have also misled subsequent generations into thinking that parents were more tyrannical than they probably were during the period, certainly more than they were supposed to be. Many authorities writing in Shakespeare's time insisted that, although parents should be consulted, they should never force a child into an unwanted marriage. Besides *Romeo and Juliet*, another play that has led some to think that fathers in particular were all powerful is *A Midsummer Night's Dream*, in which Egeus demands that his daughter Hermia marry Demetrius instead of Lysander. In the play, Duke Theseus tells Hermia she must yield to her father or else suffer one of two consequences: death or perpetual virginity. He counsels her to view her father "as a god; / One that compos'd your beauties; yea, and one / To whom you are but as a form in wax, / By him imprinted, and within his power, / To leave the figure, or disfigure it" (1.1.47–51). In fact, though Shakespeare's audiences would have agreed that a father's authority in some ways resembles God's, they would not have viewed it as absolute, especially on the matter of marriage. This episode in *A Midsummer Night's Dream* is in part a dramatic exaggeration and is also based on the ancient dramatic convention of conflict between young love and parental authority. It is worth noting that the young people end up marrying according to their wishes and that Theseus overrules Hermia's father.

Shakespeare's plays also exaggerate the degree and intensity of conflict among family members. Or perhaps more accurately, the plays present in condensed and heightened form the sort of conflicts with which his audience might have been familiar. Clandestine marriages, sibling rivalry, and marital conflict certainly took place in Shakespeare's England, but events as gripping and troubling as those found in many of his plays would have been unusual. Some of the plots would have had virtually no parallel in his audience's experience. For instance, interracial and intercultural marriages of the sort that take place in *The Merchant of Venice* and *Othello* would have been virtually unheard of in early modern England. But milder versions of the phenomenon may have been familiar—for instance, marriage between partners of different social rank, greatly different ages, or different religious persuasions.

One reason that Shakespeare chose to portray unusual events is that they lend themselves to theatrical presentation by making certain situations (and the ideas and feelings that accompany them) more vivid and memorable. Another reason his depiction of family life sometimes departs from the details of real life is that he has shaped the events to fit a play's genre. As a result, the role family plays in Shakespeare depends a great deal on whether we are looking at a comedy, tragedy, history, or romance.

The Comedies

In comedy, the typical pattern is the progress of two or more young couples toward matrimony. Along the way, they must overcome various obstacles, sometimes (for instance, in *A Midsummer Night's Dream* and *The Merry Wives of Windsor*) including parental resistance. *The Merchant of Venice* presents an interesting case: Shylock of course opposes Jessica's marriage to a Christian, but Portia also faces an obstacle created by her father—the requirement that suitors choose the right one among three caskets. That obstacle, however, is apparently inspired: it allows Portia to marry the suitor she loves and tests his ability to see beyond appearances and recognize the need to "give and hazard all" in marriage (2.7.9). Young lovers face other obstacles as well: confusion about identity in *The Comedy of Errors* and *Twelfth Night*, the unusual forest situation in *As You Like It* (and for one of the secondary characters, Phebe, gender confusion as well), and rivalry and betrayal in *The Two Gentlemen of Verona*.

In this last play and others, the greatest obstacles may be the lovers themselves. In *A Midsummer Night's Dream*, once the young lovers are in the woods, they must work through a series of changing love triangles, brought about by Puck and Oberon but perhaps representing the typical confusion and changeability of young love. In *Much Ado about Nothing*, the lovers obviously bring their own obstacles, including Beatrice and Benedick's resistance to marriage and Claudio's quick loss of faith. The course of love runs relatively smoothly for the two main couples in *As You Like It*. In a sense, they are simply waiting until they can return to civilization. But in the meantime, they learn important lessons, especially the ones Rosalind in disguise teaches Orlando about how marriage in real life will differ from his fantasy version.

Much Ado about Nothing can be read as an examination of the pros and cons of marriage. Benedick claims to want nothing less than a perfect woman and is wary of marital conflict and possible betrayal. Marriage also means a loss of independence: to be married is to "thrust [one's] neck into a yoke" and "sigh away Sundays," apparently because one is stuck at home (1.1.200–202). Beatrice does not want to marry and especially does not want to be governed by an imperfect human—she will not marry "till God make men of some other mettle than earth"—and stretching the forbidden degrees to the fullest, she jokingly argues that she is too closely related to any man for marriage to be lawful (2.1.59–65). Both characters learn that marriage has some compensating features, including the emotional fulfillment that can come once "pride and scorn" are overcome (3.1.108). Besides, as Benedick puts it, "the world must be peopled" (2.3.242). To an extent, these characters discuss the pros and cons of marriage as a way of avoiding entry into the married condition itself. Like Claudio in the same play, they must undergo a transformation—involving a willingness to risk and lose themselves in an intimate relationship with someone else—before they are ready for a genuine marriage.

The theme of transformation is present in other comedies as well. Petruchio and Katherina change; Proteus and Valentine (in *Two Gentlemen of Verona*) are "metamorphis'd" by love (1.1.66, 2.1.30). But the transformation of Claudio and Hero in *Much Ado* is one of the most moving examples. Claudio is transformed by grief, humiliation, and submission to the requirements Hero's father has set. Hero's ordeal requires her to undergo a kind of symbolic death and rebirth. When the young lovers are brought together again at the end, Hero says, "And when I liv'd, I was your other wife, / And when you lov'd, you were my other husband" (5.4.60–61), indicating that both have become new beings.

The theme of transformation affects other relationships besides that of young lovers, including those of siblings and husband and wife. Often, personal transformation is required before conflicts can be resolved. In *As You Like It,* the conflict between brothers, fueled by envy and malice as well as by the problem of inheritance discussed earlier, is overcome when certain characters undergo fundamental changes. In one case, Duke Frederick, while coming into the forest with an army against his brother, is converted by "an old religious man" (5.4.160). Oliver's conversion is more complicated—in despair, he too has entered the forest and is about to be attacked by a lioness when he is saved by his brother Orlando. Though Orlando has cause to hate Oliver, he is impelled to save him by "nature, stronger than his just occasion" (4.3.129). Oliver, transformed by his trials and by Orlando's example, is once again a natural, loving brother, and the two are reconciled.

Married couples must sometimes overcome jealousy—portrayed essentially as a form of selfishness—in order to find happiness. Francis Ford in *The Merry Wives of Windsor* is stricken with unreasonable jealousy but finally sees the error of his ways and is movingly reconciled with his wife. Jealousy is also an issue in *The Comedy of Errors*, this time in the guise of Adriana, a jealous wife who in fact has some reason to question her husband's loyalty. Yet she too (we are led to believe) must make some changes if the marriage is to be happy. In the last scene, the Abbess, who turns out to be Adriana's mother-in-law, lectures her on the miseries of jealousy and the need for patience and kindness.

Several comedies, including most of those already discussed, present social as well as personal transformations, with both sorts linked to the marriages with which the plays end. The marriages in such plays are communal events and, in the case of *As You Like It,* even have cosmic reverberations. At the end of that play, Hymen, the god of marriage, enters to celebrate the prospective marriages and the restoration of social harmony. He announces that heaven rejoices when earthly relationships are set right and notes that marriage "peoples every town," thus making civilized life possible (5.4.143). Though the plots of this and other comedies focus on the young lovers, the symbolic and thematic implications go much further, setting marriage and family life in a larger social, natural, and spiritual context.

A few comedies deliberately break from the patterns that most follow. For instance, in *Love's Labor's Lost,* a group of men try to renounce women and romantic love only to find themselves falling for a group of available women. But the play does not end with marriages. The women argue that marriage is too serious to decide on quickly and set tasks the men must undertake during the following year before their suits can be reconsidered. The character Berowne notes the play's failure to follow the usual comedic pattern: "Our wooing doth not end like an old play: / Jack hath not Gill" (5.2.874–75).

Another set of plays contradicting the usual pattern has been labeled the "dark comedies" or "problem comedies" because they differ from the lighter comedies in tone and subject matter as well as plot. *Troilus and Cressida,* which some question calling a comedy at all, takes a cynical or at best troubling view of love. *All's Well That Ends Well* differs from the usual comedic pattern in having a young woman take the lead in the courtship and in having her prospective mother-in-law assist rather than oppose her. The young man refuses the marriage until the King of France forces him into it, and then he runs away until his wife fulfills the conditions he has set for acknowledging her as his wife, by tricking him into sleeping with her.

The last of the dark comedies, *Measure for Measure*, has a similarly problematic plot. Much of the action takes place in prison or in a brothel. A young man (Claudio) is to be executed for fornication, and the deputy (Angelo) who has been put in charge attempts to force himself on the young man's sister (Isabella), who is preparing to become a nun. As in *All's Well*, a bed-trick is used to force a young man (in this case Angelo) into marriage, this time with his former fiancée Mariana. The play ends with as many as four marriages, but two are forced (in addition to Angelo and Mariana, the Duke requires another character to marry a prostitute who has had his child), and another—between Claudio and his bride Juliet—was interrupted by pregnancy and imprisonment before it could be made official. In addition, the Duke proposes to Isabella. Because Shakespeare does not provide Isabella a response, many modern interpretations make the ending inconclusive. Thus, though the play powerfully explores justice, mercy, and human frailty, it is hardly a typical comedy.

Two of the comedies have a romance framework that connects them with Shakespeare's romances, discussed later. Both *The Comedy of Errors* and *Twelfth Night* tell the story of family members separated in a shipwreck and later reunited. The endings of these plays fulfill the characters' intense desire for family connection. In *The Comedy of Errors*, a brother who has left home to find his family compares himself to a drop of water seeking another drop: "So I, to find a mother and a brother, / In quest of them (unhappy), ah, lose myself" (1.2.39–40). In *Twelfth Night*, a twin brother and sister, believing each other to be dead for most of the play, view the shipwreck and their eventual reunion as a kind of death and rebirth or resurrection. The reunion raises questions of identity—if they look alike, how can they be different people?—but more significantly demonstrates that their bond is founded on something deeper than similar appearance. What links them is a shared family history, including their shared loss of a father. Like other comedies, *Twelfth Night* involves various kinds of transformations, but by ending with a family reunion achieved after various trials and by endowing this reunion with a sense of wonder, the play resembles Shakespeare's romances. In these later plays, as in *The Comedy of Errors* and *Twelfth Night*, family relationships inspire feelings of awe as well as happiness.

The Tragedies

The settings of Shakespeare's tragedies range from the ancient world to nearly contemporary Italy. Family relationships are central to most of them, but as befits the tragic genre, families are subjected to horrific strains, including betrayal, deception, egotism, jealousy, hatred, violence, and the accidents and assaults of fortune, nature, and human frailty. Although the families succumb, in many cases, to these strains, the plays nevertheless demonstrate the value of families—otherwise we would not be moved by the tragic outcomes—as well as the powerful emotions, both positive and negative, associated with family life. The tragedies also deal with ethical and philosophical issues, including the nature of familial love, the relation of family and personal identity, and the role of family in social and political life and in the cosmos.

Titus Andronicus, probably Shakespeare's earliest tragedy, is also his most gruesome, with rape, mutilation, cannibalism, and a variety of violent deaths. The play depicts family solidarity but also political and romantic rivalry between brothers. Titus kills two of his own children, one for disobedience, the other because she has been raped. Through most of the play, he has a tender relationship with that daughter, Lavinia, which prefigures in some ways King Lear's relationship with his daughter Cordelia. The play also depicts Titus's close relationship with his young grandson, even mentioning his habit of "danc[ing]" him "on his knee" (5.3.162). Family loyalty and honor motivate much of the play's action, including the cycle of revenge that leaves most of the characters dead, among them Titus and all but one of his children.

Except for *Coriolanus* (discussed later), family is less important in the other Roman tragedies, *Julius Caesar* and *Antony and Cleopatra*, though in the latter, Mark Antony's marriage to Caesar's sister shows the uses and dangers of family alliances in the political world. Family plays no significant role in Shakespeare's last tragedy, *Timon of Athens*, set in ancient Greece and possibly never performed in Shakespeare's time. In all the other tragedies, family is one of the main concerns.

Romeo and Juliet begins with the phrase "two households" and shows these households—the Capulets and Montagues—engaging in a violent conflict that has lasted for years if not generations. Besides providing a detailed picture of family life in upper-class households, the play shows the dangers that family loyalty poses to civil harmony. Tybalt in particular has a keen sense of family honor, and his killing of Mercutio and then his death at the hands of Romeo lead to the play's tragic outcome. Yet the play presents family not only as a source of discord but also as a potential source of social harmony, through the young couple's love that links the families and through the revelation at the end that Mercutio and Paris, each allied with a different household and both now dead, were both related to Escalus, Prince of Verona.

In part because of its focus on family relationships, *Hamlet* has proven to have an enduring appeal that transcends the original medieval setting of the story. The play's portrayal of revenge, in addition to connections with violence in early modern England, draws on theatrical tradition and has deep roots in the Bible and classical mythology as well as in Germanic culture. Claudius sees himself as a Cain figure. Hamlet is fascinated by the story of Troy, including Hecuba's grief as a wife and mother and the sinister revenge Achilles' son undertakes on behalf of his father. Revenge for a father's death is, of course, a central issue not only for Hamlet but also for Laertes and Fortinbras. The tragedy results in large part from the intensity of family feeling, manifesting itself both in revenge and in "the poison of deep grief" that leads to Ophelia's madness and death (4.5.75). But Hamlet's anguish also comes from his sense that his mother is deficient in family feeling, failing to grieve adequately for his father and marrying a close relative, with the result that the marriage is incestuous, as it would have been according to English standards. Even apart from that issue, Hamlet is troubled by the confusion of family roles: Claudius and Gertrude are now his "uncle-father and aunt-mother" (2.2.376). Of course, Hamlet wants no one to substitute for his dead father. Yet despite his disillusionment and anger, his bond with his mother is tender and strong.

With its second family, that of Polonius and his children, the play depicts the brother–sister bond and a father's concern for his children, as well as the perils of courtship involving royalty. Polonius appears overbearing with Ophelia, and he later criticizes himself for being too possessive. His attempts to counsel and spy on his son show him to be a loving but flawed father. Though *Hamlet* also deals with a wide array of other issues—political, philosophical, and psychological, among others—it remains one of world literature's richest and most fascinating treatments of family life.

Othello focuses on marriage and the destructive power of jealousy but also touches on courtship, racial and cultural issues, and the father–daughter bond. The racial and cultural differences between Othello and Desdemona are not their main problem, but along with the difference between his age and Desdemona's, they do make Othello more vulnerable to Iago's plotting. The play shows jealousy to be irrational, self-generating, and consuming. As it takes over, Othello makes his greatest mistakes—demanding proof, failing to trust and communicate, focusing on his own pain, and assuming the role of a minister of justice. Desdemona's elopement with Othello may make her an undutiful daughter, but the play portrays her as virtually an ideal wife. Some have found her too passive, but at many points she is confident and assertive. No one doubts her goodwill and good intentions, and some see her determination to return good for evil as an expression of Christlike love.

King Lear presents the tragedy of two families, those of Lear and Gloucester. The families' resemblances help make their problems—egotism, rivalry, betrayal, misunderstanding—seem universal. Lear and Gloucester are both flawed fathers who learn from what they suffer and are finally reconciled with a child they have mistreated. For many readers and viewers, the conflict between the generations will seem hauntingly familiar. Though Goneril and Regan become thorough villains by the end, they begin as reasonably typical adult children trying to deal with a demanding, irrational father. Lear, who is about 80, wants to be taken care of and independent at the same time. As his daughters' condescending, self-protective stance enrages him, he grapples with deeper issues: How can children not feel natural love and loyalty for a parent who has given them everything? Who is he if he is not being treated with respect as a king and father?

Lear eventually recognizes the foolishness of disowning his youngest daughter Cordelia and makes some progress in overcoming the pride and anger that had blinded him to her love. Though the play initially grounds the parent–child bond in nature, duty, and reciprocity, by the end, when Lear and Cordelia are reconciled, it becomes something of even greater value and significance. Both Lear and Cordelia had earlier used language that associated love with quantity and with a dutiful return of favors received. But in their reconciliation scene, which many have found one of the most powerful moments in dramatic literature, they use the language of repentance, forgiveness, and unconditional love. Cordelia asks for her father's blessing, and he kneels to ask for her forgiveness. Soon after, Lear and Cordelia are captured, and Cordelia is hanged, and so their happiness is short-lived. But the last scene in which Lear carries in the body of his daughter remains one of literature's great expressions of parental grief.

Macbeth presents a strong marriage relationship that turns bad, in part because a dominating or (in some interpretations) sexually manipulative wife persuades her husband to overcome his moral scruples. Macbeth and his wife are apparently childless, though Lady Macbeth mysteriously refers to having nursed a child. Their childlessness associates them with death and sterility, whereas others who have children—Duncan, Banquo, and others—are able to live on even beyond death. The play includes many references to children, infancy, and milk and associates these with nature, innocence, life, and hope for the future. When Macbeth orders the killing of Macduff's family, the deed is such a violation of moral norms that Macbeth's defeat soon seems inevitable. Meanwhile, Macbeth's moral hardening and his wife's despair have estranged them from each other, and Macbeth is hardly moved when he learns of his wife's suicide. Though apart from Macbeth's marriage, the play does not give a detailed picture of family life, it presents family as an essential element in the natural and moral structure of the universe, and it shows how evil can destroy even apparently strong familial bonds.

Coriolanus, one of Shakespeare's last tragedies, is set in Rome and presents the story of a warrior who fails to meet the challenges of political life in his city. Despite the military and political emphasis, family is an important and pervasive aspect of the play. Coriolanus's father has died, but he has a close bond with a strong, perhaps dominating mother. He also delights in his son, who at one point kneels for a father's blessing. And he has a faithful, loving bond with his wife. But the play repeatedly gives priority to his relationship with his mother, and both of the times he kneels to ask her blessing, he expresses fervent love for her.

The closing scenes test his family loyalty. Banished from Rome and having made an alliance with a former enemy, Coriolanus is about to attack his native city. Though he is determined not to be affected by family feeling, when his family come before him pleading for Rome, he is moved. He finally yields when they all kneel and his mother complains that he has never loved her. But he knows his decision is fatal. He cannot return to Rome, and when he goes to rejoin his former enemy, the townspeople kill him.

The play raises the question of whether family relationships are an essential part of our identity. Coriolanus tries to create an identity without the aid of family ties, insisting he will "never / Be such a gosling to obey instinct, but stand / As if a man were author of himself, / And knew no other kin" (5.3.34–37). Yet "Great Nature" speaks to him through his mother, wife, and son, and he finds himself incapable of ignoring the appeal. Furthermore, when he returns to the enemy city, his killers want to take revenge for the family members he has killed: "He kill'd my son!—My daughter!—He kill'd my cousin Marcus!—He kill'd my father!" (5.6.121–22). Though here and in the other tragedies, family bonds are sometimes a destructive force, it appears that family is inescapable.

The Histories

Kinship is particularly important in the history plays, where large households are common and where lineage plays an essential role. The royal and aristocratic characters of the history plays are commonly identified by their family relationships with other characters and by the titles and responsibilities that come with those relationships. Alliances are based mainly on family bonds. With some notable exceptions, fathers and sons, brothers, and even uncles, nephews, and close cousins tend to be on the same side.

The conflicts in the history plays come mainly from one of two sources: competing claims to the throne and revenge for wrongs done to one's "house"—that is, to one's kin. The whole house of York, of course, is seeking revenge for wrongs done to their ancestors. But the Lancastrians also remember the wrongs done to them. Clifford insists on being allowed to kill the Duke of York "for my father's sake" (*3 Henry VI* 1.4.109). He also kills young Rutland, not because of anything Rutland himself has done but because he belongs to the enemy house. The killing of Rutland then becomes an additional reason for the Yorkists to take revenge on Clifford.

Contention takes place within families as well as between them. In fact, the conflicts in the history plays are to one degree or another family conflicts, between brothers or other close relatives (as in *Richard III*) or between more distant relatives (as in the dynastic struggles of the *Henry VI* plays or the civil strife of *Henry IV*, parts 1 and 2). Even the wars with the French in *Henry V* are between cousins, for King Henry is fourth cousin once removed, as well as future son-in-law, to the king of France. In virtually every case, the conflicts in the history plays have to do with descent from a common ancestor and questions of precedence and power that arise as competing claims are made on the basis of that descent. The Salic Law discussion in *Henry V* and the war that follows are attempts to sort out such claims, and competing claims to the throne give rise to the whole War of the Roses. The curse that Henry Bolingbroke's usurpation has brought upon the house of Lancaster is partly the result of his having overthrown an anointed king but also a result, though he is King Richard's cousin, of his claiming the throne more by right of conquest than by right of descent.

The violence in the history plays inevitably becomes fratricidal or even parricidal. The memorable scene in *3 Henry VI* 2.5, in which a father has killed his son, and a son has killed his father, is clearly symbolic of the conflict between

Lancaster and York as a whole. The fact that the characters in this scene are unnamed commoners suggests that the war between Lancaster and York has precipitated family conflict at every level of society. The history plays thus assert that social conflict is fundamentally related to family conflict.

Family members may also be allies, of course. Prince Hal is reconciled to his father and saves his life. When Hal becomes king, his brothers are among his closest associates. Family relationships, besides being a field of conflict, may thus be useful both to individuals and to the needs of the kingdom. But family ties may serve either the virtuous or the cynically self-seeking. Richard of Gloucester uses his family connections, and makes new ones through marriage, to facilitate his acquisition of power. He then drops or destroys family members as quickly as he has used them. The fact that Richard ultimately acknowledges no family loyalty is a sign of his depravity.

At their best, family relationships serve as a model for harmony in the kingdom. Familial harmony may even betoken and foster international harmony. Marriages are viewed throughout the history plays as ways of making alliances between families and countries, and though the purpose is often pragmatic, the parties involved still talk of the marriages in terms of love and harmonious personal attachment. An example is the marriage announced at the end of *Richard III*. This marriage resolves the conflict between the houses of Lancaster and York that this and three previous plays have traced.

Henry Richmond, who has led the Lancastrian forces, announces that he will marry Elizabeth of York. He presents this news as part of a design, smiled on by heaven, to "unite the White Rose and the Red" and end England's suffering, which he describes in familial terms:

> England hath long been mad and scarr'd herself:
> The brother blindly shed the brother's blood,
> The father rashly slaughter'd his own son,
> The son, compell'd, been butcher to the sire.
> All this divided York and Lancaster,
> Divided in their dire division,
> O now let Richmond and Elizabeth,
> The true succeeders of each royal house,
> By God's fair ordinance conjoin together! (*Richard III* 5.5.19, 23–31)

He then prays that "their heirs" may "enrich the time to come with smooth-fac'd peace, / With smiling plenty, and fair prosperous days!" (32–34), suggesting that family in the sense of lineage will be England's salvation.

Shakespeare's last history play, *Henry VIII*, ends with a prophecy that Elizabeth Tudor, descendant of Richmond and Elizabeth, will bring "a thousand thousand blessings" on the land (5.4.19). With this play, Shakespeare has managed to trace English history almost up to his own day. As a group, his history plays give one version of how, for two hundred years, from the overthrow of Richard II to the reign of Elizabeth, family bonds, marriages, and royal descent shaped and fulfilled the destiny of England. For all that can be said about the importance of politics and war in these plays, it must be said that family is also crucially important and is often the means by which politics and war operate or the setting in which their consequences are suffered.

The Romances

Originally classified with Shakespeare's comedies or tragedies, the group of late plays now called his "romances" (*Pericles*, *Cymbeline*, *The Winter's Tale*, and *The Tempest*) combine elements of tragedy and comedy and have a strong religious and symbolic dimension. All of them present families that are separated and finally reunited and that suffer various calamities and adventures along the way. These plays are strongly influenced by the Greek romances—ancient tales about long-lost children, strange adventures, and the trials of young love. Some of these tales survived into the Middle Ages and helped promote the romanticized view of love that is now common in the Western world. *Pericles* is in fact based on one of these tales, *Apollonius of Tyre*.

Though each of the romances includes a young couple, the plays do not end with three or four couples ready to marry in the fashion of many of Shakespeare's comedies. In fact, most of the romances emphasize the older generation, and two of them end with a marriage restored between a husband and wife who have been separated for years. All end with other family members restored as well: Pericles is reunited with his daughter Marina, years after he left her in the care of foster parents. In *Cymbeline*, the king is reunited with his long-lost sons, stolen by a courtier who had been falsely accused and banished. In *The Winter's Tale*, Leontes and Hermione are reunited with their daughter Perdita after 16 years of separation. And in *The Tempest*, Prospero is reunited with the brother who had usurped his dukedom, and after a brief separation, King Alonso is reunited with his son Ferdinand.

Several of these reunions are presented as symbolic instances of death and rebirth. Apparently dead after giving birth, Pericles's wife Thaisa is thrown into the sea but survives and becomes a priestess. Pericles is reunited with her when he comes to her temple, years later, to give thanks. Pericles himself is in a sense brought back to life—rescued from despair and madness—by his daughter. In *Cymbeline*, Imogen and Posthumus are each thought to be dead for a time, and more significantly, their love, which had been destroyed by deception and jealousy, is revived. In *The Winter's Tale*, Perdita survives after being abandoned as a baby and is eventually reunited with her parents. Her mother Hermione appears to die soon after Perdita's birth but is restored to life in a moving scene of symbolic resurrection soon after Perdita's return. In *The Tempest*, Alonso and Ferdinand each think the other has died in the shipwreck that landed them on Prospero's island. Prospero uses this apparent death to prepare Alonso for a different kind of loss: he and Alonso have both lost their children "in this last tempest" (5.1.153). Though using the imagery of storm and shipwreck, his meaning is clear: his daughter and Alonso's son have fallen in love and will soon leave the parental home to start life on their own. The death and rebirth symbolism of the romances thus has a variety of meanings: among other things, it refers to the passage from one generation to the next, to the restoration of separated families and damaged love, and to the rediscovery of hope.

The father–daughter bond is important in all the romances, and the mother–daughter bond in two of them. All end with one or more parental blessings. These ritual acts mark the joyful reunion of loved ones and also convey a sense of the sacred. More than any of Shakespeare's other plays, the romances associate family with holiness and divine power. Besides the blessing ritual, visions in some of the plays—especially Posthumus's vision of his dead parents and brothers in *Cymbeline*—help make this association. Furthermore, in all the romances, the family serves as an instrument of providential design. That is, the gods, though allowing humans to suffer in various ways, reward their patience with a restoration of the blessings that seemed to be lost and with the addition of new ones. These events take place in and through family relationships: the blessings that are restored are mainly the blessings of familial love and happiness, and the new blessings include the joy of seeing children grow and begin families of their own. At the same time, the romances include tragic events—sin, suffering, and even the loss of loved ones. In *The Winter's Tale*, young Mamillius, son of Leontes and Hermione, dies of grief, and Antigonus, the character forced to abandon Perdita in Bohemia, is killed. Neither of these characters is restored to life, and the others are still mourning their loss as the play ends. The endings of *The Winter's Tale* and the others romances thus combine happiness with a somber recognition that aging and death bring real losses. Prospero will regain his dukedom, but as *The Tempest* comes to an end, he says, "Every third thought shall be my grave" (5.1.312).

The romances introduce a variety of other details relevant to family life: one or more mention childbirth and nursing or include stepmothers and foster parents. In *Pericles*, incest is an issue (but the incestuous couple are destroyed by fire from heaven), and Pericles's daughter spends some time in a brothel (but she converts all the customers to virtue). In most of the romances, human wrongdoing is a more serious concern than accidental separation, and so the stories involve repentance, forgiveness, and redemption as well as reunion. In *The Tempest*, Prospero struggles to forgive his brother but finally does. Jealousy afflicts characters in *Cymbeline* and *The Winter's Tale*. This last play explores the destructive power of jealousy at length and also points to the insecurity and egotism from which it springs. In the last scene, Leontes is told, "It is requir'd / You do awake your faith" (5.3.94–95). The surface meaning is that he must have faith that his wife can be raised from the dead. But the lines also suggest that he must exercise faith in the sense of trust in order to experience the happiness of a loving marriage and family life.

CONCLUSIONS

Shakespeare's treatment of family is marked above all by rich variety. The family has political and religious functions; it is an essential element of the cosmos; it connects individuals with the past and future and with each other as members of communities. In the tragedies, families are often the victims and sources of violence and misery; in the comedies and romances, families, though threatened, are healed and celebrated. Shakespeare often reflects realistic details from family life in his time, yet the plays also use family for dramatic purposes and explore its symbolic and philosophical implications.

Through all this variety, there are continuing threads. Several of Shakespeare's poems and plays explore the relation of family to individual identity. Shakespeare's first 17 sonnets suggest that a parent's identity is reborn in a child. To have a child is "to be new made when thou art old, / And see thy blood warm when thou feel'st it cold" (Sonnet 2). These sonnets are addressed to a young man who is called his "mother's glass" (Sonnet 3) in the sense that she can see herself in him. The sonnets encourage this young man to marry because otherwise his memory will be lost, and time and death will destroy the beauty he has inherited from his parents.

In several plays, the relation of family and identity is more complicated. In the plays with twins (*The Comedy of Errors* and *Twelfth Night*), family both establishes and threatens to dissolve separate identity. In other plays, characters wonder how parentage can be the source of children's identity when siblings are so different. Lear wonders whether Goneril and Regan are truly his daughters and even calls Goneril a "degenerate bastard" (*Lear* 1.4.254). For her part, Cordelia establishes a separate identity not only by being different from her sisters but by defying her father in the first scene. Nevertheless, in this and virtually every other play, characters see themselves not as entirely separate individuals but as deeply connected with each other, especially as members of families.

The plays present family as a product of nature but also (because nature comes from God) as a divine creation. Macbeth decides at first not to kill King Duncan because he is his kinsman, king, and guest, all three being sacred relationships (*Macbeth* 1.7.12–16). In *King Lear,* Kent similarly calls the bonds of family "holy cords" and then goes on to assert that these "holy cords" are "t[oo] intrinse t' unloose" (2.2.74–75)—that is, too intricately interconnected to undo except by treachery or violence. Because family relationships are so close and potentially so strong, they can affect characters powerfully for either good or ill. They fulfill the deep human need to belong—to be connected with others—a need suggested in *The Winter's Tale* when Paulina is described as weeping for lost loved ones while fervently embracing Perdita "as if she would pin her to her heart, that she might no more be in danger of losing" (5.2.77–78). Similar feelings are expressed in many plays, often by those who share literal family relationships but sometimes (as in the case just cited) by those who do not. The plays suggest that feelings as strong as those within the family can sometimes be shared by foster parents and children, friends, and others. Yet the plays also present cases of instinctive affection between family members who do not realize they are related—for instance, Imogen and her brothers in *Cymbeline*.

But family bonds are also dangerous, as Shakespeare's many stories of familial jealousy, hatred, and violence show. The danger comes in part from the very strength of the bonds. Neither Hamlet nor Ophelia, for instance, would suffer so tragically if they did not find themselves so deeply connected with family members. The violent revenge that many plays depict is usually prompted by family loyalty. In this way family loyalty actually leads to the destruction of families as members of opposing families seek revenge for each offense the other offers. *Romeo and Juliet* shows how such violent loyalty not only destroys families but damages an entire community.

Though external enemies and natural forces sometimes assault the family, the plays show the main threat as lying within the family itself. The greatest trials families undergo result from the egotism and insecurity that afflict some of their members, egotism that seeks to dominate and insecurity that views others in the family as threats. In response to such problems, the plays regularly depict humility and repentance as a solution, along with the forgiveness offered by characters who have been mistreated.

Another prerequisite to family harmony is "faith," a word used in the plays to mean both trust and faithfulness. The lack of trust threatens families in a whole range of plays, including comedies (such as *Much Ado*), tragedies (such as *Othello*), and romances (such as *Cymbeline* and *The Winter's Tale*). In several of these plays, relationships are healed when a character's "faith" is reawakened. In certain plays, especially the late romances, divine providence plays a role in preserving or healing families. Though this providential pattern is often carried out by pagan gods, early modern viewers would have recognized a parallel to the Christian view that family harmony requires divine assistance. Because nature is fallen and imperfect, family, as a product of nature, requires grace—a word with many meanings, including the supernatural power that heals and redeems nature. The word *grace* is in fact a key word in many plays and is sometimes associated with the blessing ritual by which parents seek to bestow divine influence on their children.

In showing characters struggling to acquire the qualities needed for successful family life, Shakespeare draws on the early modern idea that marriage and family provide a setting for learning how to love and trust. They do so in part because they challenge characters' tendency toward self-centeredness and invite them to offer themselves in service and sacrifice for each other's good. The characters who resist this invitation are usually presented as villains—for instance, Claudius in *Hamlet* and Goneril, Regan, and Edmund in *King Lear*. Occasionally a character tries to be completely autonomous, to deny that family bonds have any value at all. For instance, Richard, Duke of Gloucester, who later becomes King Richard III, announces, "I have no brother, I am like no brother; / . . . / . . . I am myself alone" (*3 Henry VI* 5.6.80–83), and in fact he goes on in a later play to kill family members as part of his scheme to get the throne. In a similar way, Coriolanus tries (though unsuccessfully) to be "author of himself" and ignore his bond with family (*Coriolanus* 5.3.36).

Other plays present the contrary pattern of characters' willing submission to family bonds. In *As You Like It*, Rosalind offers herself in this way when she says to her father and her future husband, "To you I give myself, for I am yours" (5.4.116–17). Husbands and husbands-to-be in Shakespeare's plays regularly make a similar offer—for example, Berowne in *Love's Labor's Lost* ("O, I am yours, and all that I possess!" [5.2.383]), Claudio in *Much Ado* ("Lady, as you are mine, I am yours. I give away myself for you, and dote upon the exchange" [2.1.308–9]), and the Duke in *Measure for Measure* ("if you'll a willing ear incline, / What's mine is yours, and what is yours is mine" [5.1.536–37]). Some of these characters, of course, still have much to learn as the plays' events test their impulse to offer themselves. An example is Posthumus in *Cymbeline*, a loving husband who succumbs to jealousy but who eventually is willing to offer his life in exchange for his wife's.

In various ways, Shakespeare's plays suggest that seeking our own lives—our own interests and desires in opposition to those of others—is self-destructive and that finding our lives, finding self-fulfillment, requires that we, in a sense, lose our lives. The inscription on the lead casket in *The Merchant of Venice*—"Who chooseth me must give and hazard all he hath" (2.9.21)—suggests that the highest self-fulfillment is found not in complete autonomy or absolute freedom but in the free offering of the self to others. Often, especially in the plays' scenes of reunion and reconciliation, these "others" are linked to the self by the ties of marriage and family.

Because Shakespeare's depiction of violence and betrayal within the family is so memorable, many wonder whether the plays should be described as taking a positive approach to family life. Yet it can be argued that Shakespeare's negative depictions of family make sense only because they represent the violation of positive ideals that Shakespeare shared with his contemporaries. In other words, the suffering and violence in the tragedies would not be tragic if it were not felt that families can and ought to be happy and harmonious. And in fact, the plays include many examples of love, loyalty, and happiness within families.

As with other issues, Shakespeare's approach can best be described as a combination of realism and idealism. Sonnet 8 presents the positive view by comparing a family to musical harmony:

> Mark how one string, sweet husband to another,
> Strikes each in each by mutual ordering;
> Resembling sire [father], and child, and happy mother,
> Who all in one, one pleasing note do sing. . . .

Many plays contrast the positive and negative elements of family life, for instance, showing love and devotion alongside jealousy and violence (as in *Othello*), misery and death followed by joy and renewal (as in *The Winter's Tale* and other romances), and egotism and betrayal along with humility and forgiveness (as in *King Lear*). In *Much Ado about Nothing*, Claudio's idealism is shattered but later restored at a more mature level. In some plays, such as *All's Well That Ends Well*, it is unclear how much characters learn from their mistakes. Yet the ideals of trust and self-sacrifice are still present as the standards against which the characters' failures are measured.

Many readers and viewers may want to question or complicate the foregoing generalizations. In fact, as the next two chapters make clear, Shakespearean performances and critical studies over the past four hundred years have taken widely different views of his depiction of gender, marriage, and family. But what is beyond dispute is that it is often in terms of family relationships that Shakespeare's works explore the great ethical, philosophical, political, and other issues of life.

REFERENCES

Brooke, Arthur. *Romeus and Juliet*. 1562. *Narrative and Dramatic Sources of Shakespeare*. Ed. Geoffrey Bullough. 8 vols. London: Routledge and Kegan Paul; New York: Columbia University Press, 1957–75. 1:284–363.

Cressy, David. "Foucault, Stone, Shakespeare and Social History." *English Literary Renaissance* 21 (1991): 121–33.

"The Form of Solemnization of Matrimony" (from The Book of Common Prayer, 1559). *Religion and Society in Early Modern England: A Sourcebook*. Ed. David Cressy and Lori Anne Ferrell. 2nd ed. London: Routledge, 2005. 61–64.

Harbage, Alfred. *William Shakespeare: A Reader's Guide*. New York: Farrar, Straus and Giroux, 1963.

Harding, Davis P. "Elizabethan Betrothals and 'Measure for Measure.'" *JEGP* 49 (1950): 139–58.

Laslett, Peter, ed. *Household and Family in Past Time*. Cambridge: Cambridge University Press, 1972.

Mack, Maynard. "Rescuing Shakespeare." International Shakespeare Association Occasional Paper No. 1. Oxford: Oxford University Press, 1979.

Mendelson, Sara, and Patricia Crawford. *Women in Early Modern England, 1550–1720*. Oxford: Clarendon Press, 1998.

Painter, William. "Rhomeo and Julietta." *The Second Tome of the Palace of Pleasure*. London, 1567. 218–47.

Stone, Lawrence. *The Crisis of the Aristocracy, 1558–1641*. Oxford: Oxford University Press, 1965.

Thomas, Keith. "Age and Authority in Early Modern England." *Proceedings of the British Academy* 62 (1976): 205–48.

Young, Bruce W. "Haste, Consent, and Age at Marriage: Some Implications of Social History for *Romeo and Juliet*." *Iowa State Journal of Research* 62 (1987–88): 459–74.

4

FAMILY LIFE IN PERFORMANCE

Shakespearean performance provides a remarkably illuminating way of tracing the changes in family life over the past five centuries. Early productions, influenced by the prevailing view that family is both a necessary and a natural aspect of life, often emphasized the ways characters fulfilled or failed to fulfill their family duties. Later productions, especially beginning in the twentieth century, have sometimes minimized the role of family or have presented it as an obstacle to individual happiness. Yet family has proven difficult either to ignore or to treat with complete hostility, and in recent decades, family has often taken a more positive role on the Shakespearean stage.

In each generation, actors, directors, and producers have used various techniques to emphasize issues of contemporary concern and to offer interpretations that confirm or challenge prevailing attitudes. In general, theatrical professionals have aimed to please audiences, but sometimes they have tried to enlighten or shock them. In either case, they have had to consider audiences' desires, values, and anxieties, including those related to family. Given the fact that Shakespeare's plays were first performed hundreds of years ago, a modern production must choose among several alternatives. It may ignore how family life has changed; it may highlight the differences between Shakespeare's time and ours in ways that will enhance the play's meaning or impact; or it may transform the details so as to make the action of the play more familiar or relevant to a modern audience.

In addition to reflecting a culture's attitudes and way of life, performances have also reflected changing theatrical practices, and these too have influenced how family is portrayed. From the all-male casts of Shakespeare's days to the often innovative practices of recent times, theatrical conventions have affected how courtship and marriage are presented, how formally or informally family members have interacted on stage, whether family in general is viewed positively or negatively, and a host of other matters. In some ways, performance is more telling than literary criticism. Whereas critics can consider various ways of interpreting a scene or a character without necessarily committing themselves to a single interpretation, those putting on a performance have to make definite choices. It is fascinating and revealing to look at such choices and see how these help create a production's overall vision of family life.

FROM SHAKESPEARE'S TIME THROUGH THE NINETEENTH CENTURY

Before the London theaters were closed in 1642, Shakespeare's plays were performed at public theaters (including the Globe), at Blackfriars (for a somewhat more select audience), and occasionally at court. The costumes were usually colorful and elaborate, and plays set in the past would often combine historically appropriate costumes with contemporary, but not casual, clothing. Costuming may have had the effect of both distancing the action (because the costumes were more elaborate than what most in the audience were wearing) and bringing it closer (because plays set in the past would still look somewhat contemporary). Costuming and other elements of performance style would have helped make the plays' portrayal of family life at once familiar and larger than life.

Shakespeare's plays were performed by an all-male cast, with women's parts played by young men. Some have speculated that this practice added to an audience's interest in gender issues, perhaps highlighting ways that social convention and outward appearance help to shape people's perception of gender. In several of the comedies (including *Twelfth Night, As You Like It,* and others), a young woman disguised as a man interacts with a man she is in love with as well as with a woman who falls in love with her, neither of whom knows her true gender until the end of the play. The fact that the actors playing these young women were in fact young men makes the gender questions all the more slippery and complicated. But it may be that audiences in Shakespeare's time simply suspended their disbelief and accepted the female characters as purely and simply female, despite the fact that they were played by young men.

Some have also speculated that, because all parts were played by men, the relationship between the young lovers and between husbands and wives on Shakespeare's stage would have been more intellectual and verbal than physical. It is certainly true that language is the primary medium through which all of Shakespeare's characters relate to each other. Yet gestures played an important role as well, along with the skillful use of body language and tone of voice. Certainly, despite the all-male casts, Shakespeare managed to present some of the theater's greatest pairs of lovers in such a way that their relationships have convincing emotional and even physical depth.

Comments from Shakespeare's contemporaries make it clear that many were moved by the joys and woes of Shakespeare's lovers and that some saw in the characters' stories reflections of their own lives. For instance, Leonard Digges wrote of how enthusiastically playgoers responded to the story of Othello ("the jealous Moore") and to Beatrice and Benedick (lovers in *Much Ado about Nothing*). Another account tells of how a performance of *Othello* by Shakespeare's company "drew tears not only by their speech, but also by their action. Indeed

Desdemona . . . moved us especially in her death when, as she lay on her bed, her face itself implored the pity of the audience" (qtd. in Tillotson 494). Other plays about which such comments have survived include *Romeo and Juliet* and *Love's Labor's Lost*. A poet who attended the latter play lamented that, during the performance, he suffered the same fate as the characters, namely, being rejected by the woman he loved (see Marston; Tofte).

Most scholars think that the style of performance on Shakespeare's stage was more formal and exaggerated than it is today. In certain ways such a style corresponded to a more formal way of life, one in which ritual and performance were emphasized. That may be one reason Shakespeare used the parental blessing ritual in so many of his plays. It has an innately theatrical quality, with the gestures of kneeling and placing hands on the kneeling child's head, and for Shakespeare's early audiences, it was associated with powerful emotions and ideas. It is likely that early performances presented the blessing ritual with a high degree of formality and solemnity—except, of course, in comic uses (for instance, when Launcelot Gobbo asks for his father's blessing in *The Merchant of Venice*), in which cases the comedy would come largely from the absence of the expected formality.

Several of Shakespeare's plays, including *A Midsummer Night's Dream* and *The Tempest,* were apparently performed in connection with a royal or aristocratic wedding. Such an occasion would automatically have granted a contemporary relevance to these plays. *A Midsummer Night's Dream* ends with fairies blessing the bridal beds of the play's three pairs of newlyweds and calling for loving marriages, happy offspring, and protection against deformities in their children. If, as is likely, the play was written to celebrate an aristocratic wedding (or possibly a double wedding) taking place in 1596, the real couple or couples who had just married, along with their families, would have found the play and especially the marriage blessing at the end highly relevant. Similarly, certain passages in *The Tempest*—for instance, songs blessing the young couple in the play with a prosperous marriage and honorable offspring—would have had a special significance for the Princess Elizabeth and her husband, whose wedding festivities in 1612 and 1613 included a performance of the play.

In 1642, soon after civil war had broken out in England, Parliament ordered the closing of the theaters. When the theaters reopened with the restoration of the monarchy in 1660, several changes took place: women's parts were now played by women; audiences became somewhat more exclusive; playhouses were enclosed (the Globe had been open to the air); and more elaborate scenery came into use. For a time some of Shakespeare's plays with great female roles (such as Cleopatra, Hermione, and Rosalind) were performed rarely or not at all, perhaps because the roles as Shakespeare wrote them did not fit the kind of performances expected from the new actresses. Others of Shakespeare's plays continued to be staged but now competed with newer plays. Furthermore, many felt the language and plots of Shakespeare's plays were in need of improvement, and so several of the plays as performed on stage were heavily rewritten.

One of the best examples is Nahum Tate's version of *King Lear,* first published in 1681. Tate clarified the language, omitted the Fool, simplified and in some cases drastically changed the action and the characters' motives, and gave the play a happy ending. Among the details of the original that Tate retained were Cordelia's request for a father's blessing and Lear's later reference to that ritual. Though the custom of giving parental blessings had become less common, it was apparently still familiar enough in the later 1600s that Tate could expect audiences to understand what was happening in these scenes. But Tate modified many other details related to marriage and family life.

In Shakespeare's play, Cordelia's motives in the first scene can be interpreted in various ways but mainly have to do with her unwillingness to flatter her father and her anger at her sisters' empty and self-serving expressions of love. In Tate's version, Cordelia, who is in love with Edgar, deliberately provokes her father to disown her so that she can avoid being forced to marry Burgundy. The love affair between Cordelia and Edgar (entirely Tate's invention) is highly idealized. All the main characters are simplified. In particular, Edmund is a less complex and sympathetic villain, and his illegitimate status, rather than drawing sympathy, is mainly an indication of his evil character. By the end, only the villains have died; the older characters, Lear, Gloucester, and Kent, remain alive but will retire to a life of meditation; Cordelia, instead of dying tragically as in Shakespeare's version, will marry Edgar and succeed her father as ruler. To modern ears, Tate's version seems far less moving and profound than Shakespeare's original. Because Tate draws the lines more clearly between good and evil, the conflict between family members, though still strongly present, is less complex and would be less likely to remind audiences of their own family conflicts, as Shakespeare's version often does in troubling ways. Tate's Lear, though wrong in disowning Cordelia, is a less deeply flawed father than in the original and goes through a less heart-wrenching process of repentance. Perhaps because Tate's version was relatively simple and undemanding, it ruled the stage in England for over 150 years. In the early 1800s, the original version was gradually restored to the stage.

Other attempts to improve Shakespeare during the late 1600s included Thomas Otway's *The Fall of Caius Marius*, which places the story of Romeo and Juliet amid political conflicts in ancient Rome; John Dryden's version of *Troilus and Cressida*, which makes Cressida a simpler and more sympathetic character; and a version of *The Tempest* by Dryden and William Davenant that gives Miranda a sister and adds a young man who, like Miranda, has never seen anyone of the opposite sex. Most of these modified versions are simpler and in some cases lighter than Shakespeare's originals or (as in *Caius Marius*) make Shakespeare's story of young love and family conflict secondary to other concerns. Another play revised during this period was *Measure for Measure*. A version by Davenant has Angelo merely test Isabella's virtue rather than seriously try to seduce her, and in a version by Charles Gildon, Angelo and Mariana have secretly married prior to the play's action. Both revisions removed elements that audiences of the period might have found disturbing, especially those related to illicit sexual behavior. Even when plays were not drastically rewritten, the relatively exclusive audience and, especially in the early 1700s, the insistence on a dignified and heightened acting style may have diminished the sense that the troubles of Shakespeare's families had much to do with everyday life. Shakespeare's plays were certainly viewed as "images of nature," but of nature in a heightened and idealized form.

Some of Shakespeare's plays continued to be performed during the early 1700s, but the mid- and late 1700s saw a remarkable growth in his popularity and reputation. Something close to Shakespeare's *Romeo and Juliet* reappeared in the 1740s and proved popular through the rest of the century, especially David Garrick's version, which focuses on the young lovers, heightens the pathos of their story, and eliminates references to Rosaline, Romeo's previous love. Also in the 1740s, several neglected plays were revived, including two in which young women are disguised as men (*As You Like It* and *Twelfth Night*) and two others with strong female parts (*All's Well That Ends Well* and *The Winter's Tale*). The importance of family life in these plays, as well as in another revival (*The Merchant of Venice*), greatly broadened audiences' sense of how Shakespeare dealt with family. The popularity of contemporary plays dealing with domestic situations among middle-class characters may have allowed audiences to identify more closely with similar situations in Shakespeare's plays, despite his use of mostly upper-class characters.

Romeo and Juliet by William Shakespeare with Garrick as Romeo and G. Anne Bellamy as Juliet by Christian Frederick Zincke (?). The painting shows David Garrick and Anne Bellamy in an eighteenth-century production of the play. Art Archive / Garrick Club (The Picture Desk, Inc.).

Yet even as a broader range of Shakespeare's plays became available, productions continued to simplify the plays as Shakespeare had written them. One of the greatest concerns of the period was decorum—that is, the expectation that each character should fit a relatively clear and consistent type and that the higher characters, at least, should act and speak with appropriate dignity. This concern led to productions of *Othello*, for instance, from which much of the language considered indelicate (including sexual references) was removed, foreshadowing an even greater disapproval of such matters during the nineteenth century. The tendency to simplify characters and their relationships can be found in the standard eighteenth-century interpretations of Macbeth and his wife: Macbeth, especially as acted by David Garrick, was noble and sympathetic; Hannah Pritchard, Sarah Siddons, and others played Lady Macbeth as a terrible and dominating figure, a monster—or, as the play itself puts it, a "fiend-like queen"—who drives her husband to murder.

By the late 1700s, playhouses in London held much larger audiences than they had a century earlier. Though this may have helped increase and diversify interest in Shakespeare, the size of the playhouses and the use of a proscenium arch separating the stage from the audience also put a greater distance between spectators and actors and required of actors a more formal and heightened style than they could have used in a different kind of theater. Nevertheless, some actors managed to present Shakespeare's characters with impressive effect. Sarah Siddons, for instance—one of the most popular actresses of the late 1700s and early 1800s—played such wives and mothers as Lady Macbeth, Volumnia, and Hermione with power and passion.

The 1800s witnessed several important changes in Shakespearean performance. Many plays were restored to something much closer to what Shakespeare had written. Realism, including detailed historical realism, became an aim of many productions, though the historical realism tended to focus on externals (such as costume and scenery) rather than more elusive matters (such as customs, relationships, and attitudes). The style of acting became more sentimental and romantic. The result was that actors presented family relationships, as well as the relationships of young lovers, with a stronger emphasis on deep and tender feelings, an emphasis that accompanied an increasingly sentimental attitude toward family in life outside of the theater.

John Philip Kemble, in the late 1700s and early 1800s, had already played Hamlet as weeping when he speaks of his dead father. The tradition continued throughout the nineteenth century. Edmund Kean's "voice trembled" at the word *father* and he drew tears from his audiences. Johnston Forbes-Robertson made the word a "heartrending, almost sobbing entreaty." And in America, Edwin Booth expressed similar "tenderness and filial awe" (Rosenberg, *Masks of Hamlet* 301; Dawson 51). Performances of *King Lear* were likewise filled with emotion. In the scene of Lear's reunion with Cordelia, for instance, "Kean staggered, sobbing with tenderness and joy, into [Cordelia's] waiting arms" (Rosenberg, *Masks of King Lear* 289).

In 1838, William Charles Macready finally presented a version of *King Lear* with the tragic ending and with Shakespeare's language. In presenting this and other plays, however, Macready and others removed scenes or language they judged inappropriate. Shakespeare as restored in the nineteenth century thus was often Shakespeare cleansed of elements audiences might have found objectionable, including some of the more violent action and indecent language. Such "cleansing" brought Shakespeare's picture of family life closer to the idealized view of family that prevailed during this period.

Besides coarse language and violence, among the elements sometimes omitted were sexual references, even innocent ones. Victorian productions of *The Winter's Tale* sometimes eliminated references to Hermione's pregnancy, and some productions of *Romeo and Juliet* (for instance, Charlotte Cushman's) dropped the Nurse's lines about breast-feeding Juliet. As we might expect, less innocent references were often eliminated as well. For instance, Samuel Phelps's 1854 production of *Pericles* omitted references to incest between the princess and her father, a relationship essential to later events. Violence was sometimes minimized so that male characters would appear more "gentlemanly," especially in their treatment of women. Besides excluding language that was not in accordance with "good taste," Augustin Daly's New York production of *The Taming of the Shrew* in 1887 reduced the number of taming incidents. On occasion Othello's treatment of Desdemona was softened—for instance, Edwin Booth's Othello sometimes did not strike his wife as the text calls for in act 4, scene 1.

The idealizing tendency of this period carried over into the portrayal of Shakespeare's female characters, who were often played with an emphasis on their innocence and femininity—in other words, so as to make them fit the Victorian picture of the ideal woman. Ellen Terry, probably the best-loved actress of the latter part of the century, was known and admired for her highly feminine and idealized characters. Though she successfully played Shakespeare's assertive Portia (in *The Merchant of Venice*), Terry was more strongly associated with such vulnerable characters as Ophelia.

Not surprisingly, certain characters—Lady Macbeth in particular—proved difficult to reconcile with the period's ideal of pure, self-sacrificing womanhood. Traditionally, Lady Macbeth had been played as a monster, someone entirely unlike a normal woman. In 1842, Helen Faucit added a strain of womanliness to the character, making her vulnerable and loving while at the same time determined and ambitious. In the later 1800s, though the traditional ideal of womanhood still dominated, this ideal was becoming increasingly controversial. Many felt anxious and defensive concerning the "woman question," which involved, among other things, the question of a woman's role in society and in the family. Such concerns help explain why many audience members found two of the period's interpretations of Lady Macbeth disturbing, though in different ways. In 1884, Sarah Bernhardt played her as seductive and manipulative, with a sensuality that contradicted the passive, innocent feminine ideal and shocked some spectators. Perhaps just as disturbing was Ellen Terry's attempt in 1888 to bring to Lady Macbeth the idealized womanhood she used successfully with other characters. Terry played the character as a tenderly loving, self-sacrificing wife, sincerely trying to make her husband happy. Though she speaks of being willing to dash out an infant's brains, she finds it so difficult to say this that she begins to weep.

Ellen Terry as Lady Macbeth (1889) by John Singer Sargent. The painting, with a majestic Lady Macbeth holding the Scottish crown, was inspired by Ellen Terry's enactment of the role but does not picture an actual moment in the performance. Tate, London / Art Resource, NY.

To many audience members, it was jarring to see Lady Macbeth portrayed as an ideal Victorian wife while at the same time being aware of the evil, violent deeds she sets in motion.

Another character many in the nineteenth century found difficult to deal with was Hamlet's mother Gertrude. Through much of the century, her role in the play and especially her relationship with her son were de-emphasized, and she tended to be played as a stereotypical "fallen woman, whom Hamlet kept at arm's length even as he tried to reform her" (Rosenberg, *Masks of Hamlet* 74). Later in the century some productions made Gertrude more attractive and even (for instance, in Wilson Barrett's 1884 production) emphasized her loving marriage with Claudius. But audiences were apparently taken off guard by such interpretations.

Although productions during the nineteenth century were in some ways becoming more faithful to Shakespeare's texts, certain trends—for instance, the tendency to idealize and the emphasis on spectacle and on sentiment—had an opposite effect. During the late nineteenth and early twentieth centuries, especially in London productions by Henry Irving and Herbert Beerbohm Tree, audiences saw scenery so elaborate and realistic that it often overpowered the text, which had to be cut to allow time for scene changes and sometimes the addition of spectacle. Irving was the leading Shakespearean actor of the late 1800s and brought an intensely personal interpretation to his parts. Especially in certain plays, his interpretations required audiences to take a new—and often more sympathetic—look at the characters' marital and family relationships. Irving's Hamlet was more a melancholy lover than a revenger, and like actors earlier in the century, Irving emphasized the word *father* when he encountered the Ghost. Rather than portraying Shylock as a villain, Irving played the part with great pathos, adding a scene in which Shylock returns home to find his daughter gone, thus focusing on the character as a loving and wronged father and in doing so, in the opinion of many, contradicting the text.

Predictably, from the reopening of the theaters in 1660 to the end of the nineteenth century, the treatment of family in Shakespeare's plays changed with changing attitudes and performance conditions. The general trend toward larger audiences and the performance of a greater number of Shakespeare's plays eventually made available a richer sense of Shakespeare's vision of family. Yet at the same time prevailing attitudes about family limited what audiences were likely to learn.

Productions during the late seventeenth and eighteenth centuries tended to simplify the plays and make characters either noble and virtuous or the opposite. The portrayal of family dynamics was similarly simplified to fit that pattern. A greater interest in complex characters during the nineteenth century led to productions in which the family dynamics were more complicated. Yet the emphasis on tender feeling and the practice of eliminating the plays' more objectionable features deprived nineteenth-century spectators of some of the harsher aspects of Shakespeare's picture of family life. Attitudes toward family during this period were highly colored by romantic and sentimental ideals, and productions tended to modify the plays' picture of family life to fit those attitudes. Especially during the nineteenth century, Shakespeare's plays were widely performed in America and elsewhere, and such performances usually followed the trends found in England.

As the twentieth century began, feelings toward Shakespeare's portrait of family life were mixed. Some productions, such as those featuring Sarah Bernhardt and Ellen Terry as Lady Macbeth, brought out aspects of the plays that many found troubling, especially during a time when traditional family roles were being challenged. Yet many continued to find in Shakespeare's plays evidence for the value of family life and for the possibility of love and happiness in family relationships. Though some performances exaggerated such ideals, the plays contain much that supports a positive view of family. Such interplay between the plays and prevailing attitudes should remind us that the plays were not merely inert material to be reshaped by each generation. Through the centuries since the plays were first performed, Shakespeare's vision of family had in fact influenced cultural attitudes as much as such attitudes had influenced how Shakespeare was performed.

THE TWENTIETH AND TWENTY-FIRST CENTURIES

During the early twentieth century, yet another attempt was made to return Shakespearean production to its roots. Three men—William Poel, Gordon Craig, and Harley Granville-Barker—helped lead a revolt against the elaborate scenery and heavily cut texts of the late 1800s and early 1900s. They favored much simpler staging (including minimal scenery or, for Poel, no scenery at all) and some approximation to the performance conditions of Shakespeare's time. Though productions through the rest of the twentieth century would not always follow their lead, these men had a permanent effect on Shakespearean performance by returning emphasis to Shakespeare's words and opening the door to more innovative and flexible staging.

Shakespeare was widely popular on the early twentieth-century stage but became even more so during the latter part of the century, especially after World War II, when Shakespearean productions greatly increased in number. Shakespeare was performed in London at the Old Vic and later at a newly built National Theatre. In Stratford the plays were performed by the Royal Shakespeare Company (RSC), which also played at a succession of theater spaces in London. In addition, Shakespearean festivals were founded at various locations in America and Canada, and Shakespeare began to be performed widely on college campuses and in both English and translation in theaters around the world. Throughout the century, but especially from the 1940s onward, Shakespeare was also performed on film, and with the advent of television, performances were made available through that medium. Though the great number of productions makes it difficult to generalize about how family has been presented during the twentieth and early twenty-first centuries, it is clear that changing attitudes have had an impact at times more startling than at any point in the past.

In their treatment of family life, productions during this period have tended to combine tradition and innovation in varying degrees. The widespread modern practice of setting Shakespeare's plays in different historical periods has had a variety of effects, often making Shakespeare's portrait of family seem more distant when a play is given an older or more exotic setting and making it seem closer and more relevant when a play's setting is recent or familiar. Among productions that have set Shakespeare's plays in the distant past, one of the most striking was a 2007 production of *King Lear* (performed at the Folger Theatre by the Classical Theatre of Harlem), which set the story thousands of years ago in ancient Mesopotamia. Often, by contrast, the plays are given a modern setting. There have been several famous modern-dress *Hamlets*, including London productions in 1925 and 1938 and one in New York (starring Richard Burton) in 1963–64 that was filmed for release around the United States. Several recent productions of *The Winter's Tale* have been done in modern dress as well, suggesting that this story of jealousy, familial loss, and restoration has relevance for modern families. Many other plays have also been performed not only with modern dress but with modern props, ranging from telephones to automobiles.

One well-known recent instance of modernization is Baz Luhrmann's 1996 film version of *Romeo and Juliet*, in which guns replace swords and which opens and closes with a television newscast. Though the text's reference to Juliet's age (just shy of 14) is deleted, the film—with its contemporary setting and popular young stars—was clearly meant to appeal to teenage viewers, who would presumably find in it a reflection of their own experiences and desires. (Luhrmann's interpretation was anticipated 10 years earlier by an RSC production, directed by Michael Bogdanov, that included a pool party, rock music, and a press conference.)

Michael Almereyda's 2000 film version of *Hamlet* similarly updates the setting, making Gertrude and Claudius heads of a modern "Denmark Corporation." Hamlet and Ophelia come across as emotionally scarred modern young people with dysfunctional families. Polonius's stature as a father is markedly reduced. Laertes hardly pays attention as Polonius speaks the words of farewell blessing. Ophelia's line to her father, "I shall obey, my lord," is deleted. Though Hamlet and his mother seem to genuinely love each other, their interaction in the closet scene is very rough (she slaps him; he pushes her against a mirror and yells at her), and he is miserable throughout, especially when forced to watch his mother and stepfather's displays of affection.

A less well-known film, Christine Edzard's 1992 version of *As You Like It,* gives that play a modern urban setting, with the inhabitants of the Forest of Arden presented as homeless city dwellers and with other scenes placed in office buildings or at cocktail parties. Orlando's love poems to Rosalind, instead of being attached to trees, are graffiti written on walls. The courtship of Rosalind and Orlando and Rosalind's interaction with her father gain poignancy by taking place in a contemporary homeless urban setting.

The potential effectiveness of a familiar setting was demonstrated in a 1999 RSC production of *Macbeth* (preserved on film in 2001) that used spare sets and modern dress to give its domestic scenes, especially the one with Lady Macduff, a contemporary feel. In this production, Lady Macduff is played as a modern middle-class mother. Just before thugs enter to slaughter her and her children, she is giving two of the children a bath while her baby is crying in a crib. This familiar domestic atmosphere lends an immediacy to the scene that heightens the horror and pathos we feel.

Besides modernizing the settings and costuming, directors have innovated in other ways—for instance, having women play the role of Hamlet or King Lear, adding unusual musical or visual motifs, or introducing concepts from psychoanalysis or contemporary politics. International productions have been among the most innovative. A version of *King Lear* performed in Tokyo in 1991 combined diverse performance styles, including rock music and Chinese opera, and at the same time reinterpreted the story. For instance, "Edmund's grudge was foregrounded, almost justified," and he marries a prostitute, in part to express his resentment at how his father treated his unmarried mother (Aya). Another production of *Lear,* in 1989 in India, interpreted the scene of Lear's "rebirth" and reunion with Cordelia with a striking bit of stage business that reflects the deep father–daughter bond in Indian culture but that also can be viewed as having a Freudian twist: "Lear is in [Cordelia's] lap and awakens with a scream with foetus like movements," while "Cordelia watching him goes into labour" (Lear's rebirth; see the photograph on page 112). The point of this stage business, of course, is to suggest that the parent–child roles have been reversed and that Cordelia has become a life-giving mother to Lear.

In addition to theatrical innovations of the various kinds described, modern productions have used the choice of plays, the cutting of lines and scenes, and subtler changes in emphasis and style to create distinctive interpretations of family life. In particular, Shakespearean performances over the past hundred years have differed markedly from earlier ones in their treatment of sexual matters and in their emphasis on violence and conflict. The harsher aspects of Shakespeare's picture of family that had been neglected in the nineteenth century were given more than adequate attention in the twentieth.

In the 1950s, for instance, Peter Brook successfully staged *Titus Andronicus*, one of Shakespeare's most violent plays, and displayed the play's full array of horrors, including rape, cannibalism, revenge, and the killing of children, more than once at the hands of a parent. Family relationships are both the cause and the victim of most of these horrors. Later (1962–63), Brook presented an intensely bleak *King Lear,* in which the destruction of families takes place in a world seemingly bereft of hope and redemption. In this case, however, to achieve this result, Brook had to eliminate some of the play's more positive lines and add disturbing stage business—for instance, having Edgar carry his brother's body off stage "like a slaughtered pig" (Speaight 284). Brook's film version, released in 1971, was not quite so brutal but was still bleak. Filmed in a desolate landscape and gloomy interiors, the film emphasizes suffering and destruction. The blinding of Gloucester

King Lear curls in a fetal position in Cordelia's lap, symbolizing his rebirth through his daughter's intervention in a 1989 Indian production of *King Lear* directed by Amal Allana. Theatre and Television Associates, reproduced by the Shakespeare Centre Library.

is presented in its full horror and is deprived of most of the lines that set the evil deed in a moral context. The more positive moments in the film are subdued. The reunion of Lear and Cordelia, for instance, is played quietly, with little obvious emotion—Lear and Cordelia do not even share a frame until well into the scene—and the request for a father's blessing is removed.

Along with a relatively negative presentation of family life, many modern productions have emphasized the plays' sexual content. Beginning in the latter half of the twentieth century, Shakespearean productions often became much more sexually explicit than they ever had been in the past. The sexual element has sometimes been used as part of a celebration of love and life in which marriage and family are treated positively. But at times productions have used sexually explicit action or imagery, along with other elements, to present family in a cynical or harsh light. This has been done, for instance, by demeaning characters who have traditionally been idealized, as Joseph Papp did when he presented a sex-obsessed Ophelia (not to mention a wildly ridiculous title character) in his 1968 New York production of *Hamlet*. Desdemona has suffered a similar fate. Paula Vogel's *Desdemona: A Play about a Handkerchief*—a revision of *Othello* first produced in 1979 and widely performed since then—makes Desdemona a would-be prostitute who has slept with everyone except Cassio.

A famous example of the more positive use of sexual imagery is Peter Brook's 1970 production of *A Midsummer Night's Dream*. In this colorful and energetic interpretation, the characters are filled with sexual passion, and witty phallic symbolism emphasizes the sexual element in the love of Bottom and the Queen of the Fairies. Later stagings of the play have often followed Brook's lead in emphasizing the sexual content, and other plays have received similar treatment. In the 1998–99 RSC production of *The Winter's Tale*, the dancing at the sheep-shearing festival included explicit phallic images. Though some audience members doubtless found this detail offensive or at least distracting, it was probably intended to create an atmosphere of fertility and sexual excitement that would correspond to these same elements in the love between Perdita and Florizel, love that we are assured will lead to a faithful, happy marriage.

In the same production, sexual imagery was used more negatively to emphasize Leontes's jealousy. Antony Sher made clear the sexual basis for the character's torment by adding obscene bodily gestures to his words about earth being a "bawdy planet" on which adultery is widespread. Such sexually suggestive gestures are commonly used in modern productions to clarify or emphasize Shakespearean language that audiences might otherwise find obscure.

Sometimes the sexual elements are not so much positive or negative as simply strange and shocking. In a 2006 production of *Twelfth Night* (performed in Stratford by an innovative group named Filter), the twin brother and sister (Sebastian and Viola) were played by a female actor who seemed to combine the two into a single character. At the end of the play, arm in arm with both a man (Orsino) and a woman (Olivia) and kissing them in succession, this combined Sebastian-Viola appeared to be in love with them both. The effect was mind-bending, with a possible suggestion of bisexuality. The 2007 RSC production of *Coriolanus* used sexual identity (specifically hints of a homoerotic bond) for clearer thematic purposes: Coriolanus hardly touches his wife, but at one point he gives Aufidius, his former enemy and now his ally, an extended kiss on the mouth. In this production at least, Coriolanus belongs to the world of men rather than to the more feminized realm of the family.

Nudity has been used occasionally, mainly for shock value, as in a 1976 film version of *Hamlet* (directed by Celestino Coronado) and in Derek Jarman's 1979 film version of *The Tempest*. Jarman's film, despite being set vaguely in the past, has a contemporary feel resulting not only from the nudity but also from the relatively young age of the actors and especially the portrayal of Miranda as a giggly and sometimes sassy teenager. Jarman omits Prospero's speech exhorting the young couple to practice premarital chastity, perhaps because the speech would have detracted from the contemporary feel.

The tendency of modern Shakespearean productions to emphasize the harsh and sordid aspects of family life probably reached a high point in the 1960s and 1970s. Since then, though there have been frequent exceptions, there has been a noticeable trend toward more positive and affirmative presentations of family. Kenneth Branagh's 1993 film version of *Much Ado about Nothing* is a straightforward celebration of love and marriage, and Trevor Nunn's *Twelfth Night* (1996) is similarly positive and moving in its picture of the bond between brother and sister. Branagh's *As You Like It* (2007) shows the dark side of family conflict but concludes with happiness and harmony as brothers are reconciled, lovers anticipate marriage, and a father and daughter are reunited. Branagh adds a detail to emphasize the mood: as almost all the characters run through the forest singing and dancing, Rosalind's cousin Celia pauses briefly when she sees her father, who has turned from villainy to a solitary religious life, and tenderly kisses his head.

Recent productions of the tragedies, too, have affirmed the value of family life, presenting the love between parents and children or husband and wife as genuine and moving. For instance, Michael Elliott's 1983 television production of *King Lear* (starring Sir Laurence Olivier) has far more vibrant emotional content than Brook's bleak version, first staged 20 years earlier. Though much of the emotional content in Olivier's *Lear* is negative—it is after all a tragedy—the reunion between Lear and Cordelia is filled with tenderness, forgiveness, and love, and the relationship between Edgar and Gloucester is similarly moving. In a comparable way, Branagh's film version of *Hamlet* (1996) focuses on family relationships and shows family members as deeply bonded with each other, despite all the horrors they experience. As portrayed in this production, even the love of Claudius and Gertrude seems genuine.

Stage productions of Shakespeare have shared in the positive trend. Trevor Nunn's 1978 production of *The Comedy of Errors*, spiced throughout with music and high spirits, ends with moving reunions and joyful, enthusiastic celebration. A recent Royal Shakespeare Company adaptation of *The Merry Wives of Windsor*—titled *Merry Wives: The Musical* (2007)—has similar high spirits, along with tender scenes of young romantic love, and ends, for the mature

Hamlet (Kenneth Branagh) stares past his mother Gertrude (Julie Christie) at his father's ghost in Branagh's 1996 film production of *Hamlet*. Columbia Pictures/Photofest.

couple whose marriage has been troubled by jealousy and misunderstanding, with a warm embrace of reconciliation.

Several recent productions have brought an element of transcendence to their treatment of family life. Adrian Noble's *Midsummer Night's Dream* (1994–95) sought to produce a feeling of wonder and even sanctity at the end, when the marriage beds are blessed and the couples anticipate conceiving new life. In 2003 the RSC production of *As You Like It* ended with even more explicit religious feeling: as the lights dimmed and solemn music played, all the couples knelt and listened as Hymen, the god of marriage, spoke on behalf of the heavens, joining the couples and restoring familial and social harmony.

The popularity of Shakespeare's late romances in the late twentieth and early twenty-first centuries is further evidence of a positive trend. All of these plays emphasize family, move toward reunions and reconciliations, and—if the director and actors allow it—end with a sense of wonder and transcendence. In particular, during recent decades, stages around the world have seen several outstanding productions of *The Winter's Tale*. Two of the best, produced by the RSC in 1986 and 1992–93, used music throughout to heighten the atmosphere and especially at the end to emphasize the feeling of magic and emotional warmth. In the 1986 production, as Leontes and Hermione embrace, they are surrounded by the other characters holding hands in a circle, suggesting that the healing of the marriage brings harmony to the whole social order.

Over the past generation there have been emphatically positive interpretations of Shakespeare's other late romances as well, including the traditionally neglected *Pericles*. The 2002 production of this play in Stratford and London presented the reunion of separated family members with intense feeling and, in the final scene in the temple of Diana, with a sense of sanctity and wonder, emphasized by the sweet, solemn music playing in the background.

Though productions that give family relationships a grim or cynical twist still take place, the recent trend has clearly been toward a more positive treatment of family. In part, this trend may simply be a reaction to the excesses of the 1960s and 1970s. But it may also reflect a recognition that family life, despite the severe questioning and stresses it has undergone over the past century, is still one of the most important and widely valued elements of human life. Perhaps one reason Shakespeare's late romances in particular have appealed to recent audiences is their combination of idealism and realism. Though heavier in tone than most of the comedies and dealing with many of the harsh realities found in the tragedies, the romances nevertheless end with happiness and hope, thereby appealing to audiences who seek the same values in a world that is not entirely family-friendly.

SPECIFIC ISSUES IN PERFORMANCE

Besides taking part in the general trends already described, performances over the past five centuries have also differed in their treatment of specific issues related to family. To give a sense of the great variety of approaches taken by different performances, especially over the past hundred years, this chapter now looks at some of the more important and challenging of these issues, such as teenage and interracial marriage, marital conflict (including power issues raised by feminism), and other kinds of family conflict or even abuse. Included along the way will be an exploration of how various productions have handled some of the plays' more controversial moments related to family.

Teenage Marriage

Of the many teenage brides in Shakespeare, the best known and most influential is the 13-year-old Juliet in *Romeo and Juliet*. Even without giving the play a contemporary setting, modern productions have tended to present the young couple's relationship as highly relevant to contemporary audiences. One way they have done this is to have young actors play the parts. Traditionally, Romeo and Juliet were played by mature actors, some of them well into middle age, including, through the eighteenth and nineteenth centuries, Romeos played by David Garrick (in his thirties) and Henry Irving (in his forties) and Juliets played by Susannah Cibber, Anne Bellamy, Ellen Terry, and others (in their twenties and thirties). As late as 1936, the actors playing the young couple in an American film version were 49 and 31. But in 1968, the play received one of its most memorable film treatments when Franco Zeffirelli cast a 16-year-old as Romeo and a 15-year-old as Juliet. The beautiful Renaissance Italian setting helped make the film popular, but its appeal was heightened even more by its lively depiction of youthful passion, enhanced by actors who, not surprisingly, were convincing teenagers.

Although Zeffirelli's version followed the tradition of romanticizing young love and, by implication, discounting the dangers of teenage marriage, other recent productions have countered that tradition. Luhrmann's 1996 film, with its contemporary setting, presents the young couple sympathetically but reveals the perils young people are exposed to in a world filled with impulsive desire and violence. Some productions have tried even more pointedly to make the connection between young love and violence. For instance, a 1986 production cosponsored by the Folger Shakespeare Theater and the Youth Suicide National Center started with the assumption that the play "addresses a tragic crisis facing our nation—teen suicide" (program note qtd. in Barnet 237).

Interracial and Intercultural Marriage

Through much of the course of Shakespearean production, interracial marriage has been even more controversial than marriage between teenagers. Past productions of *Othello* (the main play that raises the issue) sometimes muted the

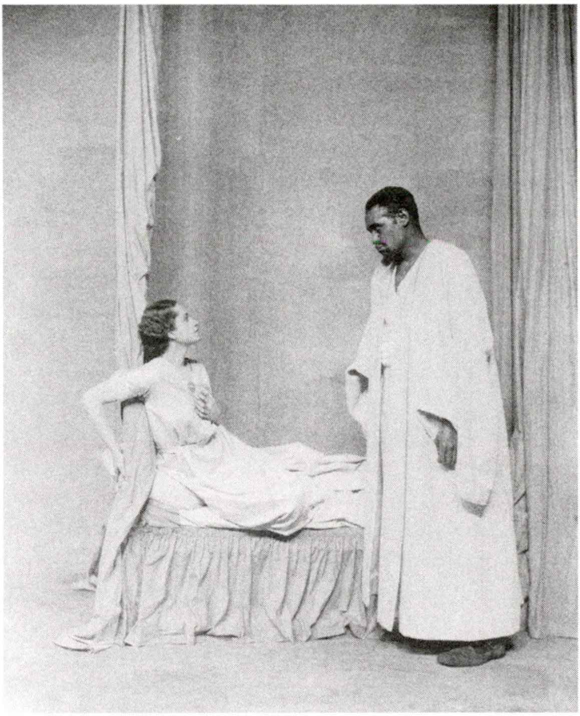

Paul Robeson as Othello stands over Peggy Ashcroft as Desdemona in a 1930 London production of *Othello*. Bettmann/CORBIS.

controversy by making Othello a mildly dark-skinned northern African rather than clearly black. For centuries, even when the racial differences were not minimized, the title role was almost always played by a white man made up to appear brown or black. Even in the twentieth century, Othello was played by such white actors as Laurence Olivier, Orson Welles, Richard Burton, and (in the 1981 BBC television version) Anthony Hopkins. Apart from the brief and unsuccessful attempt made in the 1700s by Ignatius Sancho, an Afro-Briton, and the mixed success of Ira Aldridge in the 1800s, the first black to play Othello in a major theater in the English-speaking world seems to have been the American actor Paul Robeson. In 1930, unable to perform the part in America, where prejudice against interracial marriage was especially high, he played Othello in London. Even there, the woman playing Desdemona had to justify allowing a black man to kiss her on stage. By 1943, Robeson was able to perform the role in the United States, and the production was in fact extremely successful. Though both white and black actors have played Othello from the 1940s onward, since the 1980s it has become almost obligatory for a black man to play the role.

Some recent productions have highlighted the issue of interracial marriage. Janet Suzman directed the play in South Africa in the 1980s, when apartheid was still in force, and her use of black African John Kani as Othello, both on stage and in a 1988 televised production, emphasized the relevance of racial relations for contemporary audiences. In a less obvious but still thought-provoking way, the American Civil War setting that Trevor Nunn gave the play in his 1989 stage production (followed by a 1990 television adaptation) helped to heighten the issue of racial difference and thus emphasize one problematic aspect of Othello's marriage. A 1997 production gave the play an unusual twist by having Patrick Stewart star as a white Othello, with the other characters, including Desdemona, played as black.

Modern productions of *The Merchant of Venice* have explored similar issues, this time considering how religious and cultural differences affect courtship and family dynamics. Like Desdemona, Shylock's daughter Jessica elopes, and in both cases the father disapproves of the marriage because of cultural differences. The rift with the father is much stronger in Jessica's case, though, because she abandons her Jewish heritage in order to marry a Christian. In Shakespeare's time and even later, most spectators would have viewed this marriage as simply comic, one of the ways the Christians triumph over Shylock. But with modern sensibilities attuned to greater respect for cultural difference, recent productions have often made Jessica ambivalent about her decision.

The text indicates that Jessica hates life with her father and is eager to elope. Yet some modern productions have incorporated moments of tenderness between father and daughter, sometimes by having them take part together in Jewish family rituals. Trevor Nunn's production, adapted for television in 2000, has the two sing tenderly together; Shylock even strokes Jessica's hair. Moments later, he explodes and slaps her, but he immediately regrets it. Jessica clearly wants to escape but feels torn. As she speaks of being "ashamed to be [her] father's child," she holds a picture of her mother. In this production, once she elopes, Jessica seems to abandon her Jewishness thoroughly, with striking changes in her hairstyle and clothing. Yet at the very end, as she reads the document indicating all she will inherit from her father, she is grief-stricken and begins singing a Jewish melody. This ending strongly resembles that of an earlier production, Jonathan Miller's 1973 television adaptation starring Laurence Olivier, in which Jessica remains alone at the end, sadly reading of her father's losses, while we hear a voice singing the Kaddish, a Jewish prayer of mourning, hinting both at her father's loss of his daughter and at Jessica's loss of her heritage.

Marital Dynamics

The importance of marriage in Shakespeare's plays has always been obvious, but the feminist movement of the late twentieth century brought renewed attention to how the plays deal with marriage, especially with the relative power of husbands and wives. Nowhere is the struggle for power between spouses more obvious than in *The Taming of the Shrew*. Productions of this play have ranged from celebrations of wifely submission to grim depictions of physical and mental abuse. Some have gone in yet other directions to suggest that both Petruchio and Kate are tamed or that Kate is actually Petruchio's equal but learns to play the game of conforming outwardly to social convention. Kate's final speech about her duty to obey has often been delivered with a degree of irony. For instance, in the 1929 film with Mary Pickford and Douglas Fairbanks, Pickford winks at the audience to let them, but not her husband, know she is giving the speech as a ploy. Few recent productions have taken the play's premise that wives should obey their husbands entirely seriously, a notable exception being Jonathan Miller's 1980 BBC television version, which presents the play in what Miller takes to have been its original social context. He claims the play "is about the setting up of a sober household and the necessity for marital obedience in order to maintain it" (Miller and Hallinan 138). Furthermore, perhaps because he finds it hard to imagine a Renaissance father as loving, Miller presents Petruchio as healing a Katherina who has been damaged by her father's lack of love.

By contrast, the 1966 film version with Richard Burton and Elizabeth Taylor (directed by Franco Zeffirelli), though a reasonably straightforward interpretation, does several things that minimize the seriousness with which we can take the idea of wifely submission. Set in Renaissance Italy, the production emphasizes the characters' clownish antics and physical violence, mainly for the sake of broad humor. It also makes Kate spirited throughout and shows the couple eventually as being genuinely in love. Kate gives the final speech on a wife's duty seriously but then leaves the banquet ahead of Petruchio, indicating that she is far from tamed, though she can play the game when she needs to.

Stage productions have often given the play a similar interpretation but using different means. A 2003 RSC production shows Kate falling in love with Petruchio and balancing submissiveness with spirit. Though she gives quite a straight rendition of her final controversial speech, she delivers it while holding a riding whip and wearing breeches under her dress, and she puts emphasis on the fact that a wife must be obedient to her husband's *honest* will. With Petruchio for a moment appearing ready to step on her extended hand, she seems to regret having made the offer. But as she comes to him, he kneels with her and embraces her, suggesting that in reality this is a marriage of mutual submission.

Another way recent productions have softened the play's apparent validation of male dominance is to use the frame story of the drunken Christopher Sly with which Shakespeare's text originally began, sometimes adding an end to the frame, which the text leaves unfinished. The frame makes the story of Kate and Petruchio an entertainment that Sly is watching, presented as part of a scheme to make him think he is a nobleman. A 1999 RSC production used the frame both to distance the story and to remind audiences of its relevance to contemporary concerns. A giant computer screen at the back of the stage displayed images and phrases, including "politics of power," before being used to show Sly the play about Kate and Petruchio. Though live actors soon replaced the computer images, the computer screen appeared again after the interval and then again at the end, reminding audiences that the entire story was a fantasy, set in the Renaissance, for the benefit of a more or less contemporary Sly. When Sly wakes after falling asleep at the end, he claims he has learned how to tame his wife, but it is clear she is the dominant partner in the marriage. A 1995 production directed by Gale Edwards also used the Sly frame but did so to close the play on a positive note. This production ended with Sly kneeling before his wife, grateful to finally understand her love for him.

Some productions have given the play a darker interpretation, presenting Kate's taming as cruel and humiliating and emphasizing the power of men over women. Charles Marowitz's 1973 production was especially negative, portraying Petruchio as sadistic, Kate eventually as a brainwashed wreck (her final speech is a mechanical, memorized recitation), and the consummation of the marriage as a nightmarish rape. Michael Bogdanov's 1978 production was less extreme and single-minded but similar in its treatment of some parts of the story. Though for the most part enthusiastically entertaining, this production presented the taming as a brutal process that leaves Katherina broken. At the end Petruchio casually allows her to kneel before him and put her hand under his foot. By presenting the play in modern dress and with the apparent aim of entertaining, Bogdanov made the misogynistic elements all the more obvious and troubling. These and other productions, coming at the height of the modern feminist movement, responded effectively to contemporary concerns. Yet few later productions have followed their lead, perhaps because most audiences prefer a more comic vision in which courtship and marriage are shown to be complicated yet ultimately positive. An interesting exception was a 1989 Turkish production of the play in which Katherina slit her wrists rather than submit to Petruchio.

The idea that Petruchio is himself tamed is hinted at in the 1966 film and in many other versions. It is most obvious in sequels to Shakespeare's play that purportedly show what happens to Petruchio after he has married Katherina. The first of these sequels was written about 1611 by John Fletcher, a younger contemporary of Shakespeare. Titled *The Woman's Prize, or The Tamer Tamed,* it shows

Kate (Paola Dionisotti) kneeling to Petruchio (Jonathan Pryce) in a 1978 production of *The Taming of the Shrew* by the Royal Shakespeare Company. Joe Cocks Studio Collection. Shakespeare Birthplace Trust.

Petruchio with a second wife who refuses to sleep with him until he becomes submissive. A witty twentieth-century television play also titled *The Tamer Tamed* (1956) depicts Petruchio and Katherina a year after their marriage. Katherina is pleasant but strongly asserts her "woman's reasons," which Petruchio rejects with disastrous results. Finally, he learns to trust her, and they win yet another wager made by her father. It makes sense that modern audiences, with their expanded view of women's roles, would appreciate such a sequel, responding as it does to *The Taming of the Shrew* from a woman's perspective. But the fact that Fletcher's play made a similar point in the early seventeenth century may indicate that audiences even then felt a need for a balanced picture of power relations in marriage. Two other bits of evidence point in the same direction: John Lacy's revision of *The Taming of the Shrew* in the late 1600s reduced Kate's speech of submission to two lines, and a popular eighteenth-century version—David Garrick's *Catherine and Petruchio* (1754)—treated Kate sympathetically and included a line in which she asserts that she will tame Petruchio.

Though *The Taming of the Shrew* presents the power dynamics of marriage in an unusually striking form, directors and actors have used other plays to explore the same issues. Like *The Shrew, The Comedy of Errors* presents a wife learning to yield to her husband and being instructed (this time by her sister) in a wife's duty. Modern productions have often treated this instruction comically or have otherwise tried to make it more palatable to audiences. In Trevor Nunn's 1978 production, the sister (Luciana) reads the advice from a book—thus stressing its conventional character—and then makes it part of a high-spirited song-and-dance routine.

Many other plays, even without explicit speeches about marital duties, have allowed directors to explore the husband–wife bond. In his version of *Romeo and Juliet*, for instance, Zeffirelli heightens the tension between Lord and Lady Capulet, having Lady Capulet glare at her husband from across a courtyard while he and Paris converse about young marriages ("Younger than she are happy mothers made." "And too soon marr'd are those so early made" [1.2.12–13]). By contrast, Zeffirelli presents the Montagues as a close, harmonious couple. In Baz Luhrmann's film version, both couples appear unhappy—in fact, both families are dysfunctional. While in a car together, the Montagues sit apart and do not look at each other. A neurotic Lady Capulet drinks and pops pills, apparently unable to cope with being either a wife or a mother. In 3.5, Lord Capulet not only grabs and pushes his daughter but also hits his wife.

The marital dynamics in *Macbeth* have proven especially fascinating to modern audiences. Directors and actors have to decide whether to make Macbeth and his wife equals or to make Macbeth weak and submissive (a reversal of what many suppose traditional roles to have been). They also have to consider Lady Macbeth's motivation: is she simply a monster, or does she love her husband? If Lady Macbeth is made the dominant figure, directors and performers also must consider what gives her power over her husband.

In a memorable but unduly neglected 1997 film version (directed by Jeremy Freeston), Macbeth and his wife are played as a young couple who openly display their strong mutual attraction. This version depends on the powerful sexual bond between husband and wife to explain how a good man could turn to evil. In place of the play's original closing lines, this production ends with Lady Macbeth's voice, saying "Hie thee hither" (a line from earlier in the play), as if inviting her husband to join her in death. Immediately after those words, Macbeth's head is struck off and the screen goes black.

Roman Polanski's 1971 film version, best known for its graphic violence, similarly presents Macbeth and his wife as young and physically attractive. In Trevor Nunn's 1979 television production (based on his stage version), Ian McKellen and Judi Dench play the couple as older but likewise emphasize their sexual bond. Their conversations are often mingled with passionate kissing, and when Macbeth seems unwilling to kill the king, his wife uses a combination of tenderness and contempt to revive his willingness.

By contrast, Gregory Doran's 1999 stage version made the couple's relationship close but, with one or two momentary exceptions, not obviously passionate or sexual. Lady Macbeth is ambitious for her husband and seems desperate to persuade him. But Macbeth appears the stronger of the two from the beginning. His wife is easily shaken, and at least early on, Macbeth is the one who uses their marriage bond to reassure her.

Sibling Relationships

In contrast to the often negative treatment of marriage in recent productions, which have sometimes gone well beyond the Shakespearean text in stressing marital tension or unhappiness, recent productions have generally been balanced in their treatment of sibling relationships. In particular, the bond between brother and sister—prominent in *Hamlet* and *Twelfth Night*—often comes across as positive. Virtually every major film version and many stage productions of *Hamlet*, for instance, present the relationship between Laertes and Ophelia as affectionate, friendly, comfortable, and genuinely happy. Other plays, though—especially those with brothers—show the sibling bond to be strained by conflict or separation. Directors have used a variety of techniques to emphasize sibling conflicts or to show that, despite the conflicts, the bond between siblings is still strong. A 2006 production of *Much Ado about Nothing* in Stratford added a frame in which Don Pedro's rebellious brother Don John is to be executed. At the beginning the execution turns out to be a joke, and the brothers embrace. At the end of the play, Don John is once again brought on stage for execution, but the stage goes dark before we know the outcome.

Perhaps more than any of the other plays, *King Lear* is rife with sibling conflict, between sisters as well as brothers. Some recent productions of the play have sought to make the villainous siblings Goneril, Regan, and Edmund understandable and even sympathetic, usually through subtle details of performance (that was Peter Brook's approach) but sometimes through wholesale modernization. For instance, a 2002 adaptation of *King Lear* for television stresses the apparent normality of the siblings and their motivations by setting the story in nineteenth-century America, making Lear a rancher, and retitling the story *King of Texas*.

Shakespeare's plays with twins—*Comedy of Errors* and *Twelfth Night*—are usually performed not only to explore the nature of the sibling bond but also to draw on the plays' potential for both comedy and pathos. Though most versions of *The Comedy of Errors* play up the farcical confusion for laughs, a remarkable 1996 production in Stratford stressed the larger story of a family separated and reunited and, in doing so, created a somber, haunting atmosphere as well as a sense of holiness at the end. When the two sets of twins finally appeared on stage together, they looked at each other in wonder as tender music played. The last words of the two Dromios—"We came into the world like brother and brother; / And now let's go hand in hand, not one before another"—lines usually played for laughs, were spoken warmly and seriously in this production.

Plays with siblings offer directors the choice of emphasizing the siblings' differences or their similarities, the latter sometimes stressed through doubling. Trevor Nunn's 1996 film version of *Twelfth Night* emphasizes the differences between the brother–sister twins (for instance, by showing in detail the efforts Viola has to engage in to appear male). Ultimately—after a certain amount of comic confusion—the effect is to make the twins' reunion all the more realistic and moving. By contrast, a 1969 television production of *Twelfth Night* had Joan

Plowright play both twins, with the perhaps unintended effect of depriving the ending of any genuine scene of reunion.

Branagh's 2007 version of *As You Like It* uses doubling more effectively, with Brian Blessed playing both dukes. The two are clearly distinguished—Duke Frederick has black hair combed straight back and is dressed in samurai attire; Duke Senior has graying hair and appears to be a nineteenth-century European gentleman. But beneath these surface differences, the strong resemblance between the two (stressed by having Blessed play both) reminds viewers that, for all its virulence, the play's fundamental conflict is between brothers who are deeply bonded and more similar than they are different. The doubling also helps to prepare for and justify Duke Frederick's eventual repentance. A similar effect is produced by having the play's other set of warring brothers—Oliver and Orlando—played by black actors, in contrast to the Japanese and white actors who take the other parts.

Parent–Child Relationships

The image of parent–child relations in recent productions has been remarkable for its variety, ranging from tender sympathy to extremes of parental abusiveness. Though the more negative interpretations have sometimes gone well beyond a plain reading of the text and certainly have not reflected ordinary life in Shakespeare's time, the range of images are faithful to the plays in a fundamental way: whether positive or negative, they draw their power from the innate intensity of the parent–child bond and from the assumption that this bond ought to be loving and mutually beneficial.

Among productions presenting this bond in a negative light is Zeffirelli's 1968 *Romeo and Juliet*, which stressed the gap between the generations by making Juliet's mother cold and distant, especially in contrast to Juliet's warmly sympathetic nurse. Juliet's father loses his temper to the point of violence, yelling his lines and pushing Juliet into a corner, while his wife tries to calm him and the Nurse tries to protect Juliet.

Prospero in *The Tempest*, traditionally played as a wise and loving father, has recently been portrayed as conflicted and prone to anger, an interpretation for which there is textual evidence that older performances had tended to ignore. But the older view has proven difficult to shake. Peter Hall has recounted his partly unsuccessful efforts in 1973 to get John Gielgud to break from the tradition of making Prospero an ideal father and instead to play him "neurotically" ("Sir Peter Hall Directs").

Recent productions have often presented a range of parental attitudes, even within a single play. For instance, in Branagh's 1993 film version of *Much Ado*, Leonato appears shockingly unfeeling when he throws his daughter Hero to the ground, but he soon sympathizes with her. In contrast to Peter Brook's restrained presentation of the bond between Cordelia and Lear (on stage in the 1960s, on film in 1971), most recent productions of *King Lear* have emphasized both the conflict at the beginning and the tenderness of their reconciliation. For instance, in a 1993–94 RSC performance, Robert Stephens stumbled over his daughter's name ("I think this lady to be my child Cordelia"), movingly suggesting that he is both hopeful and stricken with guilt.

Several plays—in particular *Coriolanus* and *Hamlet*—have lent themselves to productions that emphasize the strength of parental influence. Without portraying the title character as weak, recent productions of *Coriolanus* have stressed his bond with his mother and her power over him. This emphasis has a long tradition. An eighteenth-century adaptation was subtitled *The Roman Matron*, giving Volumnia equal weight with her son in the title. The mother's dominating presence became overtly physical in a 2007 Utah Shakespearean Festival production in which the actress playing Volumnia was much taller than the actor playing her son. A 1994–95 RSC production emphasized the mother–son bond by making Volumnia seem almost resentful at having to share Coriolanus with his wife and by having her cling to him when he was about to leave in exile. Later in the play, Coriolanus fell to his knees before her and, weeping, held her tightly around the waist. Though the kneeling is specified in Shakespeare's texts, directors have added and emphasized other gestures to put even greater stress on the mother–son bond.

Productions of *Hamlet* can focus on any one of several parent–child bonds and often on all of them: the bonds between Hamlet and either of his parents and between Polonius and his children. The bond between Hamlet and his mother is usually played as strong but ambivalent, and beginning in the twentieth century, it was often presented through a Freudian lens as an example of the Oedipus complex. The early twentieth-century director Tyrone Guthrie was apparently taken with the theory and gave an Oedipal interpretation to his productions. In Laurence Olivier's 1948 film version, Hamlet and his rather young-looking mother kiss lingeringly in a way that obviously exceeds the normal mother–son bond. The sexual element in their bond became more explicit in the 1980 BBC television production and Zeffirelli's 1990 film version, in both of which Hamlet holds his mother and violently imitates lovemaking to show his disgust with her second marriage.

Many other productions, finding the Oedipal interpretation excessive or without adequate textual basis, make Hamlet's love for his mother intense but not sexual. Kozintsev's Hamlet and Gertrude (1964) are warmly but not perversely affectionate. Both Richard Burton (1964) and Kenneth Branagh (1996) portray the bond between Hamlet and Gertrude as troubled but still warm, strong, and appropriate for a mother and son. In both versions of the closet scene, Hamlet treats his mother roughly and angrily but finally embraces her. Some productions—both Olivier's and Almereyda's film versions, for instance—have emphasized Gertrude's devotion to Hamlet by apparently having her deliberately drink from the poisoned cup in the last scene in order to save her son's life.

The Ghost of Hamlet's father has been portrayed in various forms ranging from the dominating martial figure in Branagh's film to the quieter, melancholy version in Zeffirelli's. Depending on the portrayal, Hamlet's response to his father can range from awe or even terror to pity. Some directors and actors have gone to strange though sometimes effective extremes to emphasize the bond between father and son. In Coronado's 1976 film, twins (Anthony and David Meyer) play Hamlet and his father. In a Royal Court Theatre production in 1980, Jonathan Pryce played a Hamlet who, as if possessed by his father's spirit, speaks the Ghost's lines as well as his own. Such portrayals not only reveal the strength of the father–son bond but also make it seem disturbed or even demonic.

The bond between Polonius and his children, especially his daughter Ophelia, has been treated with a similar range of interpretations. Zeffirelli's Ophelia (played by Helena Bonham Carter) speaks the words "I shall obey" with defiance and anger. In Branagh's film version, both Ophelia and Laertes obviously love their father. Yet Polonius finally comes across as an unsavory character. He has a mistress (Branagh's addition to the text) yet gives his son moral advice. And he becomes violent and coercive with his daughter, shoving her while he warns her about Hamlet's intentions. Nevertheless, Ophelia in Branagh's version (played by Kate Winslet) remains respectful and obedient and, after her father's death, is shown screaming as his body is taken away. Other productions present Polonius more sympathetically, often as a well-intentioned busybody who genuinely cares about his children. When Polonius gives Ophelia advice in Kozintsev's version, he is a bit gruff but not unkind; for her part, Ophelia is respectful and affectionate.

Recent productions of *The Winter's Tale* have used various techniques to emphasize the bonds between parents and children, usually presenting them as both powerful and positive. Several versions have started the play with added stage business introducing us to the boy Mamillius—for instance, the 2002 RSC production in which he plays magic tricks for the adult characters. The effect is to make his death even more poignant and troubling. Props have sometimes been used to emphasize the play's references to childhood. For instance, the 1969 RSC production introduced a giant rocking horse (on which both Mamillius and Leontes ride), a schoolboy's top, and even a yo-yo, the latter two in the hands of Polixenes, reminding us of his childhood friendship with Leontes.

The Winter's Tale concludes, of course, with the reunion of Perdita and her parents, but even before the last scene, some productions have added details to emphasize the connection between mother and daughter. For instance, in the 1992–93 RSC production, while the baby Perdita is being placed on the shores of Bohemia, Hermione hovers angel-like over the stage as if to protect her daughter. Another method sometimes used to emphasize the mother–daughter bond is having the same actor play Hermione and Perdita. In Trevor Nunn's 1969 RSC production, Judi Dench played both mother and daughter. A 1951 production directed by Peter Brook achieved essentially the same effect by having Perdita appear strikingly similar (especially in dress and hair) to Hermione as presented earlier in the play.

Though recent productions commonly emphasize the strength of the bond between parents and children, they sometimes neglect details that could enhance that emphasis. The parental blessing, for instance, one of Shakespeare's most striking embodiments of the parent–child bond, rarely receives the sort of

Prince Mamillius (Sam Rich) rides a rocking horse with his father King Leontes (Barrie Ingham) as his mother, Queen Hermione (Judi Dench), observes, in a 1969 production of *The Winter's Tale* by the Royal Shakespeare Company. Reg Wilson. Royal Shakespeare Company.

emphasis in modern productions that it would have had in Shakespeare's time. The full array of gestures accompanying the ritual as originally performed—with the child kneeling and the parent placing hands on the child's head—are only sporadically in evidence. Occasionally the blessing is removed entirely (e.g., in Jarman's film version of *The Tempest* and in many versions of *The Merchant of Venice*, including Jonathan Miller's 1973 television production). Sometimes, though the words of blessing are included, no distinctive gestures are used. For instance, the 2004 RSC production of *Hamlet*, despite putting the characters in Renaissance costume, gives no hint that a ritual action from the period is being performed: Laertes stands while Polonius speaks the words of blessing to him, and the two never touch. More often, modern productions replace the original gestures of blessing with less formal ones. The parent and child hold hands or embrace, or a father may place his hands on his son's shoulders while speaking to him (as in the 1998 RSC production of *The Tempest*) or may kiss him on the cheek or forehead (as Polonius does to Laertes in Richard Burton's and Kenneth Branagh's film versions of *Hamlet*). Whatever the gestures, the effect is almost always relatively casual in comparison to the historical ritual.

When the lines make it clear that the child should kneel before the parent, modern productions often include that action. This is especially true of productions of *King Lear* and *Coriolanus*, where the texts make much of the kneeling gesture. Sometimes, though, the lines referring to kneeling are ignored or removed. Productions that do this tend to diminish the sense of parental authority and filial submission and sometimes even shift focus away from the parent–child bond. In the 2004 RSC *All's Well That Ends Well*, the Countess is played impressively by Judi Dench, yet she lacks some of the authority the blessing gestures would give. Bertram does not kneel as the Countess blesses him. Instead, he stands throughout, and she holds his hand and then embraces him as they bid farewell. By contrast, in a 1989–90 production, Gwen Watford—pictured in the photograph on this page—played an authoritative, as well as affectionate, Countess who blesses a kneeling Bertram. The 1992 RSC production of *The Winter's Tale* omits the lines in which Paulina directs Perdita to kneel and has Hermione continue embracing Leontes as she pronounces words of blessing on her daughter, after which she finally goes to Perdita to give her an embrace. This production ends with the focus more on Hermione's marriage than on her bond with her daughter.

Occasionally, a modern production will present the blessing ritual with something of its original formality and religious power. In his film version of *Hamlet*,

Gwen Watford as the Countess of Rossillion blesses her son Bertram, played by Paul Venables, in a 1990 production of *All's Well That Ends Well* by the Royal Shakespeare Company (Barbican, London). Donald Cooper/Photostage.co.uk. By permission of Photostage Ltd.

Kozintsev has Laertes kneel while Polonius makes the sign of the cross over him—not something parents did in Shakespeare's time but nevertheless a gesture that makes the moment appropriately solemn. The 2002 RSC *Winter's Tale* has Hermione hold both hands up as she blesses her kneeling daughter, finally placing one hand on Perdita's head as she says the words "upon my daughter's head." A production in 1990 of the same play at Brigham Young University used the full historical gestures to create what is reported to have been "a moment of intimate human contact" that also conveyed a "sense of the sacred": "as she performed the ritual, Hermione became a priestess-like figure, endowed with heavenly authority, stationed between the heavens and her kneeling daughter" (Young 208).

The BBC versions of the plays made for television in the 1970s and 1980s take varying approaches to the blessing ritual. The productions of *All's Well That Ends Well* and *King John* use none of the traditional gestures. Several—for instance, *Coriolanus*, *Richard II*, and *The Tempest*—have the child kneel but omit the parents' gestures of blessing. A few have something close to the full ritual: for instance, *Titus Andronicus*, *Richard III*, *The Merchant of Venice*, and *Hamlet*. The series' most authentic rendition of the custom appears at the end of *The Winter's Tale* where Perdita kneels and Hermione places both hands on her head.

Of course, even without the historically authentic gestures, productions may use the idea of blessing to emphasize the parent–child bond. Ian McKellen's 1996 film version of *Richard III* omits any of the gestures of blessing, perhaps appropriately, given its mid-twentieth century setting. Yet it is clear both that Richard's mother blesses him and that he mocks the blessing, and when (later in the film) she curses him, he is visibly shaken, though he quickly pretends not to care.

Relationships in Combination and Conflict

Family issues rarely exist in isolation, of course. For instance, many of Shakespeare's plays deal with both marriage and parent–child bonds, often showing the connections and conflicts between these two sets of relationships. *As You Like It*, along with various other comedies and romances, ends with a parent and child reunited and the child about to marry. As we have already seen, *Othello* and *The Merchant of Venice* each include a daughter who elopes and whose father disapproves of the marriage because of cultural differences. The emphasis on the daughter's Jewish heritage in modern productions of *The Merchant of Venice* complicates both her marriage and her relationship with her father. Some plays add sibling relationships to the mix: for instance, *The Comedy of Errors*, with an entire family reunited, and *The Taming of the Shrew*, with sibling rivalry added to parent–child conflict and a tempestuous courtship. *Hamlet* presents an even fuller array of family dynamics, adding Claudius's roles of uncle and stepfather (and Hamlet's corresponding roles of nephew and stepson) to the list of courtship, marriage, parent–child, and sibling bonds.

Part of what makes Shakespeare's so-called problem comedies problematic is the way they connect and stretch a variety of family relationships. One of these plays—*Measure for Measure*—has had a number of interesting and sometimes controversial modern productions focusing on the play's sibling bonds and prospective marriages. The crucial moment for the play's siblings is in act 3, scene 1, when Isabella visits her brother Claudio, who is in prison, condemned to death for fornication. Some have claimed that, from a modern point of view, Isabella's desire to preserve her chastity does not give her sufficient motivation to turn on her brother when he asks her to give herself to Angelo in exchange for his life. Yet contemporary feminist attitudes have, if anything, heightened audiences' sympathy with Isabella and her efforts to resist pressure from men.

Modern directors have to decide how angry to make Isabella as well as how close the sibling bond should be before it is threatened. A 2003 RSC production made the bond weak and relatively unemotional, except for the anger. Aside

Isabella (Estelle Kohler) slaps her brother Claudio (Ben Kingsley) in a 1970 production of *Measure for Measure* by the Royal Shakespeare Company. Reg Wilson. Royal Shakespeare Company.

from a brief embrace midway through the scene, Isabella and Claudio speak from a distance. Isabella is stern from the start, and when she realizes Claudio is willing to have her lose her chastity, she strikes him—an action that also took place in a 1970 RSC production. Apart from these two memorable instances, however, such physical violence is a rarity in modern interpretations of the scene, and though all productions make Isabella angry, most set this anger in contrast to the strong affection between siblings demonstrated earlier and later in the play.

Another controversial moment is at the end when the Duke proposes marriage to Isabella. Traditionally, Isabella yields happily to the proposal, despite being given no lines to speak. Nineteenth-century productions in particular made the last scene more romantic by adding stage business (for instance, having the Duke kiss Isabella's hand) and expanding his proposal to include gallant explanations and an extended expression of his passion. Modern productions, by contrast, often make Isabella's response ambivalent, if not clearly negative. In John Barton's 1970 RSC production, for instance, Isabella responded to the proposal with what appeared to be shocked silence and then was left on stage, alone and apparently confused—an ending imitated by later productions, including the 1975 version at Canada's acclaimed Stratford Festival Theatre.

Though having Isabella reject the proposal might seem a modern innovation, the text as Shakespeare wrote it gives several openings for such a response. For one thing, the text gives Isabella nothing to say. Furthermore, the Duke proposes twice, and he interrupts the first proposal by saying, "But fitter time for that." Even productions that end with Isabella kissing the Duke may make Isabella's response to the first proposal unclear—for instance (as in Adrian Noble's 1983 production), by having Isabella fail to offer her hand, though the Duke has just asked for it. In the 1979 BBC version made for television, Isabella—apparently taken off guard—gives no response to the first proposal and accepts the second (smiling and offering her hand) only after a long pause.

A powerful television production of the play (directed by David Thacker in 1994) has Isabella respond to the Duke's first proposal with uncertainty. Just after he proposes again—"I have a motion much imports your good, / Whereto if you'll a willing ear incline, / What's mine is yours, and what is yours is mine"—the screen freezes on the picture of the two of them, alone on the stage, with Isabella still unresponsive. The production ends with this picture and thus leaves the issue completely unresolved.

An RSC stage production, also in 1994, was inconclusive in a more complicated way. The Duke takes Isabella's hand when he first proposes, but she hardly notices because she is focused on her brother. When the Duke repeats the offer at the end, she slaps him, then kisses him, and then turns away as if ashamed or confused. The two then look at each other uncertainly as the lights go out.

Despite this tendency to make the ending inconclusive, recent productions of *Measure for Measure* have not been cynical about the family in general. Two of the most striking productions—the 1979 BBC television production and Thacker's 1994 version—add a positive detail to the conclusion: Juliet, Claudio's lover and now his wife, appears on stage holding their baby. In the BBC version, Juliet and Claudio embrace joyfully, forming—along with their child—the beginnings of a family. Sexual activity, troubled and sordid through most of the play, is now shown to be, at least potentially, a source of life and love.

CONCLUSION

From Shakespeare's time to the present, changing performance conditions have influenced the presentation of family in his plays. Large theaters and lavish productions heavy on spectacle have generally portrayed family relationships with broad and simple strokes. Film is capable of both more spectacular and more intimate effects than the stage, and Shakespearean films have gone in both directions. During the late twentieth century, however, the trend both on stage and in film seems to have been toward greater intimacy and a corresponding emphasis on family as opposed to political or philosophical concerns. Branagh's film versions of *Hamlet* and *Much Ado*, for example, along with their visual appeal, emphasize the subtleties of courtship and marital and family relationships. According to one critic, the 1992 RSC production of *Hamlet* (starring Branagh and setting the stage for his film version) likewise "emphasized the domestic over the political, family over state" (Crowl 5).

This trend was prompted in part by new, often smaller performance spaces that allowed for more intimate performances. One such location was the Other Place, a theater in Stratford seating fewer than 150. In 1975, a memorable production of *Hamlet* in that theater, starring Ben Kingsley, used the increased intimacy to explore "the complexity of personal and family relationships in the play, indicating," according to Sally Beauman, "that the RSC was now moving away from the epic style of the Sixties, with its emphasis on relationships of state, to the interior world of the plays, to the network of cousins, brothers, fathers, daughters, and sons" (329–30). In a similar way, Trevor Nunn's 1989 production of *Othello*, also performed at the Other Place, used the setting to emphasize the play's domestic elements.

These are only a few examples of the ways changes in production practices have affected the way family is presented on stage or in film. The great variety of interpretations marking Shakespearean performances over the centuries obviously reflects changes in attitudes and, in some cases, customs related to family life. Yet beneath the variety, there has also been continuity, especially in the persistent appeal of Shakespeare's stories focused on family. The changes in interpretation have generally had more to do with changing fashions in theatrical production and acting style than with a fundamental shift in values.

But changing attitudes have left their mark, from the desire for an orderly, simplified vision of family life in the generation after Shakespeare to the sentimentalizing of family during the nineteenth century to the more casual and questioning attitudes that followed. As the family came under fire during the twentieth century, a number of bleak, cynical, or sexually explicit productions seemed to reflect the beleaguered state of the family or sometimes to join in the attack. The return to more affirmative interpretations by the end of the century suggests not only that the family has survived but that it continues to be valued by most audiences.

During the past few decades, actors and directors have made it clear that they view Shakespeare's plays as relevant to modern-day marriage and family life. Commenting on his own 1994–95 production of *King Lear,* Adrian Noble praised Shakespeare's ability to combine the particular and the universal and compared Lear to a contemporary father awakening from an accident to see an estranged daughter. While preparing to play Leontes in *The Winter's Tale* (1998–99), Antony Sher became persuaded that the play accurately portrays a medical condition known as "morbid jealousy" that often afflicts men in their forties. Gregory Doran, who directed the production, likewise viewed the play as relevant to modern audiences, not only because it provides acute psychological insights but also because it appeals to "a profound desire in everyone, the desire for there to be a second chance, for there to be forgiveness, for there to be some kind of redemption" ("Casebook").

One lesson to be drawn from this survey of Shakespearean performances is that the plays are so rich and variable that every age can find relevance in them. Especially from the mid-twentieth century onward, Shakespearean productions have drawn on the diversity within the plays to portray family life in every mode ranging from painful realism to transcendent idealism and often mixing elements from both ends of the spectrum. Especially on a global scale, Shakespeare's appeal has never been greater than at present, now that plays are available on film as well as on stage. Much of that appeal certainly has to do with how the plays can be used in production, often with great insight and emotional power, to depict the various dimensions of family life.

REFERENCES

Aya, Mimura. "Japanese Rock Opera *Hamlet*." 1998. 21 Aug. 2008. http://sia.stanford.edu/japan/INTRO/ROCKHAML.HTM.

Barnet, Sylvan. "*Romeo and Juliet* on Stage and Screen." *Romeo and Juliet*. By William Shakespeare. Ed. J. A. Bryant Jr. The Signet Classic Shakespeare. New York: New American Library, 1987. 227–38.

Beauman, Sally. *The Royal Shakespeare Company: A History of Ten Decades*. Oxford: Oxford University Press, 1982.

"Casebook." The Royal Shakespeare Company Production of *The Winter's Tale:* The Complete Edition. DVD. Heritage Theatre, 1999.

Crowl, Samuel. "Hamlet 'Most Royal': An Interview with Kenneth Branagh." *Shakespeare Bulletin* 12.4 (1994): 5–8.

Dawson, Anthony B. *Hamlet: Shakespeare in Performance*. Manchester: Manchester University Press, 1995.

Digges, Leonard. "Poets are borne not made" (1640). *The Riverside Shakespeare*. Ed. G. Blakemore Evans, J.J.M. Tobin, et al. 2nd ed. Boston: Houghton Mifflin, 1997. Appendix C, item 26. 1972.

[Lear's rebirth.] Notes (describing a scene in *King Lear,* New Delhi, India, Feb. 22–25 and March 2–4, 1989, directed by Amal Allana) on photograph P.72.17/1989 India Delhi, at the Shakespeare Centre Library, Stratford, England.

Marston, John. Excerpt from *The Scourge of Villaine* (1598). *The Riverside Shakespeare*. Ed. G. Blakemore Evans, J.J.M. Tobin, et al. 2nd ed. Boston: Houghton Mifflin, 1997. Appendix C, item 15A. 1963.

Miller, Jonathan, and Tim Hallinan. "Interview: Jonathan Miller on the Shakespeare Plays." *Shakespeare Quarterly* 32 (1981): 134–45.

Noble, Adrian. Commentary on *King Lear* (1994–95). *Great Performances Volume 1*. The Royal Shakespeare Company. Videocassette. Princeton, NJ: Films for the Humanities & Sciences, 1995.

Rosenberg, Marvin. *The Masks of Hamlet*. Newark: University of Delaware Press, 1992.

———. *The Masks of King Lear*. Berkeley: University of California Press, 1972.

"Sir Peter Hall Directs Shakespeare's Last Plays." *South Bank Show*. Dir. Chris Hunt. London Weekend Television. ITV, London. 24 Apr. 1988.

Speaight, Robert. *Shakespeare on the Stage: An Illustrated History of Shakespearian Performance*. Boston: Little, Brown, 1973.

Tillotson, Geoffrey. "*Othello* and *The Alchemist* at Oxford." *Times Literary Supplement* 20 July 1933. Cited in Marvin Rosenberg, *The Masks of Othello: The Search for the Identity of Othello, Iago, and Desdemona by Three Centuries of Actors and Critics*. Berkeley: University of California Press, 1961. 5.

Tofte, Robert. Excerpt from *Alba: The Month's Mind of a Melancholy Lover* (1598). *The Riverside Shakespeare*. 2nd ed. Ed. G. Blakemore Evans, J.J.M. Tobin, et al. Boston: Houghton Mifflin, 1997. Appendix C, item 15B. 1964.

Young, Bruce. "Parental Blessings in Shakespeare's Plays." *Studies in Philology* 89 (1992): 179–210.

Stage, Film, and Television Productions and Adaptations

All's Well That Ends Well. Dir. Barry Kyle. Perf. Gwen Watford and Paul Venables. Royal Shakespeare Company. Royal Shakespeare Theatre, Stratford-upon-Avon. Oct. 10, 1989.

All's Well That Ends Well. Dir. Elijah Moshinsky. British Broadcasting Company, 1981.

All's Well That Ends Well. Dir. Gregory Doran. Perf. Judi Dench. Royal Shakespeare Company. Gielgud Theatre, London. Feb. 18, 2004.

As You Like It. Dir. Christine Edzard. Sands Films, 1992.

As You Like It. Dir. Gregory Thompson. Royal Shakespeare Theatre, Stratford-upon-Avon. Mar. 20, 2003.

As You Like It. Dir. Kenneth Branagh. BBC Films, 2007.

Catharine and Petruchio. Dir. David Garrick. London, 1754. (Adaptation of *The Taming of the Shrew*.)

Comedy of Errors. Dir. Philip Casson. Writ. Trevor Nunn. Royal Shakespeare Company. Independent Television (ITV). Apr. 18, 1978.

The Comedy of Errors. Dir. Tim Supple. Royal Shakespeare Company. The Other Place, Stratford-upon-Avon. July 3, 1996.

Coriolanus. Dir. David Thacker. Royal Shakespeare Company. Swan Theatre, Stratford-upon-Avon. May 24, 1994; Newcastle Playhouse, Newcastle-upon-Tyne. Mar. 3–19, 1995.

Coriolanus. Dir. Gregory Doran. Royal Shakespeare Company. Royal Shakespeare Theatre, Stratford-upon-Avon. Mar. 6–31, 2007.

Coriolanus. Dir. Henry Woronicz. Utah Shakespearean Festival. Adams Shakespearean Theatre, Cedar City, UT. June 21–Sept. 1, 2007.

Coriolanus: The Roman Matron. Attrib. Thomas Sheridan. Covent Garden, London. Dec. 1754. (Adaptation of *Coriolanus*.)

Davenant, William. *The Law Against Lovers*. Lincoln's Inn Fields, London. 1662. (Adaptation of *Much Ado about Nothing* and *Measure for Measure*.)

Davenant, William, and John Dryden. *The Tempest; Or, the Enchanted Island*. London. 1670. (Adaptation of *The Tempest*.)

Dryden, John. *Troilus and Cressida*. London. 1679. (Adaptation of *Troilus and Cressida*.)

Fletcher, John. *The Tamer Tamed or, The Woman's Prize*. 1611. ("Sequel" to *The Taming of the Shrew*.)

Hamlet. Dir. Bill Colleran and John Gielgud. Perf. Richard Burton. Video by NFTA/BFI. Electronovision Theatrofilm, 1964.

Hamlet. Dir. Celestino Coronado. Perf. Anthony Meyer and David Meyer. Royal College of Art, 1976.

Hamlet. Dir. Franco Zeffirelli. Perf. Mel Gibson and Glenn Close. Warner Bros., 1990.

Hamlet. Dir. Grigori Kozintsev. Lenfilm Studios, 1964.

Hamlet. Dir. Joseph Papp. Public Theater, New York. 1968.

Hamlet. Dir. Kenneth Branagh. Castle Rock Entertainment, 1996.

Hamlet. Dir. Laurence Olivier. Carlton International Media Limited, 1948.

Hamlet. Dir. Michael Almereyda. Perf. Ethan Hawke and Julia Stiles. Miramax, 2000.

Hamlet. Dir. Michael Boyd. Royal Shakespeare Company. Royal Shakespeare Theatre, Stratford-upon-Avon. July 21–Oct. 16, 2004; Theatre Royal, Newcastle-upon-Tyne. Nov. 1–6, 2004; Arlbery Theatre, London. Nov. 23–Dec. 11, 2004.

Hamlet. Dir. Peter Brook. Facets Video, 2001.

Hamlet. Dir. Richard Eyre. Perf. Jonathan Pryce. Royal Court Theatre, London. Apr. 1980.

Hamlet. Dir. Rodney Bennett. Perf. Derek Jacobi, Patrick Stewart, and Claire Bloom. British Broadcasting Company, 1980.

Hamlet. Dir. Tyrone Guthrie. Old Vic, London. 1936–37, 1938–39, 1943–44.

Hamlet. Dir. Wilson Barrett. Princess Theatre, London. Oct. 16, 1884.

King Lear. Dir. Adrian Noble. Perf. Robert Stephens. Royal Shakespeare Company. Royal Shakespeare Theatre, Stratford-upon-Avon. May 5, 1993.

King Lear. Dir. Adrian Noble. Royal Shakespeare Company. Theatre Royal, Newcastle-upon-Tyne. Feb. 21–26, 1994; Barbican Theatre, London. May 31, 1994.

King Lear. Dir. Alfred Preisser. Classical Theatre of Harlem. Folger Theatre, Washington DC. Jan. 11–Feb. 18, 2007.

King Lear. Dir. Amal Allana. Pragati Maidan, New Delhi, India. Feb. 22–25, Mar. 2–4, 1989.

King Lear. (*Jikken Ongaku Geki: Ria O—An Experimental Musical Play: King Lear*.) Dir. J. A. Seazer. Ban'yu Inryoko. Panasonic Globe Theatre, Tokyo. Aug. 15, 1991. (Adaptation of *King Lear*.)

King Lear. Dir. Jonathan Miller. British Broadcasting Company, 1982.

King Lear. Dir. Michael Elliot. Perf. Laurence Olivier. Kultur, 1984.

King Lear. Dir. Peter Brook. Perf. Paul Scofield. Columbia Pictures, 1971.

King Lear. Dir. William Charles Macready. Covent Garden, London. Jan. 25, 1838.

King of Texas. Dir. Uli Edel. Perf. Patrick Stewart. Turner Network Television, 2002. (Adaptation of *King Lear*.)

King Richard the Second. Dir. David Giles. British Broadcasting Company, 1978.

The Life and Death of King John. Dir. David Giles. British Broadcasting Company, 1984.

Macbeth. Dir. Gregory Doran. Perf. Antony Sher and Harriet Walter. Royal Shakespeare Company. The Roundhouse, London. Channel 4. Jan. 1, 2001.

Macbeth. Dir. Gregory Doran. Royal Shakespeare Company. Swan Theatre, Stratford-upon-Avon. Nov. 16, 1999.

Macbeth. Dir. Henry Irving. Perf. Ellen Terry. Lyceum Theatre, London. Dec. 29, 1888.

Macbeth. Dir. Jeremy Freeston. Perf. Jason Connery and Helen Baxendale. CJP Public Relations, 1997.

Macbeth. Dir. Trevor Nunn. Perf. Ian McKellen and Judi Dench. Royal Shakespeare Company. A&E, 1978.

Macbeth. Dir. William Charles Macready. Perf. Helen Faucit. Dublin. May 28, 1842.

Macbeth. Trans. M. Jean Richepin. Perf. Sarah Bernhardt. Edinburgh. June 1884.

Measure for Measure. Dir. Adrian Noble. Royal Shakespeare Company. Royal Shakespeare Theatre, Stratford-upon-Avon. Oct. 4, 1983.

Measure for Measure. Dir. David Thacker. British Broadcasting Company. Nov. 5, 1994.

Measure for Measure. Dir. Desmond Davis. British Broadcasting Company, 1979.

Measure for Measure. Dir. John Barton. Royal Shakespeare Company. Royal Shakespeare Theatre, Stratford-upon-Avon. Apr. 1, 1970.

Measure for Measure. Dir. Sean Holmes. Royal Shakespeare Company. Royal Shakespeare Theatre, Stratford-upon-Avon. May 2, 2003; Theatre Royal, Newcastle-upon-Tyne. Nov. 25, 2003.

Measure for Measure. Dir. Steven Pimlott. Royal Shakespeare Company. Royal Shakespeare Theatre, Stratford-upon-Avon. Oct. 20, 1994.

Measure for Measure, or Beauty the Best Advocate. Dir. Charles Gildon. 1700. (Adaptation of *Measure for Measure*.)

Merchant of Venice. Dir. Chris Hunt and Trevor Nunn. The Performance Company, 2001.

The Merchant of Venice. Dir. Jack Gold. British Broadcasting Company, 1980.

Merchant of Venice. Dir. and Adapt. John Sichel. Perf. Laurence Olivier. ITC Distribution, 1973.

Merry Wives: The Musical. Dir. Gregory Doran. Perf. Judi Dench. Royal Shakespeare Company. Royal Shakespeare Theatre, Stratford-upon-Avon. Dec. 2–Feb. 10, 2007. (Adaptation of *The Merry Wives of Windsor*.)

A Midsummer Night's Dream. Dir. Adrian Noble. Royal Shakespeare Company. Royal Shakespeare Theatre, Stratford-upon-Avon. Aug. 3, 1994.

A Midsummer Night's Dream. Dir. Peter Brook. Royal Shakespeare Company. Roundhouse Theatregoround Festival. Oct. 29–Dec. 12, 1970.

Morgan, Elaine. *The Tamer Tamed*. British Broadcasting Company. Feb. 7, 1956. ("Sequel" to *The Taming of the Shrew*.)

Much Ado about Nothing. Dir. Kenneth Branagh. MGM Home Entertainment, 1993.

Much Ado about Nothing. Dir. Marianne Elliot. Swan Theatre, Stratford-upon-Avon. May 18, 2006.

Othello. Dir. Elijah Moshinsky. Perf. Anthony Hopkins, Bob Hoskins, and Penelope Wilton. British Broadcasting Company, 1981.

Othello. Dir. Janet Suzman. Perf. John Kani. Market Theatre, Johannesburg. 1988.

Othello. Dir. Jude Kelly. Perf. Patrick Stewart. Shakespeare Theatre Company. Lansburgh Theatre, Washington DC. 1997.

Othello. Dir. Stuart Burge. Perf. Laurence Olivier. Eagle Films, 1965.

Othello. Dir. Trevor Nunn. Perf. Ian McKellen and Imogen Stubbs. Primetime Television Ltd. June 23, 1990.

Othello. Dir. Trevor Nunn. Royal Shakespeare Company. The Other Place, Stratford-upon-Avon. Aug. 24, 1989.

Othello. Perf. Edwin Booth, Henry Irving, and Ellen Terry. Lyceum Theatre, London. 1881.

Otway, Thomas. *The History and Fall of Caius Marius*. Dorset Garden Theatre, London. 1680. (Adaptation of *Romeo and Juliet*.)

Pericles. Dir. Adrian Noble. Royal Shakespeare Company. The Roundhouse, London. July 5–13, 2002. Royal Shakespeare Theatre, Stratford-upon-Avon. Aug. 8–Nov. 2, 2002.

Pericles. Dir. Samuel Phelps. Sadler's Wells Theatre, Islington. 1854.

Richard III. Dir. Richard Loncraine. Perf. Ian McKellen. United Artists, 1995.

Romeo+Juliet. Dir. Baz Luhrmann. Perf. Leonardo DiCaprio and Claire Danes. Twentieth Century Fox, 1997.

Romeo and Juliet. Dir. David Garrick. Drury Lane and Covent Garden, London. 1748.

Romeo and Juliet. Dir. Franco Zeffirelli. BHE Films, 1968.

Romeo and Juliet. Dir. Michael Bogdanov. Royal Shakespeare Company. Royal Shakespeare Theatre, Stratford-upon-Avon. Apr. 8, 1986.

Romeo and Juliet. Perf. Charlotte Cushman. The Haymarket, London. 1845.

The Shrew. Dir. Charles Marowitz. Perf. Thelma Holt and Malcolm Tierney. Open Space Theatre, London. 1973. (Adaptation of *The Taming of the Shrew*.)

The Taming of the Shrew. Dir. Augustin Daly. Daly's Theatre on Broadway, New York. 1887.

The Taming of the Shrew. Dir. Franco Zeffirelli. Perf. Elizabeth Taylor and Richard Burton. Columbia Pictures, 1967.

The Taming of the Shrew. Dir. Gale Edwards. Royal Shakespeare Company. Royal Shakespeare Theatre, Stratford-upon-Avon. Apr. 21, 1995.

The Taming of the Shrew. Dir. Gregory Doran. Royal Shakespeare Company. Royal Shakespeare Theatre, Stratford-upon-Avon. Apr. 4–Nov. 8, 2003.

The Taming of the Shrew. Dir. John Lacy. Theatre Royal, London. 1667.

The Taming of the Shrew. Dir. Jonathan Miller. British Broadcasting Company. Ambrose Video Publishing, 1980.

The Taming of the Shrew. Dir. Lindsay Posner. Royal Shakespeare Company. The Pit, London. Oct. 27, 1999.

The Taming of the Shrew. Dir. Michael Bogdanov. Royal Shakespeare Company. Royal Shakespeare Theatre, Stratford-upon-Avon. May 4, 1978.

The Taming of the Shrew. Dir. Sam Taylor. Perf. Mary Pickford and Douglas Fairbanks. United Artists, 1929.

Tate, Nahum. *The History of King Lear*. London, 1681. (Adaptation of *King Lear*.)

The Tempest. Dir. Adrian Noble. Royal Shakespeare Company. Theatre Royal, Newcastle-upon-Tyne. Oct. 6–10, 1998; Royal Shakespeare Theatre, Stratford-upon-Avon. Feb. 25, 1998; Theatre Royal, Plymouth. Nov. 10–14, 1998.

The Tempest. Dir. John Gorrie. British Broadcasting Company, 1980.

The Tempest. Dir. Peter Hall. Perf. John Gielgud. Old Vic, London. 1974.

Titus Andronicus. Dir. Jane Howell. British Broadcasting Company, 1985.

Titus Andronicus. Dir. Peter Brook. Royal Shakespeare Company. Shakespeare Memorial Theatre, Stratford-upon-Avon. Aug. 16, 1955.

The Tragedy of Coriolanus. Dir. Elijah Moshinsky. British Broadcasting Company, 1984.

The Tragedy of Macbeth. Dir. Roman Polanski. Perf. John Finch and Francesca Annis. Columbia Pictures, 1971.

The Tragedy of Othello, the Moor of Venice. Dir. Orson Welles. Mercury Productions, 1952.

The Tragedy of Richard the Third. Dir. Jane Howell. British Broadcasting Company, 1983.

Twelfth Night. Dir. John Sichel. Perf. Joan Plowright. Associated Television, 1969.

Twelfth Night. Dir. Sean Holmes. Perf. Polly Frame. Filter. The Cube, Royal Shakespeare Theatre, Stratford-upon-Avon. Nov. 2, 2006.

Twelfth Night. Dir. Trevor Nunn. Image Entertainment, 1996.

Vogel, Paula. *Desdemona: A Play about a Handkerchief*. New York, 1979.

William Shakespeare's The Tempest. Dir. Derek Jarman. Second Sight Films, 1979.
The Winter's Tale. Dir. Adrian Noble. Royal Shakespeare Company. Royal Shakespeare Theatre, Stratford-upon-Avon. July 1, 1992.
The Winter's Tale. Dir. Adrian Noble. Royal Shakespeare Company. Theatre Royal, Newcastle- upon-Tyne. Mar. 23–27, 1993.
The Winter's Tale. Dir. Gregory Doran. Perf. Antony Sher. Royal Shakespeare Company. Royal Shakespeare Theatre, Stratford-upon-Avon. Jan. 6–Feb. 26, 1999; Barbican Theatre, London. Mar. 25, 1999.
The Winter's Tale. Dir. Jane Howell. British Broadcasting Company, 1981.
The Winter's Tale. Dir. Matthew Warchus. Royal Shakespeare Company. The Roundhouse, London. Apr. 12, 2002; Royal Shakespeare Theatre, Stratford-upon-Avon. July 31, 2002.
The Winter's Tale. Dir. Peter Brook. Phoenix Theatre, London, 1951.
The Winter's Tale. Dir. Robert A. Nelson. Brigham Young University, Provo, UT. 1990.
The Winter's Tale. Dir. Terry Hands. Royal Shakespeare Company. Royal Shakespeare Theatre, Stratford-upon-Avon. Apr. 30, 1986.
The Winter's Tale. Dir. Trevor Nunn. Perf. Judi Dench. Royal Shakespeare Company. Royal Shakespeare Theatre, Stratford-upon-Avon. May 15, 1969.

5

SCHOLARSHIP AND CRITICISM

Family has always been one of the concerns of Shakespearean criticism, though naturally it figures more prominently for some critics than for others. As critical fashions have changed, so has the place of the family. At times it has been considered one of the great universals of human experience that Shakespeare excelled in portraying, at other times a social construction shaped by the conditions of its culture. Critics have also differed as to whether family life, either in the plays or in Shakespeare's time, should be called happy or unhappy and whether the family provides a strong or fragile foundation for human life. Some have sought to set the family in the context of Shakespeare's time; others, in the context of more general psychological or social patterns. Still others have preferred to view it aesthetically or morally.

Several themes recur in the course of Shakespearean criticism, though with occasional but significant disagreement: Shakespeare's skill in rendering family life believable and moving; his moral insight; and his potent dramatic, symbolic, and even philosophical uses of the family. The effect of race and gender on family life has been a concern from the beginning. Some early critics, especially in the first part of the nineteenth century, were troubled by the idea of interracial marriage in *Othello*. Shakespeare's female characters have always drawn attention, viewed at times as ideal wives, mothers, daughters, and sisters, but with the advent of feminist criticism, viewed either as trapped by historical expectations or as defying them. With more accurate and sympathetic study of early modern life, instead of being identified with either of these polar opposites, they have come to be seen as having something of the variety of actual women in Shakespeare's time or ours.

Some critics have attempted to identify Shakespeare's values—his attitudes about family's role in life, about individuals' roles in the family, and about the sources of family's capacity to bless or do harm. Some view Shakespeare as a source of help with current challenges; others see him as part of the problem. Despite disagreement on such issues, most Shakespearean critics from his time onward have viewed his treatment of family as being relevant in one way or another to present concerns.

THE SEVENTEENTH AND EIGHTEENTH CENTURIES

The earliest recorded comments on Shakespeare's plays date from the 1590s, but such comments remain relatively brief until the later 1600s. Those who wrote about Shakespeare in the later 1600s and early 1700s often noted his skill in representing human nature and emotion. Though they rarely discussed Shakespeare's depictions of family directly, sometimes they singled out emotions especially relevant to courtship and marriage, such as romantic love and jealousy, and some commented on Shakespeare's ability to create convincing male and female characters.

Writing in 1664, Margaret Cavendish praised Shakespeare for describing his characters so well that "Readers might think they were Well acquainted with them," even giving the impression that he "had been Transformed into every one of those Persons he hath Described" (14). She prefigures Virginia Woolf, who in the twentieth century wrote of Shakespeare's "androgynous mind" (Woolf 98–99), by saying that Shakespeare seems to have "been Metamorphosed from a Man to a Woman," and she praises him for his vivid and realistic portraits of the wives in *The Merry Wives of Windsor,* Beatrice in *Much Ado*, and other female characters (Cavendish 14).

John Dryden, the leading English literary figure of the late 1600s, admired Shakespeare especially for his lively depictions of human nature, despite finding fault with his language. In an essay published in 1679, he bestowed special praise on Shakespeare's understanding of "the nature of the Passions" (18), including the passion of love (though he claimed Shakespeare excelled in "the more manly passions" [21]). A few years later, in an account of Shakespeare's life prefacing his edition of the plays (1709), Nicholas Rowe made a similar claim, praising Shakespeare's depiction of Ford's "unreasonable Jealousie" in *The Merry Wives of Windsor* (10). Rowe was one of the first to comment specifically on Shakespeare's treatment of family relationships. He interprets *Romeo and Juliet* as having as its dominant theme "the Punishment of [the] two Families, for the unreasonable Feuds and Animosities that had been so long kept up between 'em, and occasion'd the Effusion of so much Blood" (17–18). But he also praises the play for showing "something wonderfully Tender and Passionate in the Love-part" (18). Writing about *Hamlet*, he assumes that Gertrude was involved in the murder of her husband, something the play in fact leaves ambiguous. Rowe compares *Hamlet* to Sophocles' play *Electra* on the grounds that both include a guilty mother and a murdered father whose son must take revenge. But he notes a striking difference: whereas the son in Sophocles' play takes revenge on his mother, Hamlet is explicitly forbidden to do so. Though "he has the same Abhorrence for his Mother's Guilt, which, to provoke him the more, is heighten'd by Incest," Shakespeare "restrains him from doing Violence to his Mother" (18).

Not all writers of the period praised Shakespeare's depiction of marriage and family life. Thomas Rymer's notorious discussion of *Othello* (published in 1693) calls the play "a bloody farce" and mocks the lessons that he supposes one is to draw from the play. The "moral" of the play, he writes, is threefold: "First, this may be a caution to all maidens of quality how, without their parents' consent, they run away with blackamoors"; "secondly, this may be a warning to all good wives that they look well to their linen"—an allusion to Desdemona's stolen handkerchief; and finally, "this may be a lesson to husbands that before their jealousy be tragical the proofs be mathematical" (i.e., absolutely irrefutable) (210, 202). Rymer is especially critical of the role played by the handkerchief, seeing it as an inadequate cause for Othello's jealousy: "So much ado, so much stress, so much passion and repetition about a handkerchief. Why was not this called 'The Tragedy of the Handkerchief'? . . . Had it been Desdemona's garter, the sagacious Moor might have smelled a rat; but the handkerchief is so remote a trifle no booby on this side Mauritania could make any consequence from it" (208). The reference to Mauritania is an allusion to Othello's possible origin in northern Africa and hints at Rymer's racially biased view that reasonable Europeans would not have fallen into jealousy as easily as Othello does.

By the mid-eighteenth century, Shakespeare's works were acknowledged classics, and for the most part, critics continued to esteem his portrait of human nature as being realistic and universal. Writing about *The Tempest* in 1753, Joseph Warton praised his "intimate knowledge of the heart of man" (53) and listed as among the impressive features of the play "the resentment of Prospero for the matchless cruelty and wicked usurpation of his brother" and "his parental affection and solicitude for the welfare of his daughter" (58). He also found *King Lear* impressive, including its portrait of "the intolerable affronts, indignities and cruelties [Lear] suffers" from two of his daughters. He calls the daughters' lack of gratitude "unnatural," showing that the early modern concept of "natural" familial feeling was still alive 150 years after Shakespeare's time. Yet Warton wonders "whether the cruelty of the daughters is not painted with circumstances too savage and unnatural." Though such "monstrous barbarity" may at times occur in real life, he quotes Boileau as saying, "Some truths may be too strong to be believed" (60, 69).

In 1769, Elizabeth Montagu, an important figure in London literary and social circles, published *An Essay on the Writings and Genius of Shakespeare*, defending Shakespeare against the criticism of the French writer Voltaire. In the course of her essay, she notes Shakespeare's ability to convey tender feelings connected with family ties. Lady Macbeth, for instance, is realistically human as well as typically feminine, according to Montagu, in being unable to kill Duncan because "he resembled her father while he slept" (201). Macduff's response to the killing of his family is "a just imitation of natural sentiments on such a tender occasion" and, by being simple and brief, "is more pathetic than chosen terms and studied phrases" (202).

Probably the most important writer on Shakespeare during the eighteenth century was Samuel Johnson, who produced an edition of the plays (published in 1765) that included a famous preface and valuable notes. Like other critics of his time, Johnson discusses many aspects of the plays, including Shakespeare's moral and political insights and his fascinating and realistic characters. But more than many of his predecessors and contemporaries, Johnson emphasizes family relationships as well, arguing that Shakespeare's depiction of these relationships provides much of the plays' appeal. Earlier in the century, some had argued that King Lear goes mad because he has lost his royal dignity. But Johnson asserts that the play "would move our compassion but little, did we not rather consider the injured father than the degraded king" (*Selections* 240). Johnson refers with approval to another writer of the time, Arthur Murphy, who had argued that if we read the play carefully, it is clear that the "behaviour of [Lear's] Children is always uppermost in his Thoughts," far surpassing any concern he has with his kingdom. Johnson's emphasis on family in *King Lear* derives from his belief that literature is most effective when it appeals to the most general and foundational aspects of life. In a letter written in 1770, he argued that "the passions rise higher at domestick than at imperial tragedies"—we respond more powerfully, that is, to tragedies about common life in a family or household than to those about kings. This is so because "what is nearest us, touches us most" (*Letters* 1:345).

In the notes in his edition of Shakespeare, Johnson comments on many details related to family. He commends the double plot in *King Lear* for "connecting [Gloucester's] wicked son with [Lear's] wicked daughters" (*Selections* 239). He praises the "skill in human nature" shown in Shakespeare's depiction of love and jealousy in *Othello* (358). But he is less impressed by Shakespeare's "dark comedies" (*All's Well That Ends Well* and *Measure for Measure*), finding Bertram in *All's Well* an especially unattractive character "who marries Helen as a coward, and leaves her as a profligate: when she is [reported to be] dead by his unkindness, sneaks home to a second marriage, is accused by a woman whom he has wronged, defends himself by falshood [*sic*], and is dismissed to happiness" (148).

THE NINETEENTH CENTURY

Critics during the Romantic period admired Shakespeare for his psychological and moral insights and creative power. They began a trend that continued for a century or more of focusing on the inner life of particular characters, especially in the tragedies. For instance, writing in 1811, Charles Lamb described the plays as presenting "the internal workings and movements of a great mind, of an Othello or a Hamlet for instance" (191). Even when characters interact, that interaction, according to Lamb, is "only a medium" for revealing to us "the inner structure and workings of mind in a character" (194). Sometimes—for Lamb and for later critics—this emphasis on individual characters and their inner life meant ignoring the importance of family relationships in establishing those characters' identities and in shaping the plots. Lamb, who found stage productions too clumsy for conveying the plays' subtleties, preferred to enter into Lear's mind rather than contemplate his family circumstances. He considered the external action in *King Lear* "painful and disgusting": all we see is "an old man tottering about the stage . . . turned out of doors by his daughters in a rainy night," but in reading the play, by contrast, we are inside of Lear, experiencing his thoughts and feelings (204–5).

Though Lamb recognized that the characters' inner lives work themselves out in a context of relationships, he consistently emphasized the characters' perceptions. Viewing Hamlet as essentially noble, Lamb excuses his rough handling of Ophelia, arguing that his feelings for her, though ambivalent, are at core loving. *Othello* provides another example. Seeing a white woman in love with a black man on the stage is offensive, according to Lamb (a view others of the time, including Coleridge, shared), but as we read the play, Lamb says, "we see with Desdemona's eyes" and can overlook her husband's color (207).

The great Romantic poet and critic Samuel Taylor Coleridge shared Lamb's view that Shakespeare's plays are above all works of the imagination, yet he was quicker than Lamb to see their connection with real life. Like critics of the previous century, he views Shakespeare as writing of realities "grounded in our common nature" (Selected 241). Coleridge exaggerates Hamlet's status as a solitary intellect, but in dealing with other characters, he is sensitive to their familial roles. These are roles that acquire their meaning from universally shared feelings and moral judgments: "Shakespeare's fathers are roused by ingratitude, his husbands stung by unfaithfulness; in him, in short, the affections are wounded in those points in which all may, nay, must, feel" (238). Prospero is in some ways a fantastic character, yet "any thing that might have been disagreeable to us in the magician, is reconciled and shaded in the humanity and natural feelings of the father" (242). In Lear, he sees egotism that craves expressions of love and later "parental anguish from filial ingratitude" (254). In Othello, he sees not jealousy but the agonized disillusionment of a loving nature. He regards the young love in *Romeo and Juliet* as being true to life, including the way Romeo switches to Juliet from Rosaline, "a mere creation of his fancy" (251). Even Lady Macbeth views "no tie so tender as that which connected her with her babe" ("*Macbeth*" 219)—that is what makes her speech about being willing to dash its brains out so horrible. In these and other plays, Coleridge finds the expression of feelings that "[have] been, and ever will be, close and native to the heart of man" (Selected 254). Coleridge's emphasis on the emotions that accompany familial roles is not unusual. Critics from the 1600s on had mentioned such "passions" or emotions. What makes Coleridge's approach different is the way he enters into the subtleties and complexities of these emotions, seeing them as adapted to individual character and circumstances, even though they spring from our common human nature.

Critics during this period tended to neglect the historical context in which Shakespeare's plays were originally written. Shakespeare's women, for instance, especially the quieter and more passive ones, were supposedly expressions of the ideal essence of womanhood. William Hazlitt, Coleridge's contemporary, was unusual for his time in taking a different approach—namely, looking to historical circumstances to explain the "want of prominence and theatrical display in Shakespear's female characters." He grants that Shakespeare's women "seem to exist only in their attachment to others." Yet this is not because they represent the essence of womanhood. Rather, Hazlitt argues, the manners of Shakespeare's time prevented women from "exhibiting themselves in public, and confined them to the relations and charities of domestic life" (304–5). Although his explanation is in part right—women of Shakespeare's time did not normally act on the public stage, for instance—his comment shows that a lack of detailed historical information had begun to exaggerate in many people's minds the limitations imposed on early modern women.

Other critics noticed in Shakespeare's female characters something quite different from this image of quiet femininity and in fact viewed these characters as showing how women had been "emancipated, exalted, ennobled" with the advent of Christianity in comparison with previous ages and been made "the sister and co-equal of man." In this view, taken by Thomas De Quincey, Shakespeare's women are ideal in the sense that they anticipate a flowering of women's potential. Shakespeare's greatness includes his ability to portray "the beauty of the female mind" (342, 345).

German critics had begun to take an interest in Shakespeare starting in the late eighteenth century, and a translation of Shakespeare was soon undertaken by August Wilhelm Schlegel, one of the leading figures of German Romanticism. In 1808, as part of an influential series of lectures on Shakespeare and other writers, Schlegel commented on the importance of intense family feeling in *King Lear.* The happy ending of Nahum Tate's revised version of *King Lear,* which, as Schlegel notes, still ruled the stage in England, was inappropriate for a play whose entire aim, he argues, is to arouse compassion for the most intense suffering. Such suffering often involves feelings related to family. Lear "is dishonoured by the cruel ingratitude of his unnatural daughters" and left with nothing but "the capability of loving and suffering beyond measure." And "the meeting of Edgar with the blinded Gloster," he writes, "is equally heart-rending; nothing can be more affecting than to see the ejected son become the father's guide" (411–12). Schlegel also defends the play's double plot. Not only are the stories of the two families carefully connected, but in addition, "two such unheard-of examples" of filial betrayal "have the appearance of a great commotion in the moral world: the picture becomes gigantic, and fills us with such alarm as we should entertain at the idea that the heavenly bodies might one day fall from their appointed orbits" (412).

Through the remainder of the nineteenth century, many critics in England and elsewhere continued to focus on Shakespeare's characters and their feelings. Added to that was an increasing tendency to interpret the plays in moral terms. The German critic Gottfried Gervinus, for instance, faulted Othello and Desdemona for hiding their marriage from her father, who might have been pacified "if his daughter had not rebelled against him; and he might have given her in her new home his blessing, if not his good will" (qtd. in Eastman 121). Gervinus was only one among many who subjected family relationships to moral judgment as well as an analysis of feeling.

In England, the latter half of the nineteenth century included such Shakespearean critics as Edward Dowden, Algernon Swinburne, and Walter Pater. Dowden is best known for his speculative analysis of Shakespeare's personality. But his criticism also includes much acute insight into Shakespeare's characters and dramatic craftsmanship, as well as into the plays' ethical implications. A few examples related to family must stand for the wide range of his comments. What Dowden says about Ophelia may seem one-sided and sentimental: she is "Laertes' little sister," "a tender little fragile soul" who can do nothing for Hamlet (138). But most of the comments are illuminating. Juliet "deliver[s] Romeo from his dream of self-conscious egoistic feeling into the reality of anguish and of joy" (138). Helena in *All's Well That Ends Well*, allowed to choose a husband for herself, "impose[s] herself on Bertram as the blessing that he requires" (88). Shakespeare attributes only "one human tie" to Richard III, a "memory of his father" that "supplies him with a family pride which, however, does not imply attachment or loyalty to any member of his house": "contemptuous to his mother, indifferent to the life or death of [his brothers] Clarence and Edward, except as their life or death may serve his own attempt upon the crown, cynically loveless towards his feeble and unhappy wife, Richard admires with an enthusiastic admiration his great father" (188). In such comments as these, Dowden shows not only the significance of family ties but also the ethical and psychological particularities of specific relationships in the plays.

The poet Algernon Swinburne took a more aesthetically attuned approach, but he also comments on characters and their relationships, sometimes noting details relevant to family life. In connection with *Coriolanus*, for instance, he makes a perceptive comment echoing Samuel Johnson's view of *King Lear*: *Coriolanus* is "rather a private and domestic than a public or historical tragedy. . . . The subject of the whole play is not the exile's revolt, the rebel's repentance, or the traitor's reward, but above all it is the son's tragedy." That tragedy, Swinburne says, can be summed up with an inscription to "Volumnia Victrix" (qtd. In Eastman 153)—that is, the hero's mother Volumnia is the "victrix" (feminine form of "victor") because she has overpowered her son and thereby caused his downfall.

Walter Pater, another important critic from the last part of the century, reveals some of the limitations from which an aesthetic approach suffers when dealing with family relationships. Rather than looking at *Romeo and Juliet* from a historical, ethical, or psychological point of view as the story of young love or of two families in conflict, he calls the play a "perfect symphony," a dramatic poem "approach[ing] to something like the unity of a lyrical ballad, a lyric, a song, a single strain of music" (210–11). In another essay, Pater calls "the relation of Claudio and Isabella" the "main interest in *Measure for Measure*," noting how "Isabella plays upon Claudio's well-recognized sense of honour" and how her "ardent natural affection" for her brother is "poured as sudden hatred" on him when "he welcomes for a moment the chance of life through his sister's shame" (183–87). Yet apart from these brief comments, there is little in Pater's essay about the brother–sister relation itself. For the most part, the two characters stand in splendid isolation, analyzed for their individual qualities and the impression these qualities make on readers.

George Bernard Shaw began writing about Shakespeare in the late nineteenth century and continued well into the twentieth. He had a distinctly modern skepticism about Shakespeare's greatness. *Othello* is an operatic rather than realistic picture of a marriage. The characters in *As You Like It* are not like real people but are mere stage figures. On the other hand, the fortune-hunting Petruchio of *The Taming of the Shrew*, in wanting to "take an ugly and ill-tempered woman off her father's hands," is "an honest and masterly picture of a real man, whose like we have all met." But Shaw finds the last scene, with Kate's speech about a wife's duty, "altogether disgusting" (*Dramatic Opinions* 361). At the same time, Shaw was one of the first modern critics to appreciate Shakespeare's "dark comedies," viewing the complicated marriage relationship in *All's Well*, for instance, as comparable to the marriages in Ibsen's problem plays.

Shaw had famously mixed feelings about *Cymbeline*. He praises Posthumus for criticizing "slavery to an inhuman ideal of marital fidelity" but calls most of the last act "a tedious string of unsurprising *dénouements* sugared with insincere sentimentality" ("Foreword to *Cymbeline Refinished*" 135). In fact, Shaw's revised version of the last act, *Cymbeline Refinished* (1936), instead of presenting a series of happy family reunions and reconciliations, leaves many of the complications unresolved. Cymbeline's long-lost sons, for instance, are not inclined to accept him as their father. And Imogen refuses to forgive her husband for losing faith in her and trying to have her killed.

Shaw's approach illustrates how changing attitudes about gender and family affected Shakespearean criticism on these subjects. Throughout most of the nineteenth century and even before, most critics had assumed that familial feelings were natural and that criticism of Shakespeare's portrayal of family life could be grounded on universally accepted moral norms. In the course of the nineteenth century, these attitudes remained relatively constant, even as various changes in emphasis took place—for instance, the analysis of character became more subtle, and some critics stressed characters' inner life while others looked more at their relationships. But as Shaw's criticism reveals, by the early twentieth century, conventional ideas about family were being subjected to questioning, so that characters and scenes to which readers and viewers had previously responded positively could now be reinterpreted either as negative or as irrelevant to modern life. Though many disagreed with Shaw's pronouncements, it was clear that his criticism signaled fundamental changes in social attitudes.

THE TWENTIETH CENTURY AND BEYOND

The twentieth century saw a series of changes in critical fashion, along with great variety at every stage. All of these affected the interpretation of family in Shakespeare's plays. Early critics treated the plays realistically and continued the nineteenth-century tradition of analyzing the characters' inner lives. Later, in reaction, critics of a formalist bent looked at the plays as dramatic structures that made sense without reference to the outside world and at the characters as elements in those structures rather than as imitations of real people. By the end of the century, a host of new approaches had arisen, from archetypal criticism to deconstruction and feminism.

The twentieth century was also a period of intense historical research. Such research had begun in the nineteenth century and even before, but it became a much stronger element in Shakespearean criticism in the twentieth century. Family relationships came to be interpreted in terms of what were assumed to be the attitudes and practices of Shakespeare's time. Unfortunately, little information was easily available until later in the century, and when historians of the family began to make their pioneering contributions in the 1960s and 1970s, some of their early work gave an inaccurate and unbalanced view of family life that left a lasting mark on Shakespearean criticism. That trend began to change in the 1990s. Though some studies still depend on earlier and more negative sources, critics are increasingly aware that recent historical work has provided a more balanced and complicated picture of early modern family life.

The Early Twentieth Century

Two critics early in the century, Leo Tolstoy and A. C. Bradley, took very different approaches. Tolstoy, who had become disillusioned with much of the literary tradition, including his own earlier work, attacked Shakespeare in an essay published in 1906. Like Shaw, he believed that Shakespeare's plays are morally faulty and often poorly written. He focuses on *King Lear,* arguing for the superiority of an earlier anonymous version of the story—a version, incidentally, that had a happy ending (like Nahum Tate's later revision of Shakespeare's play). The family relationships in *King Lear,* he says, like the jumble of sensational incidents they are part of, lack rational, let alone moral, grounding and are unworthy of imitation. According to Tolstoy, "the reader, or spectator, can not conceive that a King, however old and stupid he may be, could believe the words of the vicious daughters, with whom he had passed his whole life, and not believe his favorite daughter, but curse and banish her." As a result, no one can identify with the characters or "share [their] feelings" (14). The characters all speak a "pretentious, and unnatural language," including Lear when he says "that he would divorce his wife in the grave should Regan not receive him," something that, Tolstoy says, "no living men could or can say" (53). The scene of reconciliation "between Lear and his daughter [Cordelia] might have been touching," though not as good as in the earlier play, if not preceded by the stupidity and monotony of what had gone before. In the last scene, Lear "continues to utter the same senseless, inappropriate words, as, for example, that in prison he will sing with Cordelia, she will ask his blessing, and he will kneel down" and "ask her forgiveness" (39–41). Tolstoy offers abundant additional examples to make his point.

About the same time, A. C. Bradley published what has proven to be one of the century's most influential books of criticism, *Shakespearean Tragedy* (1904). Bradley deals thoroughly with four of Shakespeare's tragedies as well as with the impression these plays make on us. He also offers exhaustive discussions of the characters. Though he has been accused of being overly literal-minded, in fact he is aware that these tragedies are only plays.

Family is not one of the main concerns of his criticism, but he touches on it repeatedly when his discussion of other matters requires it. A few examples: On the basis of textual evidence, he defends Gertrude from culpability in her husband's death but calls her a "very dull and very shallow" woman, with "a soft animal nature" (Bradley 141). He argues that Hamlet's love for Ophelia is sincere but, after she rejects him, "mingled with suspicion and resentment" (133). Hamlet is engaged in a "work of vengeance" that he finds "repugnant" but is "at home" in the "higher work" of trying to save his mother's soul (115). Bradley traces the course of Othello's jealousy and argues there is no reason to condemn Desdemona as an undutiful daughter or for marrying outside her race. He discusses the relationship and motivations of Lear and Cordelia (including her unwillingness to bend in the first scene) and also of Gloucester and his sons. Lady Macbeth is arguably "the most commanding and perhaps the most awe-inspiring figure that Shakespeare drew," yet she has "traces of feminine weakness and human feeling" (322, 325). In notes at the end of the book, Bradley discusses where Hamlet was when his father died, Othello's courtship (suggesting that Desdemona is not as forward as the text makes her seem), Iago's suspicions about his wife, Lear's reunion with Cordelia, the phrase "he has no children" (applied to Macbeth), and other matters. Throughout, Bradley provides a rich context for interpreting family issues, combining character criticism with attention to relationships, dramatic construction, and the general atmosphere of each play. Though in general his view of family in the plays reflects traditional attitudes, he subjects every element of the plays to rigorous analysis and thereby makes clear to what extent these attitudes are grounded in the details of the text.

In an essay published in 1933, L. C. Knights implicitly criticizes Bradley with the title *How Many Children Had Lady Macbeth?*—a question, incidentally, that Bradley never asks and that Knights never discusses either. Knights's point is that Shakespeare's plays are "dramatic poems" that must be understood as structures of themes and values, not as reflections of real life. One effect of this essay was that character criticism of the traditional kind became far less popular during the remainder of the century, especially criticism of the kind that had speculated about the early home life of characters and other details not specified in the texts.

The view Knights presents had in certain respects been anticipated by T. S. Eliot in an essay titled "Hamlet and His Problems" (1919). Eliot argues that the problems are not so much with the character as with the play, which "is most certainly an artistic failure." The play deals "with the effect of a mother's guilt upon her son," but according to Eliot, "Shakespeare was unable to impose this motive successfully" on the material he derived from earlier versions of the story. As a result, "Hamlet (the man) is dominated by an emotion which is inexpressible, because it is in *excess* of the facts as they appear." He is confronted by "the difficulty that his disgust is occasioned by his mother, but that his mother is not an adequate equivalent for it"—for one thing, Gertrude's guilt is implied rather than clearly delineated. This makes the play an artistic failure because successful drama must provide something concrete—what Eliot calls "an *objective correlative*"—to evoke the desired emotions (788–90). Eliot speculates that Shakespeare's attempt to express the inexpressible must have derived from some experience of his life, probably related to his own family relationships. Thus, despite Eliot's emphasis on *Hamlet*'s formal qualities, he also points, at least indirectly, to common human emotions and relationships to which such qualities must be linked if a play is to achieve artistic success.

As Eliot's essay and many others indicate, criticism that viewed characters as part of a dramatic structure continued to find favor. Another variety of character criticism that flourished during the twentieth century, despite Knights's warnings, was based on the theories of Sigmund Freud. In fact, Freud's influence made possible a new way of viewing Shakespeare's depiction of family life as realistic. In part because it viewed the plays in this way, psychological criticism became, along with historical criticism, one of the two most important approaches to family in Shakespeare through most of the twentieth century. Some critics came to interpret Shakespeare's picture of family relationships in terms of what Freud called the "family romance," a pattern of childhood development in which children first identify with and then are disillusioned by their parents. One of Freud's most popular concepts was the Oedipus complex, and this too was imported into Shakespearean criticism, especially in connection with *Hamlet*. Freud himself had made the connection, arguing that Hamlet's hesitations, which seem unmotivated, derive from that fact that he "is able to do anything—except take vengeance on the man who did away with his father and took that father's place with his mother, the man who shows him the repressed wishes of his own childhood realized" (264–65).

Freud's disciple Ernest Jones helped popularize the idea in an article titled "The Oedipus-Complex as an Explanation of Hamlet's Mystery," published in 1910 and later, in 1949, expanded into the book *Hamlet and Oedipus*. Despite prolonged resistance and criticism, this theory has retained persistent vitality. According to Jones, Hamlet's delay results from repressed desires, now unconsciously revived, for his mother and for his father's death. In this view, Hamlet finds himself paralyzed at the thought of killing the very man who has done what he himself wished to do, and so, without knowing why, he keeps making lame excuses and putting off his "duty."

It is Hamlet's relationship with his mother that draws the greatest attention from this approach. Jones argues that Hamlet's relationship with his mother is unusually close: "As a child Hamlet had experienced the warmest affection for his mother," affection with "a disguised erotic quality," while at the same time Gertrude possessed a "markedly sensual nature" and a "passionate fondness for her son" (*Hamlet and Oedipus* 91). In Ophelia, Hamlet finds a kind of replacement for his mother. Jones speculates that the Oedipus complex in the play derives from Shakespeare's troubled relationship with his own mother.

Many, of course, have criticized the Oedipal theory—Harold Goddard, for instance, who believed Hamlet's "attachment to his mother was neither too strong nor too prolonged" (1:344), and René Girard, who argued that the Oedipus complex is a dangerous myth projecting onto children the envy and hostility felt by adults ("Freud and the Oedipus Complex"). Furthermore, Girard and others have argued that Shakespeare's play does not endorse revenge but shows its futility and destructiveness (e.g., Girard, "Hamlet's Dull Revenge"; England; Landis).

The effect of such readings is to diminish the authority of the Ghost and set family loyalties in a larger ethical context. It also makes an Oedipal reading unnecessary.

Historical criticism and scholarship—another way of connecting the plays with real life—became increasingly sophisticated in the course of the century, helping, among other things, to set Shakespeare's treatment of family life in a context of early modern beliefs and practices. One early effort of this kind was J. W. Draper's *The Hamlet of Shakespeare's Audience* (1938), which attempted with only partial success to interpret Shakespeare's characters—in particular, the young lovers and the parents and children—in terms of Elizabethan culture. Draper draws his information in part from L. L. Schücking, a German scholar who published an article titled "Die Familie bei Shakespeare" ("The Family in Shakespeare") in 1927. This article provides historical information of limited accuracy on arranged marriages, the behavior expected of dutiful children, and other matters that help explain what happens in Shakespeare's plays.

Better-known and more fruitful work was soon being done in a field known as "the history of ideas." Two books, both published in the 1940s, helped familiarize critics and students with a broad sense of how Shakespeare and his contemporaries viewed the world: Theodore Spencer's *Shakespeare and the Nature of Man* (1942) and E.M.W. Tillyard's *The Elizabethan World Picture* (1943). Describing the early modern understanding of Nature both as an ideal moral and material order and as a fallen reality, Spencer notes the interdependence of all elements in the system, including human beings as they perform their social and familial roles. He then shows how these ideas illuminate the plays. The incest in *Hamlet* affects the state and even the universe because the family, state, and universe are interdependent. The tragedy in *King Lear* begins as the daughters fail "to fulfill the natural law by honoring their father" (141). (Spencer notes, incidentally, the prominence of the word "unnatural" in this play.) And in *Timon of Athens*, Timon's curse on his city includes an overturning of social and familial order, inviting a "Son of sixteen" to "Pluck the lin'd crutch from [his] old limping sire" and use it to "beat out his brains" (181, citing *Timon* 4.1.13–15).

Tillyard's book spends less time with Shakespeare, though it includes frequent quotations from the plays. And he says virtually nothing about the family's place in "the Elizabethan world picture." Nevertheless, he explained and helped to popularize many of the concepts that are now used to understand the early modern family: "degree" (hierarchical order), the chain of being, the "cosmic dance," and the macrocosm-microcosm concept with its correspondences between the human body, the state, and the cosmos. Though Tillyard's book and to a lesser extent Spencer's run the risk of oversimplifying early modern ideas, they help provide a context for understanding family life. Yet at the same time, they tell us a good deal more about how people thought than about how they lived.

In 1952, Alfred Harbage explored early modern attitudes in a much different kind of book. *Shakespeare and the Rival Traditions* examines the popular and coterie (i.e., exclusive, upper-class) theaters and Shakespeare's role in the first of these. In the course of this examination, Harbage discovers the kinds of values

Shakespeare affirms. These include premarital chastity, fidelity in marriage, and a single sexual standard (both men and women are expected to be chaste). All of these join in affirming the value of marriage and family. Many of Shakespeare's characters, especially the sympathetic ones, are eager for a fruitful marriage, one that is expected to provide offspring as well as spiritual and physical companionship. As Harbage put it in an earlier book, "The characters seem to desire children simply because children are a good thing to have" (*As They Liked It* 198). Once children arrive, the parents respond to them with tenderness and delight. Furthermore, the happy endings of the plays often involve "the reunion of kinsmen or restoration of concord among them" (188). These conclusions, though some could be more nuanced, are in fact borne out by the bulk of Shakespeare's plays. Yet despite Harbage's generally subtle and detailed presentation of the evidence, many later critics have ignored his findings. But that may say more about the critics, and even about prevailing social attitudes, than about Shakespeare.

The Later Twentieth Century

Along with approaches that continued—for instance, historical and psychoanalytic—the second half of the century brought a variety of new or retooled ones. For example, criticism related to myth and symbol, though it had its roots earlier in the century, became especially popular during the 1950s and 1960s when it was linked with Jung's theory of archetypes and sometimes with anthropological ideas. Among Shakespearean critics associated with this kind of criticism are G. Wilson Knight, Northrop Frye, and C. L. Barber.

Knight, who wrote mainly from the 1930s through the 1950s, interprets the plays as great visionary poems. When he writes of family relationships, he does so in thematic and symbolic terms. In *The Winter's Tale*, for instance, the relations of parents and children join with seasonal imagery and references to resurrection to become part of a great pattern of rebirth. The play's children "are nature's miracles"; "planted between heaven and earth," they "beget 'wonder'"; they "are copies of their parents" and thus suggest renewal (440). Family is thus one important element in the plays. But because family relationships are viewed as elements in larger patterns and also because Knight tends to view characters as embodiments of absolute qualities rather than as particularized individuals, family relationships become, for him, more symbolic than realistic. Much the same can be said of other varieties of mythic and archetypal criticism.

Besides theorizing from the 1940s on about the roles of myth and archetype in literature, Northrop Frye wrote specifically about Shakespeare. For instance, in *A Natural Perspective* (1965), he traces the patterns in Shakespeare's comedies and romances, including the triumph of heterosexual love over various obstacles, such as lust and male friendship; the father who either aids or impedes his daughter's progress toward happiness; the achievement of a new identity as two become one in marriage; and reunion and reconciliation between family members. Like several other critics, he pays special attention to the father–daughter bond in the late romances.

C. L. Barber's approach, especially in *Shakespeare's Festive Comedy* (1959), may be called anthropological: he looks at the roots of Shakespeare's comic patterns in the ancient traditions and rituals of his culture. For instance, he finds in *A Midsummer Night's Dream* the pattern of old age opposing youthful desire, leading the young couples to go "to the woods as an escape from the inhibitions imposed by parents and the organized community" (125–26). At the end of the play, he sees allusions to "festival custom" and religious ritual in the fairies' blessing of the marriage beds (139).

By the time Barber took up the subject of family in 1976 (in "The Family in Shakespeare's Development: Tragedy and Sacredness"), his approach had become mainly psychoanalytic. In this later essay, he interprets the plays as fantasies of psychic identification and struggle so that, though he connects the plays' action with real life, that action takes place mainly in an inner psychic world. Barber writes of fraternal rivalry, of male conflicts as Oedipal ones, of sons' identification with but also rage against their fathers, of women as threats to the male ego, and of the incest taboo and ways Shakespeare confronted it. Yet the fantasies of family also have a positive side, especially in the romances and their "visionary reunions," which dramatize "the fulfillment of the need men have to be validated by feminine presences" (191). At the same time, Barber gives Shakespeare's treatment of family a religious resonance, though one that has been transferred to the secular realm. Noting "the intensity of [Shakespeare's] investment" in the family, he argues that Shakespeare has made the human family a kind of substitute for "the Holy Family of Christianity" (188)—that is, St. Joseph (or even God himself), the Virgin Mary, and Jesus—and thus has made it sacred, though still humanly vulnerable. According to Barber, the plays' emphasis on family does much to make their contents "comprehensible to the widest variety of auditors" (200) and at the same time makes the plays moving, as we witness the supreme value placed on the family and as we feel pathos at its destruction.

Barber turned again to family in his last book, *The Whole Journey* (1986), which was published after his death. The book begins with a revised version of the essay written in 1976 (the chapter is titled "The Family and the Sacred") and then pursues many of the same themes in connection with various plays. One remarkable early chapter, titled "Domestic Comedy," shows how central the family is to *The Comedy of Errors* and how Shakespeare has made the "family-centered energies that animate the action . . . enjoyable" (67). The book also shows some influence of the feminist criticism that had become so consequential since his earlier work.

In the 1970s, Shakespearean criticism underwent a fundamental change. Literary theory, much of it from France, began to influence criticism in general, and among Shakespeareans, the older tradition of moral and humanistic criticism rapidly went out of fashion. Attacks on older approaches came in a variety of forms: poststructuralism, which questioned the stability of language, writers' authority to establish meaning, and critics' ability to discern it; Marxism and allied approaches, which saw literary texts as implicated in a struggle for power; and new forms of psychoanalytic criticism, which uncovered further conflicts and entanglements. Another factor in this change of fashion, and one that strongly influenced interpretations of the family, was the rise of feminist criticism. For more information on this change in Shakespeare studies, especially as it relates to work on the family, one of the best places to look is an article by Lynda Boose whose long title begins "The Family in Shakespeare Studies." Published in 1987, a decade or more after the change had taken place, this article describes how radically the new work differed from what came before it.

Even with the change in critical fashion, a few important studies of a more traditional kind appeared. Historical scholarship continued to analyze details relevant to the plays. For instance, marriage contracts, the subject of articles published in 1950 and 1960 (by Davis Harding and Ernest Schanzer), were revisited in 1979 and 1982 (by Karl Wentersdorf and Margaret Scott). Various kinds of traditional criticism appeared in book form. In 1971, in *Shakespeare's History Plays: The Family and the State*, Robert B. Pierce discussed the family's thematic and structural importance in the history plays, where the family is "a microcosm of the state and an echo of its values" (242). In Sarup Singh's *Family Relationships in Shakespeare and the Restoration Comedy of Manners* (1983), bits of historical information are scattered throughout, but the book is really grounded in literary rather than political or social history. In this comparison-contrast study of Shakespeare's plays and late seventeenth-century comedy, Singh sees confirmation of the familiar view that the family became less authoritarian over time. In *Shakespeare's Romances and the Royal Family* (1985), David M. Bergeron in some ways bridges the older and newer approaches, looking at the family of King James I as a "text" that Shakespeare "re-presented" on the stage. This book shows an awareness of Jacobean history and of recent theoretical developments (Bergeron mentions critics taking the "cultural materialist" approach, among others), but the connections it draws between the plays and the royal family are generally unconvincing.

More satisfactory than any of these books were several shorter pieces that appeared between 1979 and 1986. One is especially remarkable, Thomas McFarland's essay titled "The Image of the Family in *King Lear*" (1981). McFarland suggests that in *Lear*, Shakespeare drew from both contemporary events and literary sources to create an image of the family quite different from the one found in *Hamlet:* instead of the highly dramatic and mythically potent family situation of the earlier play, we find in *Lear* the concerns and relationships of ordinary life, including the complicated emotions involved in parent–child relations, raised to a tragic level. McFarland also introduces some historical context, but he does not let it overwhelm his sensitive and detailed reading of the play.

Three other pieces from this period are also worth attention: Margaret Ranald's discussion of marriage in Shakespeare's plays in terms of contemporary matrimonial law ("'As Marriage Binds, and Blood Breaks': English Marriage and Shakespeare"); David Daniell's discussion of positive elements of the marriage in *The Taming of the Shrew* ("The Good Marriage of Katherine and Petruchio"); and Thomas Hennings's interpretation of *The Comedy of Errors* as a celebration of the Christian ideal of marriage and family ("The Anglican Doctrine of the Affectionate Marriage in *The Comedy of Errors*"). Though persuasive and illuminating, these articles ran against the trends inspired by newer theoretical approaches. One additional short piece from the 1980s could be added: a note by Eric Rasmussen showing how in *Hamlet* Shakespeare has carefully balanced four pairs of fathers and sons (two of the pairs being present in the form of classical allusions) and has emphasized Hamlet's dilemma by having the pairs evenly divided between revengers and non-revengers.

Overshadowing the more traditional approaches in influence, however, have been studies bringing new theories to bear on the plays. Although few studies of the family in Shakespeare have taken a poststructural approach in the narrow sense (using the methods of deconstruction, for example), the influence of poststructuralism during the past generation has been pervasive. This may be seen in the frequent emphasis on "subjectivity," the experience of personal identity viewed in contemporary thought as being constructed by language and social forces and therefore, unlike the traditional "self," as being unstable and incoherent. Some critics have emphasized the way early modern "subjectivity" meant subjection to social expectations, including familial roles. Though, for such critics, the early modern period was a time when modern subjectivity did not exist or was only emerging, they have sometimes blamed family bonds for depriving the plays' characters of whatever tenuous subjectivity they have. For instance, Janet Adelman argues that Shakespeare, by reuniting Cordelia with her father, dissolves her identity into his. Her subsequent death effects "the ultimate silencing of her subjectivity" so that "at the end, . . . having evacuated Cordelia's subjectivity, the play takes even her death from her" (126–27).

Adelman's emphasis, though, is mainly psychological. In her best-known work, *Suffocating Mothers: Fantasies of Maternal Origin in Shakespeare's Plays*, she argues that the plays betray anxiety and ambivalence toward mothers, presenting them as powerful but sometimes "suffocating" figures who produce anger and fear in men, especially in their sons, who see them as nurturing but also as threatening. Various plays work through such anxieties and resolve them, often through the fantasy of escaping from or destroying the mother. For instance, Adelman interprets Volumnia in *Coriolanus* as a "devouring" mother who has imposed deprivation on her son, to which he responds with rage that he transfers to the city of Rome (147–61). She views Gertrude as another negative mother figure, guilty of adultery (a charge the text does not explicitly support) and of having "put an intolerable strain on Hamlet" by failing to mourn her first husband properly (30, 13). The positive mother figures are positive precisely because they are safe—they are placid or sexless women "in whose presence masculine identity and the family can safely be reconstituted" (9–10).

Another recent writer, Deborah Willis, has presented a similar view but with some qualifications. In *Malevolent Nurture: Witch-Hunting and Maternal Power in Early Modern England*, Willis argues that the plays link mothers with "a malevolent, persecutory power" that threatens order by making men feel powerless (8). She differs from Adelman, however, in suggesting that the plays do not aim to gratify male fantasies in a way that would rid them of these feelings. Though Willis draws on Kleinian psychology, her book is as much historical and feminist as it is psychological. As both her book and Adelman's indicate, in fact, many recent studies of the family in Shakespeare use elements of various approaches.

Two more strictly psychoanalytic books appeared during the 1980s: David Sundelson's *Shakespeare's Restorations of the Father* (1983) and Kay Stockholder's *Dream Works: Lovers and Families in Shakespeare's Plays* (1987). Sundelson argues that the loss and restoration of a father figure is the central pattern in Shakespeare's plays and is related to Shakespeare's commitment to patriarchal (i.e., fatherly) authority. Stockholder examines how the plays deal with sexual and familial anxieties. Her book ranges widely through Shakespeare's plays but is not really about family life itself—rather it views the plays as "dreams" and explores the effect of family relationships on the individual psyche.

Other important studies taking a psychological approach include several collected in *Representing Shakespeare*. Besides C. L. Barber's essay, already discussed, these include Sundelson's "So Rare a Wonder'd Father: Prospero's *Tempest*," in which he views the "psychological structure of the play" as "making [us] feel the power of a father and the vulnerability of a child" (51), and Coppélia Kahn's "The Providential Tempest and the Shakespearean Family," in which she argues that the late romances, though imperfectly in the case of *The Tempest*, "articulate the ambivalent wish to get free of the family . . . while at the same time to stay within it, nurtured by its loves" (239).

A different kind of psychological approach, one combined with insights from anthropology, is taken by Marjorie Garber in *Coming of Age in Shakespeare* (1981). Garber examines the rites of passage—or more loosely, the stages of development—that Shakespeare's characters undergo, many of them involving family relationships. Similarly, several recent studies have interpreted the plays as presenting characters' development in terms of Freud's "family romance" pattern—for instance, essays by Gary Waller and by Harry Berger ("*King Lear*," "Text Against Performance"). We may also link with the psychological approach two books (along with several articles) that emphasize the presence, sometimes only hinted at, of incest in the plays: Mark Taylor's *Shakespeare's Darker Purpose: A Question of Incest* (1982) and Marc Shell's *The End of Kinship:* Measure for Measure, *Incest, and the Ideal of Universal Siblinghood* (1995). This last book, however, despite its connections with psychology, is mainly historical and philosophical in its orientation.

Marxism in a strict, classical sense has rarely been used in recent Shakespearean criticism. But approaches influenced by Marxism have been very important. One of these, the "new historicism," combines concepts from various sources in an attempt to interpret literary texts as historically "situated"—as both influencing and influenced by the cultures they are part of and as implicated in relations of power and oppression in those cultures. Family, as viewed through a new historicist lens, is one of many interlinked systems of such power relations.

In 1981 an important figure in new historicism, Louis Montrose, published an article on the conflict between brothers in *As You Like It*, drawing abundantly on primary and secondary historical sources. But rather than viewing historical information as "background" for a discussion of themes and characters, Montrose uses it to show how cultural tensions related to primogeniture are at work in the play. Though considered a classic new historicist essay, the article's emphasis on economic issues also gives it affinities with cultural materialism.

A decade later, Lisa Jardine (who in preceding years had famously criticized more optimist forms of feminist criticism) published an essay in the cultural materialist vein titled "'No Offence i' th' World': *Hamlet* and Unlawful Marriage." Taking Gertrude and her "unlawful marriage" as an example, Jardine shows how female guilt is culturally constructed and uses history as a way of "restor[ing] agency to groups hitherto marginalised," including "non-élite men and all women" (125).

Many of the studies already mentioned drew on Lawrence Stone and other pioneers in the field of family history. Bergeron, for instance, cites Philippe Ariès for evidence that family life was not greatly valued until the seventeenth century, and he draws from Stone the idea that sixteenth-century families suffered from "psychic numbing" and an inability "to establish close emotional ties," accompanied by increasingly authoritarian "patriarchy" (Bergeron 29–32). Stone was especially influential on feminist criticism, which became one of the most thriving areas of literary study during the last part of the century. The feminist studies of this period emphasized gender but viewed family as the context in which many gender issues play themselves out. Many of these studies assumed, and some used historical evidence in an attempt to demonstrate, that the family in Shakespeare's time was male-dominated, even cruelly so.

Shakespearean criticism with a feminist bent published earlier had often taken the form of fairly traditional studies of character and theme. For instance, Carolyn Heilbrun's first published essay, "The Character of Hamlet's Mother" (1957), acknowledged Gertrude's sensuality but otherwise praised her. Even in the early 1980s, feminist criticism sometimes used familiar methods, though it was more sensitively attuned than previous criticism had been to the restrictions placed on women by critics or by the plays themselves. Irene Dash, in *Wooing, Wedding, and Power: Women in Shakespeare's Plays* (1981), claimed that the plays, unlike many critics, invite us to take "new attitudes toward women . . . seeing them as full, complex individual characters" (30). Carol Thomas Neely, in *Broken Nuptials in Shakespeare's Plays* (1985), noticed more of the limits the plays impose on women. Focusing on gender relations and especially the problematic course of courtship and marriage in many of the plays, Neely introduces some historical background and refers repeatedly to the supposedly patriarchal character of Renaissance culture. Yet her book is not heavily informed by historical evidence. Instead, it deals with its subject mainly in terms of dramatic and thematic structure.

Historical evidence played a moderate role in another book from this period, Diane Dreher's *Domination and Defiance* (1986). The title alludes to Dreher's view that the plays "are filled with anxious and angry fathers who insist on controlling their daughters' futures" (43). Yet despite its title, this is a reasonably balanced book, with most of its positive insights coming from its use of modern psychological concepts. The book also provides some historical information, but Dreher's reliance on the work of Lawrence Stone limits the usefulness of her interpretation. The same can be said of a host of other studies appearing during the 1980s and beyond. For instance, Mary Beth Rose's intriguing article tackling the question "Where Are the Mothers in Shakespeare?" is dependent in part on Stone's work, and Coppélia Kahn's article on a similar theme ("The Absent Mother in *King Lear*") argues that Stone's view of the family is essentially right.

Stone's best-known book, *The Family, Sex and Marriage in England 1500–1800*, was groundbreaking when it appeared in 1977. Yet many historians found it deeply flawed. According to Stone, marriage in Shakespeare's time was a practical rather than a romantic affair, "the husband and father" was a "legalized petty tyrant within the home," and family life was at best marked by "coolness and distance" (7, 217). Stone also catalogues many of the horrors recorded in connection with family life in the period, failing to note that they were often recorded precisely because of their exceptional nature. In his assessment of Stone's book, Ralph Houlbrooke argues that "much evidence of love, affection and the bitterness of loss dating from the first half of Stone's period"—that is, the period most relevant to Shakespeare—"has simply been ignored" and that, despite its admirable breadth and energy, the book is marred by its questionable assumptions about the connection between "ideals and practice" and by its "perpetuation of sociological myths" (15). Alan Macfarlane demonstrates at length how the book "ignores or dismisses contrary evidence, misinterprets ambiguous evidence, fails to use relevant evidence, imports evidence from other countries to fill gaps, and jumbles up the chronology" (113). Many historians understandably consider this Stone's "most dangerous and controversial" book (Cressy 128). Some have gone so far as to call it "unconvincing," "a compendium" of "distortions," even a "disaster" (Macfarlane 106, 123; Thompson 500).

Shakespearean critics, however, generally either were unaware of these criticisms or discounted them, and many used the book eagerly to provide historical grounding for their interpretations. From Stone they borrowed the idea—now dismissed by most historians—that the family had gone through several stages between 1500 and 1800 that could be identified with the following labels: first, "the open lineage family" (a fairly loose structure emphasizing extended family ties); second, "the restricted patriarchal nuclear family" (a heavily authoritarian structure that supposedly prevailed in Shakespeare's time); and finally, "the closed domesticated nuclear family" (a later family structure with greater emotional bonds and kinder treatment of children). This last stage also included what Stone called "companionate marriage," a term to which he gave the new meaning of marriage based on friendship and mutual affection. Stone asserted, despite abundant evidence to the contrary, that this kind of marriage was unusual until the late 1600s.

Though Stone was by no means the only influence, his work helped encourage a darker view of family life in Shakespeare's time and also helped popularize the negative connotations of the word *patriarchal*. That word, which earlier had milder meanings (such as "having to do with a venerable, old man"), had gradually taken on the connotation of male dominance that it has today. Stone helped add to that sense of the word associations with self-serving despotism and even violent abuse.

By the 1980s, many Shakespearean critics had adopted this use of the word. In 1985, for instance, Kathleen McLuskie described the "patriarchal misogyny" found in both Shakespeare's plays and his culture (98), and Carol Thomas Neely, in 1990, referred to "the brutality of the patriarchal family" and "the patriarchal oppressions in the plays" ("Epilogue" 244, 249). Even when they did not give the word such negative associations, many critics during the 1980s and beyond—including feminist, new historicist, and others—simply assumed that Stone's picture of life in Shakespeare's time was true. In his article on *As You Like It*, Louis Montrose claims that Stone's view of the family in Renaissance England as "profoundly patriarchal remains . . . undisputed" (35, note 18). Peter Erickson's book on *Patriarchal Structure in Shakespeare's Drama* (1985) uses the word *patriarchal* throughout and restates with approval Stone's assertion that the "reinforcement of patriarchy" was "a central organizing principle" of Shakespeare's time (x). As a result, Erickson views even the comic scenes and closures as instruments whereby patriarchy subdues the female characters. Marilyn Williamson, in *The Patriarchy of Shakespeare's Comedies* (1986), likewise pictures the family and English culture in Shakespeare's time as "patriarchal" and argues that patriarchal authority aimed, among other things, at controlling female sexuality. Another example of this kind of criticism is an article published in 1986 in which Karen Newman examines "Renaissance family politics" as they appear in *The Taming of the Shrew* and views the play's "patriarchal master narrative" as a key to interpreting it (50).

Studies that made no serious attempt at historical inquiry sometimes adopted the prevailing negative tone. Harry Berger Jr., in a piece first published in 1982 ("Against the Sink-a-Pace"), took a cynical view of the ending of *Much Ado*, asserting that none of the characters is genuinely transformed but that all are still implicated in the sexual and family politics of their culture. Max H. James's *"Our House Is Hell": Shakespeare's Troubled Families* (1989), a short, insistently negative book, is not well known but is a good example of the view that dominated at the time.

Yet even some of the earliest critics to use Stone were aware of a disjunction between his picture of family life and Shakespeare's plays. In an article published in 1981, Marianne Novy sets Stone's view of emotional distance in early modern families against "the warm affectionate families in Shakespeare" and wonders, "Are Shakespeare's plays evidence that Stone must be wrong?" ("Shakespeare and Emotional Distance" 317). She comes to the somewhat more complicated conclusion that Stone, though "one-sided," is partly right but that Shakespeare's plays allow the expression of familial feelings that may have been suppressed in real life (325). Lynda Boose took a simpler view, starting an article published in 1982 by quoting Stone's assertions about patriarchal tyranny and then claiming that much evidence from the time supports his "hypothesis of the absence of affect" in families of Shakespeare's time. Yet her article goes on to demonstrate the importance of the father–daughter bond in Shakespeare, a bond that Stone might lead us to believe is "the least valued." Boose comments, "When we measure Stone's assertion against the Shakespeare canon, the plays must seem startlingly ahistorical" ("The Father and the Bride" 325).

By the end of the 1980s, some Shakespeareans had misgivings about Stone, so much so that a panel of historians was invited to a meeting of Shakespeareans in 1990 to urge caution in accepting Stone's assertions and to recommend looking at other authorities (see Cressy 121–22). Since that time, some Shakespearean criticism has challenged Stone directly. Already in 1990, Debora Shuger had demonstrated that fatherly love, not tyranny, was the early modern cultural ideal and had used that ideal to provide an illuminating reading of *King Lear* and other texts. Further into the 1990s, studies were published showing the parental blessing's association with affection and goodwill, in contrast to Stone and the critics depending on him, who had viewed the ritual as an indication of children's subjection to and fear of their parents (see Young, "Parental Blessings"). The following decade saw the publication of further work showing the relevance, even in tragedies such as *Hamlet* and *King Lear,* of positive views about marriage and family in early modern England (Young, "*King Lear,*" "Teaching *Hamlet*").

In general, however, Shakespearean criticism in the 1990s and beyond was marked by a great variety of attitudes about family. In 1991, Ann Jennalie Cook published *Making a Match: Courtship in Shakespeare and His Society*, a book detailing the customs of Shakespeare's time and their relevance to his plays. She quotes Stone along with other authorities but is well aware of the variety of views about marriage and family both among historians and in the plays. In 1992, in "Shakespeare's Maimed Birth Rites," Jeanne Addison Roberts discussed a topic also taken up by others before and after her: Shakespeare's use of pregnancy and childbirth. Despite the cautions given two years earlier, her essay is distinguished by her fairly frequent references to "patriarchy."

In 1995, Michael Friedman argued that the Duke in *Measure for Measure* proposes marriage to Isabella not because he loves her but in order to restore her honor. Whatever the merits of this view, Friedman's case is weakened by his argument that "mutual romantic attachment" was not the accepted grounds for marriage in Shakespeare's time (462). In 1997, Emily Detmer looked at *The Taming of the Shrew* for evidence of changing views on domestic violence. She concludes that although wife beating was generally disapproved of in Shakespeare's time, Petruchio's more "civilized" and nonviolent tactics are still abusive. Another article appearing in 1997 reported on a panel discussion on "*King Lear* and Fathering" (see Mayers et al.), showing that Shakespearean criticism was touched, at least lightly, by the field of men's studies that had arisen in response to feminism.

A book that appeared in 1998—Lisa Hopkins's *The Shakespearean Marriage: Merry Wives and Heavy Husbands*—reveals much about the state of criticism on Shakespeare and family life in the late 1990s. First of all, Hopkins acknowledges the limitations of Lawrence Stone's work and balances it with information from other sources. She also acknowledges her own "historical positioning," which (she says) makes her "aware of the provisionality of all [her] readings" (15). In this book, at least, she reads Shakespearean marriage "as both redemptive and painful" and as being perhaps "socially indispensable" but certainly not "natural." And surprisingly, granted how often Shakespeare romanticizes marriage, she sees him as allied more closely "with an aristocratic ethos, which minimised the role of love within marriage, and stressed instead compatibility of background" (9).

The following year, a book specifically on family in Shakespeare was published: Catherine Belsey's *Shakespeare and the Loss of Eden: The Construction of Family Values in Early Modern Culture*. Belsey, like Hopkins, acknowledges Stone's limitations. Interestingly, considering her stature as a cultural materialist, her method is often psychoanalytic, with many references to Freud and the neo-Freudian writer Jacques Lacan. But she does attempt to give a sense of cultural values in Shakespeare's time and to show how the "loving nuclear family," though idealized, was fragile and unstable (100). Something of the same sense of fragility is conveyed in a fine book by Heather Dubrow, also published in 1999, titled *Shakespeare and Domestic Loss*.

The Twenty-first Century

Several valuable articles on the family in Shakespeare have been published since the turn of the century. In 2001, Marliss Desens showed how, by marrying below themselves in class, the women in some of the plays attain a degree of equality or even dominance in marriage. In "*Othello:* Portrait of a Marriage" (2002), David Bevington wrote of the dangers of Othello's possessive love. The article takes a fresh look at the play by combining traditional moral insight with some of the concerns that feminism has emphasized. Also in 2002, Catherine Belsey returned to her theme of the family's vulnerability, especially in the tragedies ("Gender and Family").

In two recent articles with overlapping content and concerns—"Multiple Parenting in Shakespeare's Romances" (2002) and "Adopted Children and Constructions of Heredity, Nurture, and Parenthood in Shakespeare's Romances" (2006)—Marianne Novy has shown how the romances reflect experiences familiar to many of Shakespeare's contemporaries: parental death, remarriage, wet-nursing, apprenticeship, and other exchanges of children, all resulting in familial and quasi-familial relationships outside the nuclear family but also, apparently, a desire for reunion with birth parents and grief and guilt at children's deaths. These articles exemplify some of the most valuable trends in recent criticism dealing with family life: in contrast to some earlier studies in which historical information was either absent or used to support preconceived notions, here historical details are used sensitively and fairly in an attempt to discern how Shakespeare's plays relate to the complex experiences and attitudes of his contemporaries.

Obviously, family continues to be a significant topic in Shakespearean criticism. After several decades of debate over Shakespeare's values and the character of family life in his time, it is likely that attention will turn more to the finer details and nuances of those subjects—the relation of family life to religion, for instance, or the experience of children, or specific courtship or mourning practices. Critics will continue to apply to Shakespeare's treatment of the family new ways of looking at his structure and style. And the tentative connections that have already been made between performance studies and study of the family may become more frequent and fruitful.

Critics using history to illuminate Shakespeare's texts now generally accept Deborah Willis's contention that understanding early modern England requires taking into account its "multiple, often inconsistent or contested" cultural discourses, including those related to gender and family (20, note 26). It is also now generally recognized that none of us—historians, critics, readers, or playgoers—can avoid looking at Shakespeare and his time from our own limited, personal locations. That is one reason that much of the best contemporary criticism dealing with Shakespeare and family life combines an effort to understand the past accurately and sympathetically with an acknowledgment of present concerns. In addition, rather than narrowly applying a single approach, many critics now draw on whatever methods or information most illuminate their subjects. At its best, historical study will continue to be linked with close attention to Shakespeare's text. Moral inquiry, which has now returned to favor in Shakespearean criticism, will certainly continue to enrich our understanding of family in the plays. It is difficult to forecast what controversies may arise in the coming years. But for now, with the benefit of a rich critical legacy, much recent historical work, and various ways of looking at the text, Shakespearean critics are well equipped to continue exploring family life as a topic of deep interest among readers and playgoers as well as an inescapable feature of human experience and of Shakespeare's works.

REFERENCES

Adelman, Janet. *Suffocating Mothers: Fantasies of Maternal Origin in Shakespeare's Plays,* Hamlet *to* The Tempest. New York: Routledge, 1992.

Ariès, Philippe. *Centuries of Childhood: A Social History of Family Life*. Trans. Robert Baldick. New York: Vintage Books, 1962.

Barber, C. L. "The Family in Shakespeare's Development: Tragedy and Sacredness." *Representing Shakespeare: New Psychoanalytic Essays*. Ed. Murray M. Schwartz and Coppélia Kahn. Baltimore: Johns Hopkins University Press, 1980. 188–202.

———. *Shakespeare's Festive Comedy: A Study of Dramatic Form and Its Relation to Social Custom*. Princeton, NJ: Princeton University Press, 1959.

Barber, C. L., and Richard P. Wheeler. *The Whole Journey: Shakespeare's Power of Development*. Berkeley: University of California Press, 1986.

Belsey, Catherine. "Gender and Family." *Cambridge Companion to Shakespearean Tragedy*. Ed. Claire Elizabeth McEachern. New York: Cambridge University Press, 2002. 123–41.

———. *Shakespeare and the Loss of Eden: The Construction of Family Values in Early Modern Culture*. New Brunswick, NJ: Rutgers University Press, 1999.

Berger, Harry, Jr. "Against the Sink-a-Pace: Sexual and Family Politics in *Much Ado about Nothing*." *Making Trifles of Terrors*. Stanford: Stanford University Press, 1997. 10–24.

———. "*King Lear*: The Lear Family Romance." *Making Trifles of Terrors*. Stanford: Stanford University Press, 1997. 25–49.

———. "Text Against Performance: The Gloucester Family Romance." *Making Trifles of Terrors*. Stanford: Stanford University Press, 1997. 50–69.

Bergeron, David M. *Shakespeare's Romances and the Royal Family*. Lawrence: University Press of Kansas, 1985.

Bevington, David. "*Othello*: Portrait of a Marriage." *Othello: New Critical Essays*. Ed. Philip C. Kolin. New York: Routledge, 2002. 221–31.

Boose, Lynda. "The Family in Shakespeare Studies; or—Studies in the Family of Shakespeareans; or—The Politics of Politics." *Renaissance Quarterly* 40 (1987): 707–42.

———. "The Father and the Bride in Shakespeare." *PMLA* 97 (1982): 325–47.

Bradley, A. C. *Shakespearean Tragedy*. 1904. 3rd ed. New York: St. Martin's Press, 1992.

Cavendish, Margaret. Letter CXXIII. 1664. *Shakespeare Criticism: A Selection, 1623–1840*. Ed. D. Nichol Smith. London: Oxford University Press, 1946. 13–15.

Coleridge, Samuel Taylor. "*Macbeth*." *Coleridge on Shakespeare*. Ed. Terence Hawkes. Harmondsworth, UK: Penguin Books, 1969. 208–19.

———. [Selected criticism.] *Shakespeare Criticism: A Selection, 1623–1840*. Ed. D. Nichol Smith. London: Oxford University Press, 1946. 213–72.

Cook, Ann Jennalie. *Making a Match: Courtship in Shakespeare and His Society*. Princeton, NJ: Princeton University Press, 1991.

Cressy, David. "Foucault, Stone, Shakespeare and Social History." *English Literary Renaissance* 21 (1991): 121–33.

Daniell, David. "The Good Marriage of Katherine and Petruchio." *Shakespeare Survey* 37 (1984): 23–31.

Dash, Irene G. *Wooing, Wedding, and Power: Women in Shakespeare's Plays*. New York: Columbia University Press, 1981.

De Quincey, Thomas. "A Summary Survey." 1838. *Shakespeare Criticism: A Selection, 1623–1840*. Ed. D. Nichol Smith. London: Oxford University Press, 1946. 337–50.

Desens, Marliss. "Marrying Down: Negotiating a More Equal Marriage on the English Renaissance Stage." *Medieval and Renaissance Drama in England* 14 (2001): 227–55.

Detmer, Emily. "Civilizing Subordination: Domestic Violence and *The Taming of the Shrew*." *Shakespeare Quarterly* 48 (1997): 272–94.

Dowden, Edward. *Shakspere: A Critical Study of His Mind and Art*. 2nd ed. London, 1876.

Draper, J. W. *The Hamlet of Shakespeare's Audience*. Durham, NC: Duke University Press, 1938.

Dreher, Diane. *Domination and Defiance: Fathers and Daughters in Shakespeare*. Lexington: University Press of Kentucky, 1986.

Dryden, John. From the Preface to *Troilus and Cressida*. 1679. *Shakespeare Criticism: A Selection, 1623–1840*. Ed. D. Nichol Smith. London: Oxford University Press, 1946. 18–22.

Dubrow, Heather. *Shakespeare and Domestic Loss*. Cambridge: Cambridge University Press, 1999.

Eastman, Arthur M. *A Short History of Shakespearean Criticism*. New York: Norton, 1968.

Eliot, T. S. "Hamlet and His Problems." *Critical Theory Since Plato*. Ed. Hazard Adams. New York: Harcourt Brace Jovanovich, 1971. 788–90.

England, Eugene. "*Hamlet* Against Revenge." *Literature and Belief* 7 (1987): 49–62.

Erickson, Peter. *Patriarchal Structures in Shakespeare's Drama*. Berkeley: University of California Press, 1985.

Freud, Sigmund. *The Interpretation of Dreams*. 1900. *The Standard Edition of the Complete Psychological Works of Sigmund Freud*. Trans. and ed. James Strachey. Vols. 4–5. London: Hogarth Press, 1953.

Friedman, Michael D. "'O, Let Him Marry Her!': Matrimony and Recompense in *Measure for Measure*." *Shakespeare Quarterly* 46 (1995): 454–64.

Frye, Northrop. *A Natural Perspective: The Development of Shakespearean Comedy and Romance*. New York: Harcourt, Brace & World, 1965.

Garber, Marjorie. *Coming of Age in Shakespeare*. London: Methuen, 1981.

Girard, René. "Freud and the Oedipus Complex." *Violence and the Sacred*. Trans. Patrick Gregory. Baltimore: Johns Hopkins University Press, 1977. 169–92.

———. "Hamlet's Dull Revenge." *Stanford Literature Review* 1 (1984): 159–200.

Goddard, Harold C. *The Meaning of Shakespeare*. 2 vols. Chicago: University of Chicago Press, 1951.

Harbage, Alfred. *As They Liked It: A Study of Shakespeare's Moral Artistry*. 1947. Harper Torchbook edition. New York: Harper & Brothers, 1961.

———. *Shakespeare and the Rival Traditions*. New York: Macmillan, 1952.

Harding, Davis P. "Elizabethan Betrothals and 'Measure for Measure.'" *JEGP* 49 (1950): 139–58.

Hazlitt, William. From *Characters of Shakespeare's Plays*. 1817. *Shakespeare Criticism: A Selection, 1623–1840*. Ed. D. Nichol Smith. London: Oxford University Press, 1946. 273–305.

Heilbrun, Carolyn G. "The Character of Hamlet's Mother." *Hamlet's Mother and Other Women*. New York: Columbia University Press, 1990. 9–17.

Hennings, Thomas P. "The Anglican Doctrine of the Affectionate Marriage in *The Comedy of Errors*." *Modern Language Quarterly* 47 (1986): 91–107.

Hopkins, Lisa. *The Shakespearean Marriage: Merry Wives and Heavy Husbands*. New York: St. Martin's Press, 1998.

Houlbrooke, Ralph A. *The English Family 1450–1700*. London: Longman, 1984.

James, Max H. *"Our House Is Hell": Shakespeare's Troubled Families*. Westport, CT: Greenwood Press, 1989.

Jardine, Lisa. "'No Offence i' th' World': *Hamlet* and Unlawful Marriage." *Uses of History: Marxism, Postmodernism, and the Renaissance*. Ed. Francis Barker, Peter Hulme, and Margaret Iversen. Manchester: Manchester University Press, 1991. 123–39.

Johnson, Samuel. *The Letters of Samuel Johnson*. Ed. Bruce Redford. 5 vols. Hyde edition. Princeton, NJ: Princeton University Press, 1992–94.

———. *Selections from Johnson on Shakespeare*. Ed. Bertrand Bronson. New Haven, CT: Yale University Press, 1986.

Jones, Ernest. *Hamlet and Oedipus*. New York: Norton, 1949.

———. "The Oedipus-Complex as an Explanation of Hamlet's Mystery: A Study in Motive." *American Journal of Psychology* 21 (1910): 72–113.

Kahn, Coppélia. "The Absent Mother in King Lear." *Rewriting the Renaissance: The Discourses of Sexual Difference in Early Modern Europe*. Ed. Margaret Ferguson, Maureen Quilligan, and Nancy J. Vickers. Chicago: University of Chicago Press, 1986. 33–49.

———. "The Providential Tempest and the Shakespearean Family." *Representing Shakespeare: New Psychoanalytic Essays*. Ed. Murray Schwartz and Coppélia Kahn. Baltimore: Johns Hopkins University Press, 1980. 217–43.

Knight, G. Wilson. "'Great Creating Nature': An Essay on *The Winter's Tale*." *Shakespeare: Modern Essays in Criticism*. Ed. Leonard F. Dean. Revised ed. London: Oxford University Press, 1967. 423–55.

Knights, L. C. *How Many Children Had Lady Macbeth? An Essay in the Theory and Practice of Shakespeare Criticism*. Cambridge, UK: Gordon Fraser, The Minority Press, 1933.

Lamb, Charles. "On the Tragedies of Shakespeare." 1811. *Shakespeare Criticism: A Selection, 1623–1840*. Ed. D. Nichol Smith. London: Oxford University Press, 1946. 190–212.

Landis, Joan Hutton. "Shakespeare's Poland." *Hamlet Studies* 6 (1984): 8–17.

Macfarlane, Alan. Review of Lawrence Stone, *The Family, Sex and Marriage in England 1500–1800*. *History and Theory* 18 (1979): 103–26.

Mayers, Ozzie J., Clark Hendley, Philip Kronebusch, and Glen Palm. "*King Lear* and Fathering: A Panel Discussion." *Journal of Men's Studies* 6 (1997): 103–14.

McFarland, Thomas. "The Image of the Family in King Lear." On King Lear. Ed. Lawrence Danson. Princeton, NJ: Princeton University Press, 1981. 91–118.

McLuskie, Kathleen. "The Patriarchal Bard: Feminist Criticism and Shakespeare: *King Lear* and *Measure for Measure*." *Political Shakespeare: New Essays in Cultural Materialism*. Ed. Jonathan Dollimore and Alan Sinfield. Ithaca, NY: Cornell University Press, 1985. 88–108.

Montagu, Elizabeth. *An Essay on the Writings and Genius of Shakespear*. 1769. Rpt. London: Frank Cass & Co., 1970.

Montrose, Louis Adrian. "'The Place of a Brother' in *As You Like It*: Social Process and Comic Form." *Shakespeare Quarterly* 32 (1981): 28–54.

Murphy, Arthur. [From *Gray's-Inn Journal*, 1754.] *Shakespeare Criticism: A Selection, 1623–1840*. Ed. D. Nichol Smith. London: Oxford University Press, 1946. 120, note 1.

Neely, Carol Thomas. *Broken Nuptials in Shakespeare's Plays*. New Haven, CT: Yale University Press, 1985.

———. "Epilogue: Remembering Shakespeare, Revising Ourselves." *Women's Re-Visions of Shakespeare*. Ed. Marianne Novy. Chicago: University of Illinois Press, 1990. 242–52.

Newman, Karen. "Renaissance Family Politics and Shakespeare's *The Taming of the Shrew*." *Fashioning Femininity and English Renaissance Drama*. Chicago: University of Chicago Press, 1991. 33–50.

Novy, Marianne. "Adopted Children and Constructions of Heredity, Nurture, and Parenthood in Shakespeare Romances." *Childhood and Children's Books in Early Modern Europe, 1550–1800*. Ed. Andrea Immel and Michael Witmore. New York: Routledge, 2006. 55–74.

———. "Multiple Parenting in Shakespeare's Romances." *Domestic Arrangements in Early Modern England*. Ed. Kari Boyd McBride. Pittsburgh: Duquesne University Press, 2002. 188–208.

———. "Shakespeare and Emotional Distance in the Elizabethan Family." *Theatre Journal* 33 (1981): 316–26.

Pater, Walter. *Appreciations*. London: Macmillan, 1895.

Pierce, Robert B. *Shakespeare's History Plays: The Family and the State*. Columbus: Ohio State University Press, 1971.

Ranald, Margaret Loftus. "'As Marriage Binds, and Blood Breaks': English Marriage and Shakespeare." *Shakespeare Quarterly* 30 (1979): 68–81.

Rasmussen, Eric. "Fathers and Sons in *Hamlet*." *Shakespeare Quarterly* 35 (1984): 463.

Roberts, Jeanne Addison. "Shakespeare's Maimed Birth Rites." *True Rites and Maimed Rites: Ritual and Anti-Ritual in Shakespeare and His Age*. Ed. Linda Woodbridge and Edward Berry. Urbana: University of Illinois Press, 1992. 123–44.

Rose, Mary Beth. "Where Are the Mothers in Shakespeare? Options for Gender Representation in the English Renaissance." *Shakespeare Quarterly* 42 (1991): 291–314.

Rowe, Nicholas. "Some Account of the Life, etc., of Mr. William Shakespear." 1709. *Eighteenth Century Essays on Shakespeare*. Ed. D. Nichol Smith. 2nd ed. Oxford: Clarendon Press, 1963. 1–22.

Rymer, Thomas. "A Bloody Farce." [Excerpts from A *Short View of Tragedy* (1693).] *Othello*. Ed. Edward Pechter. Norton critical edition. New York: Norton, 2004. 201–10.

Schanzer, Ernest. "The Marriage-Contracts in *Measure for Measure*." *Shakespeare Survey* 13 (1960): 81–89.

Schlegel, A. W. *A Course of Lectures on Dramatic Art and Literature*. 1811. Trans. John Black. London, 1846.

Schücking, L. L. "Die Familie bei Shakespeare." *Englische Studien* 62 (1927): 187–226.

Scott, Margaret. "'Our City's Institutions': Some Further Reflections on the Marriage Contracts in *Measure for Measure*." *ELH* 49 (1982): 790–804.

Shaw, Bernard. *Dramatic Opinions and Essays*. London: Archibald Constable & Co., 1907.

———. Foreword to *Cymbeline Refinished*. *Geneva, Cymbeline Refinished, & Good King Charles*. New York: Dodd, Mead, 1947. 133–38.

Shell, Marc. *The End of Kinship:* Measure for Measure, *Incest, and the Ideal of Universal Siblinghood*. Baltimore: Johns Hopkins University Press, 1995.

Shuger, Debora Kuller. "Nursing Fathers: Patriarchy as a Cultural Ideal." *Habits of Thought in the English Renaissance: Religion, Politics, and the Dominant Culture*. Berkeley: University of California Press, 1990. 218–49.

Singh, Sarup. *Family Relationships in Shakespeare and the Restoration Comedy of Manners*. Delhi: Oxford University Press, 1983.

Spencer, Theodore. *Shakespeare and the Nature of Man*. 1942. 2nd ed. New York: Macmillan, 1961.

Stockholder, Kay. *Dream Works: Lovers and Families in Shakespeare's Plays*. Toronto: University of Toronto Press, 1987.

Stone, Lawrence. *The Family, Sex and Marriage in England 1500–1800*. New York: Harper & Row, 1977.

Sundelson, David. *Shakespeare's Restorations of the Father*. New Brunswick, NJ: Rutgers University Press, 1983.

———. "So Rare a Wonder'd Father: Prospero's *Tempest*." *Representing Shakespeare: New Psychoanalytic Essays*. Ed. Murray Schwartz and Coppélia Kahn. Baltimore: Johns Hopkins University Press, 1980. 33–53.

Taylor, Mark. *Shakespeare's Darker Purpose: A Question of Incest*. New York: AMS Press, 1982.

Thompson, E. P. "Happy Families." Review of *The Family, Sex and Marriage in England 1500–1800*, by Lawrence Stone. *New Society* (8 September 1977): 500.

Tillyard, E.M.W. *The Elizabethan World Picture*. London: Chatto and Windus, 1943.

Tolstoy, Leo. *Tolstoy on Shakespeare: A Critical Essay on Shakespeare*. Trans. V. Tchertkoff and I[sabella] F[yvie] M[ayo]. New York: Funk & Wagnalls, 1906.

Waller, Gary. "The Late Plays as Family Romance." *Approaches to Teaching Shakespeare's* The Tempest *and Other Late Romances*. Ed. Maurice Hunt. New York: Modern Language Association of America, 1992.

Warton, Joseph. From *The Adventurer*, 1753–54. *Shakespeare Criticism: A Selection, 1623–1840*. Ed. D. Nichol Smith. London: Oxford University Press, 1946. 52–69.

Wentersdorf, Karl. "The Marriage Contracts in *Measure for Measure:* A Reconsideration." *Shakespeare Survey* 32 (1979): 129–44.

Williamson, Marilyn. *The Patriarchy of Shakespeare's Comedies*. Detroit, MI: Wayne State University Press, 1986.

Willis, Deborah. *Malevolent Nurture: Witch-Hunting and Maternal Power in Early Modern England*. Ithaca, NY: Cornell University Press, 1995.

Woolf, Virginia. *A Room of One's Own*. 1929. San Diego: Harcourt Brace Jovanovich, 1981.

Young, Bruce W. "*King Lear* and the Calamity of Fatherhood." *In the Company of Shakespeare: Essays on English Renaissance Literature in Honor of*

G. *Blakemore Evans*. Ed. Thomas Moisan and Douglas Bruster. Madison, NJ: Fairleigh Dickinson University Press, 2002. 43–64.
———. "Parental Blessings in Shakespeare's Plays." *Studies in Philology* 89 (1992): 179–210.
———. "Teaching *Hamlet* as a Play about Family." *Approaches to Teaching Shakespeare's* Hamlet. Ed. Bernice Kliman. New York: Modern Language Association, 2002. 107–12.

PRIMARY DOCUMENTS

One of the best ways to get a sense of family life in Shakespeare's time is to look at documents written during the period. The present collection includes excerpts from a wide variety of sources: sermons, pamphlets, poems, ballads, advice books on marriage and family life, and legal handbooks, among others. The writers represent different classes and religious persuasions and include clergymen, lawyers, and poets. Most selections are by men, but a few (see Documents 13, 22, 24) are by women, and others purport to represent women speaking (Documents 7, 19, and 20). Some documents reflect views authorized by the Church of England. Many are by Puritans, a significant and influential portion of the English Church that was intensely interested in living a godly life, in the home as elsewhere. England was officially Protestant during Shakespeare's lifetime, but a few selections are by Roman Catholics. Ben Jonson, for instance, was Catholic for part of his life (see Documents 30 and 31).

Printed sources, of course, often represent the ideals rather than the reality of family life. Nevertheless, the selections provided here reflect the interests, attitudes, and experiences of a great variety of readers. One selection was written by an aristocratic woman, the Countess of Lincoln (see Document 22), and like most of the documents, was intended mainly for middle- and upper-class readers. A few selections, however, such as the ballads and the pamphlet on *Two Horrible and Inhumane Murders* (Documents 7, 17, 20), were aimed at a popular audience. Two items (Documents 19 and 27) are in dialogue form and give a vivid sense of what real-life conversations about family life may have sounded like.

The documents are organized into six sections by topic. The first section ("The Family in General") includes four brief statements that define the family, describe its problems, prescribe general remedies, and survey the basic relationships that make up family life. The second section ("Family and Religion: Religious Texts and Rituals") presents two fundamental documents that would have been familiar to virtually everyone in the period: the marriage ceremony prescribed by the Book of Common Prayer and *An Homily of the State of Matrimony*, the Church of England's official sermon on marriage. The next two sections ("Courtship and

Betrothal" and "Marriage: Love, Duty, Conflict") illustrate the steps leading to marriage and the many dimensions of married life, from the wedding night (described in Document 11) to attitudes about women and the roles of husband and wife to marital conflict and proposed solutions. The fifth section ("Parents and Children") presents advice about nursing, parenting, and children's duties and reveals how parents responded to their children's deaths. The final section ("Siblings and Inheritance") indicates the sorts of conflicts that sometimes arose between siblings, especially on the issue of inheritance.

Besides the kinds of documents included here, diaries, letters, and other unpublished material also shed light on family life in early modern England. Modern scholars have produced several fine collections of such material. Two of the best are *English Family Life, 1576–1716: An Anthology from Diaries* (Oxford: Basil Blackwell, 1988), edited by Ralph Houlbrooke, and Linda Pollock's *A Lasting Relationship: Parents and Children over Three Centuries* (London: Fourth Estate, 1987).

With one exception (a nineteenth-century edition of the 1559 Book of Common Prayer), the following selections are transcribed from sixteenth- and seventeenth-century texts. Spelling has been modernized, and for the sake of clarity, some changes have been made in punctuation, paragraphing, and other details. The original spelling has been kept, however, for Document 11 (Spenser's *Epithalamion*), given that Spenser often used spelling for poetic effect.

THE FAMILY IN GENERAL

John Dod (1550–1645) **and Robert Cleaver** (1561/2–c. 1625). Written by two Puritan clergymen, *A Godly Form of Household Government* was one of many manuals on family life published during the early modern period, and like most, it has a religious emphasis, viewing the family as designed by God to bring about his purposes. As its subtitle indicates, the book details "the several duties of the husband towards his wife, and the wife's duty towards her husband, the parents' duty towards their children, and the children's towards their parents, the master's duty towards his servants, and also the servants' duty toward their masters." The following selection draws the standard parallel between the family and the larger social unit of the state or "commonwealth." (*A Godly Forme of Houshold Government for the Ordering of Private Families, according to the Direction of Gods Word.* London, 1621. A7r.)

Document 1: From *A Godly Form of Household Government*

An household is as it were a little commonwealth, by the good government whereof, God's glory may be advanced, and the commonwealth which standeth [consists] of several families benefited; and all that live in that family receive much comfort and commodity [benefit].

Matthew Griffith (1599?–1665). Griffith, an Anglican clergyman, published a long treatise on family life in 1633. By calling his book *Bethel* (a Hebrew word meaning "house of God"), he signaled that a good family must be built on a religious foundation. In this brief excerpt, Griffith presents his book as a cure for contemporary neglect of family duties. Such duties, he believed, were linked to the larger duty to maintain social order, a view that helps explain why (unlike many of the Puritans who wrote about the family) he was a strong supporter of the king during the English Civil War. (*Bethel: or, A Forme for Families in which All Sorts, of Both Sexes, are So Squared, and Framed by the Word of God, as They May Best Serve in Their Severall Places, for Usefull Pieces in God's Building.* London, 1633. 2.)

Document 2: From *Bethel: or, A Form for Families*

Now the sickness wherewith this age is generally infected, is caused by a supine neglect, if not by a willful contempt of family-duties: and what marvel though the whole city be foul, and the people generally profane, when we will not begin reformation at home; and every one sweep before his own door? That I may therefore cure the indevotion of these times, and prevent this disease, before it grow epidemical, I'll here endeavor (by God's grace) with all possible plainness, and perspicuity, to teach all such as are willing to learn, how they may best serve God, as members of his family.

William Perkins (1558–1602). Perkins was an important and widely published clergyman and theologian and a leading figure among the moderate Puritans who made up a significant part of the Church of England. *Christian Economy,* which he wrote in Latin, was translated into English and published after his death. The book surveys all the relationships and responsibilities of a household (*economy* originally meant "household management"). In the excerpt presented here, Perkins focuses on the essential character of a good family, namely, that all the members will perform both their temporal and spiritual duties and so make the household not only a pragmatic success but even "a kind of paradise upon earth." (*Christian Oeconomie: or, A Short Survey of the Right Manner of Erecting and Ordering a Familie according to the Scriptures.* London, 1609. 7–9.)

Document 3: From *Christian Economy*

Wherefore, those families wherein this service of God is performed, are, as it were, little churches, yea even a kind of paradise upon earth. . . . On the other side, where this duty of God's service is not used, but either for the most part, or altogether neglected, a man may term those families, no better than companies of profane and graceless atheists, who as they deny God in their hearts, so they are known by this note, that they "do not call upon the name of the Lord" (Psalm 14:4). Yea such families are fitly compared to an herd of swine, which are always feeding upon the mast with greediness, but never look up to the hand that beateth it down, nor to the tree from whence it falleth.

The other duty concerning the house itself, is, that every member in the family, according to their ability, employ themselves in some honest and profitable business, to maintain the temporal estate and life of the whole.

Thomas Gataker (1574–1654). In 1623, Gataker, a moderate Anglican minister, published a volume containing "two marriage sermons." In the following excerpt, from the first of the sermons *(A Good Wife God's Gift)*, Gataker describes the various relationships of family life, which he ranks in ascending order of strength and intimacy. The lowest is between servants and masters (with *family* understood to mean household, servants would have counted as family members); above that is the bond between siblings; and then come the relationships between parents and children and finally between husband and wife, who should be as united as a single body or as the mingled water of a single river. Like Pierre de La Primaudaye (see **Document 32**), Gataker compares friends and brothers, noting that although friends may be closer than brothers, the natural bond between brothers makes their conflict harder to heal. (*A Good Wife Gods Gift and, A Wife Indeed. Two Mariage Sermons*. London, 1623. 3–5.)

Document 4: From *A Good Wife God's Gift*

In a man's own family there are some nearer than others. A son is nearer than a servant, and a wife than a son. . . . Brethren are nearer than friends. And howsoever Solomon truly saith, that a friend sometimes sticketh closer to a man than a brother [Proverbs 18:24]: yet in nature a brother is nearer than any friend is or can be. There is a civil knot only between friend and friend; there is a natural bond between brother and brother. And therefore, a brother offended is harder to win than a strong city; and their contentions are as bars of brass. It is easier gluing again of boards together, that have been unglued, than healing up the flesh that is gashed and divided: and the reason is, because there was but an artificial connection before in the one, there was a natural conjunction in the other: so it is easier reconciling of friends than of brethren, there being a civil bond only broken in the dissension of the one, a natural tial [bond, tie] violated in the dissensions of the other.

But children they are yet nearer than either friends or brethren. They are *partes nostri, viscera nostra;* they are as our very bowels, and part of our selves. And therefore no marvel if Solomon say, that a foolish son is a cause for sorrow to his father, and an heaviness to his mother [Proverbs 10:1, 17:25]. And, he that begetteth a fool, begetteth himself sorrow: and the father of a fool shall have no joy [Proverbs 17:21]. . . .

. . . Husband and wife are nearer than friends, and brethren; or than parents and children. Children, though they spring from their parents, yet they abide not always with them. They are as rivers rising from one head, but taking several ways, making several streams, and running apart in several channels. But man and wife must bide by it. They are as two streams, that rising from several heads, fall the one into the other, mingle their waters together, and are not severed again till they are swallowed up in the sea. Children are as branches shooting out of one stem, divided and severed either from other, or as grafts and scions [shoots for grafting] cut off, or boughs and branches slipped off from their native stock, and either planted or engrafted elsewhere. Man and wife are as the stock and scion the one engrafted into the other, and so fastened together, that they cannot again be sundered. . . . And therefore, saith the Holy Ghost, shall a man leave father and mother, and be glued unto, or cleave fast to his wife: and they two shall be one flesh [Genesis 2:24].

FAMILY AND RELIGION: RELIGIOUS TEXTS AND RITUALS

The Book of Common Prayer. The Book of Common Prayer, created under the direction of Archbishop Thomas Cranmer in 1549, was one of the first great products of the English Reformation. Revised under Queen Elizabeth in 1559, it contained the ceremonies used in the Church of England, including baptism, marriage, the churching of women, and the burial of the dead. Though a valid marriage could be entered into privately, the Church expected couples to take part in the public ceremony outlined here, in part to ensure that no impediments would render the marriage invalid. After the asking of the banns (the public announcement of a forthcoming marriage), the ceremony would take place in church, beginning with the priest's review of the purposes of marriage, which was followed by the couple's exchange of vows, the giving of a ring (a detail opposed by some Puritans), and further prayers and exhortation. (*Liturgical Services of the Reign of Queen Elizabeth*. Ed. William Keatinge Clay. Cambridge, 1847. 217–24.)

Document 5: From "The Form of Solemnization of Matrimony"

First the banns [announcement of the coming marriage] must be asked three several Sundays or holy days, in the time of service, the people being present after the accustomed manner.

And if the persons that would be married dwell in diverse parishes, the banns must be asked in both parishes, and, the curate of the one parish shall not solemnize matrimony betwixt them, without a certificate of the banns being thrice asked from the curate of the other parish. At the day appointed for solemnization of matrimony, the persons to be married shall come into the body of the church with their friends and neighbors. And there the priest shall thus say:

Dearly beloved friends, we are gathered together here in the sight of God, and in the face of his congregation, to join together this man and this woman in holy matrimony, which is an honorable estate, instituted of God in paradise, in the time of man's innocency: signifying unto us the mystical union, that is betwixt Christ and his church: which holy estate Christ adorned and beautified with his presence and first miracle that he wrought in Cana of Galilee [John 2], and is commended of Saint Paul to be honorable among all men, and therefore is not to be enterprised [undertaken], nor taken in hand unadvisedly, lightly or wantonly, to satisfy men's carnal lusts and appetites, like brute beasts that have no understanding; but reverently, discreetly, advisedly, soberly, and in the fear of God: duly considering the causes for the which matrimony was ordained. One was, the procreation of children, to be brought up in the fear and nurture of the Lord, and praise of God. Secondly, it was ordained for a remedy against sin, and to avoid fornication, that such persons as have not the gift of continency [self-restraint], might marry, and keep themselves undefiled members of Christ's body. Thirdly, for the mutual society, help and comfort, that the one ought to have of the other, both in prosperity and adversity: into the which holy estate these two persons present come now to be joined. Therefore if any man can show any just cause, why they may not lawfully be joined together, let him now speak: or else hereafter for ever hold his peace.

And also speaking to the persons that shall be married, he shall say:

I require and charge you (as you will answer at the dreadful day of judgment, when the secrets of all hearts shall be disclosed) that if either of you do know any impediment why ye may not be lawfully joined together in matrimony, that ye confess it. For be ye well assured, that so many as be coupled together otherwise than God's word doth allow, are not joined together by God, neither is their matrimony lawful.

At which day of marriage, if any man do allege and declare any impediment why they may not be coupled together in matrimony by God's law or the laws of this realm: and will be bound, and sufficient sureties with him, to the parties, or else put in a caution to the full value of such charges as the persons to be married doth sustain to prove his allegation: then the solemnization must be deferred unto such time as the truth be tried. If no impediment be alleged, then shall the curate say unto the man,

N. [Name of the groom] Wilt thou have this woman to thy wedded wife, to live together after God's ordinance in the holy estate of matrimony? Wilt thou love her, comfort her, honor and keep her, in sickness, and in health? And forsaking all other, keep thee only to her, so long as you both shall live?

The man shall answer, I will.

Then shall the priest say to the woman,

N. [Name of the bride] Wilt thou have this man to thy wedded husband, to live together after God's ordinance in the holy estate of matrimony? Wilt thou obey him and serve him, love, honor, and keep him, in sickness and in health, and forsaking all other, keep thee only unto him, so long as you both shall live?

The woman shall answer, I will.

Then shall the minister say,

Who giveth this woman to be married unto this man?

And the minister receiving the woman at her father or friend's hands, shall cause the man to take the woman by the right hand, and so either to give their troth [promise] to other.

The man first saying:

I, N. [name] take thee, N. [name] to my wedded wife, to have and to hold from this day forward, for better, for worse, for richer, for poorer, in sickness, and in health, to love and to cherish, till death us depart, according to God's holy ordinance: and thereto I plight thee my troth.

Then shall they loose their hands, and the woman taking again the man by the right hand shall say:

I, N. [name] take thee, N. [name] to my wedded husband, to have and to hold from this day forward, for better, for worse, for richer, for poorer, in sickness, and in health, to love, cherish, and to obey, till death us depart, according to God's holy ordinance: and thereto I give thee my troth.

Then shall they again loose their hands, and the man shall give unto the woman a ring, laying the same upon the book with the accustomed duty to the priest and clerk. And the priest taking the ring, shall deliver it unto the man, to put it upon the fourth finger of the woman's left hand. And the man taught by the priest shall say.

With this ring I thee wed: with my body I thee worship: and with all my worldly goods I thee endow. In the name of the Father, and of the Son, and of the Holy Ghost. Amen.

Then the man leaving the ring upon the fourth finger of the woman's left hand, the minister shall say.

O eternal God, creator and preserver of all mankind, giver of all spiritual grace, the author of everlasting life: Send thy blessing upon these thy servants, this man and this woman, whom we bless in thy name; that as Isaac and Rebecca lived faithfully together, so these persons may surely perform and keep the vow and covenant betwixt them made, whereof this ring given and received is a token and pledge, and may ever remain in perfect love and peace together, and live according unto thy laws: through Jesus Christ our Lord. Amen.

Then shall the priest join their right hands together, and say:

Those whom God hath joined together, let no man put asunder.

Then shall the minister speak unto the people:

Forasmuch as N. [name] and N. [name] have consented together in holy wedlock, and have witnessed the same before God and this company, and thereto have given and pledged their troth, either to other, and have declared the same by giving and receiving of a ring, and by joining of hands: I pronounce that they be man and wife together. In the name of the Father, and of the Son, and of the Holy Ghost. Amen.

And the minister shall add this blessing:

God the Father, God the Son, God the Holy Ghost, bless, preserve, and keep you: the Lord mercifully with his favor look upon you, and so fill you with all spiritual benediction and grace, that you may so live together in this life, that in the world to come you may have life everlasting. Amen. . . .

[After a psalm and prayers, the minister offers the following prayer, unless the woman is past childbearing years:]

O merciful Lord and heavenly Father, by whose gracious gift mankind is increased: we beseech thee assist with thy blessing these two persons, that they may both be fruitful in procreation of children, and also live together so long in godly love and honesty, that they may see their children's children, unto the third and fourth generation, unto thy praise and honor: through Jesus Christ our Lord. Amen.

O God, which by thy mighty power hast made all things of naught; which also, after other things set in order, didst appoint that out of man (created after thine own image and similitude) woman should take her beginning: and knitting them together, didst teach that it should never be lawful to put asunder those, whom thou by matrimony hadst made one: O God which hast consecrated the state of matrimony to such an excellent mystery, that in it is signified and represented the spiritual marriage and unity betwixt Christ and his church: Look mercifully upon these thy servants, that both this man may love his wife, according to thy word (as Christ did love his spouse the church, who gave himself for it, loving and cherishing it even as his own flesh:) And also that this woman may be loving and amiable to her husband as Rachel, wise as Rebecca, faithful and obedient as Sara, and in all quietness, sobriety, and peace be a follower of holy and godly matrons: O Lord, bless them both, and grant them to inherit thy everlasting kingdom: through Jesus Christ our Lord. Amen.

Then shall the priest say,

Almighty God, which at the beginning did create our first parents Adam and Eve, and did sanctify and join them together in marriage: pour upon you the riches of his grace, sanctify and bless you, that ye may please him both in body and soul, and live together in holy love, unto your lives' end. Amen.

Then shall begin the Communion, and after the gospel shall be said a sermon, wherein ordinarily (so oft as there is any marriage) the office of a man and wife shall be declared, according to holy scripture: or if there be no sermon, the minister shall read this that followeth:

All ye which be married, or which intend to take the holy estate of matrimony upon you: hear what holy scripture doth say, as touching the duty of husbands toward their wives, and wives toward their husbands. Saint Paul (in his epistle to the Ephesians, the fifth chapter) doth give this commandment to all married men:

Ye husbands love your wives, even as Christ loved the church, and hath given himself for it, to sanctify it purging it in the fountain of water, through thy word, that he might make it unto himself a glorious congregation, not having spot or wrinkle, or any such thing, but that it should be holy and blameless. So men are bound to love their own wives as their own bodies. He that loveth his own wife, loveth himself: for never did any man hate his own flesh, but nourisheth and cherisheth it, even as the Lord doth the congregation: for we are members of his body, of his flesh and of his bones.

For this cause shall a man leave father and mother, and shall be joined unto his wife, and they two shall be one flesh. This mystery is great: but I speak of Christ and of the congregation. Nevertheless, let every one of you so love his own wife, even as himself.

Likewise the same Saint Paul (writing to the Colossians [3:19]) speaketh thus to all men that be married: Ye men, love your wives, and be not bitter unto them.

Hear also what Saint Peter the apostle of Christ, which was himself a married man, saith unto all men that are married: Ye husbands, dwell with your wives according to knowledge: Giving honor unto the wife as unto the weaker vessel, and as heirs together of the grace of life, so that your prayers be not hindered [1 Peter 3:7].

Hitherto ye have heard the duty of the husband toward the wife. Now likewise, ye wives, hear and learn your duty toward your husbands, even as it is plainly set forth in holy scripture.

Saint Paul (in the forenamed epistle to the Ephesians, fifth chapter) teacheth you thus: Ye women, submit yourselves unto your own husbands as unto the Lord: for the husband is the wife's head, even as Christ is the head of the church. And he is also the Savior of the whole body. Therefore as the church or congregation is subject unto Christ, so likewise let the wives also be in subjection unto their own husbands in all things. And again he saith: Let the wife reverence her husband. And (in his epistle to the Colossians [3:18]) Saint Paul giveth you this short lesson: Ye wives, submit yourselves unto your own husbands, as it is convenient in the Lord.

Saint Peter also doth instruct you very godly, thus saying: Let wives be subject to their own husbands, so that if any obey not the word, they may be won without the word by the conversation of the wives, while they behold your chaste conversation coupled with fear: whose apparel let it not be outward, with braided hair and trimming about with gold, either in putting on of gorgeous apparel: but let the hid man which is in the heart, be without all corruption, so that the spirit be mild and quiet, which is a precious thing in the sight of God. For after this manner (in the old time) did the holy women which trusted in God apparel themselves, being subject to their own husbands: as Sara obeyed Abraham, calling him lord; whose daughters ye are made, doing well, and being not dismayed with any fear [1 Peter 3:1–6].

The new married persons (the same day of their marriage) must receive the Holy Communion.

An Homily of the State of Matrimony. The "homilies" were sermons prescribed for reading in the Church of England. Written by various clergymen and published in two volumes (the first in 1547 and the second in 1563, with many later editions), these homilies are considered one of the foundational documents of Anglicanism, the others being the Bible, the Thirty-Nine Articles (a summary of doctrine), and the Book of Common Prayer. Near the end of a series of over 30 sermons on scripture, salvation, faith, works, repentance, the sacraments, prayer, and many other topics comes a sermon on "the state of matrimony," emphasizing the purposes of marriage, the duties of husband and wife, and the dangers of marital conflict. As an expression of official views on these matters, the homily straightforwardly calls for wives' obedience and attributes marital conflict to sin. Yet it also advises patience and love on the part of both spouses. Later discussions of these topics often took a more nuanced approach, suggesting that Shakespeare's contemporaries, though quite familiar with the homily, did not always find that it matched their own view or experience of marriage. (*The Second Tome of Homilies . . . Set Out by the Authority of the Late Queenes Majestie: and to Be Read in Every Parish Church Agreeablie*. London, 1623. 239–48.)

DOCUMENT 6: FROM *AN HOMILY OF THE STATE OF MATRIMONY*

The word of Almighty God doth testify and declare, whence the original beginning of matrimony cometh, and why it is ordained. It is instituted of God, to the intent that man and woman should live lawfully in a perpetual friendship, to bring forth fruit, and to avoid fornication. By which means a good conscience might be preserved on both parties, in bridling the corrupt inclinations of the flesh, within the limits of honesty. For God hath straightly forbidden all whoredom and uncleanness, and hath from time to time taken grievous punishment of this inordinate lust, as all stories and ages have declared. Furthermore it is also ordained, that the church of God and his kingdom might by this kind of life be conserved and enlarged, not only in that God giveth children by his blessing, but also in that they be brought up by the parents godly, in the knowledge of God's word, that thus the knowledge of God and true religion might be delivered by succession from one to another that finally many might enjoy that everlasting immortality. Wherefore, forasmuch as matrimony serveth us as well to avoid sin and offence, as to increase the kingdom of God: you, as all other which enter the state, must acknowledge this benefit of God, with pure and thankful minds, for that he hath so ruled your hearts, that ye follow not the example of the wicked world, who set their delight in filthiness of sin, but both of you stand in the fear of God, and abhor all filthiness. . . . For the devil will assay to attempt all things to interrupt and hinder your hearts and godly purpose, if ye will give him any entry. For he will either labor to break this godly knot once begun betwixt you, or else at the least he will labor to encumber it with divers griefs and displeasures.

And this is the principal craft [trick], to work dissension of hearts of the one from the other: That whereas now there is pleasant and sweet love betwixt you, he will in the stead thereof, bring in most bitter and unpleasant discord. And surely that same adversary of ours, doth, as it were from above, assault man's nature and condition. For this folly is ever from our tender age grown up with us, to have a desire to rule, to think highly of our self, so that none thinketh it meet to give place to another. That wicked vice of stubborn will and self-love, is more meet to break and to dissever the love of heart, than to preserve concord. Wherefore married persons must apply their minds in most earnest wise to concord, and must crave continually of God the help of his Holy Spirit, so to rule their hearts, and to knit their minds together, that they be not dissevered by any division of discord. This necessity of prayer, must be oft in the practice and using of married persons, that oft times the one should pray for the other, lest hate and debate do arise betwixt them. And because few do consider this thing, but more few do perform it (I say to pray diligently) we see how wonderful the devil deludeth and scorneth this state, how few matrimonies there be without chidings, brawlings, tauntings, repentings, bitter cursings, and fightings. Which things whosoever doth commit, they do not consider that it is the instigation of the ghostly [spiritual] enemy, who taketh great delight therein: For else they would with all earnest endeavor, strive against these mischiefs, not only with prayer, but also with all possible diligence. . . .

But to this prayer must be joined a singular diligence, whereof Saint Peter giveth this precept, saying, You husbands, deal with your weaker vessel, and as unto them that are heirs also of the grace of life, that your prayers be not hindered (1 Peter 3:7). This precept doth particularly pertain to the husband: for he ought to be the leader and author of love, in cherishing and increasing concord, which then shall take place, if he will use moderation and not tyranny, and if he yield some thing to the woman. For the woman is a weak creature, not endowed with like strength and constancy of mind, therefore they be the sooner disquieted, and they be the more prone to all weak affections and dispositions of mind, more than men be, and lighter they be, and more vain in their fantasies and opinions. These things must be considered of the man, that he be not too stiff, so that he ought to wink at some things, and must gently expound all things, and to forbear.

Howbeit the common sort of men doth judge, that such moderation should not become a man: For they say that it is a token of womanish cowardness, and therefore they think that it is a man's part to fume in anger, to fight with fist and staff. Howbeit, howsoever they imagine, undoubtedly Saint Peter doth better judge what should be seeming [appropriate] to a man, and what he should most reasonably perform. For he saith, reasoning should be used, and not fighting. Yea he saith more, that the woman ought to have a certain honor attributed to her, that is to say, she must be spared and borne with, the rather for that she is the weaker vessel, of a frail heart, inconstant, and with a word soon stirred to wrath. And therefore considering these her frailties, she is to be the rather spared. By this means, thou shalt not only nourish concord: but shalt have her heart in thy power and will. For honest natures will sooner be retained to do their duties, rather by gentle words, than by stripes. But he which will do all things with extremity and severity, and doth use always rigor in words and stripes, what will that avail in the conclusion? Verily nothing, but that he thereby setteth forward the devil's work, he banisheth away concord, charity, and sweet amity [friendship], and bringeth in dissension, hatred, and irksomeness, the greatest griefs that can be in the mutual love and fellowship of man's life. Beyond all this, it bringeth another evil therewith, for it is the destruction and interruption of prayer: For in the time that the mind is occupied with dissension and discord, there can be no true prayer used. For the Lord's Prayer hath not only a respect to particular persons, but to the whole universal, in the which we openly pronounce, that we will forgive them which have offended against us, even as we ask forgiveness of our sins of God, which thing how can it be done rightly, when their hearts be at dissension? How can they pray each for other, when they be at hate betwixt themselves? . . .

Now as concerning the wife's duty. What shall become her? Shall she abuse the gentleness and humanity of her husband and, at her pleasure, turn all things upside down? No surely. For that is far repugnant against God's commandment, For thus doth Saint Peter preach to them, Ye wives, be ye in subjection to obey your own husbands (1 Peter 3:1). To obey, is another thing than to control or command, which yet they may do, to their children, and to their family [household]: But as for their husbands, them must they obey, and cease from commanding, and perform subjection. For this surely doth nourish concord very much, when the wife is ready at hand at her husband's commandment, when she will apply herself to his will, when she endeavoreth herself to seek his contentation [contentment], and to do him pleasure, when she will eschew [avoid] all things that might offend him: For thus will most truly be verified the saying of the poet, A good wife by obeying her husband, shall bear the rule, so that he shall have a delight and a gladness, the sooner at all times to return home to her. But on the contrary part, when the wives be stubborn, froward [perverse], and malapert [impudent], their husbands are compelled thereby to abhor and flee from their own houses, even as they should have battle with their enemies. Howbeit, it can scantly be, but that some offences shall sometime chance betwixt them: For no man doth live without fault, specially for that the woman is the more frail party. Therefore let them beware that they stand not in their faults and willfulness: but rather let them acknowledge their follies, and say, My husband, so it is, that by my anger I was compelled to do this or that, forgive it me, and hereafter I will take better heed. Thus ought the woman more readily to do, the more they be ready to offend. And they shall not do this only to avoid strife and debate: but rather in the respect of the commandment of God, as Saint Paul expresseth it in this form of words, Let women be subject to their husbands as to the Lord: for the husband is the head of the woman, as Christ is the head of the church (Ephesians 5:22–23). Here you understand, that God hath commanded that ye should acknowledge the authority of the husband, and refer to him the honor of obedience. . . .

. . . Let not therefore the woman be too busy to call for the duty of her husband, where she should be ready to perform her own, for that is not worthy any great commendations. And even so again, let not the man only consider what belongeth to the woman, and to stand too earnestly gazing thereon, for that is not his part or duty. But as I have said, let either party be ready and willing to perform that which belongeth especially to themselves. For if we be bound to hold out our left cheek to strangers which will smite us on the right cheek: how much more ought we to suffer an extreme and unkind husband? But yet I mean not that a man should beat his wife, God forbid that, for that is the greatest shame that can be, not so much to her that is beaten, as to him that doth the deed. But if by such fortune thou chancest upon such an husband, take it not too heavily, but suppose thou, that thereby is laid up no small reward hereafter, and in this life time no small commendation to thee, if thou canst be quiet. But yet to you that be men, thus I speak, Let there be none so grievous fault to compel you to beat your wives. But what say I, your wives? No, it is not to be borne with, that an honest man should lay hands on his maid servant to beat her. Wherefore if it be a great shame for a man to beat his bondservant, much more rebuke it is, to lay violent hands upon his freewoman. And this thing may be well understood by the laws which the paynims [pagans] have made, which doth discharge her any longer to dwell with such an husband, as unworthy to have any further company with her that doth smite her. For it is an extreme point, thus so vilely to entreat her like a slave, that is fellow to thee of thy life, and so joined unto thee before time in the necessary matters of thy living. And therefore a man may well liken such a man (if he may be called a man, rather than a wild beast) to a killer of his father or his mother. And whereas we be commanded to forsake our father and mother, for our wives' sake, and yet thereby do work them none injury, but do fulfill the law of God: How can it not appear then to be a point of extreme madness, to entreat her despitefully, for whose sake God hath commanded thee to leave parents? Yea, who can suffer such despite [outrage]? Who can worthily express the inconvenience that is, to see what weepings and wailings be made in the open streets, when neighbors run together to the house of so unruly an husband, as to a Bedlam-man [madman; "Bedlam" was a hospital for the insane], who goeth about to overturn all that he hath at home? Who would not think that it were better for such a man to wish the ground to open, and swallow him in, than once ever after to be seen in the market? But peradventure thou wilt object, that the woman provoketh thee to this point. But consider thou again that the woman is a frail vessel, and thou art therefore made the ruler and head over her, to bear the weakness of her in this her subjection. And therefore study thou to declare the honest commendation of thine authority, which thou canst no way better do, than to forbear to urge her in her weakness and subjection. . . .

Whensoever any displeasant [unpleasant] matter riseth at home, if thy wife hath done aught amiss, comfort her, and increase not the heaviness. For though thou shouldest be grieved with never so many things, yet shalt thou find nothing more grievous than to want the benevolence of thy wife at home. What offence soever thou canst name, yet shalt thou find none more intolerable, than to be at debate with thy wife. And for this cause most of all oughtest thou to have this love in reverence. And if reason moveth thee to bear any burden at any other men's hands, much more at thy wife's. For if she be poor, upbraid her not, if she be simple, taunt her not, but be the more courteous: for she is thy body, and made one flesh with thee. But thou peradventure wilt say that she is a wrathful woman, a drunkard, and beastly, without wit and reason. For this cause bewail her the more. Chafe not in anger, but pray unto Almighty God. Let her be admonished and helped with good counsel, and do thou thy best endeavor, that she may be delivered of all these affections [inclinations]. But if thou shouldest beat her, thou shalt increase her evil affections: For frowardness [perversity] and sharpness, is not amended with frowardness, but with softness and gentleness. . . .

Do the best ye can of your parts, to custom your selves to softness and meekness, and bear well in worth such oversights as chance [happen]: and thus shall your conversation be most pleasant and comfortable. And although (which can no otherwise be) some adversities shall follow, and otherwhiles [sometimes] now one discommodity, now another shall appear: yet in this common trouble and adversity, lift up both your hands unto heaven, call upon the help and assistance of God, the author of your marriage, and surely the promise of relief is at hand. . . .

COURTSHIP AND BETROTHAL

Martin Parker (flourished 1624–1647). Broadside ballads were a popular feature of life in Shakespeare's time. *Broadside* refers to the large single sheet on which a ballad was printed. Intended for singing, ballads touch on various topics, including political events, current scandals, and marvels that strain belief. Many deal with the trials of young love, courtship, and marriage (see also **Document 20**). In *The Wooing Maid,* we hear the complaint of a young woman desperate to marry. Now over 20, she claims that "most marry at fourteen" and many shortly after. Like *Romeo and Juliet,* the ballad portrays a possible but highly exaggerated situation. In fact, few married at 14. Most married in their twenties, with 25 or 26 being the average age for women. Nevertheless, the ballad gives a vivid sense of attitudes and customs related to courtship in the early 1600s. *The Wooing Maid* is attributed to Martin Parker, who produced scores of popular ballads between the 1620s and 1640s. (*The Wooing Maid.* London, 1635.)

Document 7: *The Wooing Maid*

The Wooing Maid;
Or,
A fair maid neglected,
Forlorn and rejected,
That would be respected:
Which to have effected,
This general summon
She sendeth in common;
Come tinker, come *broom-man: ***street-sweeper***
She will refuse no man.

To the tune of *If 'be the dad on't.*

I am a fair maid, if my glass do not flatter,
Yet, by the effects, I can find no such matter;
For every one else can have suitors great plenty;
Most marry at fourteen, but I am past twenty.
Come gentle, come simple, come foolish, come witty,
Oh! if you lack a maid, take me for pity.

I see by experience—which makes me to wonder—
That many have sweethearts at fifteen, and under,
And if they pass sixteen, they think their time wasted;
O what shall become of me? I am out-casted:
Come gentle, come simple, come foolish, come witty,
Oh! if you lack a maid, take me for pity.

I use all the motives my sex will permit me.
To put men in mind, that they may not forget me:
Nay, sometimes I *set my commission o' th' tenters, ***put my authority on tenterhooks or on the rack (i.e., strain my authority)***
Yet let me do what I will, never a man ventures.
Come gentle, &c.

When I go to weddings, or such merry meetings,
I see other maids how they toy with their *sweetings, ***sweethearts***
But I sit alone, like an abject forsaken;

Woe's me! for a husband what course shall be taken?
Come gentle, &c.

When others to dancing are courteously chosen,
I am the last taken among the half dozen,
An yet among twenty not one can excel me;
What shall I do in this case? some good man tell me.
Come gentle, &c.

'Tis said that one wedding produceth another—
This I have heard told by my father and mother—
Before one shall scape me, I'll go without bidding;
O that I could find out some fortunate wedding!
Come gentle, &c.

Sure I am unfortunate, of all my kindred,
Else could not my happiness be so long hindered:
My mother at eighteen had two sons and a daughter,
And I'm one and twenty, not worth looking after.
Come gentle, &c.

My sister, that's nothing so handsome as I am,
Had six or seven suitors, and she had to deny them;
Yet she before sixteen was luckily married:
O Fates! why are things so unequally carried?
Come gentle, &c.

My kinswoman Sisly, in all parts misshapen,
Yet she had a husband by fortune did happen
Before she was nineteen years old, at the furthest;
Among all my lineage am I the unworthiest?
Come gentle, &c.

There are almost forty, both poorer and younger,
Within few years married, yet I must stay longer.
Within four miles compass—O is't not a wonder?
Scant none above twenty, some sixteen, some under.
Come gentle, &c.

I hold my self equal with most in the parish
For feature, for parts, and what chiefly doth cherish
The fire of affection, which is store of money;
And yet there is no man will set love upon me.
Come gentle, &c.

Who ever he be that will ease my affliction,
And cast upon me an auspicious affection,
Shall find me tractable still to content him,

That he of his bargain shall never repent him.
Come gentle, &c.

I'll neither be given to scold nor be jealous,
He ne'er shall want money to drink with good fellows:
While he spends abroad, I at home will be saving,
Now judge, am I not a lassie worth the having.
Come gentle, &c.

Let none be offended, nor say I'm uncivil,
For I needs must have one, be he good or evil;
Nay, rather than fail, I'll have a tinker or broom-man,
A peddler, an ink-man, a mat-man or some man.
Come gentle, come simple, come foolish, come witty,
Oh let me not die a maid, take me for pity.

John Stockwood (died 1610). The title *A Bartholomew Fairing* refers to a popular fair held annually in London. In this book, Stockwood, a minister and schoolmaster, argues that children should not marry without their parents' consent and that parents should provide good matches for their children. At the same time, because marriage should be founded on love, he condemns parental tyranny and advises young people who are in love to seek their parents' permission to marry as they wish. The vigor of Stockwood's argument indicates that parents were often not as involved in their children's courtship and marriage as he might have liked. (*A Bartholmew Fairing for Parentes to Bestow upon Their Sonnes and Daughters*. London, 1589. 76–78.)

Document 8: From *A Bartholomew Fairing for Parents*

[Using Martin Luther as his source, Stockwood argues the following:] Parents ought to provide their sons and daughters of honest marriage: Although . . . parents do sometimes abuse their power and authority, and will compel their children to marry with those, whom they love not, the which cometh often to pass in the great families of noble men. They are to be found fault withal, because they carry no spark of a fatherly mind and affection, but are blocks and stocks, they have not that same natural love towards their children. In such a case let the pastor of the church, or the civil magistrate set in their authority; because that this is not a fatherly power, but a tyranny. . . .

Furthermore, let children know that they are to ask their [the parents'] advice and to know their pleasure. Let not a young man, whose age is fit for marriage, be afraid to open his mind unto his parents: that he is in love with an honest maiden, and desire, that they will give her him to wife. For albeit [although] this seem to be a token of lust scarce comely [proper], yet let them know that God his mercy doth cover the same in marriage, and hath given a remedy for this disease. Let them therefore humble themselves before their parents, and plainly and freely say unto them: My dear father, my good mother, give me such a young man, or such a maiden, whom I love. And if she be worthy to be matched with thee, or worthy of thine affinity [relationships by marriage], or thy parents', thine honest parents will not deny thee, albeit the dowry or wealth be not answerable. Such marriages cannot choose but be happy and prosperous, and God of his infinite goodness doth bless, pardon, and cover the heat of lust as it were with the cover of marriage.

The Law's Resolutions of Women's Rights. The author of this collection of legal opinions related to women is unknown but, according to the volume's preface, died before its publication. Modern authorities have named several possible writers, including John More, Sir John Doddridge, and Thomas Edgar. Whoever the writer is, he describes women's vulnerable legal position and presents himself as a defender of their rights. In the following excerpts, from sections 1, 3, and 4 of the second book, he defines marriage and discusses both public and secret "sponsion" (his term for spousal or the promise to marry), including the dangers of the latter. (*The Lawes Resolutions of Womens Rights: or, The Lawes Provision for Woemen.* London, 1632. 51–54.)

DOCUMENT 9: FROM *THE LAW'S RESOLUTIONS OF WOMEN'S RIGHTS*

Section I. Of marriage, according to the civil and common law

Marriage is defined to be a conjunction of man and woman, containing an inseparable connection and union of life. But as there is nothing that is begotten and finished at once, so this contract of coupling man and woman together, hath an inception first, and then an orderly proceeding. The first beginning of marriage (as in respect of contract, and that which law taketh hold on) is when wedlock by words in the future tense is promised and vowed, and this is but *sponsio* or *sponsalia* [a solemn promise]. The full contract of matrimony, is when it is made by words *de praesenti* [in the present tense] in a lawful consent, and thus two be made man and wife existing without lying together, yet matrimony is not accounted consummate until there go with the consent of mind and will conjunction of body.

Section III. Of public sponsion [promise to marry]

This sponsion (in which as it stands, is no full contract of matrimony, nor any more, save only an obligation, or being bound in a sort to marry hereafter) may be public or secret: . . . it is now received a general opinion that the good-will of parents is required in regard of honesty, not of necessity, according to the canons which exact necessarily none other consent but only of the parties themselves, whose conjunction is in hand, without which the conclusion of parents is of none effect. . . .

Section IV. Of secret sponsion

Those spousals which are made when a man is without witness, *solus cum sola* [the man alone with the woman], are called secret promising or desponsation [betrothal], which though it be tolerated when by liquid [evident] and plain probation [examination] it may appear to the judge, and there is not any lawful impediment to hinder the contract, yet it is so little esteemed of (unless it be very manifest) that another promise public made after it shall be preferred and prevail against it. The cause why it is misliked, is the difficulty of proof for avoiding of it, when for offense her just cause of refusal, the one or other party might seek to go loose and perhaps cannot, but must stand haltered from any other marriage, and the judge in suspense what to determine.

Henry Swinburne (c. 1551–1624). Swinburne, who held judicial positions in York, was a lawyer specializing in ecclesiastical (church) law, which governed such matters as marriage, divorce, and inheritance. He is best known for two works, *A Brief Treatise of Testaments and Last Wills* and *A Treatise of Spousals, or Matrimonial Contracts*. The excerpts presented here are from the second book, in which he discusses betrothal, marriage, and divorce. Among other things, he states emphatically that a valid marriage requires the consent of the bride and groom. Though published in 1686, *A Treatise of Spousals* must have been written before 1624, when Swinburne died. (*A Treatise of Spousals, or Matrimonial Contracts*. London, 1686. 5, 11–14, 193–95.)

DOCUMENT 10: FROM *A TREATISE OF SPOUSALS*

Section II. The definition of spousals

. . . Spousals are a mutual promise of future marriage, being duly made between those persons, to whom it is lawful. In which definition I observe three things especially: One, that this promise must be mutual; Another, that it must be done right, duly: The last, by them to whom it is lawful.

First, whereas this promise is described to be mutual, it proveth that it is not sufficient if either of the parties alone do promise: And therefore if the man (for example) say to the woman, "I do promise that I will marry thee": But if the woman doth not make the like promise to the man; or contrariwise, the woman doth promise, but not the man, this is a lame contract (having as it were but one leg) and so not being able to walk upright, is not of any force of law.

Section IV. Of the great importance of the first division or distinction betwixt spousals *de futuro* and spousals *de praesenti*

When we shall view the small difference betwixt those words, whereby spousals *de futuro* [in the future tense], or *de praesenti* [in the present tense] are contracted, it cannot but seem strange that from so small difference of forms, so great diversity of effects should proceed: for in truth, so very little (very often) is the odds betwixt the form of words of these two contracts, that the best learned are at greatest variance, whether such words make spousals *de futuro*, or *de praesenti*. Neither is it unknown to the youngest students in this faculty, that words of future time do not evermore import spousals *de futuro;* neither words of present time always spousals *de praesenti*. Again, that some words are so untoward [awkward, stiff], that it is a question whether they make any kind of spousals at all; and contrariwise, some words so flexible that they may easily be stretched to make, either the one or the other. . . .

. . . Understand therefore, that that man and that woman, which do contract spousals *de futuro*, as "I will take thee to my wife; I will take thee to my husband," are not very [truly] husband and wife, neither so reputed in law except in certain cases hereafter expressed, which excepted, they may by mutual agreement dissolve those spousals, and safely match themselves elsewhere; or if but the one of them alone shall renounce, and thereupon adventure [venture] indeed to marry otherwise, or to contract spousals *de praesenti* with some other person, in these cases by the laws civil and ecclesiastical, this marriage or contract *de praesenti* shall stand firm and lawful, notwithstanding the pre-contract of spousals *de futuro:* The reason is, because, like as when a man doth promise he will sell his land, the land is not thereby sold in deed, but promised to be sold afterwards; so while the parties do promise only, that they will take, or will marry; they do not thereby presently take or marry: but deferring the accomplishment of that promise until another time, the knot in the meantime is not so surely tied, but that it may be loosed, while the matter is in suspense and unperfect. But that woman, and that man, which have contracted spousals *de praesenti;* as, "I do take thee to my wife" and "I do take thee to my husband" cannot by any agreement dissolve those spousals, but are reputed for very husband and wife in respect of the substance and indissoluble knot of matrimony; and therefore if either of them should in fact proceed to solemnize matrimony with any other person, consummating the same by carnal copulation, and procreation of children: this matrimony is to be dissolved as unlawful, the parties marrying to be punished as adulterers, and their issue in danger of bastardy.

The reason is, because here is no promise of any future act, but a present and perfect consent, the which alone maketh matrimony, without either public solemnization or carnal copulation; for neither is the one, nor the other of the essence of matrimony, but consent only.

Section XIV. Of public and private spousals

Fourthly, spousals be either public or private; public spousals are they which are contracted before sufficient witnesses, and wherein are observed all other solemnities requisite by the ecclesiastical law: For so careful were the ancient law-makers to avoid those mischiefs, which commonly attend upon secret and clandestine contracts, that they would have the same solemnities observed in contracting spousals, which be requisite in contracting matrimony; Which solemnities what they are shall afterwards be declared: Private spousals are they, at the contracting whereof, are omitted some of those solemnities aforesaid, but especially when as there be no witnesses present at the contract: In which case these questions following are usually propounded.

First, whether such secret contracts be good in law, yea, or no? And it seemeth they are not good. . . . But the law doth forbid all persons to make secret contracts of spousals, or matrimony; and that justly, considering the manifold discommodities [inconveniences] depending thereupon, namely, for that hereby it cometh to pass oftentimes, that the parties secretly contracting, are otherwise formally affianced [engaged], or so near in blood that they cannot be married; or being free from those impediments, yet do they alter their purposes, denying and breaking their promises, whence perjuries, adulteries, and bastardies, with many more intolerable mischiefs do succeed; and therefore such secret pacts, covenants, and contracts are worthily reputed, as if they had not been made at all. . . . Wherefore seeing secret contracts cannot be proved, it is all one in effect, as if they were not.

Others are of another opinion, holding the contract for firm and indissoluble; for the confirmation whereof, they allege a very round [neatly expressed] text, extant in the body of the law, the words are these. . . . Secret marriages are done indeed against the law, but being contracted, cannot be dissolved; Yielding this reason, that because these solemnities are not of the substance of spousals, or of matrimony, but consent only; for (as another text saith) . . . Naked consent is sufficient to make spousals.

MARRIAGE: LOVE, DUTY, CONFLICT

Edmund Spenser (1552?–1599). Spenser is one of England's major poets, greatly admired for his lyric poetry and for his great romantic epic *The Faerie Queene,* an allegorical fantasy with religious, moral, political, and philosophical import. Along with many other topics, Spenser deals with romantic love and marriage, especially in Book 3 of *The Faerie Queene* and in his *Amoretti* and *Epithalamion.* In the *Amoretti,* Spenser portrays his own courtship of Elizabeth Boyle. The *Epithalamion* celebrates their marriage. The *Amoretti,* a series of sonnets, use elements derived from the Italian poet Petrarch, who wrote of the joy and misery of being in love with an unapproachable, idealized woman. But Spenser departs from the Petrarchan pattern by depicting a courtship that finally leads to marriage. Spenser's *Epithalamion,* based on ancient Greek and Roman models, describes the wedding day and (in the selection provided here) the wedding night. Frankly describing the couple's sexual "delight," the poet calls for heaven's blessing on the marriage and gives their bond cosmic, social, and spiritual significance, tying their hope to conceive a child with the vitality of nature and anticipation of "a large posterity" who will enjoy both earthly happiness and heavenly bliss. Though I have modified some of the poem's typographical features, I have followed the conventional practice of retaining Spenser's spelling. (*Amoretti and Epithalamion.* London, 1595. H4v, H5v–H7r.)

Document 11: From *Epithalamion* (lines 315–33, 353–426)

Now welcome night, thou night so long expected,
that long daies labour doest at last defray,
And all my cares, which cruell love collected,
Hast sumd in one, and cancelled for *aye: ***ever***
Spread thy broad wing over my love and me,
that no man may us see,

And in thy sable mantle us enwrap,
From feare of perrill and foule horror free.
Let no false treason seeke us to entrap,
Nor any dread disquiet once annoy
the safety of our joy:
But let the night be calme and quietsome,
Without tempestuous storms or sad *afray: ***fear***
Lyke as when Jove with fayre *Alcmena lay, ***the mother of Hercules***
When he begot the great *Tirynthian groome: ***Hercules***
Or lyke as when he with *thy selfe did lie, ***with night***
And begot Majesty.
And let the mayds and yongmen cease to sing:
Ne let the woods them answer, nor theyr eccho ring.

. . . .

But let stil Silence trew night watches keepe,
That sacred peace may in assurance rayne,
And tymely sleep, when it is tyme to sleepe,
May poure his limbs forth on your pleasant playne,
The whiles an hundred little winged *loves, ***Cupids***
Like divers fethered doves,
Shall fly and flutter round about your bed,
And in the secret darke, that none reproves,
Their prety stealthes shal worke, & snares shal spread
To filch away sweet snatches of delight,
Conceald through covert night.
Ye sonnes of Venus, play your sports at will,
For greedy pleasure, carelesse of your *toyes, ***amorous play***
Thinks more upon her paradise of joyes,
Then what ye do, albe it good or ill.
All night therefore attend your merry play,
For it will soone be day:
Now none doth hinder you, that say or sing,
Ne will the woods now answer, nor your Eccho ring.

Who is the same, which at my window peepes?
Or whose is that faire face, that shines so bright,
Is it not *Cinthia, she that never sleepes, ***Cynthia or Diana, goddess of the moon and patroness of childbirth***
But walkes about high heaven al the night?
O fayrest goddesse, do thou not envy
My love with me to spy:
For thou likewise didst love, though now unthought,
And for a fleece of *woll, which privily, ***wool***
The *Latmian shepherd once unto thee brought, ***Endymion***
His pleasures with thee wrought.
Therefore to us be favorable now;
And sith of wemens labours thou hast charge,

And generation goodly dost enlarge,
Encline thy will t'effect our wishfull vow,
And the chast wombe informe with timely seed,
That may our comfort breed:
Till which we cease our *hopefull hap to sing, *hoped for good fortune*
Ne let the woods us answere, nor our Eccho ring.

And thou great Juno, which with *awful might *awe-inspiring*
the lawes of wedlock still dost patronize,
And the religion of the faith first plight
With sacred rites hast taught to solemnize:
and *eeke for comfort often called art *also*
Of women in their *smart, *pain of childbirth; labor*
Eternally bind thou this *lovely band, *loving*
And all thy blessings unto us impart.
And thou glad *Genius, in whose gentle hand, *god or spirit of procreation*
The bridale bowre and *geniall bed remaine, *life-giving, pertaining to marriage*
Without blemish or staine,
And the sweet pleasures of theyr loves delight.
With secret ayde doest succour and supply,
Till they bring forth the fruitfull progeny,
Send us the timely fruit of this same night.
And thou fayre *Hebe, and thou *Hymen free, *goddess of youth . . . god of marriage*
Grant that it may so be.
Til which we cease your further prayse to sing,
Ne any woods shal answer, nor your Eccho ring.

And ye high heavens, the temple of the gods,
In which a thousand torches flaming bright
Doe burne, that to us wretched earthly clods:
In dreadful darknesse lend desired light;
And all ye powers which in the same remayne,
More then we men can *fayne, *feign (i.e., pretend or imagine)*
Poure out your blessing on us plentiously,
And happy influence upon us raine,
That we may raise a large posterity,
Which from the earth, which they may long possesse,
With lasting happinesse,
Up to your *haughty pallaces may mount, *exalted, lofty*
And for the *guerdon of theyr glorious merit *reward*
May heavenly tabernacles there inherit,
Of blessed Saints for to increase the count.
So let us rest, sweet love, in hope of this,
And cease till then our tymely joyes to sing,
The woods no more us answer, nor our eccho ring.

But let stil Silence trew night watches keepe,
That sacred peace may in assurance rayne,

And tymely sleep, when it is tyme to sleepe,
May poure his limbs forth on your pleasant playne,
The whiles an hundred little winged *loves, ***Cupids***
Like divers fethered doves,
Shall fly and flutter round about your bed,
And in the secret darke, that none reproves,
Their prety stealthes shal worke, & snares shal spread
To filch away sweet snatches of delight,
Conceald through covert night.
Ye sonnes of Venus, play your sports at will,
For greedy pleasure, carelesse of your *toyes, ***amorous play***
Thinks more upon her paradise of joyes,
Then what ye do, albe it good or ill.
All night therefore attend your merry play,
For it will soone be day:
Now none doth hinder you, that say or sing,
Ne will the woods now answer, nor your Eccho ring.

William Austin (c. 1587–1634). Though *Haec Homo* was not published until after his death, Austin, a lawyer, may have written it about 1620. Like a host of other writers during this period, Austin took part in the controversy over gender issues, examining the nature of men and women and asking which of the two is superior. Writing in praise of women, Austin focuses on the biblical story of Adam and Eve. Whereas some had used this story against women, interpreting Eve as responsible for the fall of mankind, Austin views the story as showing that women are essentially equal to men and in some respects even superior. Austin was one of many who used Eve's creation from Adam's rib as an indication that marriage should be both an intimate and an egalitarian companionship. The title *Haec Homo,* Latin for "this man" or "this human being" but with "this" in the feminine form, apparently asserts women's full humanity alongside men. (*Haec Homo: Wherein the Excellency of the Creation of Woman, Is Described*. London, 1637. 6–7, 39–41, 43.)

Document 12: From *Haec Homo*

She [woman] hath not only the same name with him [man]; but, they are both of one figure; made by one workman; of one substance; in one place; in one day; so that, there is no such general difference between them, that can give excuse to man to esteem basely and meanly of her, but that he must needs (therein) touch himself: since she was made so equal with him, and so like him. Notwithstanding, there may be observed some nice [subtle] differences between them in their creation: but indeed, they are such, as rather much increase her praise, than detract the least scruple from her worth and excellency. . . .

And as a rib cannot be divided from the body of man, but by death; or by extreme violence: So cannot woman be divided from that sacred conjunction, (in which she is made one body with her husband,) but by death, or adultery; which is the extreme violation of the nuptial bed. . . .

... He should remember, that she is one rib of his, and no more; and, that the rest of her body (in the composition) was added and supplied by the Lord himself, whose (indeed) she is by right: and who hath only lent her unto him, as a fellow-helper; and not as a servant. . . .

Moreover, she was taken from his side; not only to give ease and rest to him, but also, to give dignity and honor unto her: For (as it hath been observed,) as she was not made of his head, (to sit above, and rule him;) so, was she not made of his feet; (to be despised, and trodden under him:) but, from his side; (to be equal with him,) so that, though he be her head; she is not his feet: but may go side by side with him.

Rachel Speght (born 1597?). Both men and women took part in the debate about marriage and gender roles that surfaced periodically in early modern England. As its full title indicates, Speght's contribution, in 1617, was a response to a notorious antifeminist pamphlet titled *The Arraignment of Women,* published two years earlier. In *A Muzzle for Melastomus* (*Melastomus* means "black mouth"), Speght energetically and learnedly defends women (mainly on religious grounds), argues that a husband should help with household chores and that his position as head should be one of love and service, and describes the ideal unity of husband and wife. Speght, the daughter of a London minister, wrote this pamphlet at age 19. (*A Mouzell for Melastomus, the Cynicall Bayter of, and Foule Mouthed Barker against Evahs Sex. Or an Apologeticall Answere to That Irreligious and Illiterate Pamphlet Made by Io. Sw. [John Swetnam] and by Him Intituled,* The Arraignement of Women. London, 1617. 12–17, 20–21.)

Document 13: From *A Muzzle for Melastomus*

The other end for which woman was made, was to be a companion and helper for man; and if she must be an helper, and but an helper, then are those husbands to be blamed, which lay the whole burden of domestical affairs and maintenance on the shoulders of their wives. For, as yoke-fellows they are to sustain part of each other's cares, griefs, and calamities. . . .

Seeing then that these unreasonable creatures [animals], by the instinct of nature, bear such affection each to other, that without any grudge, they willingly, according to their kind [nature], help one another, I may reason . . . that much more should man and woman, which are reasonable creatures, be helpers each to other in all things lawful. . . . So that neither the wife may say to her husband, nor the husband unto his wife, I have no need of thee, no more than the members of the body may so say each to other, between whom there is such a sympathy, that if one member suffer, all suffer with it. . . .

Marriage is a merry-age, and this world's paradise, where there is mutual love. . . .

. . . With God is no respect of persons, nations, or sexes: For whosoever, whether it be man or woman, that doth believe in the Lord Jesus, such shall be saved. And if God's love even from the beginning, had not been as great toward woman as to man, then would he not have preserved from the deluge of the old world as many women as men; nor would Christ after his resurrection have appeared unto a woman first of all other, had it not been to declare thereby, that the benefits of his death and resurrection, are as available, by belief, for women as for men; for he indifferently died for the one sex as well as the other: Yet a truth ungainsayable [undeniable] is it, that the man is the woman's head; by which title yet of supremacy, no authority hath he given him to domineer, or basely command and employ his wife, as a servant; but hereby is he taught the duties which he oweth unto her: For as the head of a man is the imaginer and contriver of projects profitable for the safety of his whole body; so the husband must protect and defend his wife from injuries: For he is her head, as Christ is the head of his church, which he entirely loveth, and for which he gave his very life. . . . Secondly, as the head doth not jar or contend with the members, which being many, as the apostle saith, yet make but one body; no more must the husband with the wife, but expelling all bitterness and cruelty he must live with her lovingly, and religiously, honoring her as the weaker vessel. Thirdly, and lastly, as he is her head, he must, by instruction, bring her to the knowledge of her creator, that so she may be a fit stone for the Lord's building.

Great was the unthankfulness of Pharaoh's butler [see Genesis 40] . . . But far greater is the ingratitude of those men toward God, that dare presume to speak and exclaim against woman, whom God did create for man's comfort. . . . Let men therefore beware of all unthankfulness, but especially of the superlative ingratitude, that which is towards God, which is no way more palpably declared, than by the contemning [scorning] of, and railing against women, which sin, of some men (if to be termed men) no doubt but God will one day avenge, when they shall plainly perceive, that it had been better for them to have been born dumb and lame, than to have used their tongues and hands, the one in repugning [contending], the other in writing against God's handiwork, their own flesh, women I mean, whom God hath made equal with themselves in dignity, both temporally and eternally, if they continue in the faith: which God for his mercy sake grant they always may, to the glory of their Creator, and comfort of their own souls, through Christ, amen.

William Gouge (1575–1653). Gouge's *Of Domestical Duties* is a large volume discussing the duties of various family members. Gouge, a well-known Anglican minister and preacher, views the subject (as would most of his contemporaries) in religious terms and supports his advice with frequent scriptural quotations. Among other things, he wrote against wife beating and noted that a wife's duty to obey her husband was not absolute. In the following excerpts, he discusses the "remedies against adultery" and "mutual love betwixt man and wife." Gouge views sexual relations in marriage (which he calls "due benevolence," using the biblical phrase) not only as a remedy against adultery and a source of offspring but also as producing affection and mutual delight. Most of Gouge's contemporaries would have agreed with these views, as well as with his assertion that the love between husband and wife is the highest human love. On another issue—the advisability of second marriages—opinion was divided. Gouge writes favorably of such marriages, noting that death produces "an utter dissolution of the marriage bond," freeing the surviving partner to remarry, and advising that love of a second spouse should take precedence over memories of the first. Interestingly, after his own wife's death while giving birth in 1625, he never remarried. (*Of Domesticall Duties Eight Treatises*. London, 1622. 221–22, 225–27.)

DOCUMENT 14: FROM *OF DOMESTICAL DUTIES*

Of Remedies against Adultery, and in particular of Due Benevolence, and of Defect or Excess Therein

. . . One of the best remedies [against adultery] that can be prescribed to married persons (next to an awful fear of God, and a continual setting of him before them, wheresoever they are) is, that husband and wife mutually delight each in other, and maintain a pure and fervent love betwixt themselves, yielding that due benevolence [i.e., sexual relations] one to another which is warranted and sanctified by God's word [see 1 Corinthians 7:3], and ordained of God for this particular end. This due benevolence (as the apostle styleth it) is one of the most proper and essential acts of marriage: and necessary for the main and principal ends thereof: as for preservation of chastity in such as have not the gift of continency [self-restraint], for increasing the world with a legitimate brood, and for linking the affections of the married couple more firmly together. These ends of marriage, at least the two former, are made void without this duty be performed.

As it is called benevolence because it must be performed with good will and delight, willingly, readily and cheerfully; so it is said to be due because it is a debt which the wife oweth to her husband, and he to her. For the wife hath not the power of her own body, but the husband; and likewise also the husband hath not the power of his own body, but the wife. . . .

Of Mutual Love Betwixt Man and Wife

. . . A loving mutual affection must pass betwixt husband and wife, or else no duty will be well performed: this is the ground of all the rest. In some respects love is proper and peculiar to an husband, as I purpose to show when I come to speak of an husband's particular duties. But love is also required of wives, and they are commanded to be lovers of their husbands, as well as husbands to love their wives: so as it is a common mutual duty belonging to husband and wife too: and that is true wedlock, when man and wife are linked together by the bond of love. Under love all other duties are comprised: for without it no duty can be well performed. Love is the fulfilling of the law, that is, the very life of all those duties which the law requireth. It is the bond of perfection, which bindeth together all those duties that pass betwixt party and party. Where love aboundeth, there all duties will readily and cheerfully be performed. Where love is wanting, there every duty will either be altogether neglected, or so carelessly performed, that as good not be performed at all: in which respect the apostle willeth, that all things be done in love. Love as it provoketh the party in whom it ruleth to do all the good it can; so it stirreth up the party loved to repay good for good. It is like fire, which is not only hot in it self, but also conveyeth heat into that which is near it: whence ariseth a reflection of heat from one to another. Note how admirably this is set forth betwixt Christ and his spouse in the Song of Solomon: and it is further manifested in the examples of all good husbands and wives noted in the scripture: they did mutually bear a very loving affection one to another.

. . . Man and wife therefore are each to other an especial pledge of God's favor, and in this respect above all others under God to be loved. If this be the ground (as it ought to be) of their mutual love, their love will be fervent and constant. Neither will the want, or withering of any outward allurements, as beauty, personage, parentage, friends, riches, honors, or the like, withhold or withdraw, extinguish or extenuate their love: neither will any excellencies of nature or grace in other husbands and wives draw their hearts from their own to those other: nor yet will the love of a former yoke-fellow dead and gone, any whit lessen the love of the living mate.

. . . By God's ordinance man and wife are no longer bound one to another than they live together. Death is an absolute diremption [separation], and maketh an utter dissolution of the marriage bond. If the man be dead, the wife is delivered from the law of the man, so as she may take another man. Which liberty is also given to the man. Being now free, if they marry another (that other being now a true husband or wife) their love must be as entire to that other as it was to the former: yea, and more entire, if there were any defect in the former. For as children married out of their parents' house must not retain such a love of their parents as shall swallow up their love of the party to whom they are married, but must according to the law, leave father and mother, and cleave to their yoke-fellow: so neither must the love of a former husband or wife be predominant when they are married to another. This other must be as close cleaved unto, as if they had never been joined to a former. The living husband or wife is the present pledge of God's favor. He is now thine own husband: and she is now thine own wife: and not the party that is dead. I deny not but the memory of a virtuous husband or wife ought to be precious to the surviving party: for the memorial of the just is blessed. But as the virtue of a person deceased may not be buried with the dead corpse: so neither may the person be kept above ground with the memory of his or her virtue: which after a sort is done, when love of the party deceased either taketh away, or extenuateth [weakens] the love of the living. This is to give dominion to the dead over the living: which is more than the law enjoineth.

Henry Smith (c. 1560–1591). Known as "silver-tongued Smith," the author of *A Preparative to Marriage* was a clergyman and popular London preacher. In this sermon, he discusses the purposes, joys, and duties of marriage; advises how to avoid conflict; and emphasizes loving unity of husband and wife, requiring a total sharing on both parts. Along the way, he covers many issues, including sexual relations, breast-feeding and other duties to children, the role of stepmothers, and divorce, which (like some though not all Protestants) he believed should be allowed in cases of adultery. Like many of his sermons, this one was published separately (in multiple editions) and also, after his death, as part of his collected sermons, which went through several editions. (*The Sermons of Maister Henrie Smith Gathered into One Volume*. London, 1593. 2, 7–15, 35–54, 62–69, 73.)

Document 15: From *A Preparative to Marriage*

Well might Paul say, marriage is honorable: for God hath honored it himself. It is honorable for the author, honorable for the time, and honorable for the place. Whereas all other ordinances were appointed of God by the hands of men, or the hands of angels, marriage was ordained by God himself, which cannot err. No man, nor angel, brought the wife to the husband, but God himself: so marriage hath more honor of God in this, than all other ordinances of God beside, because he solemnized it himself.

. . . In all nations the day of marriage was reputed the joyfullest day in all their life, and is reputed still of all, as though the sun of happiness began that day to shine upon us, when a good wife is brought unto us. Therefore one saith: that marriage doth signify merry-age, because a playfellow is come to make our age merry, as Isaac and Rebecca sported together. . . .

Now it must needs be, that marriage, which was ordained of such an excellent author, and in such a happy place, and of such an ancient time, and after such a notable order, must likewise have special causes for the ordinance of it. Therefore the Holy Ghost doth show us three causes of this union.

One is, the propagation of children, signified in that when Moses saith; He created them male and female: not both male, nor both female, but one male, and the other female, as if he created them fit to propagate other. And therefore when he had created them so, to show that propagation of children is one end of marriage, he said unto them; Increase and multiply. That is, Bring forth children, as other creatures bring forth their kind.

For this cause marriage is called matrimony, which signifieth mothers, because it maketh them mothers which were virgins before: and in the seminary [seed-bed] of the world, without which all things should be in vain, for want of men to use them, for God reserveth the great city [heaven] to himself, and this suburbs [the earth] he hath set out to us, which are regents by sea and by land. . . .

The second cause is to avoid fornication. . . .

Now if marriage be a remedy against the sin of fornication, then unless ministers may commit the sin of fornication, it seems that they may use the remedy as well as other: for as it is better for one man to marry than to burn, so it is better for all men to marry than to burn: and therefore Paul saith, Marriage is honorable amongst all men. And again, For the avoiding of fornication let every man have his wife. And as though he did foresee that some would except the minister in time to come; in the first epistle of Timothy, the third chapter and second verse, he speaketh more precisely of the minister's wife than of any other, saying; Let him be the husband of one wife. . . .

Lastly, if marriage be a remedy against sin, then marriage itself is no sin: . . . and if marriage be not a sin, then the duties of marriage are not sin, that is, the secret of marriage is not evil, and therefore Paul saith, not only marriage is honorable: but the bed is honorable, that is, even the action of marriage is as lawful as marriage. . . .

The third cause is to avoid the inconvenience of solitariness signified in these words, It is not good for man to be alone, as though he had said; this life would be miserable and irksome, and unpleasant to man, if the Lord had not given him a wife to company his troubles. If it be not good for man to be alone, then it is good for man to have a fellow: therefore as God created a pair of all other kinds, so he created a pair of this kind. . . .

The duties of marriage may be reduced to the duties of man and wife one toward another, and their duties toward their children, and their duty toward their servants. For themselves, saith one, they must think themselves like two birds, the one is the cock, and the other is the dam: the cock flieth abroad to bring in, and the dam sitteth upon the nest to keep all at home. So God hath made the man to travel abroad, and the woman to keep home: and so their nature, and their wit, and their strength, are fitted accordingly; for the man's pleasure is most abroad, and the woman's within. . . .

To show the love which should be between man and wife, marriage is called *conjugium* [the marriage bond (Latin)], which signifieth a knitting or joining together: showing, that unless there be a joining of hearts, and a knitting of affections together, it is not marriage in deed, but in show and name, and they shall dwell in a house like two poisons in a stomach, and one shall ever be sick of another. . . .

To begin this concord well, it is necessary to learn one another's nature, and one another's affections, and one another's infirmities, because ye must be helpers, and ye cannot help unless you know the disease. All the jars almost which do trouble this band, do rise of this, that one doth not hit the measure of the other's heart, to apply themselves to either's nature, whereby it cometh to pass, that neither can refrain when either is offended; but one sharpeneth another, when they had need to be calmed. Therefore they must learn of Paul [in 1 Corinthians 9:22] to fashion themselves one to the other, if they would win one another, and if any jar do arise, one saith; in no wise divide beds for it, for then the sun goeth down upon their wrath [see Ephesians 4:26], and the means of reconcilement is taken away. Give passions no times, for if some man's anger stand but at night, it turneth to malice which is uncurable. . . .

The man may spell his duty out of his name, for he is called the head: to show, that as the eye, and the tongue, and the ear, are in the head, to direct the whole body: so the man should be stored with wisdom, and understanding, and knowledge, and discretion, to direct his whole family: for it is not right that the worse should rule the better, but the better should rule the worse, as the best rules all. The husband saith, that his wife must obey him because he is her better, therefore if he let her be better than himself, he seems to free her from her obedience, and bind himself to obey her.

His first duty is called hearting, that is, hearty affection. As they are handfasted, so they must be heart-fasted, for the eye, and the tongue, and the hand, will be her enemies, if the heart be not her friend. As Christ draweth all the commandments to love, so I may draw all their duties to love, which is the heart's gift to the bride at her marriage. First, he must choose his love, and then he must love his choice: this is the oil which maketh all things easy. In Solomon's song, which is nothing else but a description of Christ the bridegroom, and the church his spouse, one calleth the other love, to show, that though both do not honor alike, yet both should love alike, which the man may do without subjection.

The man is to his wife in the place of Christ to his church: therefore the apostle requireth such an affection of him towards his spouse, as Christ beareth toward his spouse: for he saith; Husbands love your wives, as Christ loved his congregation, that is, with a holy love, and with a hearty love, and with a constant love, as the church would be loved of Christ. . . . So a good husband will not take occasion to love his wife less for her infirmities, but comfort her more for them, . . . that she may bear with his infirmities too.

When Christ saith, that a man should leave father and mother, and cleave to his wife, he signifieth how Christ left his Father for his spouse, and that man doth not love his wife so much as he should, until he affect her more than ever he did his father or mother. . . .

His next duty to love, is a fruit of his love: that is, to let all things be common between them, which were private before. The man and wife are partners, like two oars in a boat, therefore he must divide offices and affairs, and goods with her, causing her to be feared and reverenced, and obeyed of her children and servants like himself, for she is an under officer in his commonwealth, and therefore she must be assisted and borne out like his deputy, as the prince standeth with his magistrates for his own quiet, because they are the legs which bear him up. To show this community between husband and wife, he is to maintain her as he doth himself, because Christ saith, They are no more two but one.

Therefore when he maintaineth her, he must think it but one charge, because he maintaineth no more but himself, for they two are one. He may not say as husbands are wont to say, That which is thine is mine, and that which is mine is mine own; but that which is mine is thine and my self too. . . .

Lastly, he must tender her as much as all her friends, because he hath taken her from her friends, and covenanted to tender her for them all. . . .

This is far from civil wars between man and wife; in all his offices is found no office to fight. If he cannot reform his wife without beating he is worthy to be beaten for choosing no better: when he hath used all means that he may, and yet she is like her self, he must take her for his cross, and say with Jeremy, This is my cross, and I will bear it [see Jeremiah 10:19]. But if he strike her, he takes away his hand from her, which was the first part he gave her to join them together: and she may put up her complaint against him, that he hath taken away part of her goods. Her cheeks are made for thy lips, and not for thy fists.

. . . Adam saith of his spouse, This is flesh of my flesh, But no man (saith Paul) ever hated his own flesh. So then, if a man ask whether he may strike his wife, God saith nay; thou mayst not hate thy wife, for no man hateth his own flesh: showing, that he should not come near blows, but think his wrath too much: for Paul saith, Be not bitter to your wives, noting that anger in a husband is a vice. . . .

Likewise the woman may learn her duty of her names. . . .

Beside a yoke-fellow, she is called a helper, to help him in his business, to help him in his labors, to help him in his troubles, to help him in his sickness: like a woman physician, sometime with her strength, and sometime with her counsel: for sometime as God confoundeth the wise by the foolish, and the strong by the weak: so he teacheth the wise by the foolish, and helpeth the strong by the weak.

Therefore Peter saith, Husbands are won by the conversation of their wives. As if he should say, sometime the weaker vessel is the stronger vessel, and Abraham may take counsel of Sara, as Naaman was advised by his servant. . . .

Beside a helper, she is called a comforter too, and therefore the man is bid rejoice in his wife: which is as much to say, that wives must be the rejoicing of their husbands, even like David's harp to comfort Saul. . . .

Lastly, we call the wife "huswife": that is, house-wife, not a street wife, like Thamar [Tamar, in Genesis 38], nor a field-wife, like Dinah [Genesis 34]: but a house-wife, to show that a good wife keeps her house, and therefore Paul biddeth Titus to exhort women that they be chaste, and keeping at home: presently after chaste, he saith keeping at home, as though home were chastity's keeper. . . .

As it becometh her to keep home, so it becometh her to keep silence, and always speak the best of her head [i.e., her husband]. Other seek their honor in triumph, but she must seek her honor in reverence, for it becometh not any woman to set light by her husband, nor to publish his infirmities. For they say that is an evil bird that defileth her own nest, and if a wife use her husband so, how may the husband use the wife? Because this is the quality of that sex, to overthwart [oppose], and upbraid, and sue the preeminence of their husbands, therefore the philosophers could not tell how to define a wife, but called her, the contrary to a husband, as though nothing were so cross and contrary to a man, as a wife. This is not scripture, but no slander to many. . . .

Though a woman be wise, and painful, and have many good parts, yet if she be a shrew, her troublesome jarring in the end will make her honest behavior unpleasant, as her over-pinching at last causeth her good housewifery to be evil spoken of. Therefore although she be a wife, yet sometimes she must observe the servant's lesson, Not answering again, and hold her peace, to keep the peace. Therefore they which keep silence, are well said to hold their peace, because silence oftentimes doth keep the peace, when words would break it.

To her silence and patience, she must add the acceptable obedience, which makes a woman rule while she is ruled. This is the wife's tribute to her husband: for she is not called his head, but he is called her head. Great cause hath man to make much of his wife, for great and many are her duties to him, for Paul saith; Wives submit your selves unto your husbands, as to the Lord. Showing that she should regard his will as the Lord's will, but withal, as the Lord commandeth only that which is good and right, so she should obey her husband in good and right, or else she doth not obey him as the Lord, but as the tempter. . . .

Lastly we put the duty toward children, because they come last to their hands. . . . Before we teach parents to love their children, they had need be taught not to love them too much, for David's darling [Absalom], was David's traitor: and this is the manner of God, when a man begins to set any thing in God's room, and love it above him which gave it, either to take away it, or to take away him, before he provoke him too much; therefore if parents would have their children live, they must take heed to love them too much: for the giver is offended, when the gift is more esteemed than he.

The first duty is the mothers, that is, to nurse her child at her own breasts, as Sara did Isaac, and therefore Esay [Isaiah] joineth the nurse's name and the mother's name both in one: and calleth them nursing mothers, showing, that mothers should be the nurses. [See Isaiah 49:23.] . . .

The next duty is, catechize [instruct] a child in his youth, and he will remember it when he is old: This is the right blessing which fathers and mothers give to their children, when they cause God to bless them too. . . .

Now I speak to one which is a mother so soon as she is married: therefore peradventure you look that I should show the duty of stepmothers. Their name doth show them their duty too, for a stepmother doth signify a steadmother, that is, one mother dieth, and another cometh in her stead: therefore that your love may settle to those little ones as it ought, you must remember that ye are their steadmother, that is in stead of their mother, and therefore to love them, and tender them, and cherish them as their mother did. . . . Further, these children are orphans, and therefore you must not only regard them as children, but as orphan children. Now God requireth a greater care over widows and orphans, than over any other women or children. . . .

If these duties be performed in marriage, then I need not speak of divorcement, which is the rod of marriage, and divideth them which were one flesh, as if the body and soul were parted asunder. But because all perform not their wedlock vows, therefore he which appointed marriage, hath appointed divorcement, as it were taking our privilege from us, when we abuse it. As God hath ordained remedies for every disease, so he hath ordained a remedy for the disease of marriage. The disease of marriage is adultery, and the medicine hereof is divorcement. Moses licensed them to depart for hardness of heart, but Christ licenseth them to depart for no cause but adultery. If they might be separated for discord, some would make a commodity of strife: but now they are not best to be contentious, for this law will hold their noses together, till weariness make them leave struggling: like two spaniels which are coupled in a chain, at last they learn to go together, because they may not go asunder. . . . Nothing may dissolve marriage but fornication, which is the breach of marriage, for marriage is ordained to avoid fornication, and therefore if the condition be broken, the obligation is void. . . .

Thus have I chalked [marked] the way, to prepare you unto marriage, as the Levites prepared their brethren to the Passover [Ezra 6:20]: remember that this day ye are made one, and therefore must have but one will. And now the Lord Jesus, in whom ye are contracted, knit your hearts together, that ye may love one another like David and Jonathan [see 1 Samuel 18:1], and go before you in this life, like the star which went before the Gentiles, that ye may begin, and proceed, and end in his glory. To whom be all glory for ever, Amen.

William Perkins (see **Document 3**). In the following selection, Perkins discusses the relationship of husband and wife and their duties as master and mistress of the household. He attributes the husband's authority both to God and to nature, but he also pictures marriage as a cooperative relationship in which husband and wife share goods, counsel, responsibility, and loving companionship. He argues that sexual relations in marriage are not sinful, that they serve important purposes in addition to procreation, and that clergymen should not be forbidden to marry. Perkins's views, presented methodically and with frequent scriptural support (most of which is omitted here), would likely have been shared by most of his readers. (*Christian Oeconomie: or, A Short Survey of the Right Manner of Erecting and Ordering a Familie according to the Scriptures*. London, 1609. 11–15, 110–123, 163–74.)

Document 16: From *Christian Economy*

Of Married Folks

. . . Marriage of itself is a thing indifferent [neutral], and the kingdom of God stands no more in it, than in meats and drinks; and yet it is a state in it self, far more excellent, than the condition of single life. For first, it was ordained by God in paradise, above and before all other states of life, in Adam's innocence before the fall. Again, it was instituted upon a most serious and solemn consultation among the three persons in the holy trinity. . . . Thirdly, the manner of this conjunction was excellent, for God joined our first parents Adam and Eve together immediately. Fourthly, God gave a large blessing unto the estate of marriage, saying, Increase and multiply and fill the earth. Lastly, marriage was made and appointed by God himself, to be the fountain and seminary [seed-bed] of all other sorts and kinds of life, in the commonwealth and in the church. . . .

The end [purpose] of marriage is fourfold.

The first is, procreation of children, for the propagation and continuance of the seed and posterity of man upon the earth. . . .

The second is the procreation of an holy seed, whereby the church of God may be kept holy and chaste, and there may always be a holy company of men, that may worship and serve God in the church from age to age. . . .

The third is, that after the fall of mankind, it might be a sovereign means to avoid fornication, and consequently to subdue and slake the burning lusts of the flesh. . . . And for this cause, some schoolmen do err, who hold that the secret coming together of man and wife, cannot be without sin, unless it be done for procreation of children. Lombard [Peter Lombard] the master of the *Sentences* [an important medieval theological text] saith the contrary, namely, that marriage before the fall was only a duty, but now since the fall it is also remedy.

The fourth end is, that the parties married may thereby perform the duties of their callings, in better and more comfortable manner. . . .

Marriage is free to all orders, and sorts of men without exception, even to those that have the gift of continence [self-restraint]; but for them which cannot abstain, it is, by the express commandment of God, necessary. . . .

By which it appeareth to be a clear case, that the commandment of the pope of Rome, whereby he forbiddeth marriage of certain persons, as namely, of clergymen, is merely diabolical; for so writeth the Apostle (1 Timothy 4:1). . . .

Of the Communion of Married Folks, and of Due Benevolence

The communion of man and wife, is that duty, whereby they do mutually and willingly communicate, both their persons, and goods each to other, for their mutual help, necessity and comfort. . . .

This duty consisteth principally in the performance of special benevolence one to another, and that not of courtesy, but of due debt (1 Corinthians 7:3). . . .

Due benevolence must be showed with a singular and entire affection one towards another; and that three ways principally.

First, by the right and lawful use of their bodies, or of the marriage-bed, which is indeed an essential duty of marriage.

The marriage bed signifieth that solitary and secret society, that is between man and wife alone.

And it is a thing of its own nature indifferent; neither good nor bad. . . .

This coming together of man and wife, although it be indifferent, yet by the holy usage thereof, it is made a holy and undefiled action. . . . And it is (as all other creatures and ordinances of God are) sanctified by the word and prayer. . . . In which place it is to be observed, how the Apostle applieth the point of sanctification directly to marriage. . . .

So much for the first way of performance of due benevolence [i.e., through sexual relations].

The second way is, by cherishing one another. . . . This cherishing is the performing of any duties, that tend to the preserving of the lives one of another. Wherefore they are freely to communicate their goods, their counsel, their labors each to other; for the good of themselves and theirs.

The third way is, by an holy kind of rejoicing and solacing themselves each with other, in a mutual declaration of the signs and tokens of love and kindness. . . . This rejoicing and delight is more permitted to the man, than to the woman; and to them both, more in their young years, than in their old age.

Of the Master of the Family or Goodman of the House

. . . The goodman or master of the family, is a person, in whom resteth the private and proper government of the whole household, and he comes not unto it by election, as it falleth out in other states, but by the ordinance of God, settled even in the order of nature. The husband indeed naturally bears rule over the wife; parents over their children, masters over their servants: but that person who by the providence of God, hath the place of an husband, a father, a master in his house, the same also by the light of nature, hath the principality and sovereignty therein, and he is *paterfamilias*, the father and chief head of the family: to him therefore the true right and power over all matters domestical, of right appertaineth. The duties of the master of the family, are specially five.

I. To bear the chief stroke, and to be the principal agent, director and furtherer of the worship of God within his family. . . .

II. To bring his family to the church or congregation on the Sabbath day, to look that they do religiously there behave themselves.

III. To provide for his family meat, drink and clothing, and that they may live a quiet and peaceable life. . . .
IV. To keep order, and to exercise discipline in his house. . . .
V. To give entertainment to those that are strangers, and not of the family, if they be Christians, and believers; but specially to the ministers of the word. . . .

Of the Mistress of the Family, or Goodwife of the House

The goodwife or mistress of the house, is a person which yieldeth help and assistance in government to the master of the family. For he is, as it were, the prince and chief ruler; she is the associate, not only in office and authority, but also in advice, and counsel unto him. . . .

Her duty is two-fold.

First to govern the house, as much as concerneth her, in her place. . . . And that she doth three ways. I. By exercising herself in some profitable employments, for the good of her charge. . . . II. By appointing her maids their work, and overseeing them therein. . . . III. By ordering her children and servants in wisdom; partly by instruction, partly by admonition, when there is need.

Two Horrible and Inhumane Murders. Shakespeare's contemporaries were both shocked and fascinated by incidents of domestic violence, which contradicted the ideal image of a loving, harmonious family. The anonymous pamphlet *Two Horrible and Inhumane Murders* is based on real events. As the full title indicates, the murders were "done in Lincolnshire by two husbands upon their wives," one having "strangled his wife in her sickness, five and twenty years since, and not revealed till November last: the other having killed his wife, made a great fire, and burnt her" in 1604. The excerpt presented here is from the conclusion, in which the author exhorts husbands and wives to exercise patience and kindness and so avoid the fate of the couples described in the pamphlet. (*Two Horrible and Inhumane Murders Done in L[in]colneshire.* London, 1607. C2r.)

DOCUMENT 17: FROM *TWO HORRIBLE AND INHUMANE MURDERS*

Therefore since we daily do, or may see, the greedy desire that Satan hath to increase his kingdom, it shall be very needful for us to pray continually unto God, to make us both watchful and wary, that we come not within the Devil's claws or clutches: for if he see or perceive any hatred, discontent, or disquietness [disturbance] betwixt man and man, but especially between a man and his wife (which should be both as one) let us assure ourselves that he will not cease to set all his hellhounds to work, to make each slight occasion between them, a main step to their downfall and deep destruction.

And therefore husbands shall do well to have a special care, that they give not any just cause of offense to their honest wives: for if the hatred of a woman be once rooted in her heart, 'tis no way to be dissolved, but by death.

And for wives, they shall do as well, if in modest and mild manner, they observe the humors [temperament] of their husbands (to whom they are tied by God, not for a day or two, or so long as they list, but for term of life) not reproving them boldly or bitterly when they are very merry, very melancholy, or before company, lest they drive them to unmanly cruelty, which will (in time) prove hateful tyranny. For, as husbands are taught by the Apostle Paul, not to be bitter unto their wives: so are wives likewise instructed by the selfsame apostle to be loving and amiable to their husbands.

Which rules and directions, if husbands and wives would follow, they might surely and safely fly from all such like faults as these, and many other that the Devil doth daily tempt them unto. Which gift of grace God grant unto us all, even for his Christ's sake, amen.

William Heale (1581/2–1628). It is unclear how common wife beating was in early modern England, but though there were defenders of the practice, most argued vigorously against it, whether from a legal, moral, or religious point of view (see also **Documents 6** and **15**). William Heale's treatise is one of the best known on the subject. Titled *An Apology for Women* (*apology* here means "defense"), the book responds to a speech made in Oxford by William Gager favoring the lawfulness of wife beating. Heale, a learned clergyman, gathers arguments from scripture and classical antiquity, defends women against traditional criticisms, and portrays marriage as a loving companionship. (*An Apologie for Women.* Oxford, 1609. 12, 19, 28, 30, 46–47, 49.)

Document 18: From *An Apology for Women*

. . . In agreeing matches, where man and wife make up the sweet harmony of mutual love, in a reciprocal consent and union, ye may observe a heaven of government, the husband intent on his business, the wife employed in her house, the children brought up religiously, their attendants, their servants, every one (as Virgil's commonwealth of bees [*Georgics* 4]) busied in his place. Whence towards the autumn of their years, they gather in the fruitful harvest of true friendship, of competent riches, of good estimate, of self-content. . . .

Why then should husbands sue for a toleration to beat their wives, to whom as they are in society more nearly linked, so in love more dearly engaged than to their dearest friend? Many are the friendly offices of thy friend; many more of thy wife. She sits at thy table: she lies in thy bosom: she shares of thy grievances and lessens the burden: she participates thy pleasures and augments the joy: in matters of doubt she is thy counselor; in case of distress thy comforter: she is a com-partner with thee in all the accidents of life. Neither is there any sweeter taste of friendship, than the coupling of souls in this mutuality either of condoling or comforting. . . .

. . . For in the whole body of either law, canon or civil, I have not yet found (neither, as I think, hath any man else) let down in these or equivalent terms, or otherwise past by any positive sentence or verdict, That it is lawful for a husband to beat his wife. . . .

In the second rank are those, who out of a staid judgment and upright mind, hold it not only unlawful, but an odious, unmanly, and unseemly [unfitting] thing. Odious in respect of the breach of their faith given wedlock. Unmanly in regard of woman [woman's] weakness, and imbecility [weakness]. Unseemly for example's sake. And therefore in consideration of all is altogether unlawful. . . .

Now for further satisfaction, to prove that the laws allow not any verbal correction I have added these few reasons.

First. If a husband may lawfully beat his wife, then is the wife legally bound to endure his beating. For the law gives not authority to the punisher, but therewithal enjoins obedience on the punished. But the law binds not a wife to such blockish [senseless] patience. For in such a case it allows her to depart from her husband; and of her husband in time of her absence to obtain sufficient maintenance. Neither doth it limit her any time to return if she fear his tyranny: nor yet constrains her to live again with him, unless for her good usage be given her good security.

In answer whereof that shift will not serve, to say the law authorizeth a man to beat his wife but slightly, and not in such sort as may cause her departure. This is too coarse a salve for such a sore. For a little beating unto some women, is more than much unto others; and therefore in them it will breed the same or worse effects: and how little so ever it be they are not bound to take it. . . .

Lastly correction by way of beating (say the best you can say of it) is merely servile: and in many men's judgments so inhumane, as that a wise man whose actions flow from discreet premeditation, will not exercise it upon his slaves or swains [servants]. But servility is only to be imposed on such as are servile; and therefore not on wives who are in the law free burgesses [citizens] of the same city whereof their husbands are free, and free denizens [inhabitants] in the same land wherein their husbands are free. . . .

Robert Snawsel (dates unknown). First published in 1610, with later editions in 1619 and 1631, Snawsel's *A Looking Glass for Married Folks* is based on Erasmus's *Conjugium,* a colloquy on marriage derived in turn from Plutarch's *Conjugal Precepts*. Snawsel's version adds a strong Christian element, with emphasis on repentance and forgiveness. The book presents a dialogue in which two women seek to reconcile a quarreling husband and wife by teaching them their duties. The characters' names are significant: Xantippe is named after Socrates' wife, traditionally a shrew. Her husband's name (Ezer) is Hebrew for "help." The women who counsel them are Eulalie (from Greek roots for "speaking well") and Abigail, named for one of King David's wives, described in the Bible as "a woman of good understanding, and of a beautiful countenance" (1 Samuel 25:3). After advising Xantippe, the women turn their attention to Ezer. (*A Looking Classe for Maried Folkes*. London, 1610. G4v–H3v.)

Document 19: From *A Looking Glass for Married Folks*

Eulalie. I suppose by your speech, that you have had many bouts.

Ezer. Yea that we have, till the blood hath run down the one of our faces.

Abigail. O lamentable thing to be heard of in a Christian commonwealth between man and wife! . . .

Eulalie. . . . Thy wife is one of thy principal members; if she be uncomely [displeasing] in any way, put thou more comeliness [pleasing appearance] on; if she be not so beautiful, as thou desirest, cover it with contentation [contentment]; if not so provident as she ought, cover that with thy good husbandry; if she be not so wife, as thou wished, cover that with thy prudency. If she be not so loving as is fit, cover that with the skirts of thy love; if choleric [prone to anger], cover it with patience: and although she fail in duty, which she ought, yet she may challenge yours as due debt, as long as she is your wife you are bound to give honor to her as to the weaker vessel.

Eulalie. If these things were well considered of many men, much strife and terrible broils would be left between man and wife.

Ezer. Yea, but I must needs tell you that these things can hardly be digested; for if we should yield thus much to our wives, they would make stark fools of us.

Abigail. No, not so sir, for you should see the blessing of God upon you, which would mitigate the swelling and raging of your wife's affections [inclinations, diseases]. . . . This then is your precept, that you love your wife as he did his church.

Ezer. I will try, if that I can win her by kindness.

Abigail. That must be the way, if ever you win her, and the means whereby you must keep her being won. . . . These things I say ought to cause a man to love his wife, to cherish, maintain, and provide for her like a woman, and to comfort her, as his own bowels. Now where this true love is, there will nothing, that is either necessary, profitable, or comfortable for the wife be wanting, if that possible her husband can procure it; and I would all husbands would mark this. For according to his love, will his care be, to provide for her; and after his care, will his diligence be to please her; and as he pleaseth her, so shall he have comfort by her.

Eulalie. This may serve to reprove the corrupt, proud, and churlish affections of many men, which will rather seek to cross them in that which is good and godly.

Ezer. It is true, and much more are they to blame, that tyrannously will rule yea overrule, and that without all rule, credit, or honesty. . . .

Eulalie. The worse they are this way, the worse it is for themselves; for as it is said, the hasty man never wants woe, so I think I may say, the tyrant shall never want a shrew.

Abigail. I would such men would but a little consider how the Lord doth mitigate their authority over their wives, when he saith, that they should honor them as the weaker vessels. And again, that man and wife make but one body; and again, that they should draw the yoke equally together. . . .

Ezer. And truly neighbors it comes to my mind now, that the Lord laid these duties of loving and honoring their wives upon men, partly because they are stronger and more able to bear and support the infirmities and weaknesses of their wives, than the wives are of the husbands. And again, that the husbands should not swell too much with their authority, that they should not make their poor wives as slaves, but should account of them as themselves. For the Lord knew very well that men are of such natures (for the most part) that if he gave them power, they would stretch it to the uttermost: and therefore he abates their superiority; and makes it in some measure equal with the wives. And further he would have man to know that this is his dignity, to give honor unto the woman, lest she through the loftiness of his mind should be used crossly and unkindly.

Eulalie. Lo neighbor, lo, yonder comes your wife.

Ezer. Why how now wife, where have you been all this while?

Xantippe. Forsooth husband, I have been about some special business, that concerns you and me. . . .

Xantippe. As I was coming home, I spied a solitary place, which I went unto, and there poured forth my complaints to the Lord, praying his Majesty for pardon of my disobedience towards you, and all my abusing of you with my tongue by railing speeches, and that we might more quietly live together than we have done; for I felt such horrible gripings [pains] within me, that I thought my heart would have burst: and then came the trifling occasions of my falling out into my mind, which made such horrible broils and hurly burly [commotion] between us, the which at the first I might have stopped with a patient word, but sinful wretch that I was, I rather opened a fountain, by my railing long. . . .

Abigail. God hath promised to forgive all that unfeignedly [sincerely] repent, of whom I make no doubt, by that I have now heard from your own mouth, that you are one. . . .

Ezer. I thank God and our good neighbors, we have been well exercised here this afternoon also: for I hope they have done me more good than ever I thought women could have done to man in that kind.

Xantippe. I thank God also for it, and I rejoice at it in my soul.

Ezer. Well wife, here is my hand, and give me thine, and let us renew our covenant which we have broken with God, and toward each other. And now let us here vow both before God and our good neighbors, Abigail and Eulalie, through his grace to keep the same inviolate [unbroken] while we live.

Xantippe. Here husband, here is both my hand and my heart.

The Lamentation of a New Married Man. This anonymous ballad, a lighthearted look at the pros and cons of marriage, has two parts: *The Lamentation of a New Married Man* and *An Answer Sent to the Young Married Man, Written Most Friendly by His Gentle Wife Nan*. The first part presents common complaints made by young husbands about their wives' flaws and the end of their own independent and self-indulgent status as bachelors. The second part suggests that the complaints are at least partly unfounded: the young husband's "gentle wife" defends herself and reminds her husband of all the joys she brings, including their time together in bed. The ballad suggests that men were expected to help care for their children (note the references to the cradle) and that marriage helped establish a man's status as a respected member of the community. This document also provides evidence for some of the activities a married woman might have taken part in outside of the home. (*The Lamentation of a New Married Man, Briefely Declaring the Sorrow and Grief that Comes by Warrying [Marrying] a Young Wanton Wife*. London, c. 1628–29.)

DOCUMENT 20: *THE LAMENTATION OF A NEW MARRIED MAN*

You bachelors that brave it
So gallant in the street,
With musk and with rose water,
Smelling all so sweet:

With shoes of Spanish leather,
So *featly to your feet, ***elegant***
Behold me a married man.

Before that I was wedded,
I lived in delight,
I went unto the dancing school,
I learned at fence to fight:
With twenty other pleasures,
That now are banished quite,
I being a married young man.

When I lived single,
I knew no cause of strife,
I had my heart in quiet,
I led a pleasant life:
But now my chiefest study
Is how to please my wife,
I being a married man.

Quoth she, You do not love me,
To leave me all alone,
You must go a *gadding, ***wandering***
And I must bide at home,
While you among your minions,
Spend more than is your own:
This life leads a married man.

Do you think to keep me
So like a drudge each day,
To toil and *moil so sadly, ***work hard***
And lame me every way:
I'll have a maid, *by Lady, ***by the Virgin Mary (an oath)***
Shall work while I do play,
This life leads a married man.

Then must I give attendance
Upon my mistress' heels,
I must wait before her,
While she doth walk the fields,
She'll eat no meat but lobsters,
And pretty *grigs and eels, ***a kind of eel***
This life leads a married man.

Then must I get her cherries,
And dainty *Kathern pears, ***Catharine (a kind of pear)***

And then longs for *codlings, — *a kind of apple*
She breedeth child she swears
When God knows 'tis a cushion
That she about her bears,
This life leads a married man.

She must have *rabbit suckers, — *baby rabbits*
Without spot or speck,
I must buy her peasecods
At sixteen *groats the peck — *a small coin*
She must have eggs and white wine
To wash her face and neck:
This life leads a married man.

If once to pass it cometh,
That she is brought to bed,
Why then with many dainties
She must be daily fed,
A hundred toys and trifles
Comes then within her head:
This life leads a married man.

Against that she *is churched, — *takes part in the churching of women ritual*
A new gown she must have:

A dainty fine *rebato — *a stiff collar*
About her neck so brave:
French bodice, with a *farthingale — *a petticoat with hoops*
She never *lins to crave — *ceases*
This life leads a married man.

Abroad among her *gossips — *friends*
Then must she daily go:
Requesting of this favor
A man must not say no,
Lest that an unkind quarrel
About this matter grow
This life leads a married man.

To offerings and weddings:
Abroad that she must prance,
Whereas with lusty youngsters
This gallant dame must dance:
Her husband must say nothing,
What *hap soever chance: — *event*
This life leads a married man.

And then there is no remedy,
She must go to a play,
To purge abounding *choler.
And drive sad dumps away:
She tarries out till midnight,
She swears she will not stay,
This life leads a married man.

ill temper (or the fluid supposedly causing it)

When home at last she cometh,
To bed she gets her soon,
And there she sleeps full soundly,
Till the next day at noon,
Then must she eat a *cawdie
With a silver spoon
This life leads a married man.

small cod (?)

Therefore my friends be warned,
You that unwedded be,
The troubles of a married man
You do most plainly see,
Who likes not of his living,
Would he would change with me,
That now am a married man.

Where I was wont full often
Good company to keep.
Now I must rock the cradle,
And hush the child asleep,
I had no time nor leisure
Out of my doors to peep,
Since I was a married man.

****

The second part to the same tune. An answer sent to the young married man, Written most friendly by his gentle wife Nan.

Alack wherefore lament you,
your happy wedded state:
Therein you show great folly,
repentance comes too late
To make yourself a *mocking-stock
with every scoffing *mate
Now you are a married young man.

laughing-stock
fellow

In youth, do well remember,
Your mind was all on pride:
Deceiving sport and pleasure,
your lavish thoughts did guide,
'Tis time such foolish fancies
should now be laid aside,
Now you are a married young man.

When you lived single,
Your time you vainly spent:
Unto unlawful pastime
Your youngling wits were bent
But now you must learn wisdom,
discredit to prevent,
*Sith you are a married young man. — *since*

An *alas to *estimation, — *lamentation (for lack of) . . . reputation*

*Longs to a single life, — *belongs*
What were you but a *skipjack, — *a lively young fool*
before you had a wife,
A *mate for every *madcap, — *companion . . . reckless fellow*
a stirrer up of strife,
Till you were a married young man.

A wife hath won you credit,
A wife makes you esteemed
An *honest man through marriage — *respectable*
now are you surely deemed.
And you shall find at all times,
a wife your dearest friend,
Now you are a married young man.

Then is it right and reason,
your wife should pleased be,
It is a happy household
where couples do agree,
It doth delight the angels,
such concord for to see,
Then blest is the married young man.

If I do blame your gadding
it is for love, be sure,
Bad company doth always
Ill counsel still procure
The man that will be thrifty,
must at his work endure,
While he is a married young man.

This works his commendations
amongst the very best,
The chief men of the parish,
his *quaintance will request, — *acquaintance*
And then he shall be called
to office with the rest
When he is a married young man.

He shall be made a *headborough
unto his credit great,
At what time all neighbors,
his friendship will entreat,
And then it is most decent,
he should go fine and neat.
When he is a married young man.

parish officer comparable to a constable

Then bareheaded unto him,
a number daily flocks:
To help him by his office,
from many stumbling blocks:
Then comes he to be *constable,
and set knaves in the stocks:
Thus riseth a married young man.

officer with policeman-like duties

His wife shall then be seated
in church at her desire,
Her husband he is *sideman
and sits within the choir,
Then he is made a *churchwarden
and placed somewhat higher,
Great joy to a married young man.

an assistant to the parish churchwardens
parish officer assisting the minister

Then seeing all this credit
by marriage you do find,
Unto your wife 'tis reason,
you should be good and kind
And sometimes wait upon her
according to her mind:
As best fits a married young man.

If friendly you go with her
to walk out of the town,
Why then you may have pleasure,
to give her a *green gown.
To have so great a favor,
some men would give a crown
Which is not a married young man.

from rolling with her in the grass

As for the pears and apples,
you give me in the street,
The cherries or the codlings,
for pretty women meet,
At night I give you kindly
a thousand kisses sweet
Great joy to a married young man.

An hundred other pleasures,
I do you then beside,
In bringing forth your children
great sorrow I do bide.
For twenty gowns and *kirtles, ***skirts***
the like would not be trade,
By any fine young married man.

Why should you scorn the cradle
I tell you sir most plain,
There is not any pleasure,
but sometimes breedeth pain,
If you will not be troubled,
why then good sir refrain
To play like a married young man.

PARENTS AND CHILDREN

John Earle (born between 1598 and 1601; died 1665). A clergyman and at one point a tutor to the Prince of Wales, Earle is now best known for the book *Microcosmography,* meaning "study of the little world" (presumably the world of human nature). The book is an important contribution to a genre known as "character" writing, a character being a brief sketch describing a particular kind of person. Though these character sketches were often exaggerated and humorous, they reveal much about cultural assumptions. The following selection, describing a typical child, emphasizes children's innocence and parents' delight in their offspring. Other writers of the period drew a contrasting picture of children, seeing in their selfish and undisciplined impulses signs of their fallen nature as inheritors of original sin. (*Microcosmographie, or, A Peece of the World discovered in Essayes and Characters.* London, 1628. B1r–B2v.)

Document 21: From *Microcosmography* ("A Child")

A child is a man in a small letter, yet the best copy of Adam before he tasted of Eve, or the apple; and he is happy whose small practice in the world can only write this character. He is nature's fresh picture newly drawn in oil, which time, and much handling, dims and defaces. His soul is yet a white paper unscribbled with observations of the world, wherewith at length it becomes a blurred notebook. He is purely happy, because he knows no evil, nor hath made means by sin to be acquainted with misery. He arrives not at the mischief of being wise, nor endures evils to come by fore seeing them. He kisses and loves all, and when the smart [pain] of the rod is past, smiles on his beater. Nature and his parents alike dandle [play with] him, and entice him on with a bait of sugar, to a draught of wormwood. He plays yet, like a young prentice [apprentice] the first day, and is not come to his task of melancholy. His hardest labor is his tongue, as if he were loath to use so deceitful an organ; and he is best company with it when he can but prattle. We laugh at his foolish sports, but his game is our earnest: and his drums, rattles and hobby-horses, but the emblems, and mocking of man's business. His father hath writ him as his own little story, wherein he reads those day of his life that he cannot remember; and sighs to what innocence he has lived. The elder he grow he is a stair lower from God; and like his first father [Adam] much worse in breeches. He is the Christian's example, and the old man's relapse: The one imitates his pureness, and the other falls into his simplicity. Could he put his body with his little coat, he had got eternity without a burthen, and changed but one heaven for another.

Elizabeth Clinton, Countess of Lincoln (1574?–1630?). A noblewoman who gave birth to 18 children, about half of whom survived, Clinton wrote a treatise on nursing later in her life. Though, like many who could afford to, she had hired a wet nurse for her children, she now writes to encourage mothers to nurse. Acknowledging that illness and other problems may prevent some from nursing, she speaks sternly against those who fail to breast-feed for less weighty reasons, even calling a mother "unnatural" if she deliberately avoids nursing. For Clinton, this aspect of motherhood is a blessing for which women should be grateful. (*The Countesse of Lincolnes Nurserie.* Oxford, 1622. 1, 16–21.)

Document 22: From *The Countess of Lincoln's Nursery*

Because it hath pleased God to bless me with many children, and so caused me to observe many things falling out to mothers, and to their children; I thought good to open my mind concerning a special matter belonging to all child-bearing women, seriously to consider of: and to manifest my mind the better, even to write of this matter, so far as God shall please to direct me; in sum, the matter I mean, Is the duty of nursing due by mothers to their own children.

In setting down whereof, I will first show, that every woman ought to nurse her own child; and secondly, I will endeavor to answer such objections, as are used to be cast out against this duty to disgrace the same. . . .

I beseech all godly women to remember, how we elder ones are commanded to instruct the younger, to love their children, now therefore love them so as to do this office to them when they are born, more gladly for love sake, than a stranger, who bore them not, shall do for lucre sake. Also I pray you to set no more so light by God's blessing in your own breasts, which the Holy Spirit ranketh with other excellent blessings; if it be unlawful to trample under feet a cluster of grapes, in which a little wine is found; then how unlawful is it to destroy and dry up those breasts, in which your own child (and perhaps one of God's very elect, to whom to be a nursing father, is a king's honor; and to whom to be a nursing mother, is a queen's honor) might find food of sincere milk, even from God's immediate providence, until it were fitter for stronger meat? I do know that the Lord may deny some women, either to have any milk in their breasts at all, or to have any passage for their milk, or to have any health, or to have a right mind: and so they may be letted [prevented] from this duty, by want, by sickness, by lunacy, etc. But I speak not to these: I speak to you, whose consciences witness against you, that you cannot justly allege any of those impediments. . . .

Therefore be no longer at the trouble, and at the care to hire others to do your own work: be not so unnatural to thrust away your own children: be not so hardy as to venture a tender babe to a less tender heart: be not accessory to that disorder of causing a poorer woman to banish her own infant, for the entertaining of a richer woman's child, as it were, bidding her unlove her own to love yours. . . .

. . . Think always, that having the child at your breast, and having it in your arms, you have God's blessing there. For children are God's blessings. Think again how your babe crying for your breast, sucking heartily the milk out of it, and growing by it, is the Lord's own instruction, every hour, and every day, that you are suckling it, instructing you to show that you are his new born babes, by your earnest desire after his word; and the sincere doctrine thereof, and by your daily growing in grace and goodness thereby, so shall you reap pleasure, and profit. Again, you may consider, that when your child is at your breast, it is a fit occasion to move your heart to pray for a blessing upon that work; and to give thanks for your child, and for ability and freedom unto that, which many a mother would have done and could not; who have tried and ventured [risked] their health, and taken much pains, and yet have not obtained their desire. But they that are fitted every way for this commendable act, have certainly great cause to be thankful: and I much desire that God may have glory and praise for every good work, and you much comfort, that do seek to honor God in all things. Amen.

Edward Topsell (1572–1625). *The Reward of Religion* is a series of lectures on the biblical book of Ruth, drawing lessons of comfort for the faithful. Topsell, a clergyman, touches on various family duties, including (in the selection presented here) a mother's duty to nurse her own child. Like other writers on the subject, Topsell views breast-feeding as an expression of love and argues that it is good for the mother's health and prevents the child from acquiring "a contrary disposition and complexion" from a wet nurse. (*The Reward of Religion. Delivered in Sundrie Lectures upon the Booke of Ruth*. London, 1613. 289–90.)

Document 23: From *The Reward of Religion*

It is a sign of the want of love and natural affection in the parents (as the apostle speaketh) when the mothers do not bestow the labor to give their own children their natural milk: for if they had the same natural feeling of their duties to their children, they could not (having no occasion) commit the nourishing of their children to strangers, who can never be so inwardly kind to the infants, as the mothers either are or ought to be:

. . . These causes and more also being duly and carefully considered, you shall find it a greater sin, to give your children to other to be nursed, than heretofore you conceived of it, so that you must for this one thing, condemn the use of your breasts, (which were the creation of God, and the practice of the ancient godly women, which were every way as noble as any alive) forsake the tender love that another ought to bear to her innocent babe, bring your children's bodies to a second, yea, a contrary disposition and complexion, and stop up the plentiful conduits of streaming milk in your breasts, to the loss and hindrance of your own health: Therefore if any have any power to perform this natural duty to their children, let them practice it: for all the carnal reasons of the world, must not prevail against the least collection of the word of God. . . . But in causes [cases] of weakness in the woman, danger to the child, or sickness in either of both; it is not only a duty of necessity, but of conscience, to nourish and cherish the children of other.

Elizabeth Jocelin (1596–1622). Anticipating that she might die following childbirth (as she did), Jocelin wrote this treatise to guide her husband in raising the child she was carrying. The letter to her husband that prefaces the treatise is remarkable for her warm expressions of affection and religious faith. Raised in an upper-class family, Jocelin was well educated, yet as a woman, she depreciates her writing ability. Nevertheless, she writes confidently about familial issues, including the child's education. Her husband valued her treatise so much that he had it published after her death. (*The Mothers Legacie, to Her Unborne Childe*. London, 1624. A11r–12r, B2r–4v, B7r–B9v.)

Document 24: From *The Mother's Legacy to Her Unborn Child*

To My Truly Loving, and Most Dearly Loved Husband, Tourell Jocelin:

Mine own dear love, I no sooner conceived an hope, that I should be made a mother by thee, but with it entered the consideration of a mother's duty, and shortly after followed the apprehension of danger that might prevent me from executing that care I so exceedingly desired, I mean in religious training our child. And in truth death appearing in this shape, was doubly terrible unto me. First, in respect of the painfulness of that kind of death, and next of the loss my little one should have in wanting me.

But I thank God, these fears were cured with the remembrance that all things work together for the best to those that love God, and a certain assurance that he will give me patience according to my pain. . . .

And (dear love) as thou must be the overseer, for God's sake, when it shall fail in duty to God, or to the world, let not thy indulgence wink at such folly, but severely correct it: and that thy trouble may be little when it comes to years, take the more care when it is young. First, in providing it a nurse: O make choice, not so much for her complexion, as for her mild and honest disposition: Likewise if the child be to remain long abroad after weaning, as near as may be, choose a house where it may not learn to swear, or speak scurrilous words. . . .

Next, good sweet heart, keep it not from school, but let it learn betimes [at an early age]: if it be a son, I doubt not but thou wilt dedicate it to the Lord as his minister, if he will please of his mercy to give him grace and capacity for that great work. If it be a daughter, I hope my mother Brooke (if thou desirest her) will take it among hers, and let them all learn one lesson.

I desire her bringing up may be learning the Bible, as my sisters do, good housewifery, writing, and good works: other learning a woman needs not: though I admire it in those whom God hath blest with discretion, yet I desired not much in my own, having seen that sometimes women have greater portions of learning, than wisdom, which is of no better use to them than a main sail to a fly-boat [a small, quick-moving boat], which runs in under water. But where learning and wisdom meet in a virtuous disposed woman, she is the fittest closet for all goodness. She is like a well-balanced ship that may bear all her sail. She is—indeed, I should but shame my self, if I should go about to praise her more.

But, my dear, though she have all this in her, she will hardly make a poor man's wife: Yet I leave it to thy will. If thou desirest a learned daughter, I pray God give her a wise and religious heart, that she may use it to his glory, thy comfort, and her own salvation. . . .

But I know thou wonderest by this time what the cause should be that we two continually unclasping our hearts one to the other, I should reserve this to writing. When thou thinkest thus, dear, remember how grievous it was to thee but to hear me say, I may die, and thou wilt confess this would have been an unpleasant discourse to thee, and thou knowest I never durst displease thee willingly, so much I love thee. All I now desire is, that the unexpectedness of it make it not more grievous to thee. But I know thou art a Christian, and therefore will not doubt of thy patience.

And though I thus write to thee, as heartily desiring to be religiously prepared to die, yet, my dear, I despair not of life, nay, I hope and daily pray for it, if so God will be pleased. . . .

My dear, thou knowest me so well, I shall not need to tell thee, I have written honest thoughts in a disordered fashion, not observing method. For thou knowest how short I am of learning and natural endowments to take such a course in writing. Or if that strong affection of thine have hid my weakness from thy sight, I now profess seriously my own ignorance: and though I did not, this following treatise would betray it: But I send it only to the eyes of a most loving husband, and of a child exceedingly beloved, to whom I hope it will not be altogether unprofitable.

Thus humbly desiring God to give thee all comfort in this life, and happiness in the life to come, I leave thee and thine to his most gracious protection.

Thine inviolable, [i.e., with an unbreakable bond]

Eliza. Jocelin

The Office of Christian Parents. This anonymous work includes a "brief admonitory addition unto children" but focuses mainly on parents' duties. As the title suggests, the point of view is religious, but the book is also pragmatic, counseling parents how to most effectively influence their children at various stages, starting even before a child is born and continuing until a child is married. On the question of how vigorously to discipline children, the writer recommends a moderate course between harsh punishment and excessive indulgence. Though parents should be involved in their children's choice of a spouse, they should not force them into a marriage against their liking. (*The Office of Christian Parents Shewing*

How Children Are to Be Governed throughout All Ages and Times of Their Life. Cambridge, 1616. 46–47, 55, 61–62, 89–91, 139–40, 192–94.)

Document 25: From *The Office of Christian Parents*

Here me thinketh I see the child swaddled in clouts [pieces of cloth] ready for the cradle, the mother pointeth out to her provision for the little babe; the midwife is careful to advise the childwife [woman who has given birth], to look well to herself, and the father hearkeneth cheerfully what may be lacking, and all the house is ready to do something to show their joy for the newborn babe. And first all the care is about the natural life, they warm the clouts, they prepare pap [soft food], and there is a keeper to keep in the mother, and to look to the child. In some places there comes in the childwife's mother, and layeth things to her daughter's breasts to dry up her milk: she will not have her daughter troubled with the nursing: and the father cannot abide the crying of the child: therefore a nurse is sent for in all haste.

Here let not the parents run headlong after their fancies; children perhaps are more of value, than that a little trouble should so hastily, and so soon turn them out to a stranger; and the charge of so precious a jewel, is not so lightly to be regarded: if they did consider how far the office of parents doth bind them, and would make conscience of their ways, they could not upon so slender a cause venture the child out of their own bosom. Let them therefore hearken, first what nature speaketh to them, and then what Christian religion requireth. Nature seemeth to me to speaketh aloud, that the mother which breedeth the infant in her womb, hath therewithal, in the same body prepared two breasts full of milk, as it were two bottles to feed it being born, which is most kindly for that child, and hath no other use to serve unto. . . .

Here cometh in the mamish cockling [indulgence, as of a fond mother] of the parents, to give the child the sway of his own desires, to have whatsoever it pointeth to, and so it maketh the parents and all the house slaves, and there is no end of noise, of crying, and wailing: or else there is such severity, as the heart of the child is utterly broken. Here wise parents going between these two extremes, will at the beginning with a mild and discreet behavior, accustom the child to take what is allowed and appointed, and no more. . . .

But sometime there needeth correction, therefore the parents must beware they teach them not evil things, which they can hardly drive out with much correction: for some think it no matter what they teach children being so young, but they err most grossly. Others do absolutely deny beating, saying, that it is a foul thing and slavish, adding that there need no chastising if he that teach be continually at hand: Surely, this is a very good matter: for when children are let alone to teach themselves, they learn nothing but evil; whereas the continual eye of the parent, doth so finely enclose them within the hurdles of modesty and honesty, that seldom or never they need the use of the rod: yet is not the rod altogether to be abolished, for little children are not all of a like disposition; to some a word is sufficient, and some must have a little terror of the rod ministered with the words, which if it be not begun in that tender age, and so continued from age to age, they will wax so strong, that no instruction, admonition, or correction will take any hold on them.

. . . Christian parents ought not to enthrall themselves to their children in such a doting manner. Howbeit [however] sometime the parents are diversely affected [inclined]; The father is over-hasty, and the mother over-fond: some mothers have no other discipline but severe correction, some fathers cannot abide to hear their children cry. This is a destruction, like unto the manner of children in making a garden; when they have set flowers or herbs, ever and anon they will pull them up to see how they grow; . . . so it is when man and wife do not but join in one steady course of discipline, what the one planteth, the other pulleth up. By severity, the children being over-awed, learn to lie, dissemble [conceal], and to do any wickedness in secret. . . . So some parents are fierce and wayward, that children knowing not how to please them, devise [invent] they care not what, so they may not displease: therefore here cometh the fit place for the apostle's rule of government, Fathers provoke not your children to wrath, but bring them up in instruction and information [training] of the Lord: by which words both the austerity and cockling [pampering] of parents are reproved: for as he forbiddeth provoking of children by hard handling, so he calleth the parents from foolish indulgency, when he would have them instructed and informed [trained]; which two words do show such a guiding of children, that they teach them all good things which the Lord our God requireth, and cause them to do the same: and they are not made afraid by rigor unreasonable; neither yet wanton by cockling unseasonable [unsuitable]: which is also a reproof to the most sort of parents, they cannot correct but when they are angry, and they will seldom teach their children in due season for time and place: they will oft reprove them, till the children make no regard of their words; and chiefly then they will talk of their manners, when they should be sure to have them mannerly, namely when they are in presence of strangers, then they will slap them and chide them. . . . We must take heed that the punishment be not greater than the fault, and that for the same cause one be punished, and another be not called in question. Also anger in punishing is to be restrained; for he that cometh to punish being angry, will never keep that mediocrity [moderation] which is between too little and too much. . . .

And at this age of twelve years and forward, the parents, and namely the mother, is to use herself more familiarly with the daughter (always keeping the gravity and authority of a mother) that so the child may love her company, and be more apt to open her mind to her mother, and not by severity to cause her delight in a stranger, and to open her mind to such: for by kind usage, they shall see further into their natures, and more easily learn what need they have of marriage, and so prevent the stealing away of their child, or at least of their child's heart. And thus observing their natural disposition, on the one side they may in due time seek out an honest match for their child: and handsomely on the other side choose such a man, as their daughter may be best able to content, and be contented. For every honest or rich maid, is not fit for every honest and rich man; but there is a certain equability to be observed, that they two who by marriage are to be made one, may joyfully give due benevolence one to the other: as to musical instruments rightfully fitted, do make a most pleasant and sweet harmony in a well tuned consort. And in this case, I see many parents to do contrary to their office: for either they think not upon their children's need, or else neglect the time, or for worldly respects, cause their children to stay overlong, to their great hazard and damage many ways. . . .

Now are we come to our last period, to seek out a match for our son: . . . namely, the child son or daughter ought not to marry of their own head, without the direction and consent of their parents. . . .

Notwithstanding I do not take the authority of parents in this case to be absolute, and without limitation. For first, nature teacheth that he must use his children like a parent, that is, kindly and lovingly as son and daughter, and not as slaves or as beasts tyrannically: for if nature teach (as it is before showed in this chapter) that when children grow to ripeness of age, they should be applied to such trades, as they by natural inclination are fit, apt, and liking; then much more in the matter of marriage, the children ought to have their liking, wherein the child is to forsake father and mother, that they two may be one flesh: for what comfort is it for the child to forsake their parents, and to cleave to her to whom he hath no liking? You shall have parents when they make their children a coat, they will bid them choose the color, and yet think they lose no authority over their children: much less shall their authority be diminished, if they suffer their children to view well, and consider of the husband or wife they choose for them, that they like as well as their parents. The child must do the service which marriage requireth; therefore the parents have great reason to grant the child free liberty to like or not to like, that it may the more cheerfully perform the duty, which is unchangeable during life.

William Gouge (see **Document 14**). In this excerpt, Gouge discusses children's duties toward their parents, including the duty to provide for their physical needs. For Gouge, the basis of this duty is not only parental authority but also gratitude and "recompense" for all the benefits children have received. Elsewhere in *Of Domestical Duties,* Gouge elaborates further on children's duties but, like other writers (for example, see **Document 28**), notes that parental authority is limited and that children have a higher duty to God. (*Of Domesticall Duties Eight Treatises*. London, 1622. 469–70, 473.)

Document 26: From *Of Domestical Duties*

Of Children's Recompense

The general head whereunto all the duties which children owe to their parents in regard of their necessity, is in one word recompense, which is a duty whereby children endeavor as much as in them lieth, to repay what they can for their parents' kindness, care, and cost towards them, and that in way of thankfulness; which maketh a child think he cannot do too much for his parent, and well may he think so, for a parent doth much more for his child before it is able to do for itself, than the child possibly can do for the parent. So as if the parent's authority were laid aside, yet the law of equity requireth this duty of recompense: so also doth the law of piety and charity. Wherefore of all other duties this is most due. It is in express terms given in charge to children by the apostle, who willeth them to learn to requite [repay] their parents.

Contrary is neglect of parents in their need, which is more than monstrous ingratitude. As all ingratitude is odious to God and man, so this most of all, and yet very many are guilty thereof. In them the proverb is verified that love is weighty. For it is the property of weighty things to fall down apace, but to ascend slowly, and that not without some violence. Thus love from the parent to the child falleth down apace, but it hardly ascendeth from children to parents. In which respect another proverb saith, One father will better nourish nine children, than nine children one father. Many children in his kind do no more for their parents, than for strangers. They either consider not how much their parents have done for them; or else they conceit [imagine] that what their parents did, was of mere duty, and needeth no recompense. Fie upon such barbarous and inhumane children! . . .

Of Children's Relieving Their Parents According to Their Need

Besides bearing with parents' necessities, in such cases as parents stand in need of their children's relief and succor, they must afford it them. In sickness they must visit them, as Joseph visited his father. In time of mourning, they must comfort them, as the children of Jacob. In want, they must provide things needful for them, as the sons of Jacob, who went up to buy food for their father; and as Joseph, who sent for Jacob into Egypt, and there nourished him.

Peter (or Pierre) Erondell (flourished 1586–1609). Erondell, a Frenchman, wrote *The French Garden* to help the English (especially Englishwomen) learn French. Most of the book is in the form of dialogues, with parallel versions in English and French. The following excerpt is from the third dialogue, which presents a lady, her daughters, and a "mistress" (apparently a governess or tutor) at the beginning of a typical day. A daughter kneels and asks for her mother's blessing; then the lady and the governess discuss the ritual, noting that it is a distinctive English practice. As revealed in other documents, French and Italian visitors were impressed by the custom. It is noteworthy that the dialogue associates the English custom with the blessings given by the biblical patriarchs. (*The French Garden: For English Ladyes and Gentlewomen to Walke*. London, 1605. E7v, E8v.)

Document 27: From *The French Garden*

The Daughter. I beseech you, Mother, pray to God to bless me and give me your blessing, if it pleaseth you.

Lady. I pray the strong Almighty God to increase his graces in you, and to bless you. I marvel very much that Frenchmen (which bring up and teach their children so well) do not make them to ask their parents' blessing (I mean their father's and mother's) seeing that it is a thing that hath been used by the holy patriarchs, and also that Ecclesiasticus saith, that the blessing of the father, doth strengthen the houses of the children, and that the mother's curse doth root out the foundation thereof: What say you to it, Mistress Clemence?

Mistress. Madame, the mothers and fathers in France do not neglect to pray to God for their children, and although they use not the outward ceremony, yet they do bless them, and without doubt, God heareth their prayers, and maketh the children to prosper.

Henry Smith (see **Document 15**). In a sermon titled *The Affinity of the Faithful,* Smith considers where a Christian's greatest loyalty resides. The answer, not surprisingly, is with God. In this selection, Smith emphasizes the limited nature of parental authority and argues that all family bonds must be subordinated to moral and religious obligations. By setting conscience above social expectations, Smith exemplifies one way that Protestantism helped to loosen the traditional social structure, which had family relationships at its core. (*The Sermons of Maister Henrie Smith Gathered into One Volume*. London, 1593. 241–42.)

Document 28: From *The Affinity of the Faithful*

When Paul said, Children obey your parents in the Lord, he meaneth that we should not obey them against the Lord: as when he saith, Obey princes for conscience; he meaneth that we should not obey them against conscience. Therefore, when it cometh to this, that the earthly father commandeth one thing, and the heavenly Father commandeth another thing, then as Peter answered the rulers, so thou mayst answer thy parents, Whether is it meet to obey God or you? [Acts 5:29] then these are the hands which thou must cut off, then these are the eyes which thou must pull out; or else they should be as dear unto thee as thy hand or thine eye. In Matthew, A man must forsake his father and mother to dwell with his wife [Matthew 19:5]; but in Luke, He must forsake father and mother, and wife to dwell with Christ; for, He that forsaketh father or mother or wife for me, shall receive more (saith our Savior [Luke 18:29–30]:) nay, he which doth not hate father and mother and wife for me, cannot be my disciple (saith he again in the same evangelist [Luke 14:26]): showing that our love towards God should be so great, that in respect of it, our love towards men should seem to be but hatred. Thus he that obeyed his parents more than we, yet would have us search some sentence, some example in scripture of not obeying them too; because it is such a hard point to know how far they are to be obeyed which are set in authority over us. As none but God spake always right; so none but God must always be obeyed: we are not called only the sons of men, but the sons of God. Therefore, as Christ answered his mother when she would have him turn water into wine; Woman what have I to do with thee? [John 2:4] So we should answer father, and mother, and brethren, and sisters, and rulers, and masters, and wife too, when they will us to do that which is not meet.

A Handkercher for Parents' Wet Eyes. I. C. (or possibly J. C.) are the initials of the unknown writer of a "consolatory letter" to a friend who had lost a child. *A Handkercher* (meaning "handkerchief") *for Parents' Wet Eyes* presents reasons a parent should not be overwhelmed by grief and responds to various objections put in the mouth of the grieving parent. Yet the tone is sympathetic (the writer himself may have experienced a similar loss), and he acknowledges that deep grief is natural. The letter builds to a climax in which the writer offers religious consolation, including hope of reunion with the lost child in heaven. Many but not all grieving parents in early modern England would have entertained such a hope. The following excerpt ends with a phrase ("the hope of Israel") used by the Apostle Paul in reference to the doctrine of the resurrection (Acts 28:20). The Sadducees (a Jewish sect) and Gentiles (non-Jews), also mentioned in this excerpt, were groups portrayed in the New Testament as rejecting this doctrine. (*A Handkercher for Parents Wet Eyes upon the Death of Children. A Consolatory Letter to a Friend.* London, 1630. 1, 11, 33, 61–62, 65.)

DOCUMENT 29: FROM *A HANDKERCHER FOR PARENTS' WET EYES*

Sir, I know you do now feel what it is to be a father; and therefore to bar you altogether from lamenting and sorrowing in such an accident as this (the death of your beloved son) were as unreasonable, as to chide a man, for showing himself sensible, when a tooth is drawn, or a leg or arm is sawed off from his body. . . .

All unions in this world must be dissolved: Fathers and children must be severed; friends and friends, husbands and wives, as they had a time to come together, so they must have a time to part asunder. . . .

God may intend herein the father's trial, as well as the child's benefit. You yourself have sometimes given one of your little ones an apple, and ask it again immediately, to try his love. So God gives us dear pledges, and anon requires them from us again, to make proof which we love better, our children or him. He allows us to hold them dear, but himself must be dearer. . . .

He is not clean gone, but only gone before. His mortality is ended, rather than his life. You have lost him for a time, God hath found him for ever.

Rejoice and bless God, that you had such a son. Had him, did I say? You have him still. Not one child the fewer have you for his taking hence. . . .

There [in heaven] you shall one day see him again face to face, in that very house of clay [his body], which he laid down, when he left the world and you (though altered in quality); and (if that may make to the increase of your bliss) I am persuaded, know, and enjoy him, see heaven the richer in your seed, his joy augmented and made fuller by yours, and yours by his.

Let Sadducees deny this, and Gentiles deride it; This is the hope of Israel.

Ben Jonson (1572–1637). Jonson, a friend and rival of Shakespeare and one of the greatest writers of the period, wrote poems, plays, and prose works and often took a satirical view of his contemporaries. Yet the two poems presented here, though revealing great poetic skill, also express tender personal feeling. The first, about a daughter who died in infancy, emphasizes her innocence. The second describes Jonson's deep attachment to his son (also named Benjamin) and presents the standard view that excessive parental love may incur God's disapproval and that the child, who belongs to God, is happier in heaven. Jonson makes much of his children's names: Mary is named after "heaven's queen" (an allusion to the Virgin Mary that may derive from Jonson's Roman Catholic affiliation between 1598 and 1610); in the second poem, the first line refers to the literal meaning of the Hebrew name Benjamin, "son of the right hand." (*The Workes of Benjamin Jonson.* London, 1616. 774, 780–81.)

Document 30: "On My First Daughter"

Here lies to each her parents' *ruth,	***grief***
Mary, the daughter of their youth:	
Yet, all heaven's gifts, being heaven's due,	
It makes the father, less, to *rue.	***regret, be sorry***
At six months end, she parted hence	
With safety of her innocence;	
Whose soul *heaven's queen, (whose name she bears)	***the Virgin Mary***
In comfort of her mother's tears,	
Hath plac'd amongst her virgin-train:	
Where, while that *sever'd doth remain,	***separated (i.e., the soul separated from the body)***
This grave partakes the fleshly birth.	
Which cover lightly, gentle earth.	

Document 31: "On My First Son"

Farewell, thou child of my right hand, and joy;	
My sin was too much hope of thee, lov'd boy,	
Seven years thou wert lent to me, and I thee pay,	
Exacted by thy fate, on the just day.	
O, could I lose all *father, now. For why	***fatherly feeling***
Will man lament the state he should envy?	
To have so soon scap'd worlds, and flesh's rage,	
And, if no other misery, yet age?	
Rest in soft peace, and, ask'd, say here doth lie	
BEN JONSON his best piece of poetry.	
For whose sake, henceforth, all his vows be such,	
As what loves may never *like too much.	***please***

SIBLINGS AND INHERITANCE

Peter (or Pierre) de La Primaudaye (1546–1619?). Originally published in French in two volumes (1577 and 1583), the first English translation of *The French Academy* was published in 1586 and 1594, with several new editions appearing over the following 25 years. The book was highly influential, both directly and through the frequent borrowings other writers made from it. *The French Academy* is a vast compendium of information and opinion on various matters, including the "manners and callings" of different social positions, "the soul and body of man," a "notable description of the whole world," and the "means to eternal life." The following selection is from a chapter titled "Of the Duty of

Children towards Their Parents: Of the Mutual Love that Ought to Be among Brethren: Of the Duty of Servants towards Their Masters" (chapter 50 of the first book). The excerpt presented here notes issues, especially related to inheritance, that may lead to fraternal conflict but asserts that enmity between brothers is "most prodigious and against nature" and that brothers honor their parents by loving each other. (*The French Academie. Fully Discoursed and Finished in Foure Bookes*. Trans. Thomas Bowes. London, 1618. 222–25.)

Document 32: From *The French Academy*

Moreover, seeing we must labor to obey and to please our parents in all things, it is certain that no action, gift or disposition in us is more acceptable, or contenteth them better than to see good will, and an assured and certain friendship among brethren. . . . For if parents are offended when their children offer wrong to a servant whom they love, . . . is it likely that they could patiently abide to see their children whom they love best of all, to hate one another, to be always quarrelling one with another, to speak ill one of another, and in all their enterprises and actions to be divided, and set one against another, and to seek to supplant and defeat each other? I think no man will affirm it. Therefore contrariwise we may judge, that those brethren which love and cherish one another, which join together in one bond of selfsame wills, studies and affections, that which nature had disjoined and separated in bodies, and lastly, which have all their talk, exercises, plays, and pastimes common amongst them, they I say undoubtedly give occasion to their parents of a sweet and happy contentation [contentment] in their old age for this brotherly friendship. For no father (saith Plutarch) ever loved learning, honor or silver so much as he did his children. And therefore they never took so great pleasure to see their children good orators, rich, or placed in great office; and dignities, as to see them love one another. . . . Therefore let us utterly banish away all hatred of our brethren, which is both condemned by God who commendeth above all things concord unto us, and also a naughty nurse for the old age of fathers and mothers, and a worse for the young years of children.

And seeing we are about this matter of brotherly love, so precious and excellent, whereunto nowadays men have so small regard, I think we ought to insist and stand longer upon it, and allege some precepts and examples of ancient men, whereby to confirm us in it more and more. First, nature hath bred from our birth in regard of us the beginning and occasion of this amity, and hath taken away from our judgment all former motions, to procure love. Therefore we must beware that we seek not too exactly after the faults and imperfections one of another, but cover and bear with them, because they are of our own blood: knowing that no man's life can be sincere [pure] and clean from all vice, so that we were better to support the domestical imperfections of our brethren, than to make trial of those that are in strangers. That brother (saith Plutarch) that warreth with his brother, and seeketh to procure a stranger to friend, seemeth to me to cut off voluntarily a member of his own flesh belonging to him, that he may apply and fasten to that place one taken from another man's body. . . . All enmity breedeth within our souls a thousand passions that torment us, but especially that enmity which a man beareth towards his brother, as that which is most prodigious and against nature. And as bodies that were once joined together, if the glue or band wax loose, may be joined and glued again; but if a natural body break or rent asunder, it is hard to find any solder that is able to reunite and knit them well together again: so those mutual friendships, which we contract voluntarily with such as are not of kin or allied unto us, if peradventure they fall asunder sometimes, may easily be overtaken again; but when brethren are once estranged and fallen from that love whereby nature doth necessarily link them one with another, they are hardly reconciled again together. And if they be friends again, yet it is always with some distrust and suspicion.

Questionless [without question] it is impossible but that affairs should breed in these times wherein we live, many occasions of dissension and debate between brethren, namely, for goods and successions, as this word of "parting" [dividing an inheritance] importeth, and bringeth with it division, every one being desirous to have his own. But herein also they must suffer their matters to fight by themselves, without adding any headstrong passion, covetousness, or choler [anger], which are as a hook that taketh hold of them, and seeketh to set them together by the ears. They must, as it were in a balance consider jointly together on which side right and equity declineth, and as soon as they can possible, let them remit the judgment and deciding of their controversies to the arbitrement [judgment] of some good men. Yea, a good brother ought rather to rejoice and boast that he hath overcome and gone beyond his brother, in gracious behavior, in courtesy, in voluntary giving of place, and in every good duty towards him, than in the division of some goods. . . .

Therefore to end our present discourse, let us learn, that it is a great and commendable virtue, and beseeming [befitting] every good and gentle nature, to know how to obey well, and to give honor and service to those that occupy the degree of fathers, lords, and masters over us, as also to love our brethren with an indissoluble love, to reverence one another, the younger honoring the elder, and the elder yielding all duties of sincere love to the younger.

John Earle (see **Document 21**). Like the earlier selection from *Microcosmography* describing "A Child," the following selection purports to depict a typical "younger brother." This sketch reveals the challenges that often faced younger sons, especially those of the upper classes, as a result of primogeniture. Because the oldest son inherited the estate and title, younger sons had to find another career and sometimes resented their oldest brother. (*Micro-cosmographie, or, A Peece of the World discovered in Essayes and Characters*. London, 1628. C3v–C5v.)

Document 33: From *Microcosmography* ("Younger Brother")

His [a younger brother's] father has done with him, as Pharaoh to the children of Israel, that would have them make brick, and give them no straw; so he tasks him to be a gentleman, and leaves him nothing to maintain it. . . . His birth and bringing up will not suffer him to descend to the means to get wealth: but he stands at the mercy of the world. . . . If his annuity [yearly allowance] stretch so far, he is sent to the university, and with great heart-burning takes upon him the ministry; as a profession he is condemned to by his ill fortune. Other take a more crooked path, yet the King's high-way, where at length their vizard [mask] is plucked off, and they strike fair for Tyburn [i.e., hanging; Tyburn was an execution site]: but their brother's pride, not love, gets them a pardon. His last refuge is the Low Countries [Netherlands], where rags and lice are no scandal, where he lives a poor gentleman of a company, and dies without a shirt. The only thing that may better his fortunes, is an art he has to make a gentlewoman, wherewith he baits now and then some rich widow that is hungry after his blood [i.e., his gentlemanly status]. He is commonly discontented, and desperate, and the form of his exclamation is, "That churl [villain] my brother." He loves not his country for this unnatural custom [i.e., primogeniture], and would have long since revolted to the Spaniard, but for Kent only which he holds in admiration [because inheritance was divided equally among sons there].

GLOSSARY

This glossary lists a selection of the key terms appearing in the text related to family, literature, theater, and history. Cross-referenced words appear in **bold.**

Abandonment—See **Exposure or abandonment.**

Adultery—Sexual relations between two persons not married to each other, at least one of whom is married to someone else.

Affines—One's relatives by marriage. See **Affinity.**

Affinity—Relationship established through marriage.

Agnatic—A term referring to family relationships traced only through one's father or a more distant male ancestor and his male descendants. Relatives so defined are "agnates." See **Cognatic.**

Anglican—A term meaning, as a noun, a member of the Church of England; as an adjective, it refers to the Church of England or its doctrines or practices, especially after its break from the Roman Catholic Church in 1534. See **Puritan.**

Annulment—Also called a "decree of nullity." The legal dissolution of a marriage that is judged not to be valid, for instance, because of a prior **contract,** because the couple are too closely related, or because one or both of the parties did not consent to the match. See **Divorce, Impediment.**

Antiquity—A historical term referring to ancient times; for Europe and the lands surrounding the Mediterranean, the term usually refers to the time from the beginning of civilization until the end of the Roman Empire in the A.D. 400s.

Apprenticeship—The legal arrangement in which one person (an apprentice) is bound for a certain number of years to serve an employer, who in return is bound to instruct the apprentice in a trade or craft.

Archetype—See **Mythic and archetypal criticism.**

Arranged marriage—A marriage in which the choice of partners is made by parents or others, not by the bride or groom. See **Forced (or enforced) marriage.**

Banns—The announcement that a marriage is to take place, read in church on three Sundays or holy days preceding the wedding.

Bastardy—The state of being born out of wedlock. *Base* and *base born* are adjectives that may refer to illegitimate children. See **Whoreson.**

Bed trick—A plot motif in which one person secretly takes the place of another in a sexual encounter; usually one woman takes the place of another so that the man is tricked into having sexual relations with someone other than the woman he thought he was with. Shakespeare uses this motif in *All's Well That Ends Well* and *Measure for Measure*.

Bêt-'āb—(Hebrew, "father's house"). An extended family unit in ancient Israel, including a husband and wife and their children and grandchildren, sometimes along with servants and other unrelated members, all living in a family compound with two or three houses surrounding a courtyard.

Betrothal—A formal agreement to marry.

Bilateral kindred—A person's relatives on both the father's and mother's sides.

Birthright—Rights, especially of inheritance or preeminence, belonging to the firstborn son (or in some cases, to the firstborn child of either sex); under certain circumstances, these rights could be transferred to a younger **sibling.**

Breeching—The change from wearing gown-like "**coats**" to wearing breeches or pants; this change marked a boy's entry into the world of men and usually took place between ages 5 and 7 in early modern England. See **Unbreeched.**

Bride gift—Money or property given by a suitor to the bride, usually at the time of **betrothal.** See **Bride price** and **Morning gift.**

Bride price—Money or property given by a suitor to the bride's family; with time, it came to be given to the bride herself and was identified as a "**bride gift.**" See **Morning gift.**

Canon law—Ecclesiastical or church law, especially the body of law instituted in the Catholic Church by popes and church councils.

Child-bed privilege—The privilege granted to a woman who has just given birth of having about a month of recovery and freedom from most of her usual responsibilities.

Churching of women—Also called "purification of women" and "thanksgiving for the deliverance of women"; a ceremony of the Church of England marking a woman's return to full social activity after she has given birth.

Clan—A large group with common ancestry, usually living in the same area. See ***Genos, Mišpāḥâ*** and **Phratry.**

Clandestine marriage—Secret or concealed marriage; generally refers to a marriage lacking witnesses or solemnization by a minister or a marriage that has these but that is hidden from the couple's parents.

Coats—A gown-like outfit worn by both boys and girls in early modern England beginning in infancy; these coats were worn until about age 6 by boys and a few years longer by girls. See **Breeching.**

Cockle—To indulge or pamper, especially a child.

Cognatic—A term referring to family relationships traced through both one's father and one's mother. Relatives so defined are *cognates*. See **Agnatic.**

Collateral—A term referring to relatives (including **siblings**) not in one's direct line of descent but descending by a different line from a common ancestor.

Comedy—A play intended to amuse; it is usually lighter in tone than a **tragedy** and ends happily, with problems resolved and, in Shakespeare, often with multiple marriages. See **Romantic comedy.**

Comitatus—Among early Germanic peoples, the followers of a chieftain, who depended on these followers for military and other services and who in return provided for their needs and divided with them the spoils of battle.

Companionate marriage—A term earlier used to refer to a kind of marriage, usually childless, in which the couple can easily divorce and have no legal responsibilities to each other; more recently, it has come to mean a relatively egalitarian kind of marriage based on friendship and mutual affection.

Concubine—A woman who is not a wife in a full sense but who is viewed as belonging to a particular man and who may bear him legitimate children. *Concubinage* refers to this secondary or inferior kind of marriage.

Conjugal family—A family that consists only or primarily of a husband and wife and their children. See **Nuclear family.**

Consanguinity—Relationship by blood (i.e., by common ancestry), as opposed to relationship by marriage. See **Affinity.**

Contract—A binding agreement to marry. See **Betrothal, Handfasting, Sponsion, Spousal,** and **Troth-plight.**

Cousin, coz—Terms used in early modern England to refer to **kin** of almost any kind (except direct ancestors and descendants) outside of the immediate family; not limited to cousins in the modern sense. "Coz" was a familiar form often used in direct address.

Dark comedy—Also called "problem comedy." A type of **comedy,** especially of Shakespearean comedy, more serious and somber than most comedies, focusing on difficult issues and situations, sometimes harsh in its tone, and often dealing with unpleasant or sordid subjects and characters and taking place in unpleasant locations. Shakespeare's dark comedies include *All's Well That Ends Well*, *Troilus and Cressida*, and *Measure for Measure*; some add *The Merchant of Venice*.

Divorce—Legal termination of a marriage. Though divorce as we know it did not exist in medieval or early modern Europe, the word *divorcium* was used for two methods of ending a marriage: *divorcium a mensa et thoro* ("divorce from table and bed"), corresponding to what we would call "**separation**" (the marriage still existed, but the couple no longer lived together); and *divorcium a vinculo* ("divorce from the bond"), corresponding to what we would call "**annulment**" (i.e., a valid marriage was judged never to have existed).

Dower—A wife's right, granted by her husband's family, to benefit from a portion of her husband's inheritance, usually at the time of his death; not the same as a **dowry** or **jointure,** though Shakespeare sometimes uses the word "dower" to refer to either of these.

Dowry—Money or property given by a woman's family at the time of her marriage; generally viewed as belonging to the women, though often in the husband's control during his lifetime. Also called "portion" or "marriage portion."

Early modern period—The historical period following the **Middle Ages** in Europe, marked by a continuation of much in the medieval outlook and way of life but with changes that would eventually produce modern European culture; it is usually thought of as beginning in the 1300s in Italy and later in the rest of Europe and continuing until about 1700. The early modern period in England is usually designated as taking place from about 1500 to 1700. Sometimes also called the **Renaissance.**

Eastern family—Term used by some scholars to refer to a type of family found in eastern Europe and non-European cultures and characterized by **endogamous** marriages, very young marriage for women, separation between men and women, and exclusion of women from public life. See **Western European family.**

Endogamy—The practice of marrying within a kinship group (such as a **clan** or **tribe**), often including close relatives (such as marriage between an uncle and niece), though not usually within the immediate family. The adjective is *endogamous*.

Enforced marriage—See **Forced marriage.**

Epithalamion—(Greek, "at the bridal chamber"). A song or poem celebrating a wedding.

Exogamy—The practice of marrying outside one's kinship group (such as **clan** or **tribe**), especially avoiding marriage with close relatives.

Exposure or abandonment—The practice of leaving an infant outdoors to die or to be found and cared for by strangers.

Extended family—Refers generally to any relatives beyond the nuclear family; more specifically refers to households including such relatives and sometimes made up of several related nuclear families. See **Nuclear family.**

Family—A word with three primary meanings in early modern England: (1) members of a **household,** whether related or not (including servants as well as relatives); (2) those related by blood (**consanguinity**) or marriage (**affinity**), whether or not living together; (3) those belonging to a **lineage** (i.e., related by descent from a common ancestor).

Family romance—See **Psychoanalytic criticism**.

Feminism—A movement (especially strong in the twentieth century but with earlier predecessors) aimed at promoting the rights and interests of women. Feminist literary criticism, which became especially important beginning in the 1960s, examines and seeks increased attention and stature for writing by women, looks at women's concerns in all writing, and seeks to uncover the male bias in Western literature generally.

Forbidden degrees—Particular degrees or steps of relatedness, whether by blood (**consanguinity**) or marriage (**affinity**), that prevent a valid marriage from being contracted. Also called "prohibited degrees."

Forced (or enforced) marriage—A marriage in which one or both of the partners have been forced to marry without their consent. Since the 1100s, such marriages have been viewed as invalid and (if lack of free consent could be proved) could be **annulled.** See **Arranged marriage.**

Fornication—Sexual relations between two unmarried persons. Sometimes extended to include **adultery.**

Fosterage—The practice of sending children to live in the homes of someone other than their parents. "Foster parents" are those who act as mother or father to such children.

Friends—A term sometimes used in early modern England to refer to relatives.

Gavelkind—The custom of dividing an inheritance equally among sons, traditionally practiced in Kent and a few other places in the British Isles.

Gender studies—The academic study of issues related to gender or sexual identity in literature and other aspects of culture. Though related to **feminist criticism,** gender studies seeks to address both male and female concerns.

Genos* (plural: *gene*)**—A Greek term referring to a group of related families or households. Sometimes translated "**clan.**" See **Phratry** and ***Phyle.

Gens—A Latin term referring to a group of families claiming common ancestry.

Godfather, godmother, godparent, godson, goddaughter—Relationships (sometimes called "spiritual kinship") established in the Roman Catholic, Anglican, and certain other churches between a child at the time of baptism and persons outside the family. A godfather or godmother professes faith on behalf of the child and is responsible for the child's religious education. The child is a godson or goddaughter in relation to the godparents.

Greek romances—Also called "Greek novels." Long prose fictional narratives written in Greek between the first and the third centuries A.D., about long-lost children, strange adventures, and lovers who are separated and, after many trials, finally reunited. Important examples include Heliodorus's *Aethiopica*, Longus's *Daphnis and Chloe*, and the anonymous *Apollonius of Tyre*.

Handfasting—The act of becoming betrothed; refers to the couple's clasping hands as part of the ceremony. See **Betrothal, Contract, Sponsion, Spousal,** and **Troth-plight.**

History play—A play based on historical events. Shakespeare's history plays are based on English history and focus on events related to the monarchy.

House—In early modern England, a term referring both to a dwelling place and to a **family,** especially in the sense of **lineage.**

Household—Those living together in a house, especially in the sense that they form an organized group for economic activity; may include family members and others, such as servants.

Impediment—A condition that would prevent a valid marriage from taking place, such as a **pre-contract** or a relationship between the prospective bride and groom within the **forbidden degrees.**

Incest—Marriage or sexual relations considered unlawful within a particular society because those married or engaging in sexual relations are too closely related, either by blood (**consanguinity**) or marriage (**affinity**). Marriages within the **forbidden degrees** are considered incestuous. Some also have considered marriage between those related by "**spiritual kinship**" to be incestuous.

Jointure—Lands or income provided by the groom or the groom's family for the wife's support after her husband's death.

Kin, kindred—Those related by blood or common descent, especially those closely enough related to be recognized as having a claim on one's loyalty.

Levirate marriage—(From the Hebrew word *lēvir*, meaning "brother-in-law"). A form of marriage practiced by the ancient Hebrews in which a near kinsman, sometimes a brother, married the widow of a man who died without having children.

Lineage—A group that includes all the descendants of a particular ancestor; the relationship established by a line of descent.

Lustratio—In ancient Rome, a ceremony for the protection and purification of a newborn child taking place eight days (for girls) or nine days (for boys) after birth.

Marxist criticism—A kind of literary or cultural criticism that emphasizes the economic forces that supposedly, through a process called dialectical materialism, determine everything else in a society. Among the concepts of Marxist criticism are base (the economic forces and the social relations they produce) and superstructure (the ideological constructs that arise at the conscious level, including religion, philosophy, literature, and art).

Masque—A form of entertainment popular in the English court during the early 1600s. Masques use music, dance, and spectacle, along with words and actions, to present a message or story in symbolic terms. Shakespeare incorporated masque-like elements in some of his later plays, notably *The Tempest.*

Master, mistress—The male ("master") or female ("mistress") head of a **household.**

Matriarchal—Patterned after the older word *patriarchal,* refers to rule by women, especially in families or kinship groups supposedly dominated by a mother or other female ancestor.

Matrilineal—Tracing descent and kinship through female relatives.

Mean household size—The average number of people living in each residence in a given community or culture.

Menarche—The age at which a woman has her first menstrual period; the event of becoming fertile.

Microcosm, macrocosm—Terms meaning literally "little world" and "great world"; they refer to the **Renaissance** concept that the world is made up of smaller entities that resemble the whole world in structure and function. For instance, an individual human being may be viewed as a "little world" or microcosm resembling the "great world" or cosmos. The family can likewise be viewed as a "little world."

Middle Ages or the medieval period—The historical period in Europe from the collapse of the Western Roman Empire in the 400s until the **Renaissance** or **early modern period.** In England, the medieval period is usually thought of as including the Anglo-Saxon period, from the mid-400s to 1066, and the later Middle Ages from 1066 to about 1500.

Midwife—A woman, or sometimes a man, who assists at the delivery of a child.

Mišpāḥâ—A Hebrew word, sometimes translated **"clan,"** referring to a group of **kin** within a **tribe** generally living in the same area.

Monasticism—The way of life associated with monasteries, that is, with monks, nuns, and others who have taken vows of poverty, celibacy, and obedience with the aim of living a life higher than or separate from the world.

Monogamy—The practice of having a single spouse.

Morning gift—In older Germanic cultures (including Anglo-Saxon England), property granted by a husband to his wife after the marriage has been consummated, usually the morning or day after the wedding; this is generally in addition to the bride price or bride gift. See **Bride price** and **Bride gift.**

Mythic and archetypal criticism—A critical approach examining two closely related elements of literature: myths (sacred stories that explain the meaning and origin of the world and the things in it) and archetypes (symbols found repeatedly in myths and in later literature). According to the psychologist C. G. Jung, who influenced one version of archetypal criticism, the archetypes belong to the "collective unconscious" that all human beings share and hence are universal.

Nature—A word with several important meanings in early modern England including (1) the entire created universe; (2) the creative and life-giving power by which the universe and all things in it operate (this power was sometimes personified as a goddess); (3) the innate characteristics of any thing or class of things (for instance, human nature); (4) the original state of anything, unaffected by human activity or social convention; (5) the laws, deriving from God, that govern all things (also called "the laws of nature" or "natural laws"); (6) the ideal state of anything (its state when it is in accordance with natural law); and (7) proper love and loyalty between family members. It was viewed as "natural" for people to act in accordance with nature in the sense of familial love and loyalty and "unnatural" for them to act otherwise.

New Historicism—A form of historical criticism important especially beginning in the 1980s; opposed to traditional historical criticism, which it views as aiming for an impossible objectivity and as reducing history to "background" that literary works "reflect." Instead, this approach views literary works, criticism, and all cultural activity as historically "situated." This approach emphasizes the relationships of power and oppression in societies; in some versions, it proposes that literature takes part in a subversion-containment dialectic. "Cultural materialism" is a name for a version of this approach that has a **Marxist** orientation.

Norman Conquest—The conquest of Anglo-Saxon England in 1066 by the Norman French (from Normandy); as a result, William I (William the Conqueror) became king of England, and the Norman French became England's ruling class.

Nuclear family—A family made up of a husband and wife and their children and generally living in a single **household** apart from other families.

Nuptial, nuptials—A wedding.

Oedipus complex—See **Psychoanalytic criticism.**

Overlay or overlie—To smother a child by lying on top of it.

Parental blessing—A ritual practiced in various cultures (including early modern England) in which the father, mother, or both place their hands above or on the head of a child and say certain words to express goodwill (sometimes accompanied by advice) and to convey supernatural influence for the good of the child.

Paterfamilias—A Latin term referring to the father as head of a **household,** having authority over all his living descendants as well as his slaves and former slaves, including (in theory) power over life and property.

Patriarchal, patriarchy—Terms originally referring to the head or ancestor of a family or **tribe** (from Greek words meaning "family" or "lineage" and "head" or "origin"); later used to refer to certain forms of family organization, specifically those in which a living male ancestor heads a family group made up of several generations of descendants. More recently, the terms have been used loosely to refer to cultures in which husbands and fathers have supreme authority in families, sometimes with connotations of male domination and brutality in general. Some scholars have criticized this looser use of the terms as misleading.

Patrilineal—Tracing descent and kinship through male relatives.

Patronymic—A name derived from one's father or other male ancestor.

Phratry (or *phratria*)—A kinship group in ancient Greece comparable to a **clan** and consisting of several groups (each of which was made up of related families and called a ***genos***); the word *phratria* is sometimes translated "brotherhood." See ***Genos*** and **Phyle.**

***Phyle* (plural: *phylae*)**—Something like a **tribe,** the largest of the kinship groups that together made up the *polis* or community in ancient Greece. Each *phyle* was made up of **phratries.**

Pietas—A Latin term meaning reverence for and devotion to ancestors and country.

Polis—A Greek word referring to the community to which people in an ancient Greek city-state viewed themselves as belonging and whose laws and customs were binding on all. See ***Genos*, Phratry,** and ***Phyle*.**

Polygamy—The practice of marrying more than one spouse (see **Polygyny**); *resource polygamy* refers to polygamy practiced only by a small portion of a community with adequate means to support a large **household.**

Polygyny—Literally, "many women or wives." A form of **polygamy** in which one man is married simultaneously to more than one woman.

Portion or marriage portion—See **Dowry.**

Poststructuralism—A term for a variety of critical approaches that became prominent beginning in the 1970s; generally considered to include deconstruction and recent forms of **feminist, new historicist, psychoanalytic,** and reader-response criticism, it stresses the "decentering of the subject" (human selfhood or identity), the "death of the author" (including the idea that texts are produced by an impersonal process of writing and reading rather than by individual agents), and some degree of relativism about truth and values.

Pre-contract—An agreement to marry entered into prior to a later attempt to marry someone else; if discovered, a pre-contract would be an **impediment** to a later marriage.

Primogeniture—The practice of bestowing inheritance (including property and titles) on the oldest child or, more often, the oldest son, sometimes with lesser provision made for younger **siblings.**

Prohibited degrees—See **Forbidden degrees.**

Psychoanalytic criticism—A kind of psychological criticism based (most commonly) on the theories of Freud and using such concepts as wish fulfillment, the unconscious, repression (especially of sexual wishes), the Oedipus complex, dream symbolism, and the id, the ego, and the superego. Many psychoanalytic concepts are relevant to the study of the family, including the Oedipus complex (deriving from young boys' supposed desire to displace their fathers) and the "family romance" (a pattern described by Freud in which children first identify with and then are disillusioned by their parents).

Puritan—A term referring to a movement (Puritanism) of the late 1500s and early 1600s, Calvinist in its theology, that sought to "purify" the Church of England by bringing its doctrines and practices into harmony with Puritan understanding of the Bible, by eliminating ceremonies associated with Roman Catholicism, and by reforming contemporary morals. A Puritan is someone, either inside or outside the Church of England, associated with this movement. See **Anglican.**

Queer theory—A kind of literary criticism or theory that focuses on the experience, identity, and social status of gays and lesbians, how they are represented in literature, and literature they produce.

Reformation—Also called the Protestant Reformation. A movement in Europe of the 1500s aimed at reforming the Roman Catholic Church and resulting in the creation of a number of separate "Reformed" or "Protestant" churches.

Renaissance—The revival of interest in ancient Greek and especially Roman literature, language, and arts, beginning in Italy in the 1300s and spreading north and west through Europe; the movement became influential in England about 1500, so that the English Renaissance is often thought of as taking place from about 1500 to 1660. As a term for a historical period, *Renaissance* is now in dispute; the term *early modern* is often preferred.

Resource polygamy—See **Polygamy.**

Romance—A term that came to be applied by nineteenth- and twentieth-century critics to several of Shakespeare's later plays (*Pericles*, *Cymbeline*, *The Winter's Tale*, *The Tempest*), also known as **tragicomedies,** because they have both **tragic** and **comic** elements. These plays are called romances because they have settings, characters, situations, or events that are "romantic" in the sense of being unusual, strange, heightened, idealized, supernatural, wondrous, or awe-inspiring. Like Shakespeare's **comedies,** the romances end happily but are usually more serious in tone and sometimes present characters' deaths. They include mythic, religious, and symbolic elements, such as death and rebirth, restoration, reunion, repentance, and reconciliation.

Romantic comedy—Though the term sometimes refers to any **comedy** that involves love, especially between young lovers, many critics prefer using it to mean a type of comedy that ends happily (often with marriage, reunion, reconciliation, or good fortune) and that suggests a positive, even idealized outlook on life. Like **romances,** romantic comedies sometimes include unusual, heightened, or wondrous elements, but they are usually lighter in tone and do not include death.

Salic law—A law in older Germanic cultures prohibiting inheritance through the female line.

Separation—The condition, sometimes brought about by legal decree, in which a husband and wife cease living together as part of the same **household,** but without the marriage being legally dissolved. See **Divorce.**

Sibling—A brother or sister; siblings are children of the same parent or parents.

Spiritual kinship—See **Godfather, godmother, godparents, godson, goddaughter.**

Sponsion—A formal promise; sometimes specifically a promise to marry. See **Betrothal, Contract, Handfasting, Spousal,** and **Troth-plight.**

Spousal, spousals—The state of being married; or the ceremony by which a couple becomes betrothed or married. See **Betrothal, Contract, Handfasting, Sponsion,** and **Troth-plight.**

Strict settlement—A form of inheritance devised in England in the 1640s with the aim of protecting an estate and the rights of possible heirs by specifying what would happen to the estate under certain conditions (especially the absence of sons), with trustees appointed to ensure the carrying out of the provisions.

Swaddling bands—Bands of cloth in which infants were often wrapped beginning shortly after birth and continuing for several months and sometimes up to a year or more; these bands had the effect of preventing the child's limbs from moving.

Tragedy—A serious drama that ends in disaster, often in death (in Shakespearean tragedies, usually multiple deaths). A tragedy typically focuses on a main character who begins at the height of his fortune but then suffers unexpected reversals. According to Aristotle, such a play arouses "pity and fear" in such a way as to produce a "catharsis" (a sense of purification or release, from the Greek word for purgation).

Tragicomedy—A play that encompasses both serious elements (including the threat of disaster) and lighter or happier elements. Most often the term refers to **Renaissance** plays, mingling upper- and lower-class characters, in which a plot that seems headed for a **tragic** outcome ends happily. See **Romance.**

Tribe—A relatively large group based on common ancestry but sometimes including unrelated members. See ***Phyle.***

Troth-plight—The pledging of one's faithfulness (*troth* means "promise" or faithfulness in keeping one's word); specifically, the promise to marry. See **Betrothal, Contract, Handfasting, Sponsion,** and **Spousal.**

Tutor—A term (originally Latin) referring to a legal guardian. Later extended to refer to an instructor.

Unbreeched—Adjective referring to a young boy (usually under age 6 or 7) who has not yet started wearing breeches or pants. See **Breeching, Coats.**

Unilateral kinship—One's relatives on only one side (either the father's or the mother's) and usually including only relatives traced through men or women but not both. Sometimes called "unilineal descent group."

Verba de futuro—(Or *sponsalia per verba de futuro*, Latin for "betrothal by words in the future tense"). A form of **betrothal** in which a person promises to marry in the future, using such an expression as "I will take thee as my wife (or husband)" or "I promise to marry thee," with the name of the other person inserted after "thee." Both this and **betrothal** per ***verba de praesenti*** constituted legally binding **contracts.**

Verba de praesenti—(Or *sponsalia per verba de praesenti*, Latin for "betrothal by words in the present tense"). A form of **betrothal** in which a person uses such an expression as "I take thee to be my espoused wife [or husband]," with the person's name inserted after "thee." See ***Verba de futuro.***

Ward, wardship—A ward is a child under the government of a legal guardian; wardship refers to the condition of wards or the practice of granting control of an heir's marriage and property to a guardian until the heir reaches a certain age.

Weaning—The process of ending a child's breast-feeding.

Wergild—Literally, "man gold." An Anglo-Saxon term for a payment given by the responsible party or his family to the family of someone killed or injured.

Western European family—Term used by some scholars to refer to the type of family found in Western Europe and characterized by **exogamy,** relative closeness in age of husbands and wives, and generally free mingling of men and women. See **Eastern family.**

Wet nurse—A woman hired to nurse a child who is not her own.

Whoreson—An early-modern English term for a **bastard** or illegitimate male child.

SELECTED BIBLIOGRAPHY

HISTORICAL STUDIES OF FAMILY LIFE

Print Sources

Amussen, Susan. "The Family and the Household." *A Companion to Shakespeare*. Ed. David Scott Kastan. Malden, MA: Blackwell, 1999. 85–99.

———. *An Ordered Society: Gender and Class in Early Modern England*. New York: Columbia University Press, 1988.

Anderson, Michael. *Approaches to the History of the Western Family, 1500–1914*. London: Macmillan, 1980.

Ariès, Philippe. *Centuries of Childhood: A Social History of Family Life*. Trans. Robert Baldick. New York: Vintage Books, 1962.

Avery, Gillian. "The Voice of the Child, Both Godly and Unregenerate, in Early Modern England." *Infant Tongues: The Voice of the Child in Literature*. Ed. Elizabeth Goodenough, Mark A. Heberle, and Naomi Sokoloff. Detroit, MI: Wayne State University Press, 1994. 16–27.

Blits, Jan H. "Privacy and Public Moral Education: Aristotle's Critique of the Family." *Educational Theory* 35 (1985): 225–38.

Bonfield, Lloyd. *Marriage Settlements, 1601–1740: The Adoption of the Strict Settlement*. Cambridge: Cambridge University Press, 1983.

Boswell, John. *The Kindness of Strangers: The Abandonment of Children in Western Europe from Late Antiquity to the Renaissance*. Chicago: University of Chicago Press, 1988.

Capp, Bernard. *When Gossips Meet: Women, Family, and Neighbourhood in Early Modern England*. Oxford: Oxford University Press, 2003.

Carlson, Eric Josef. *Marriage and the English Reformation*. Oxford: Blackwell, 1994.

Casey, James. *The History of the Family*. Oxford: Basil Blackwell, 1989.

Clark, Ira. "The Marital Double Standard in Tudor and Stuart Lives and Writing: Some Problems." *Medieval and Renaissance Drama in England* 9 (1997): 34–55.

Classen, Albrecht, ed. *Childhood in the Middle Ages and the Renaissance: The Results of a Paradigm Shift in the History of Mentality*. Berlin: Walter de Gruyter, 2005.

Coster, Will. *Family and Kinship in England, 1450–1800*. Seminar Studies in History. Harlow, UK: Pearson Education, 2001.

Cox, Cheryl Ann. *Household Interests: Property, Marriage Strategies, and Family Dynamics in Ancient Athens*. Princeton, NJ: Princeton University Press, 1998.

Crawford, Sally. *Childhood in Anglo-Saxon England*. Stroud, UK: Sutton Publishing, 1999.

Cressy, David. *Birth, Marriage, and Death: Ritual, Religion, and the Life-Cycle in Tudor and Stuart England*. Oxford: Oxford University Press, 1997.

———. "Foucault, Stone, Shakespeare and Social History." *English Literary Renaissance* 21 (1991): 121–33.

Cunningham, Hugh. *Children and Childhood in Western Society since 1500*. London: Longman, 1995.

Demand, Nancy. *Birth, Death, and Motherhood in Classical Greece*. Baltimore: Johns Hopkins University Press, 1994.

deMause, Lloyd, ed. *The History of Childhood*. New York: Psychohistory Press, 1974.

Durston, Christopher. *The Family in the English Revolution*. Oxford: Basil Blackwell, 1989.

Erickson, Amy L. *Women and Property in Early Modern England*. London: Routledge, 1993.

Fitz, Linda T. "'What Says the Married Woman?' Marriage Theory and Feminism in the English Renaissance." *Mosaic* 13.2 (1980): 1–22.

Fleming, Peter. *Family and Household in Medieval England*. Social History in Perspective. Houndmills, UK: Palgrave, 2001.

Forster, Marc R., and Benjamin J. Kaplan, eds. *Piety and Family in Early Modern Europe: Essays in Honour of Steven Ozment*. Aldershot, UK: Ashgate, 2005.

French, Valerie. "Children in Antiquity." *Children in Historical and Comparative Perspective: An International Handbook and Research Guide*. Ed. Joseph M. Hawes and N. Ray Hiner. Westport, CT: Greenwood Press, 1991. 13–29.

Frye, Susan, and Karen Robertson, eds. *Maids and Mistresses, Cousins and Queens: Women's Alliances in Early Modern England*. New York: Oxford University Press, 1999.

Gardner, Jane F., and Thomas Wiedemann, eds. *The Roman Household: A Sourcebook*. London: Routledge, 1991.

Gies, Frances, and Joseph Gies. *Marriage and the Family in the Middle Ages*. New York: Harper & Row, 1987.

Gillis, John R. *For Better, for Worse: British Marriages, 1600 to the Present*. New York: Oxford University Press, 1985.

Golden, Mark. *Children and Childhood in Classical Athens*. Baltimore: Johns Hopkins University Press, 1990.

———. "Did the Ancients Care When Their Children Died?" *Greece and Rome* 35 (1988): 152–63.

Goody, Jack. *The Development of the Family and Marriage in Europe*. Cambridge: Cambridge University Press, 1983.

———. *The European Family: An Historico-Anthropological Essay*. Oxford: Blackwell, 2000.

Gottlieb, Beatrice. *The Family in the Western World from the Black Death to the Industrial Age*. New York: Oxford University Press, 1993.

Gowing, Laura. "Secret Births and Infanticide in Seventeenth-Century England." *Past and Present* 156 (1997): 87–115.

Hajnal, John. "European Marriage Patterns in Perspective." *Population in History: Essays in Historical Demography*. Ed. D. V. Glass and D.E.C. Eversley. London: Edward Arnold, 1965. 101–43.

Hanawalt, Barbara A. *Growing Up in Medieval London*. New York: Oxford University Press, 1993.

———. *The Ties That Bound: Peasant Families in Medieval England*. New York: Oxford University Press, 1986.

Hawes, Joseph M., and N. Ray Hiner, eds. *Children in Historical and Comparative Perspective: An International Handbook and Research Guide*. Westport, CT: Greenwood, 1991.

Heers, Jacques. *Family Clans in the Middle Ages*. Trans. Barry Herbert. Amsterdam: North-Holland Publishing Company, 1977.

Hellerman, Joseph H. *The Ancient Church as Family: Early Christian Communities and Surrogate Kinship*. Minneapolis: Fortress Press, 2001.

Herlihy, David. *Medieval Households*. Cambridge, MA: Harvard University Press, 1985.

Herlihy, David, and Christiane Klapisch-Zuber. *Tuscans and Their Families: A Study of the Forentine Catasto of 1427*. Yale Series in Economic History. New Haven, CT: Yale University Press, 1985.

Hess, Richard S., and M. Daniel Carroll R., eds. *Family in the Bible: Exploring Customs, Culture, and Context*. Grand Rapids, MI: Baker Academic, 2003.

Houlbrooke, Ralph A. *The English Family 1450–1700*. London: Longman, 1984.

———, ed. *English Family Life, 1576–1716: An Anthology from Diaries*. Oxford: Basil Blackwell, 1988.

———. "The Making of Marriage in Mid-Tudor England." *Journal of Family History* 10 (1985): 339–52.

Hurstfield, Joel. *The Queen's Wards: Wardship and Marriage under Elizabeth I*. Cambridge, MA: Harvard University Press, 1958.

Ingram, Martin. *Church Courts, Sex, and Marriage in England, 1570–1640*. Cambridge: Cambridge University Press, 1987.

Jones, Jeanne. *Family Life in Shakespeare's England: Stratford-upon-Avon 1570–1630*. Stratford-upon-Avon: Sutton Publishing in association with the Shakespeare Birthplace Trust, 1996.

Kelly, Henry Ansgar. *Love and Marriage in the Age of Chaucer*. Ithaca, NY: Cornell University Press, 1975.

———. *The Matrimonial Trials of Henry VIII*. Stanford: Stanford University Press, 1976.

Kertzer, David I., and Marzio Barbagli, eds. *Family Life in Early Modern Times, 1500–1789*. The History of the European Family: Vol. 1. New Haven, CT: Yale University Press, 2000.

Klapisch-Zuber, Christiane. *Women, Family, and Ritual in Renaissance Italy*. Trans. Lydia Cochrane. Chicago: University of Chicago Press, 1985.

Lacey, W. K. *The Family in Classical Greece*. London: Cornell University Press, 1968.

Lancaster, Lorraine. "Kinship in Anglo-Saxon Society." *The British Journal of Sociology* 9 (1958): 230–50, 359–77.

Laslett, Peter. *Family Life and Illicit Love in Earlier Generations*. Cambridge: Cambridge University Press, 1977.

———, ed. *Household and Family in Past Time*. Cambridge: Cambridge University Press, 1972.

———. *The World We Have Lost: Further Explored*. 3rd ed. London: Methuen, 1983.

Laslett, Peter, Karla Oosterveen, and Richard M. Smith, eds. *Bastardy and Its Comparative History*. Cambridge, MA: Harvard University Press, 1980.

Lucas, R. Valerie. "Puritan Preaching and the Politics of the Family." *The Renaissance Englishwoman in Print: Counterbalancing the Canon*. Ed. Anne M. Haselkorn and Betty S. Travitsky. Amherst: University of Massachusetts Press, 1990. 224–40.

Macfarlane, Alan. *The Family Life of Ralph Josselin, a Seventeenth-Century Clergyman*. Cambridge: Cambridge University Press, 1970.

———. *Marriage and Love in England: Modes of Reproduction, 1300–1840*. Oxford: Blackwell, 1986.

———. *The Origins of English Individualism: The Family, Property and Social Transition*. Oxford: Basil Blackwell, 1978.

———. Review of Lawrence Stone, *The Family, Sex and Marriage in England 1500–1800*. *History and Theory* 18 (1979): 103–26.

Mendelson, Sara, and Patricia Crawford. *Women in Early Modern England, 1550–1720*. Oxford: Clarendon Press, 1998.

Mertes, Kate. *The English Noble Household, 1250–1600: Good Governance and Political Rule*. Oxford: Basil Blackwell, 1988.

Murray, Alexander Callander. *Germanic Kinship Structure: Studies in Law and Society in Antiquity and the Early Middle Ages*. Toronto: Pontifical Institute of Mediaeval Studies, 1983.

Noonan, John T., Jr. "Power to Choose." *Viator* 4 (1973): 419–34.

Orme, Nicholas. *Medieval Children*. New Haven, CT: Yale University Press, 2001.

———. *Medieval Schools*. New Haven, CT: Yale University Press, 2006.

Outhwaite, R. B. *Clandestine Marriage in England, 1500–1850*. London: Hambledon Press, 1995.

———, ed. *Marriage and Society: Studies in the Social History of Marriage*. London: Europa Publications, 1981.

Ozment, Steven. *Ancestors: The Loving Family in Old Europe*. Cambridge, MA: Harvard University Press, 2001.

———. *When Fathers Ruled: Family Life in Reformation Europe*. Cambridge, MA: Harvard University Press, 1983.

Patterson, Cynthia B. *The Family in Greek History*. Cambridge, MA: Harvard University Press, 1998.

Pearson, D'Orsay W. "Renaissance Adolescent Marriage: Another Look at Hymen." *Cithara* 23.1 (1983): 17–27.

Perdue, Leo G., Joseph Blenkinsopp, John J. Collins, and Carol Meyers, eds. *Families in Ancient Israel*. The Family, Religion, and Culture. Louisville, KY: Westminster John Knox, 1997.

Pinchbeck, Ivy, and Margaret Hewitt. *Children in English Society*. 2 vols. London: Routledge & Kegan Paul, 1969–73.

Pollock, Linda A. *Forgotten Children: Parent-Child Relations from 1500 to 1900*. Cambridge: Cambridge University Press, 1983.

———. *A Lasting Relationship: Parents and Children over Three Centuries*. London: Fourth Estate, 1987.

Pomeroy, Sarah B. *Families in Classical and Hellenistic Greece: Representations and Realities*. Oxford: Clarendon Press, 1997.

Rabb, Theodore K., and Robert I. Rotberg, eds. *The Family in History: Interdisciplinary Essays*. New York: Harper & Row, 1971.

———, eds. *Marriage and Fertility: Studies in Interdisciplinary History*. Princeton, NJ: Princeton University Press, 1980.

Rawson, Beryl, ed. *The Family in Ancient Rome: New Perspectives*. London: Croom Helm, 1986.

Rousseau, Constance M., and Joel T. Rosenthal, eds. *Women, Marriage, and Family in Medieval Christendom: Essays in Memory of Michael M. Sheehan, C.S.B.* Studies in Medieval Culture 37. Kalamazoo: Western Michigan University-Medieval Institute Publications, 1998.

Satlow, Michael L. *Jewish Marriage in Antiquity*. Princeton, NJ: Princeton University Press, 2001.

Schücking, Levin L. *The Puritan Family: A Social Study from the Literary Sources*. New York: Schocken Books, 1970.

Shaw, Brent. "The Age of Roman Girls at Marriage: Some Reconsiderations." *Journal of Roman Studies* 77 (1987): 30–46.

Shuger, Debora Kuller. "Nursing Fathers: Patriarchy as a Cultural Ideal." *Habits of Thought in the English Renaissance: Religion, Politics, and the Dominant Culture*. Berkeley: University of California Press, 1990. 218–49.

Slater, Miriam. *Family Life in the Seventeenth Century: The Verneys of Claydon House*. London: Routledge & Kegan Paul, 1984.

Smith, C. J. *The Roman Clan: The Gens from Ancient Ideology to Modern Anthropology*. Cambridge: Cambridge University Press, 2006.

Stone, Lawrence. *The Family, Sex and Marriage in England 1500–1800*. New York: Harper & Row, 1977.

Thirsk, Joan. "The European Debate on Customs of Inheritance, 1500–1700." *Family and Inheritance: Rural Society in Western Europe, 1200–1800*. Ed. Jack Goody, Joan Thirsk, and E. P. Thompson. Cambridge: Cambridge University Press, 1976. 177–91.

———. "Younger Sons in the Seventeenth Century." *History* 54 (1969): 358–77.

Thomas, Keith. "Age and Authority in Early Modern England." *Proceedings of the British Academy* 62 (1976): 205–48.

———. "Children in Early Modern England." *Children and Their Books*. Ed. Gillian Avery and Julia Briggs. Oxford: Clarendon Press; New York: Oxford University Press, 1989. 45–77.

Travitsky, Betty. "Child Murder in English Renaissance Life and Drama." *Medieval and Renaissance Drama in England* 6 (1993): 63–84.

Treggiari, Susan. *Roman Marriage: Iusti Coniuges from the Time of Cicero to the Time of Ulpian*. Oxford: Oxford University Press, 1991.

Williams, Gordon. "Some Aspects of Roman Marriage Ceremonies and Ideals." *Journal of Roman Studies* 48 (1958): 16–29.

Wrightson, Keith. *English Society, 1580–1680*. London: Hutchinson, 1982.

———. "Infanticide in Earlier Seventeenth-Century England." *Local Population Studies* 15 (1975): 10–22.

Electronic Sources

"Daily Life: Home & Family." *Canaan and Ancient Israel*. University of Pennsylvania Museum of Archaeology and Anthropology. http://www.museum.upenn.edu/Canaan/Home&Family.html.

Desmet, Christy. *The Renaissance Family*. http://virtual.park.uga.edu/cdesmet/class/engl6320/FAMILY.htm.

The Family. Internet Shakespeare Editions. University of Victoria. http://internetshakespeare.uvic.ca/Library/SLT/society/familysubj.html.

Greydanus, Richard. "The Roman *Familia*." *Writings*. http://rgrydns.blogspot.com/2006/01/roman-familia.html.

Nuptiae: Roman Marriages. http://www.societasviaromana.net/Collegium_Religionis/nuptiae.php.

Orme, Nicholas. "Childhood in Medieval England, c.500–1500." *Representing Childhood*. http://www.representingchildhood.pitt.edu/medieval_child.htm.

Powers, Jennifer Goodall. *Ancient Weddings*. Classics Technology Center. http://ablemedia.com/ctcweb/consortium/ancientweddings.html.

Provencal, Vernon L. *The Family in Aristotle*. http://www.mun.ca/animus/2001vol6/provencal6.htm.

Somerville, J. P. *The Early Modern Family*. http://history.wisc.edu/sommerville/367/367-033.htm.

Witmore, Michael. "Childhood in Early Modern England, c. 1500–1700." *Representing Childhood*. http://www.representingchildhood.pitt.edu/early_modern_child.htm.

CRITICAL STUDIES ON SHAKESPEARE AND FAMILY LIFE

Print Sources

Adelman, Janet. "Bed Tricks: On Marriage as the End of Comedy in *All's Well That Ends Well* and *Measure for Measure*." *Shakespeare's Personality*. Ed. Norman N. Holland, Sidney Homan, and Bernard J. Paris. Berkeley: University of California Press, 1989. 151–74.

———. *Suffocating Mothers: Fantasies of Maternal Origin in Shakespeare's Plays,* Hamlet *to* The Tempest. New York: Routledge, 1992.

Alexander, Peter. *Hamlet, Father, and Son*. Oxford: Clarendon Press, 1955.

Barber, C. L. "The Family in Shakespeare's Development: Tragedy and Sacredness." *Representing Shakespeare: New Psychoanalytic Essays*. Ed. Murray Schwartz and Coppélia Kahn. Baltimore: Johns Hopkins University Press, 1980. 188–202.

Barber, C. L., and Richard P. Wheeler. *The Whole Journey: Shakespeare's Power of Development*. Berkeley: University of California Press, 1986.

Belsey, Catherine. "Gender and Family." *Cambridge Companion to Shakespearean Tragedy*. Ed. Claire Elizabeth McEachern. New York: Cambridge University Press, 2002. 123–41.

———. *Shakespeare and the Loss of Eden: The Construction of Family Values in Early Modern Culture*. New Brunswick, NJ: Rutgers University Press, 1999.

Berger, Harry, Jr. *Making Trifles of Terrors*. Stanford: Stanford University Press, 1997. Especially the first four chapters.

Bergeron, David M. *Shakespeare's Romances and the Royal Family*. Lawrence: University Press of Kansas, 1985.

Bevington, David. "*Othello:* Portrait of a Marriage." *Othello: New Critical Essays*. Ed. Philip C. Kolin. New York: Routledge, 2002. 221–31.

Birje-Patil, J. "Marriage Contracts in *Measure for Measure*." *Shakespeare Studies* 5 (1969): 106–11.

Boose, Lynda. "An Approach through Theme: Marriage and the Family." *Approaches to Teaching Shakespeare's* King Lear. Ed. Robert H. Ray. New York: Modern Language Association of America, 1986. 59–68.

———. "The Family in Shakespeare Studies; or—Studies in the Family of Shakespeareans; or—The Politics of Politics." *Renaissance Quarterly* 40 (1987): 707–42.

———. "The Father and the Bride in Shakespeare." *PMLA* 97 (1982): 325–47.

Brewer, Derek. "Some Examples from Shakespeare." *Symbolic Stories: Traditional Narratives of the Family Drama in English Literature*. Cambridge, UK: D. S. Brewer, 1980. 112–47.

Cacicedo, Albert. "'She Is Fast My Wife': Sex, Marriage, and Ducal Authority in *Measure for Measure*." *Shakespeare Studies* 23 (1995): 187–209.

Chedgzoy, Kate. "Wise Children and Foolish Fathers: Carnival in the Family." *Shakespeare's Queer Children: Sexual Politics and Contemporary Culture*. Manchester: Manchester University Press, 1995. 49–93.

Cook, Ann Jennalie. *Making a Match: Courtship in Shakespeare and His Society*. Princeton, NJ: Princeton University Press, 1991.

Daniell, David. "The Good Marriage of Katherine and Petruchio." *Shakespeare Survey* 37 (1984): 23–31.

Danson, Lawrence. "Shakespeare and the Misrecognition of Fathers and Sons." *Paternity and Fatherhood: Myths and Realities*. Ed. Lieve Spaas. New York: St. Martin's, 1998. 236–45.

Darcy, Robert F. "Freeing Daughters on Open Markets: The Incest Clause in *The Merchant of Venice*." *Money and the Age of Shakespeare*. Ed. Linda Woodbridge. New York: Palgrave Macmillan, 2003. 189–200.

Dash, Irene G. *Wooing, Wedding, and Power: Women in Shakespeare's Plays*. New York: Columbia University Press, 1981.

Deats, Sara Munson. "Teaching *Romeo and Juliet* as a Tragedy of the Generation Gap and of Teenage Suicide." *Approaches to Teaching Shakespeare's* Romeo and Juliet. Ed. Maurice Hunt. New York: Modern Language Association of America, 2000. 108–14.

Desens, Marliss. "Marrying Down: Negotiating a More Equal Marriage on the English Renaissance Stage." *Medieval and Renaissance Drama in England* 14 (2001): 227–55.

Detmer, Emily. "Civilizing Subordination: Domestic Violence and *The Taming of the Shrew*." *Shakespeare Quarterly* 48 (1997): 272–94.

Dolan, Frances E. *Dangerous Familiars: Representations of Domestic Crime in England, 1550–1750*. Ithaca, NY: Cornell University Press, 1994.

Dreher, Diane. *Domination and Defiance: Fathers and Daughters in Shakespeare*. Lexington: University Press of Kentucky, 1986.

Dubrow, Heather. *Shakespeare and Domestic Loss*. Cambridge: Cambridge University Press, 1999.

———. " 'This Jewel Holds His Building on My Arm': The Dynamics of Parental Loss in *Pericles*." *In the Company of Shakespeare: Essays on English Renaissance Literature in Honor of G. Blakemore Evans*. Ed. Thomas Moisan and Douglas Bruster. Madison, NJ: Fairleigh Dickinson University Press, 2002. 27–42.

Erickson, Peter. *Patriarchal Structures in Shakespeare's Drama*. Berkeley: University of California Press, 1985.

Fortier, Mark. "Married with Children: *The Winter's Tale* and Social History; or Infacticide [*sic*] in Earlier Seventeenth-Century England." *Modern Language Quarterly* 57 (1996): 579–603.

Frey, Charles. "Shakespeare's Imperiled and Chastening Daughters of Romance." *South Atlantic Bulletin* 43.4 (1978): 125–40.

Friedman, Michael D. "Male Bonds and Marriage in *All's Well* and *Much Ado*." *SEL* 35 (1995): 231–49.

———. " 'O, Let Him Marry Her!': Matrimony and Recompense in *Measure for Measure*." *Shakespeare Quarterly* 46 (1995): 454–64.

Garber, Marjorie. *Coming of Age in Shakespeare*. London: Methuen, 1981.

Gossett, Suzanne. " 'I'll Look to Like': Arranged Marriages in Shakespeare's Plays." *Sexuality and Politics in Renaissance Drama*. Ed. Carole Levin and Karen Robertson. Lewiston, NY: Edwin Mellin Press, 1991. 57–74.

———. "'You Not Your Child Well Loving': Text and Family Structure in *Pericles*." *Companion to Shakespeare's Works*. Ed. Richard Dutton. Malden, MA: Blackwell, 2003. 348–64.

Harding, Davis P. "Elizabethan Betrothals and 'Measure for Measure.'" *JEGP* 49 (1950): 139–58.

Heilbrun, Carolyn G. "The Character of Hamlet's Mother." *Hamlet's Mother and Other Women*. New York: Columbia University Press, 1990. 9–17.

Hennings, Thomas P. "The Anglican Doctrine of the Affectionate Marriage in *The Comedy of Errors*." *Modern Language Quarterly* 47 (1986): 91–107.

Holland, Norman, Sidney Homan, and Bernard J. Paris, eds. *Shakespeare's Personality*. Berkeley: University of California Press, 1989. The essays by Holland, Farrell, Novy, and Adelman are especially relevant to family.

Hopkins, Lisa. *The Shakespearean Marriage: Merry Wives and Heavy Husbands*. New York: St. Martin's Press, 1998.

Horwich, Richard. "*The Merry Wives of Windsor* and the Conventions of Companionate Marriage." *The Shakespeare Yearbook* 3 (1992): 31–43.

Hunter, Dianne. "Shakespeare's Continuity through the Daughter." *Literature and Psychology* 48.3 (2002): 38–56.

James, Max H. *"Our House Is Hell": Shakespeare's Troubled Families*. Westport, CT: Greenwood, 1989.

Janton, Pierre. "Sonship and Fatherhood in *Macbeth*." *Cahiers Elisabéthains* 35 (1989): 47–58.

Jardine, Lisa. "'No Offence i' th' World': *Hamlet* and Unlawful Marriage." *Uses of History: Marxism, Postmodernism, and the Renaissance*. Ed. Francis Barker, Peter Hulme, and Margaret Iversen. Manchester: Manchester University Press, 1991. 123–39.

———. *Still Harping on Daughters: Women and Drama in the Age of Shakespeare*. Sussex, UK: Harvester Press; Totowa, NJ: Barnes & Noble, 1983.

Jones, Ernest. *Hamlet and Oedipus*. New York: Norton, 1949.

Kahn, Coppélia. "The Absent Mother in *King Lear*." *Rewriting the Renaissance: The Discourses of Sexual Difference in Early Modern Europe*. Ed. Margaret Ferguson, Maureen Quilligan, and Nancy J. Vickers. Chicago: University of Chicago Press, 1986. 33–49.

Kaplan, Lindsay M. "Jessica's Mother: Medieval Constructions of Jewish Race and Gender in *The Merchant of Venice*." *Shakespeare Quarterly* 58 (2007): 1–30.

Kehler, Dorothea. "Jaquenetta's Baby's Father: Recovering Paternity in *Love's Labor's Lost*." *Renaissance Papers 1990*. Ed. Dale B. J. Randall and Joseph A. Porter. Durham, NC: Southeastern Renaissance Conference, 1990. 45–54.

Knapp, John V. "Family Games and Imbroglio in *Hamlet*." *Reading the Family Dance: Family Systems Therapy and Literary Studies*. Ed. John V. Knapp and Kenneth Womack. Newark: University of Delaware Press, 2003. 194–218.

Kusunoki, Akiko. "'Oh Most Pernicious Woman': Gertrude in the Light of Ideas on Remarriage in Early Seventeenth-Century England." Hamlet *and Japan*. Ed. Yoshiko Ueno. New York: AMS, 1995. 169–84.

Loberg, Harmonie. "Queen Gertrude: Monarch, Mother, Murderer." *Atenea* 24.1 (2004): 59–71.

Mack, Maynard. "Rescuing Shakespeare." International Shakespeare Association Occasional Paper No. 1. Oxford: Oxford University Press, 1979.

Mayers, Ozzie J., Clark Hendley, Philip Kronebusch, and Glen Palm. "*King Lear* and Fathering: A Panel Discussion." *Journal of Men's Studies* 6 (1997): 103–14.

McFarland, Thomas. "The Image of the Family in *King Lear*." *On* King Lear. Ed. Lawrence Danson. Princeton, NJ: Princeton University Press, 1981. 91–118.

McLuskie, Kathleen. "The Patriarchal Bard: Feminist Criticism and Shakespeare: *King Lear* and *Measure for Measure*." *Political Shakespeare: New Essays in Cultural Materialism*. Ed. Jonathan Dollimore and Alan Sinfield. Ithaca, NY: Cornell University Press, 1985. 88–108.

Montrose, Louis Adrian. "'The Place of a Brother' in *As You Like It*: Social Process and Comic Form." *Shakespeare Quarterly* 32 (1981): 28–54.

Moore, Jeanie Grant. "Riddled Romance: Kingship and Kinship in *Pericles*." *Rocky Mountain Review of Language and Literature* 57.1 (2003): 33–48.

Neely, Carol Thomas. *Broken Nuptials in Shakespeare's Plays*. New Haven, CT: Yale University Press, 1985.

Nelson, T.G.A. "'Bad Commodity' or 'Fair Posterity'? The Ambivalence of Issue in English Renaissance Comedy." *English Literary Renaissance* 15 (1985): 195–224.

Newman, Karen. "Renaissance Family Politics and Shakespeare's *The Taming of the Shrew*." *Fashioning Femininity and English Renaissance Drama*. Chicago: University of Chicago Press, 1991. 33–50.

Novy, Marianne. "Adopted Children and Constructions of Heredity, Nurture, and Parenthood in Shakespeare Romances." *Childhood and Children's Books in Early Modern Europe, 1550–1800*. Ed. Andrea Immel and Michael Witmore. New York: Routledge, 2006. 55–74.

———. "Multiple Parenting in Shakespeare's Romances." *Domestic Arrangements in Early Modern England*. Ed. Kari Boyd McBride. Pittsburgh: Duquesne University Press, 2002. 188–208.

———. "Shakespeare and Emotional Distance in the Elizabethan Family." *Theatre Journal* 33 (1981): 316–26.

Pierce, Robert B. *Shakespeare's History Plays: The Family and the State*. Columbus: Ohio State University Press, 1971.

Rackin, Phyllis. "Staging the Female Body: Maternal Breastfeeding and Lady Macbeth's 'Unsex Me Here.'" *Corps/décors: Femmes, Orgie, Parodie*. Ed. Catherine Nesci, Gretchen Van Slyke, and Gerald Prince. Amsterdam, Netherlands: Rodopi, 1999. 17–29.

Ranald, Margaret Loftus. "'As Marriage Binds, and Blood Breaks': English Marriage and Shakespeare." *Shakespeare Quarterly* 30 (1979): 68–81.

———. *Shakespeare and His Social Context*. New York: AMS Press, 1987.

Rasmussen, Eric. "Fathers and Sons in *Hamlet*." *Shakespeare Quarterly* 35 (1984): 463.

Ray, Sid. *Holy Estates: Marriage and Monarchy in Shakespeare and His Contemporaries*. Selinsgrove, PA: Susquehanna University Press, 2004.

Reynolds, Simon. "The Lawful Name of Marrying: Contracts and Stratagems in *The Merry Wives of Windsor*." *The Shakespeare Yearbook* 7 (1996): 313–31.

Roberts, Jeanne Addison. "Shakespeare's Maimed Birth Rites." *True Rites and Maimed Rites: Ritual and Anti-Ritual in Shakespeare and His Age*. Ed. Linda Woodbridge and Edward Berry. Urbana: University of Illinois Press, 1992. 123–44.

Rose, Mary Beth. "Where Are the Mothers in Shakespeare? Options for Gender Representation in the English Renaissance." *Shakespeare Quarterly* 42 (1991): 291–314.

Schanzer, Ernest. "The Marriage-Contracts in *Measure for Measure*." *Shakespeare Survey* 13 (1960): 81–89.

Schwartz, Murray, and Coppélia Kahn, eds. *Representing Shakespeare: New Psychoanalytic Essays*. Baltimore: Johns Hopkins University Press, 1980. Most of the essays deal with family, marriage, and gender relations.

Scott, Margaret. "'Our City's Institutions': Some Further Reflections on the Marriage Contracts in *Measure for Measure*." *ELH* 49 (1982): 790–804.

Shell, Marc. *The End of Kinship:* Measure for Measure, *Incest, and the Ideal of Universal Siblinghood*. Baltimore: Johns Hopkins University Press, 1995.

Singh, Sarup. *Family Relationships in Shakespeare and the Restoration Comedy of Manners*. Delhi: Oxford University Press, 1983.

Stockholder, Kay. *Dream Works: Lovers and Families in Shakespeare's Plays*. Toronto: University of Toronto Press, 1987.

Sundelson, David. "The Dynamics of Marriage in *The Merchant of Venice*." *Humanities in Society* 4.2–3 (1981): 245–62.

———. *Shakespeare's Restorations of the Father*. New Brunswick, NJ: Rutgers University Press, 1983.

Taylor, Mark. *Shakespeare's Darker Purpose: A Question of Incest*. New York: AMS Press, 1982.

Thompson, Ann, and Neil Taylor. "'Father and Mother Is One Flesh': *Hamlet* and the Problems of Paternity." *Paternity and Fatherhood: Myths and Realities*. Ed. Lieve Spaas. New York: St. Martin's Press, 1998. 246–58.

Trivedi, Achala S. *Family Relationships in Shakespeare*. Jaipur, India: Printwell, 1995.

Vanita, Ruth. "'Proper' Men and 'Fallen' Women: The Unprotectedness of Wives in *Othello*." *SEL* 34 (1994): 341–56.

Waller, Gary. "The Late Plays as Family Romance." *Approaches to Teaching Shakespeare's* The Tempest *and Other Late Romances*. Ed. Maurice Hunt. New York: Modern Language Association of America, 1992.

Wentersdorf, Karl. "The Marriage Contracts in *Measure for Measure*: A Reconsideration." *Shakespeare Survey* 32 (1979): 129–44.

Whitworth, Charles. "Wooing and Wedding in Arden: Rosalynde and *As You Like It*." *Etudes Anglaises* 50 (1997): 387–99.

Wilcockson, Colin. "Father-Directors, Daughter-Performers in Shakespeare." *Critical Survey* 3.2 (1991): 134–41.

Williamson, Marilyn. *The Patriarchy of Shakespeare's Comedies*. Detroit, MI: Wayne State University Press, 1986.

Willis, Deborah. *Malevolent Nurture: Witch-Hunting and Maternal Power in Early Modern England*. Ithaca, NY: Cornell University Press, 1995.

Willson, Robert F., Jr. "Enframing Style and the Father-Daughter Theme in Early Shakespearean Comedy and Late Romance." *Approaches to Teaching Shakespeare's* The Tempest *and Other Late Romances*. Ed. Maurice Hunt. New York: Modern Language Association of America, 1992. 38–48.

Young, Bruce W. "Haste, Consent, and Age at Marriage: Some Implications of Social History for *Romeo and Juliet*." *Iowa State Journal of Research* 62 (1987–88): 459–74.

———. "*King Lear* and the Calamity of Fatherhood." *In the Company of Shakespeare: Essays on English Renaissance Literature in Honor of G. Blakemore Evans*. Ed. Thomas Moisan and Douglas Bruster. Madison, NJ: Fairleigh Dickinson University Press, 2002. 43–64.

———. "Parental Blessings in Shakespeare's Plays." *Studies in Philology* 89 (1992): 179–210.

———. "Ritual as an Instrument of Grace: Parental Blessings in *Richard III*, *All's Well That Ends Well*, and *The Winter's Tale*." *True Rites and Maimed Rites*. Ed. Linda Woodbridge and Edward Berry. Urbana: University of Illinois Press, 1992. 169–200.

———. "Teaching *Hamlet* as a Play about Family." *Approaches to Teaching Shakespeare's* Hamlet. Ed. Bernice Kliman. New York: Modern Language Association, 2002. 107–12.

Ziegler, Georgianna. "Parents, Daughters, and 'That Rare Italian Master': A New Source for *The Winter's Tale*." *Shakespeare Quarterly* 36 (1985): 204–12.

Electronic Sources

Family / Introduction. Shakespearean Criticism. eNotes. http://www.enotes.com/shakespearean-criticism/family.

Young, Bruce. "'The Holy Cords Too Intrinse to Unloose': Families in Life and in Shakespeare." *Marriage and Families*. http://marriageandfamilies.byu.edu/issues/2002/January/holy.aspx

PERFORMANCE STUDIES ON SHAKESPEARE AND FAMILY

Print Sources

Comensoli, Viviana, and Anne Russell, eds. *Enacting Gender on the English Renaissance Stage*. Urbana: University of Illinois Press, 1999.

Cook, Ann Jennalie. "The Transformation of Stage Courtship." *The Elizabethan Theatre XI: Papers Given at 11th International Conference on Elizabethan Theatre, University of Waterloo, July 1985*. Ed. A. L. Magnusson and C. E. McGee. Port Credit, Ontario: P. D. Meany, 1990. 155–75.

Gay, Penny. *As She Likes It: Shakespeare's Unruly Women*. Gender in Performance Series. London: Routledge, 1994.

Griggs, Yvonne. "'All Our Lives We'd Looked Out for Each Other the Way Motherless Children Tend to Do': *King Lear* as Melodrama." *Literature Film Quarterly* 35.2 (2007): 101–7.

Kobayashi, Kaori. "Can a Woman Be Liberated in a 'Chauvinist's Dream'?: Michael Bogdanov's Production of *The Taming of the Shrew* in 1978." *Shakespeare Studies* (Shakespeare Society of Japan) 35 (1997): 59–102.

Orgel, Stephen. *Impersonations: The Performance of Gender in Shakespeare's England*. Cambridge: Cambridge University Press, 1996.

Rackin, Phyllis. "Androgyny, Mimesis, and the Marriage of the Boy Heroine on the English Renaissance Stage." *Speaking of Gender*. Ed. Elaine Showalter. New York: Routledge, 1989. 113–33.

Richmond, Hugh M. "*The Taming of the Shrew*, or How a Talented Woman Can Become a Successful Wife and Be Happy." *Shakespeare's Sexual Comedy: A Mirror for Lovers*. Indianapolis: Bobbs-Merrill, 1971. 83–101.

Robinson, Randal. "Family by Death: Stage Images in *Titus Andronicus* and *The Winter's Tale*." *From Page to Performance: Essays in Early English Drama*. Ed. John A. Alford. East Lansing: Michigan State University Press, 1995. 221–33.

Rutter, Carol. *Clamorous Voices: Shakespeare's Women Today*. London: Women's Press, 1988.

Shapiro, Michael. *Gender in Play on the Shakespearean Stage: Boy Heroines and Female Pages*. Ann Arbor: University of Michigan Press, 1994.

Simmons, James R., Jr. "'In the Rank Sweat of an Enseamed Bed': Sexual Aberration and the Paradigmatic Screen Hamlets." *Literature Film Quarterly* 25.2 (1997): 111–18.

Unkefer, Virginia A. "The Playwright and Actor on Stage: Mothers and Sons in *Richard III*, *Coriolanus*, and *Hamlet*." *Shakespeare Bulletin: A Journal of Performance Criticism and Scholarship* 12.3 (1994): 27–29.

Wofford, Susanne L. "'To You I Give Myself, for I Am Yours': Erotic Performance and Theatrical Performatives in *As You Like It*." *Shakespeare Reread: The Texts in New Contexts*. Ed. Russ McDonald. Ithaca, NY: Cornell University Press, 1994. 147–69.

Electronic Sources

Berens, Brad. *Shakespearean Stage History from 1660 Onwards: A Beginner's Guide*. http://www.berens.org/shakespeare/.

Designing Shakespeare. AHDS Performing Arts. http://www.ahds.ac.uk/performingarts/collections/designing-shakespeare.htm.

Exploring Shakespeare. Royal Shakespeare Company. http://www.rsc.org.uk/explore/.

An International Database of Shakespeare on Film, Television and Radio. British Universities Film & Video Council. http://www.bufvc.ac.uk/databases/shakespeare/index.html.

Lehmann, Courtney, and Lisa S. Starks. "Making Mother Matter: Repression, Revision, and the Stakes of 'Reading Psychoanalysis into' Kenneth

Branagh's *Hamlet*." *Early Modern Literary Studies* 6.1 (2000): 2.1–24. http://extra.shu.ac.uk/emls/06-1/lehmhaml.htm.

The RSC Shakespeare: Plays. http://www.rscshakespeare.co.uk/plays.html.

The RSC Shakespeare: RSC Staging Histories: A Key. http://www.rscshakespeare.co.uk/key.html.

Rusche, Harry. *Shakespeare & the Players*. Emory University. http://shakespeare.emory.edu/players_index.cfm.

The Shakespeare Globe Centre (USA) Research Archive. University of Maryland Department of Theatre. http://www.sgc.umd.edu/.

Shakespeare in Performance. Touchstone. http://www.touchstone.bham.ac.uk/performance.html.

Shakespeare in Performance. University of Victoria. http://internetshakespeare.uvic.ca/Theater/sip/index.html.

Shakespeare's Staging: Shakespeare's Performance. University of California, Berkeley. http://shakespearestaging.berkeley.edu/index.php.

GENERAL EARLY MODERN AND SHAKESPEAREAN ELECTRONIC SOURCES

Early Modern ("Renaissance") Electronic Resources

Early Modern Resources. http://www.earlymodernweb.org.uk/emr/.

EEBO (*Early English Books Online*). http://eebo.chadwyck.com/home (images of nearly 125,000 early English books). http://quod.lib.umich.edu/e/eebo/ (searchable transcriptions of over 10,000 early English books). (Note: These sites are a valuable resource for finding original printed materials in English from the early modern period [c. 1475–1700]. The complete versions of these sites are available only at institutions with subscriptions, such as certain universities and libraries.)

A New Library of Renaissance Source Materials. Tufts University. http://www.perseus.tufts.edu/sources.html.

General Shakespearean Sites

Complete Works of William Shakespeare Online. Massachusetts Institute of Technology. http://www-tech.mit.edu/Shakespeare/works.html.

Electronic Shakespeare: Resources for Researchers. http://www.wfu.edu/~tedforrl/shakespeare/#Shakespeare%20in.

Gates, Joanne E. *Expanded List of Shakespeare Links*. http://www.jsu.edu/depart/english/gates/shtragln.htm.

Internet Resources Guide. Royal Shakespeare Company. http://www.rsc.org.uk/content/3935.aspx.

Internet Shakespeare Editions. University of Victoria. http://ise.uvic.ca/index.html.

Mr. William Shakespeare and the Internet. Palomar College. http://shakespeare.palomar.edu.

Shakespeare Resource Center. http://www.bardweb.net/.

Study Materials. Shakespeare Birthplace Trust. http://www.shakespeare.org.uk/content/view/18/18/.

Touchstone: Resource for Shakespeare Studies. The British Library. http://www.touchstone.bham.ac.uk/.

The World Shakespeare Bibliography Online. http://www.worldshakesbib.org/.

INDEX

About the Author

BRUCE W. YOUNG is Associate Professor of English at Brigham Young University. His essays have appeared in such journals as *Marriage and Families* and *Studies in Philology*.